PURIFY AND DESTROY

The CERI Series in Comparative Politics and International Studies

Series editor CHRISTOPHE JAFFRELOT

This series consists of translations of noteworthy publications in the social sciences emanating from the foremost French research Centre in International Studies, the Paris-based Centre d'Etudes et de Recherches Internationales (CERI), part of Sciences Po and associated with the CNRS (Centre National de la Recherche Scientifique).

The focus of the series is the transformation of politics and society by transnational and domestic factors–globalisation, migration and the postbipolar balance of power on the one hand, and ethnicity and religion on the other. States are more permeable to external influence than ever before and this phenomenon is accelerating processes of social and political change the world over. In seeking to understand and interpret these transformations, this series gives priority to social trends from below as much as the interventions of state and non-state actors.

Founded in 1952, CERI has fifty full-time fellows drawn from different disciplines conducting research on comparative political analysis, international relations, regionalism, transnational flows, political sociology, political economy and on individual states.

JACQUES SEMELIN

Purify and Destroy

The Political Uses of Massacre and Genocide

TRANSLATED FROM THE FRENCH BY
CYNTHIA SCHOCH

Columbia University Press
New York

Columbia University Press
Publishers Since 1893
New York
Copyright © 2007 by Jacques Semelin
English translation © CERI, Paris, 2007
Translated from the French by Cynthia Schoch
All rights reserved

Library of Congress Cataloging-in-Publication Data
Semelin, Jacques.
[Purifier et détruire. English]
Purify and destroy: the political uses of massacre
and genocide/[Jacques Semelin]; translated from
the French by Cynthia Schoch.
    p. cm.
Includes bibliographical references and index.
ISBN 978-0-231-14282-3 (cloth: alk. paper) —
ISBN 978-0-231-51237-4 (e-book)
1. Genocide—Political aspects. I. Title.

HV6322.7.S4613 2007
304.6'63—dc22

2007006228

For Pierre Hassner,
whose companionship has always been an important source of
intellectual stimulation and who very wisely encouraged me to
explore the foundations of the power to destroy

Mine is a most peaceable disposition.
My wishes are: a humble cottage with a thatched roof,
but a good bed, good food, the freshest milk and butter,
flowers before my window, and a few fine trees before my door;
and if God wants to make my happiness complete,
he will grant me the joy of seeing some six or seven of my
enemies hanging from those trees. Before their death I shall,
moved in my heart, forgive them all the wrong they did me in
their lifetime.
One must, it is true, forgive one's enemies—but not before they
have been hanged.

Heinrich Heine, *Gedanken und Einfälle*

I thought of Campo dei Fiori
In Warsaw by the sky-carousel
One clear spring evening
To the strains of a carnival tune.
The bright melody drowned
The salvoes from the ghetto wall,
And couples were flying
High in the blue sky.

At times wind from the burning
Would drift dark kites along
And riders on the carousel
Caught petals in mid-air.
That same hot wind
Blew open the skirts of the girls
And the crowds were laughing
On the beautiful Warsaw Sunday.

Czeslaw Milosz, *Campo dei Fiori*

CONTENTS

III. INTERNATIONAL CONTEXT, WAR AND THE MEDIA

VI. THE POLITICAL USES OF MASSACRE
AND GENOCIDE

FOREWORD

It is not surprising that Jacques Semelin, a student of non-violence, should write the most comprehensive (and therefore upsetting) book on the subject of massacres and genocides and of their political uses. He focuses on three formidable cases: the Nazi extermination of the Jews, ethnic cleansing in the disintegrating Yugoslavia, and the massacres of the Tutsis in Rwanda. His work is a miracle of critical and probing analysis. He rejects simple explanations, catch phrases that don't help much (such as the banality of evil), and he shows the complexity of concepts such as that of genocide, a legal term that does not cover all the cases of massacres to which it has been applied. He brilliantly dissects the process that leads to the extermination of enemies within states, what he calls "the imaginary constructs of social destructiveness," which entail an ideology whose rhetoric is built around three main themes: identity, purity and security, and aims at instilling fear, hatred and the will to eliminate those enemies, with the help of conspiracy theories and paranoia. He also shows how the international system of sovereign states has contributed to the triumph of violence: wars between huge masses of citizens mobilized by their states have had a way of destroying the weak barriers painfully built by philosophers, churches and lawyers, culminating in the deliberate attacks on civilians that marked World War II, and in the thirst for revenge total war has created. Semelin, at the end of his work, invites researchers to spread as much knowledge as possible about the massacres that have so brutally and repeatedly destroyed the illusions of a peaceful or moderate world, but he himself knows too much about what may mobilize all the demons of human nature to have much faith left in the utopias of pacification through trade or globalization, or in the chances of successful prevention.

Given the persistence of massacres in a world full of failed states, of murderous states, of non-governmental terrorists, ethnic tensions and vengeful ideologies (religious as well as secular), this methodical book, based on immense learning, is one that needs to be read, for its wisdom, its fairness and an acute reasonableness that shows the influence of Raymond Aron and Pierre Hassner, and knows how to distinguish reason and rationality. There simply is no comparable work. It is brave, devastating and haunting.

STANLEY HOFFMANN

ACKNOWLEDGEMENTS

This book is the product of a long maturation process that probably began one day in July 1985 with the emotion I felt during a visit to Auschwitz-Birkenau, and subsequently fed by other travels to Poland, Germany, Rwanda and various countries in the Balkans. It is impossible for me to thank all the people who, over the years, have played important parts in the intellectual evolution of this work. But I must first mention my unforgettable meeting with the historian Leon Poliakov, pioneer of Holocaust studies in France, whose statement with regard to the genocide of the Jews has remained etched on my mind: 'Since the event had multiple causes, it is impossible to know what the cause of the event was.' This remark has always inspired my role as a scholar regarding the object under study. It has lighted my way through the social sciences, a constant reminder of the complexity of academic method and an incitement to modesty.

I also have in mind the conference on genocide and mass persecutions that I organized in Paris in March 1986 with the support and participation of Leon Poliakov himself, Yves Ternon (for Turkey under Talaat), Wladimir Berelowicth (for the USSR under Stalin), Jean-Luc Domenach (for Maoist China) and François Ponchaud (for Cambodia under Pol Pot). To my knowledge, this seminar was the first attempt at comparative analysis in France regarding the major mass murders of the twentieth century. I still recall the keen enthusiasm with which I followed the discussions, and the premises of this book probably also reside in that meeting.

But it is certainly the French political scientist and philosopher Pierre Hassner who, in the 1990s, after I had defended my postdoctoral degree entitling me to direct research in political science (which he had supervised), awakened in me the desire and the strength to undertake a new research program on this difficult theme in the framework of the National Center for Scientific Research (CNRS). For that reason I dedicate this book to him.

    In the final phase of writing I benefited hugely from the remarks
and comments of colleagues, who graciously agreed to read it and
point out shortcomings: Philippe Burrin (for Nazi Germany), Jean-
Pierre Chrétien, Marcel Kabanda and Claudine Vidal (for Rwanda),
Joseph Krulic and Joel Hubretch (for former Yugoslavia). The
analyses offered in this book have been deeply enriched by their
remarks and suggestions. Other colleagues, acquaintances and close
friends also read all or part of the manuscript: Annette Becker,
Sandrine Lefranc, Christian Mellon, Géraldine Muhlman, Valérie
Rosoux, Rafiki Ubaldo. Their incisive comments often led me to
make substantial modifications to improve the precision and clarity
of my argument. But naturally I alone remain responsible for what is
written in these pages.

    Over the years I spent preparing this book, several colleagues
played an important role in encouraging and stimulating my research.
First there are Michel Wieviorka, director of CADIS (EHESS) and
Christophe Jaffrelot, director of CERI (Sciences Po), who welcomed
me into their teams in 2000 and in 2004 respectively, thereby providing this research with an institutional framework that was essential to
its success. The 'Peacemaking: From Mass Crime to Peacebuilding'
research group which I co-chaired at CERI with Béatrice Pouligny
from 2000 to 2002 was a particularly stimulating intellectual melting
pot. Pierre Muller's support in organizing an international symposium on extreme violence in November 2001, under the auspices
of the Association Française de Science Politique, was a great encouragement. The dialogue among the disciplines represented at
this meeting provided me with insights from which this book has
benefited. The support of colleagues who hold major responsibilities in French social science research, such as Patrick Michel at the
CNRS and Gérard Grunberg at Sciences Po, was also an essential
source of recognition for this work, giving me even more energy to
complete it.

    I cannot neglect to pay tribute as well to my foreign colleagues,
mainly those I have met in the framework of the International
Association of Genocide Scholars and with whom I discussed some
of the ideas defended in this book. Foremost among them are Omer
Bartov (Brown University), Frank Chalk (Concordia University,
Montreal), Ben Kiernan (Yale University) Henry Huttenbach (City

University of New York), Eric Markusen (University of Minnesota), and Robert Melson (Purdue University).

I am indebted to Caroline Longlet, Ronald Hato and Nathalie Tenenbaum, who edited and prepared the manuscript. Nathalie, in particular, had the onerous task of working with me in the final phase of writing, reading and rereading the text, finding and completing references, and improving its presentation. Without her precious and benevolent collaboration, this book would simply not be what it is.

Even as I was still drafting the French manuscript, Michael Dwyer, director of Hurst & Co., London, showed great faith in this endeavour by offering to publish it in English. I am extremely grateful to him for giving me the possibility of making my research known to an English-speaking audience.

If this is possible today, it is thanks to Cynthia Schoch who had the enormous responsibility of translating the book, ably seconded by Philippa Bush. Throughout our collaboration I had the opportunity to appreciate both her exceptional professional consciousness and her literary talents. While remaining faithful to the author's thinking, Cynthia's writing remains flowing and elegant. I am sure her translation will serve my English-speaking readers well, for which I am particularly thankful to her.

And, in addition to my gratitude for her occasional remarks on my writing, my deepest and warmest thoughts go to Lydie, who finds herself in the particularly difficult situation of having to cope with a researcher probably too often absorbed by his attempt to understand human beings and the extremes of their behaviour.

INTRODUCTION

Understand?

I am not a German Jew, or a Tutsi from Rwanda, or a Bosnian Muslim. My ancestry stems from the Vendée region in France. But the 'fiery columns' of troops who arrived on the scene and massacred the rebel Chouans who opposed the French Revolution are not part of my family history. I am not writing in the name of any single community's history. Nor do I want to take the position of a justice-seeking historian out to avenge other peoples, brilliantly depicted by Chateaubriand.[1] If I have dedicated many years to this book, it is in my capacity as a *scholar*, in the hope that my research will help comprehend the enigma of genocides. I am sure, moreover, that a number of my contemporaries have asked themselves the same questions: How can it possibly happen? How can things reach the point of killing thousands, tens of thousands, even millions of defenceless individuals? And what is the point of making them suffer on top of it, why rape and torture them before destroying them?

We can admit, meanwhile, to being sometimes stirred by vengeful thoughts toward someone we regard as our enemy. And we may go so far as to dream of inflicting pain on him, even killing him. Fortunately, this murderous intention remains just what it is: mere fantasy. What occurs then when this fantasy manifests itself in reality? Especially when it consists of committing not just murder but mass murder? Reason totters on the edge of the chasm of human barbarism. Regarding the Holocaust, director Claude Lanzmann paraphrased these questions in an arresting statement: 'A gulf lies between the desire to kill and the act itself'.[2] This remark touches on the core problem of *crossing the threshold*, of plunging into the abyss of genocide, which is the central part of the analyses set forth in this book. We discover this moment to be in no way just a psychological impulse, but rather a highly complex process of reaching the tipping

1

point, of sliding into violence, that occurs with the interweaving of collective and individual dynamics which are political, social and psychological by nature, to name a few.

Is it not perhaps dangerous to seek to shed light on this enigma? Should we really try to find answers? There are some who would doubt the value of doing so, or even fear the outcome. They recommend keeping the memories alive, and preserving victims' accounts of their suffering. Seek to understand? Definitely not. For this would be to play into the logic of murderers and allow them a human face, invent excuses for them, and in short pardon their crimes. Such reluctance is not entirely unwarranted.

But 'understanding is not forgiving', replies American historian Christopher Browning at the very beginning of his major work on the transformation of German police officers in Hamburg into mass murderers of Polish Jews. 'Not trying to understand the perpetrators in human terms would make impossible not only this study but any history of Holocaust perpetrators that sought to go beyond one-dimensional caricature', he adds.[3] Let us recall also the words of the French historian Marc Bloch, written shortly before he was executed during the Nazi occupation of France: 'When all is said and done, a single word, "understand," is the beacon light of our research'.[4]

This quest for understanding is deeply rooted in the very experience of massacre, as victims wonder 'What is the point of all this?', 'Why me?', 'What have I done?' On arriving at Auschwitz, Primo Levi received this scathing reply: 'Here there is no why' ('*Heir ist kein warum*').[5] It is this primacy of apparent incoherence as imposed by the executioners that turns the desire to understand into a moral obligation. Refusing to seek understanding would amount to acknowledging their posthumous victory. It would amount to admitting that the intelligence of evil-doing was and remains decidedly stronger than that of attempting to untangle its mysteries. From an ethical standpoint such a position is untenable. For the sake of all those who have wondered 'why', we have a duty to apply our intellect.

Far from exonerating those who order or carry out a massacre, taking this all-embracing step ultimately involves questioning the responsibility of each and every one implicated in the killings. We cannot indeed consider that these people are necessarily always 'acted upon' by external factors, that their destructive behaviour is completely predetermined as if they were mere puppets. Nor, barring exceptions, can we perceive them as 'madmen', for as we will see, executioners come across as being very ordinary people. The question is much more to understand how they came to commit such acts, and what meaning (justification?) they invest in their involvement. In short, the question is to understand how individuals immersed in a given social situation will interpret this situation and react to it... by indulging in massacre. Max Weber's comprehensive sociology will prove especially suited to helping us specifically study these 'executioners': more than objective social causes, what counts when analysing their behaviour is primarily the meaning or meanings they ascribe to their action. Sociology's potential to aid our understanding of the process by which individuals descend into massacre are clear to see. But sociology has neglected this field of study for far too long, leaving it to the historians. In 1989 the English sociologist of Polish stock, Zygmunt Bauman, already made a case for sociology to allow itself to be queried by this 'ugly subject' in as much as the very history of the Holocaust had the potential to renew its theoretical framework.[6] More generally, I would say that over and above sociology, research in this field should be undertaken far more systematically by all branches of the social sciences, given the frequency with which civilian populations were destroyed in the twentieth century, and with the nascent twenty-first century already seeming to be following in step.

Falling within such a perspective, this book rises to a dual challenge. The first is comparison. Research on genocide is dominated by studies of the extermination of European Jews, and these are therefore impossible to leave to one side. However, to take scholarship in this field one step further, a comparative analysis is more than necessary: understanding is also comparing. The methodology of comparison offers the social sciences the rare possibility of testing their hypotheses, since submitting them to an experimental protocol is clearly impossible. So I decided to add to the case of the Holocaust those of Rwanda and Bosnia in the early 1990s. I could have turned to others. Unfortunately there is no lack of examples. I will, moreover, mention some of them occasionally, such as the Armenians

under the Ottoman Empire or Cambodia under Pol Pot. I nevertheless confined my research to these three examples the better to
undertake an in-depth inquiry, and the effort to grasp their terribly
complex histories still remained enormous.[7] Historians usually work
on a given period in a specific country with which they are extremely
familiar. But here the reader will be able to follow three histories in
parallel as their sometimes converging but most often diverging
paths are shown. For the process of comparison is indispensable
when it comes to showing, not the similarity of the cases studied but
rather, starting from a common set of questions, the specificity of
each historical instance. Comparing means differentiating.

Still, I needed one common notion to refer to in conducting my
investigation. Naturally the term 'genocide' sprang to mind, since its
use has become so commonplace. But it is precisely the frequent
misuse of this notion that makes employing it in the social sciences
problematic. Although recognising the genocidal nature of the
extermination of European Jews and the Rwandan Tutsis posed no
problem, the same was not true for Bosnia, which is considered by
some as genocide and by others as a form of ethnic cleansing. But
was I to be dogged from the start by these kinds of problem of definition, when the book's ambition was far more to do with better
identifying the processes of sliding into extreme forms of violence?
Including the case of Bosnia proved all the more interesting in this
regard, bearing in mind such quarrels. Breaking with many earlier
studies, I therefore deliberately decided to reverse the approach:
instead of tackling the controversial issue of the definition (or definitions) of genocide from the outset, I have preferred to deal with it
at the end of the book, drawing on all the reflection that comes
before.

This choice seemed all the wiser when, as my research progressed,
I realized that it was largely sufficient to use the notion of 'massacre'
as a minimal term of reference or smallest common denominator. I
will offer an empirical, typically sociological definition of massacre
as *a form of action that is most often collective and aimed at destroying non-
combatants*. Of course the objection can be levelled that this does not
solve the matter of defining genocide. My reply is that this, precisely,
is one of the aims of this book: to evaluate better in what circumstances a massacre or series of massacres can evolve toward a situation

qualified as genocidal. This approach has thus prompted me to question the relevance of the notion of 'genocide', highly instrumentalised in so many cases today, by undertaking a critical survey of nearly all the literature on the subject since the term was coined in 1944.[8]

The second challenge this book addresses is multidisciplinarity. In fact, 'massacre' as a phenomenon in itself is so complex that it requires a multidisciplinary examination: from the standpoint of not only the historian but also the psychologist, the anthropologist and so on. In this respect the work that certainly influenced me the most is one previously cited, by Christopher Browning. While he structures his book as a 'good historian', analysing murders of Jews by the German police in neat chronological order, taking care to interpret these men's conduct in each of their individual contexts, he concludes with a discussion of their behaviour in the light of certain psychological theories that could help our understanding of them. This carefully thought-out and qualified disciplinary openness definitely lends his writing depth. I have striven to proceed in a similar perspective, and have felt better qualified to do so with the acquisition over time of knowledge in multiple disciplines, ranging from psychology to political science and including contemporary history and the sociology of communication. However, the difficulty was to achieve a writing style that was not too 'disjointed' and obscure. In short, the style I sought, while deeply inspired by these various disciplines and their approaches, would strive to avoid jargon and offer a common meeting place for knowledge, while maintaining the coherent thread of a narrative. On this latter point, i.e. the common thread of the research, there is no doubt that this work focuses directly on power from an angle that is rarely analysed in political science: the power to destroy.

The more headway I made in drafting these pages, the more Michel Foucault's work came to mind, particularly his demonstration that all power seeks to leave its imprint on bodies, or conversely that the body is the privileged receptacle of power's will. We might recall that *Discipline and Punish* begins with the public execution of Damiens on the Place de Grève in Paris on 2 March 1757, he being sentenced to die by a series of unspeakable tortures for having made an attempt on the King's life.[9] This highly ritualised *mise-en-scène* of bodily suffering, Foucault instructs us, aims to restore through the spectacle of execution the full force of royal power that was momentarily wounded by the criminal's act. Partly drawing inspiration from this approach, I would argue that the act of massacring is the most spectacular practice which those in power have at their disposal to assert their ascendancy by marking, martyrising and destroying the bodies of those identified as their enemies. However, my object of study is not the suffering of a single individual but the massacre of hundreds, thousands, tens of thousands of people, if not many more. Obviously the political power discussed in this book does not appear in the same light as it would have done in the seventeenth and eighteenth centuries analysed by Foucault. Having first examined a power that tortures bodies in order to command respect and distance, he then showed how power in the following century tended to soften by inventing a new orthopaedics of discipline to ensure the docility of people's bodies and souls. What I have attempted to analyse here, instead, are the powers for whom such social control is no longer sufficient, that do not hesitate to destroy bodies in large numbers, *en masse*, basing their justifications on a rhetoric of the imaginary and the sacred. Thus whereas Foucault described a state that imprisons and controls, the purpose of the following pages is to understand how states can, under certain circumstances, inspire, organize or set in motion what we might call political practices of 'purification' and destruction of the 'social body'. Such practices are already observable in the nineteenth century with the rise of nationalist movements, but underwent a considerable upsurge in the twentieth century.

Need I add that this power to purify and destroy, even if we feel prepared to grasp it armed with the full advantage of multidisciplinary knowledge, nevertheless remains absolutely mind-boggling? There is no sidestepping this problem: the efforts of a researcher to understand can end up being paralysed by the horrifying nature of his subject matter. One might point out that he should have known what to expect, but who is ever really prepared for the shock of tales of cruelty in all their naked horror? Especially since the study of the behaviour of torturers prompts the researcher to ask himself personally a very uncomfortable question: 'What would I have done in their shoes?' It is true, however, that emotion can paralyse one's ability to think. In time the scholar recovers his wits and his distance from the subject. But he is left with the deep conviction that his work, walking the fine line between human and inhuman, is not without risk to himself. It involves an exploration of extremes, which lays bare his sensitivity, and is likely to provoke in him equally extreme attitudes of rejection or passion.

Certainly, stating that genocide is 'unthinkable' now appears to me to be the usual gross cliché of any conventional discourse on the subject. Of course genocide is thinkable—unfortunately it is too thinkable. As the reader discovers the wealth and depth of the various analyses presented and discussed here, there can be no doubt as to the pains to which scholars have already gone in attempting to grasp it. However, the monstrosity of the deeds generally associated with massacres does provoke horror and revulsion, and so the understandable refusal to tarry over them, and thus to ponder them. It is as if the closer the scholar draws to the fundamental core of human cruelty, the more he is faced with a sort of 'black hole' that resists any sort of understanding via the intellect. It might as well be said that such an apparently unfathomable universe will always call forth new research, given that human behaviour in such circumstances is so truly incredible. This also means that the researcher must show modesty in his interpretations, and always be prepared to go back to work.

I thus invite the reader to follow me along these tortuous paths that lead human beings from peace to barbarity. I have no intention of tugging at the heartstrings of cruelty or voyeurism to keep the attention; there are already far too many films and books that exploit such inclinations among the public. Of course, I will be unable to avoid describing certain facts that could not be concealed for any reason. But it is not a matter of offering them up as a spectacle, or of constructing a sort of aesthetics of horror. No, I have instead sought to lay bare—unanalysed—the processes that can lead to massive human destructivity. We will thus embark on a sort of journey, leading from countries that could be our own. They are not at war (yet?) but their domestic situation is deteriorating. In this increasingly critical context, hateful discourses are beginning to rise above the general hubbub. Then, without our noticing, suddenly the trigger of violence is pulled: one group becomes the executioner of another group, or a segment of its own. At that point anything becomes possible.

As for readers who live in a country where violence is already prevalent, where the state does not really ensure its citizens' security, or even designates some of them as its enemies, I hope they too will take some interest in reading these pages. They may be experiencing or have already experienced what I describe; they can talk about it better than I can. But perhaps they will find something new in this attempt to compare highly different countries. Sometimes it is through awareness of the misfortune of others that one manages to understand one's own condition, a little better and in a different light.

I

THE IMAGINARY CONSTRUCTS
OF SOCIAL DESTRUCTIVENESS

'Massacre'? The word evokes the sheer barbarity human beings are capable of: blood spewing everywhere, unthinkable atrocities, bodies torn asunder. Yet I will proceed to argue in the following pages that massacres are mainly born out of a mental process, a way of seeing some 'Other' being, of stigmatising him, debasing him, and obliterating him before actually killing him. This is always a complex mental process, and it usually takes time to mature. But it can also develop at astounding speed, particularly in the event of war.

Those who live in a country that is at peace today have trouble imagining the material reality of such a tragedy. The eternal question always crops up: how on earth is it possible? How can human beings suddenly become executioners of their fellow man? Yet if our own country sank into an increasingly serious economic crisis, with dismal parades of millions of unemployed, if it was harassed by a rise in terrorist attacks, each one bloodier than the last, how long would we remain impervious to this way of thinking? We would have to find enemies, not only beyond our borders but also within them, and—who knows?—maybe even right where we live: in our town, village, street, our own building. For it is my deep conviction, or rather the conclusion I have reached after years of research, that no society, when it begins to fall apart, is exempt from such processes.

The social dynamics that can lead to 'ethnic cleansing' and genocide are in fact latent in our school playgrounds or neighbourhoods. I am not even referring to such abominable graffiti as 'dirty Jew' or 'dirty Arab' that hostile hands have scribbled anonymously here and there on a letterbox, on a hoarding or in a stairwell. Such exclamations are already the hateful expression of the rejection of an 'Other' by racist individuals or groups in the very midst of our supposedly tolerant democracies. Already at a young age, don't children occasionally take pleasure in identifying a 'whipping boy'? Later, don't these youths tend to form 'clans' or gangs with a strong sense of belonging: 'us' against 'them'? And aren't our religious aspirations based on a basic quest for purity in a world perceived as impure? The dynamics of violence that end up in massacres draw on such factors: the identification of scapegoats, a radicalised antagonism between friend and enemy and, worse yet, killing as an act of purification. Of course the specific form a massacre takes always depends on the culture and the conflict that gives them shape. But they also have a universal foundation specific to our common humanity. Luckily, ideas are rarely translated into deeds. It takes a combination of many twisted detours, complex social circumvolutions and favourable political circumstances to bring about a massacre. But it always lurks as a possibility in man's future and his possible end.

Unpromising avenues

Let us start by clearing the ground to avoid detours down unpromising avenues of inquiry. The particular danger to be averted is privileging one factor—be it economics, demographics or culture—over others. For instance it is sometimes asserted that massacres have to do with the endemic poverty in some countries. This old theory correlating violence and poverty no doubt has some validity in that a serious economic crisis is likely to destabilize a social system. But poverty in and of itself does not cause mass violence, or genocide. If it did, given the number of different populations who in fact live below poverty level today, how can we explain the fact that they are not slaughtering each other?

Should the explanation be sought instead in the context of overpopulation problems affecting certain countries? Some put forward what they call the 'rabbit hutch theory': when too many rabbits are put in the same enclosure, they start killing each other to have more vital living space. The same is supposedly true of humans. Such a socio-biological approach, which tends to liken the behaviour of human beings to that of animals, is highly debatable. Indeed, no one has ever effectively demonstrated that human overpopulation necessarily leads to massacre. If it did, how could we explain the peacefulness that reigns today in the Netherlands, a small country which has one of the highest population densities in the world? The weight of demographics must certainly not be neglected, and recalling that the French war specialist Gaston Bouthoul once described war as 'deferred infanticide'.[1] And we know that underdevelopment encourages high birth rates, a factor that can be perceived as a threat by a neighbouring group in a numerical minority. Such a phenomenon can be identified in the Kosovo equation. That poor province of the former Yugoslavia is made up of 10 per cent of Serbs living alongside 90 per cent of Albanians. This statistical imbalance contributed to inducing among the Serbian minority, already apprehensive about the future, feelings of wariness and hostility toward the Albanian majority. Here the hostile perception of one group by another was based on a true demographic disproportion. But such reasoning does not apply to Germany in the 1920s. There, indeed, it is hard to see how the very small Jewish minority in this country (520,000 people, or 0.76 per cent of the total population)[2] could pose a demographic threat to the majority of non-Jewish Germans. In this case statistics are no help in understanding the rise of anti-Semitism.

Should the cause of massacres be sought then within the cultural particularity of one people or another? It is sometimes affirmed that Africans or Asians have a greater propensity to kill each other than 'civilized white' peoples. The wars around the Great Lakes region in Africa (Burundi, Rwanda, Democratic Republic of Congo) or the communal riots in India and Indonesia supposedly supply proof of these peoples' savagery. But have we forgotten the heavy history of the Europeans out to conquer other continents, crushing rebellious populations as they saw fit? And the expeditions of the English colonists taking possession of lands in North America at the Indians' expense? And in 1941 they were Europeans too, the Germans who on 29 and 30 August, in Babi-Yar, executed 33,371 Ukrainian Jews from Kiev (men, women and children). Have we also forgotten the tens of thousands dead and the atrocities committed during the civil wars in Spain (1936–9) and Greece (1943–9)? And it was again Europeans who massacred other Europeans in Srebrenica in July 1995, where Bosnian Serbs under the orders of General Mladic executed 8,000 Muslims (mostly men). Truly, in this Europe that claims to be a peaceful and pacified standard-bearer of the ideal of human rights, we have considerable trouble perceiving ourselves as 'savages', whereas our own barbaric acts are no less barbaric than those of other peoples on other continents. 'The barbarian is first of all a man who believes in barbarity,' Claude Lévi-Strauss once aptly remarked.[3]

We can discard, then, any culturalist approach that presents one people or another, on account of its culture, as predestined to perpetrate massacres. 'Culture' is not an immutable given but a dynamic construct that undergoes a wide range of transformations. In this spirit the political scientist Jean-François Bayart has offered an incisive critique of these 'illusions of cultural identity'.[4] There is no doubt that brutal cultural myths are often associated with the history of various peoples. But that doesn't mean these people will necessarily descend into savagery. However, these myths are sometimes exploited by those very individuals who call for revenge against a designated enemy.

Consequently, the idea that some sort of historical fatality has previously written massacre into the destiny of a country such as Bosnia or Rwanda is indefensible. Everything would then be rooted in clashes between age-old religious or ethnic hatreds. This so-called 'primordialist' theory interprets the development and sustaining of hostile relations between groups as being due to their different religious or ethnic identities. It views relations between them as irreconcilable because they are based on irrational affective perceptions of mutual wariness and ostracism.[5] In such a theory, identitarian sentiments specific to these groups, strongly rooted in their histories, would inevitably lead them to confrontation, and therefore to violence and massacres.

But a considerable body of empirical research shows that ethnic or religious heterogeneity does not necessarily lead to violence. As the English historian Marc Levene notes, 'Ethnic or cultural antipathies may exist without ever leading to massacre.'[6] Certainly ethnic or religious tensions sometimes result in riots that may seem spontaneous to the outside observer. But the systematic studies on this subject conducted by the American political scientist Donald Horowitz indeed show that although a spark may serve as a 'catalyst', such riots only really gain in magnitude if leaders organise them, some-times with the undercover support of certain state institutions (po-lice or the army).[7] In other words, identifying historic, ethnic or religious tensions in a given region is not enough to explain why, when and how massacres occur. Groups can experience tension and conflict between them without killing each other: there is no direct causal relation.

It is thus reasonable to think that the process leading to a massacre is the result not of one of these supposed 'causes' but instead an accu-mulation of them. This intuition is not misguided. For often enough, in countries that have experienced such events, it is common to observe a disastrous economic situation, huge social inequalities, a tendency toward overpopulation or an influx of immigrants per-ceived as foreigners, ethnic or religious tensions, and so on. However, this conjunction of 'objective' causes is still far from leading unavoid-ably to a massacre. It certainly creates a situation conducive to out-breaks of violence of one group toward another that may have already been the object of negative prejudices, or even racist attitudes.

But such a context still requires that opinion leaders, whether or not they have political power, suggest a certain interpretation of this situation and affirm: 'this is what is happening to us, this is who is responsible for our misfortune. It is *they* who are the cause of our suf-fering. We absolutely must get rid of them. We promise you that afterwards everything will be better. Just give us your support, or better yet, join in the fight to rid ourselves of this scourge.' It is truly this type of discourse that can set the stage for mass violence and accompany it. So this is the real starting point for this book.

The power of imaginary constructs

What could 1930s Germany, late 1980s Yugoslavia and early 1990s Rwanda possibly have in common? The first of these was a great 'civilised' industrial country that lost the First World War and in the following years underwent severe political instability. The 1917 Bolshevik revolution in Russia, a fantastic promise of change for some, also helped fuel an intense fear of communism which right-wing and extreme-rightwing parties made sure they exploited. The second, Yugoslavia, entered a period of political uncertainty with

the death in 1980 of its founding father, Joseph Broz, better known
as Tito, who in the aftermath of the Second World War had pulled
off the feat of building a federal state uniting different nationalities
(Serbian, Croatian, Slovene etc.). A feat of strength in the literal
sense, too, for Tito, after the war, made no bones about executing his
opponents, real or imagined, the Bleiburg and Kosevje massacres
being the best known today.[8] The vacuum left by his demise in 1980
allowed for the revival, especially in Serbia and in Croatia, of a
nationalism that the myth of the 'communist brotherhood' never
managed to eliminate entirely. In the small, mainly agricultural and
post-colonial country of Rwanda, which first came under German
and later Belgian domination, tension suddenly worsened between
the Hutus at the head of the state, and the Tutsi minority. In 1959, in
the broader context of the decolonisation of Africa, the Hutus took
power and massacred a portion of the Tutsi population, provoking
the flight of many of them into neighbouring countries (Burundi
and Uganda). A series of mirrored political crises then occurred
between Burundi, ruled by the Tutsis, and Hutu-led Rwanda, com-
pounded by each country's individual internal crises. From 1990 on,
the future became all the more threatening for the Hutus in Rwanda
when an army of Tutsi fighters, the Rwanda Patriotic Front (RPF,
mainly composed of offspring of 1959 exiles), attempted to penetrate its territory with the obvious intention of re-taking power
wrested from their parents thirty years earlier.

In these three countries, the situation was exacerbated by a serious
economic crisis that not only deprived many individuals of access to
jobs and an income, but also increased the feeling of anxiety with
respect to an uncertain future. There is no need to go over again the
traumatic effects the Great Depression had in 1929, with its millions
of unemployed, particularly disastrous in Germany. The Yugoslav
crisis in the 1980s, in the context of the successive oil crises, is
probably less well known. It was nevertheless extremely severe, with
the standard of living dropping by at least 30 per cent. An American
observer, Harold Lydall, pointed out in this regard: 'The decline in
the standard of living has been so great that it is difficult to think of
any other country that would not have responded with major
political changes, or even a revolution.'[9] In Rwanda, as early as the
1980s, agricultural production was no longer able to keep up with

the demographic curve, this country having the highest population density on the continent of Africa.[10] Food shortages, even famine, started to appear. 'Already in 1989', notes Belgian anthropologist Danielle de Lame, 'the farmers described their situation as apocalyptic. … The last satisfactory coffee bean harvest (their primary source of foreign exchange) had been in 1987 and the price on the world market was dropping at the same time.'[11] A large proportion of the nation's youth (over 57 per cent of the population was under the age of twenty at the time) owned no land and had little hope of acquiring any. They lived from hand to mouth with no job or other opportunity. How in this case can anyone believe in the future? Where could they turn?

In a situation where former points of reference seem to crumble, where threats become more and more frightening, how can the ruling elite be expected to react? Audacious economic reforms? New administrative measures? Participation in an international cooperation programme? All these technical solutions or other rescue plans do not seem up to the task in hand. For it is the very 'soul' of a disoriented and paralysed population that appears to be at stake in such circumstances. When a person has experienced severe shock or stress, a post-traumatic state can often be diagnosed. By extension we can speak of a 'collective trauma' for a nation or a community whose identity seems profoundly altered by the crisis or crises assailing it. This community's basic points of reference, which cause its members to say 'we Germans' or 'we Hutus', seem destabilised. It is these imaginary foundations of their institutions, to use Cornelius Castoriadis' terminology, that are in crisis. These imaginary constructs, which give meaning to those who share them and to what brings them together, are situated far out of reach from technical regulations. But suddenly they no longer seem to operate. That which allowed people to say 'us' is not there. The 'us' becomes a grievance, a wound, an affliction. Who can lead the group forward out of this state of crisis and offer a new perspective?

It is the social and political actors who will, of course, through their discourse and actions, take charge of the collective emotions associated with this mass trauma. They are ideally placed to be heard by the public, and the affective nature of their posture vis-à-vis the public ensures this will happen. Such actors are said to 'know how to talk to the people', using metaphors and symbols that resonate deeply with their own history. By this very fact, given a situation perceived to be threatening and chaotic, they respond to the imaginary construct that has emerged in crisis by another imaginary construct that restructures the previous one on new foundations. True, their ascendancy over public opinion is never guaranteed: other political and social actors in competition with them can champion totally different visions of the future. For instance, the latter will denounce the former's outrageous demagogy. The result is necessarily a conflict between two parties, the outcome of which is far from certain. But what is certain is that the actors who know how to tug at these strings of the *imaginaire* have in their possession a powerful weapon that lets them glimpse the possibility of seizing power.

Their imaginary rhetoric first aims to transform the collective anxiety which has more or less permeated the population into a feeling of intense fear with regard to an enemy they set out to depict as being highly dangerous. Anxiety and fear are not the same thing. One specific feature of anxiety is its indistinct, even indefinable nature, whereas the causes of fear are easier to name and thus identify. The aim of such rhetoric seems to be to make this anxiety fix on some 'enemy' who is then endowed with a real-life 'figure' denounced as being a cancer within the society. The most extreme discourses present these enemy figures as necessarily frightening, even diabolical. Thus, well before Hitler came to power, caricatures of the evil-minded 'Jew' had been in circulation for a long time. In pre-genocide Rwanda, the same was true of the 'Tutsi', and in the 1980s, before Milosevic rose to power, the rumour was circulating among the Serbs in Kosovo that the Albanians wanted simply to perpetrate 'a new genocide' against them. This attempt to channel anxiety on to an easily identifiable enemy is already a way of responding to the population's trauma: they are provided with an explanation of the source of the threat. This 'transmutation' of insidious anxiety into a fear concentrated on a hostile 'figure' serves as the foundation for hatred to develop against the evil-minded 'Other'. Hatred here is not a fundamental given defining from the outset how 'natural' relationships will be between groups. It is instead a constructed passion, a product both of the wilful action of its zealous promoters and by the circumstances encouraging it to spread. In the end the logical and dreadful outcome of this transformation of anxiety into hatred inevitably boils down to eliciting in society the desire to destroy what has been designated as the source of fear. True, it is still only a 'desire': we are still well within the realm of the *imaginaire*. But it is an *imaginaire* of death.

This operation has obvious benefits for those who initiate it. We should not lose sight of the final aim of this social-affective process: to treat the afflicted 'us' and reshape it in order to help it emerge from its state of crisis. Focusing attention on an 'enemy to be destroyed' means seeking to rebuild oneself at the expense of this dangerous 'Other'. Beyond fear and hatred, thus appears a fantasy of all-powerfulness in which this 'us' is victorious: it is regenerated by destroying 'them'. The death of an evil 'them' makes possible the omnipotence of 'us'. Such a psychological posture may seem 'primitive' or archaic-which, in fact, it is. We are still here in the realm of the *imaginaire*, but unlike that of death, it is one of omnipotence and glory. The two are inextricably linked. The two of them can be terribly effective because they affect the very foundations of the human psyche as explained, for example, by psychoanalysis.

Destructive fantasies. Can the field of psychoanalysis prove useful in understanding phenomena of extreme violence? If so, with what prerequisites? Currents in psychoanalysis are various and sometimes contradictory. Some historians and sociologists, not without good reason, are hostile towards any attempt to gain insight from this discipline. Moreover, there is always the risk of 'psychologising' or 'psychoanalysing' the conduct of historical actors when political analyses would seem much more apt to explain their behaviour. But why should the scholar deprive himself entirely of the psychological, even psychoanalytical perspective, to achieve a deeper understanding of often repugnant phenomena, when history, sociology, and political science seem at pains to account for them? Significant in this regard is the very structure of the pioneering and incisive work by Norman Cohn[12] on the roots of anti-Semitism: after a brilliant analysis of the myth of the *Protocols of the Elders of Zion*, he concludes his essay by suggesting an interpretation through 'collective psychopathology' (an expression that Sigmund Freud would certainly not reject). To some extent, this book begins where Norman Cohn's research left off.

However, we need to be clear from start that the contribution to understanding violence by the father of psychoanalysis is disappointing. Freud first saw aggression as related to sexuality (in sado-masochism, for instance). Then, after the First World War, he viewed aggressive behaviour as a component of a 'death impulse' seeking to tear apart everything that the libido has united, and to reduce to zero any impulsive tension. This death impulse, biological in origin, supposedly incites man helplessly to destroy himself or others, with no apparent escape from this tragic destiny. For lack of proof, this Freudian theory remains a postulate viewed by many, and notably by many psychoanalysts, with circumspection. Freud's reasoning in fact comes across as a fine example of pseudo-explanation, as it replies to the question 'why does man tend to destroy himself?' with the disarmingly simplistic 'because he is driven by a destructive instinct'! In his famous correspondence with Albert Einstein, who in 1932 asked him the question 'Why war?' Freud seems in fact to be conscious of the limits of his approach in this area.[13] Nonetheless, barely a year before Hitler's rise to power, he did demonstrate a certain clairvoyance in expressing his profound pessimism as to man's determination to forestall his own collective violence, even through the use of Law. He had come to believe rather that man now had the capacity to self-destruct. Freud then reformulated for the famous physicist his theory of the destructive instinct, which he claimed was not given the attention it warrants. However, at the end of his letter he indicates his own dissatisfaction with the explanations just given: 'should this exposé prove a disappointment to you, my sincere regrets'. In fact, the father of psychoanalysis did not often address the question of aggression, and even less so that of collective violence. It was his theories of human sexuality, not of violence and war, that earned him such renown.

However, followers in his footsteps have embarked on more detailed research on the question of aggression. Among them is the English psychoanalyst Melanie Klein, who set out to detect its existence among infants. According to her theory, the origin of aggressive behaviour is to be sought in the primal conflicts of early childhood and infants' destructive fantasies.[14] She devoted much of her work to studying infantile development and children's archaic fantasies of devouring and omnipotence, thereby breaking with the myth of childhood innocence.[15] She viewed the child's imaginary world as being made up of love and hate towards a mother who one minute offers the child the breast, and then refuses it.[16] These very early sensations are also said to be at the basis of our primary perceptions of good and bad, of good and evil, of friend and enemy.

Continuing along the lines of Melanie Klein's approach, the Italian psychoanalyst Franco Fornari, in an incisive yet little-known work, attempted to lay down the psychological foundations for an interpretation of war. Analysing the correspondence between Freud and Einstein, he also admits that it is 'difficult not to feel a sense of disappointment in reading Freud's reply, even if a certain tendency to relieve people of any illusions they may have by pointing out hidden and disturbing aspects at the foundation of their values is perfectly in keeping with his style.' It was from the work of Melanie Klein that Fornari drew inspiration to reflect on war. He borrows from her distinction between 'paranoid-schizoid position' and 'depressive position', that both develop in the first months of life from the good mother/bad mother dichotomy. In the depressive position, the infant 'is concerned with saving the love object through which he feels alive to the extent of sacrificing himself out of love for this object. In the paranoid-schizoid position, on the other hand, the infant is worried about saving his Self by destroying the object via which he feels destroyed.'[17] The paranoid-schizoid position precedes the depressive position. But the latter plays a fundamental role because it makes the child feel for the first time the sense of guilt that arises from the desire to kill the love object. Fornari accords the same importance to this depressive phase as Melanie Klein does. He sees in it the origin of civilisation, given the fact that the feeling of guilt introduces laws making murder illegal. But while this 'psychological organiser' can be effective for inhibiting individual violence, it doesn't prevent war.

According to Fornari, war is the epitome of a paranoid process, based on the belief that it is by killing the enemy that one will survive: 'The subject perceives the object as a threat to his own existence, a threat in and of itself illusory, but psychologically real.'[18] The paranoid violence that breaks out during war stems from a typical psychotic illusion: by killing the enemy-other, the subject believes he is overcoming death. In short, the paranoid-schizoid position boils down to this elementary equation: YOUR DEATH IS MY LIFE. For Fornari war is thus first and foremost an imaginary phenomenon related to the destructive fantasies of early childhood precisely because during the infant's emotional development, the paranoid-schizoid position occurs before the real threat arrives from a real enemy. As the American psychologist René Spitz has shown, an eight-month-old child illusorily projects an aggressive intent on an unknown person—the stranger—taking him for an enemy without the latter having ever manifested any real hostile attitude. This is why Franco Fornari has no trouble asserting: 'It might be said that societies, with respect to war, are conditioned from a psychological standpoint to situate themselves at the level of anxiety of an eight-month-old child.'[19]

This sort of regressive mechanism against an internal enemy seems to be established through such hostile representations as those of 'the Jew' or 'the Tutsi'. In these moments of severe crisis, where the mad history of a country seems to be going out of control, looms the possibility of a collective regression towards this archaic conflict. Indeed, such circumstances lead individuals to transgress the depressive position that opened them to the process of civilisation. Assailed by anxiety, and convinced they can no longer control their own fate, they end up wanting to extract from this other his evil side, which they perceive as being responsible for their suffering. They thus tend to revert to that stage of primal conflict that is so powerful because it 'speaks' to everyone, as it is a stage in everyone's personality development. This mechanism of archaic defence aims concretely at the disintegration of the evil social object—sometimes by destroying it—to restore the primal position of omnipotence in early childhood. Through this attempt to recover the ego's all-powerfulness, in a paranoid mode, individuals go through the path of their psychological development backward: they experiment with a process of de-civilisation.[20]

Political discourses generally described as being 'extremist' are also those that appear, from a psychological standpoint, to be the most regressive. They in fact draw on this matrix of the infantile imagination to 'read' and interpret the realities of the crisis. They feed on the chaos of society, whether it is at war or not, to say: 'See, we're right!' Here the relations between the imaginary and the real are not as contradictory as they appear. True, it is indeed in the imaginary representations of the executioner that the figure of the victim, 'his' victim, is first constructed. Thus the ideology of the Hutu extremists in Rwanda was first based on negative stereotypes of the Tutsi (arrogant, dominating, foreign, wicked, etc.) rooted in colonial representations that had described the supposed superiority of the 'Tutsi race'. As the Canadian scholars Frank Chalk and Kurt Jonassohn have noted, it is indeed first in the executioner's eyes that the 'other' takes on the figure of an enemy to be destroyed.[21] Good methodological sense thus dictates that we give priority to analysing this imaginary construct, its structure and its basic themes, in order to understand how the process of mass violence is triggered. Such is precisely the aim of this first chapter.

Between imaginary and real: the role of ideology. Nonetheless, we must beware of taking the above to mean that the identity of victims is pure fantasy. Indeed, if we try to grasp these phenomena solely from the standpoint of the imaginary, we might conclude that it is all an 'illusion', and that the victims themselves are unreal. But they are very real indeed: the Nazis did not invent the 'Jews', whose history is ancient, who have religious and community traditions, and so on. In this sense the notion of 'identity'—be it religious, ethnic or other— is not an invention of the future executioners. Individuals have defined themselves as 'Jews', 'Tutsis' or 'Muslims' from Bosnia-Herzegovina before being castigated and persecuted. This is why the imaginary process described here is potentially so dangerous. If it were outside the frame of any sort of reality, it would remain at the stage of a death-dealing daydream. But it plunges its roots into reality to say, with the assuredness of a statement of fact: 'Here are the people who are the cause of all our misfortunes.' In short, this *imaginaire*, which draws on the most archaic of human anxieties, feeds on real phenomena to distort the reality of those it designates as victims to make this reality truly frightening. Imaginary and real thus seem inextricably linked.

What triggers the shift from fantasy into action? How does the fear of being destroyed lead to the act of destroying another defenceless individual? This comes down to wondering how the primal psychological positions described by Franco Fornari can contribute to the appalling development of an episode of mass violence. In the course of early childhood each of us is confronted with archaic anxieties, which the various stages of psychological development should theoretically enable us to suppress. Fortunately these destructive fantasies remain precisely in the state of fantasies! Our dreams are moreover the means by which to 'realise' them in our imaginary world, if psychoanalytical theory is right. And the tales and legends our parents read to us in the course of our child-hood in fact helped us to overcome them.[22] So what causes these fantasies to be carried out in some cases? What happens to bring them about in reality?

This tipping process is fluid, complicated and, fortunately, un-certain. But in any event, in order for this *imaginaire* of destruction (and omnipotence) to be able to operate in reality, a common binding agent is required: a discourse that is perceived as coherent and credible, and able to allay individuals' anxiety. This binding agent linking together the individuals who choose to adhere to it is ideology. Through it imaginary and real interrelate. By ideology I mean a discourse based on arguments that are both rational and irra-tional, i.e. structured in opposition to this evil-minded 'Other'. In a way, ideology—or rather ideologies (because there are multiple for-mulations of them)—is an 'accretion' of imaginary representations. These discourses, in which myths and realities are intertwined, can serve as a springboard towards massacre.

Now, the basic rhetoric of these ideologies, and the vocabulary it uses, is never innocent. In the cases of Germany, Yugoslavia and Rwanda such rhetoric is built around three main themes: identity, purity and security. Since these pertain to life, death and the sacred, they can leave no-one indifferent: they 'speak' to everyone, inter-mixing imagination and reality. It is on the basis of this rhetoric that enemy figures take shape, as I would like to demonstrate now. Although these imaginary themes—identity, purity and security— are most often interconnected, for clarity's sake I would like to analyse them separately.

From the identity narrative to the figure of Traitor

Paul Valéry long ago made this remarkable observation: 'History is the most dangerous product the chemistry of the intellect has ever concocted.... It sets people dreaming, it intoxicates them, spawns in them false memories, exaggerates their reflexes, keeps old wounds open, torments them in their repose, prompts them to delusions of grandeur or deliriums of persecution, and makes nations bitter, arrogant, unbearable and vain.'[23] The French writer was pointing out here less the role of History itself, but more the way a group constructs its recollection of its own past. For it is not so much historical events that weigh on the lives of populations as the representations they construct from these events.

In the case of Germany after 1918, for instance, it was less the Treaty of Versailles that 'determined' the country's future destiny than the way in which some German political actors used their interpretation of the very unfavourable conditions this treaty offered Germany to stoke the nationalist fire. Other factors contributed to this disastrous situation: the effects of the 'Great War' on the population itself, the economic crisis, recurrent political unrest, and so on. The historian George Mosse maintains that one consequence of the particularly intense violence of the First World War was the 'brutalisation' of social relations. His analyses are insightful enough when one considers the veritable cult of violence that seemed to develop in Germany throughout the 1920s, the evidence of which he describes right down to everyday life.[24] But why wasn't France also affected by this 'war culture', given that the French, like the Germans, underwent the same torrent of gunfire and slaughter on the same massive scale? The big difference is that the Germans, unlike the French, could not obtain release from this tragedy through the collective satisfaction of victory: they had been beaten, and many of them could not accept defeat, especially on the right and extreme right. Ideological discourses wielded by these political movements tried to tap into the trauma of defeat for their own benefit by offering a narrative that could rescue the nation's honour and provide it with new incentive.

The thread of this narrative, which potentially paved the way for a new spiral of violence, consisted precisely in a reading of this 'misfortune' that had befallen the people. In other historic situations, however different they may be, this same 'explanatory' pattern can be found, based on a handful of apparently convincing assertions: 'If we are suffering today, it is not our fault: we are the victims of

History. However, the tragedy that has befallen us is not fatal. We have the means to reconquer our honour and our glory. To do so we must believe in ourselves, in our people, in its destiny.'

Then the 'afflicted us' winds up almost transcended by words that seem timeless, words that provide a way to escape this unbearable present to reunite with the everlasting soul of the people, 'our people'. There occurs a sort of *transmutation* of the initial trauma through this saving and grandiose 'us', through which individuals can draw the strength required for their collective recovery. In his reflection on the bases of the Nazi *imaginaire* the Swiss historian Philippe Burrin draws a fitting parallel between the theme of resentment, constantly ruminated by Hitler and his followers, and this quest for Germanic omnipotence. 'Resentment', he writes, 'is a sense of injustice, of being in the right and yet mocked, accompanied by an awareness of impotence as a result of which one becomes obsessed with the memory of all the unfairness suffered. But such an obsession may in some circumstances—Nietzsche's analysis springs to mind—introduce a transmutation of values whereby one may assign a negative quality to what one has previously desired yet which has remained unattainable. One does this in the name of a new set of values, antithetical to one's earlier set, and doing so can restore a positive sense of self-esteem.' And Burrin adds: 'If ever resentment resulted in such a transmutation of values, it happened in Hitler's case, for here was a loser who discovered a new basis for self-esteem in an ideology that exalted the creative power of the Aryan race. The same could be shown to apply to the Nazi party generally, for its chief political offering and principal source of success at a time of great crisis was, so to speak, the projection of a refusal to accept humiliation, on the one hand, and on the other an image of 'existential power'.'[25] This existential power was supposed to be embodied in the 'community of the people' of Aryans, destined to dominate Europe and perhaps even the world.

This kind of resentment can also be detected in the history of the peoples of Yugoslavia. Deeply felt mistrust between Croats and Serbs, for example, could not be dislodged in the first federal state (1919–41), nor in the second (1945–91). Perpetuation of this union among southern Slavs depended primarily on the capacity of these two peoples to get along despite their national differences. But the contracts conditioning it were sources of endless dispute. Croats have always felt dominated: in the nineteenth century by Vienna or Budapest, in the twentieth century by Belgrade. As for the Serbs, they have always seen themselves as the centre of the Empire. Believing that the blood they spilt during the two world wars had never been properly rewarded, they aspired to much more than just recognition and power. This basic antagonism between Croats and Serbs certainly went through periods of calm. But the reality was that it never ceased to tear the state of Yugoslavia apart, preventing it from achieving any semblance of stability.[26] Nationalist discourses on both sides seized the opportunity of the economic slump in the 1980s to break out in the open. In fact, according to English sociologist John Allcock, the Yugoslav elites proved themselves incapable at the time of resolving the economic crisis by adapting to the world market; moreover, the Communist system of self-management very likely acted as a structural obstacle to such a shift.[27] Under these conditions, the state legitimacy crisis prompted political leaders to choose between *ethnos* and *demos*, in other words between an 'imagined community' (on an ethnic basis) and a redefined 'common citizenship' (in Yugoslav terms).[28] This question having fired up the political debate, both Milosevic and Tudjman came out in favour of the ethno-national solution. Mythical representations that tended to equate a territory and a people, and the blood spilled by this people on this territory, wound up at the forefront of the political scene. The *imaginaires* of 'us', or rather *'among ourselves'*, against an 'Other', even against the 'Others', had bright days ahead.

Among Hutus in Rwanda we can also identify gradual accumulation of a painful memory feeding on a past of suffering, humiliation, forced labour, and so on, associated with the period of Tutsi domination. But the shaping of this narrative of victimisation was quite different to that of Yugoslavia. Hutu and Tutsi identities, both particularly complex, have fluctuated throughout Rwanda's history. The French historian Jean-Pierre Chrétien and the American political scientist (Ugandan by birth) Mahmood Mamdani suggest two interpretations of the phenomenon, each taking a regional perspective that includes the history of neighbouring Burundi and Uganda.[29] They concur on the fact that the arrival of colonizers in the late nineteenth century, and racial representations that the

Germans and later the Belgians projected on the populations of Rwanda, contributed to the increasing reification of these fluctuating Hutu-Tutsi identities. The country being ruled by a Tutsi king, the first anthropologists were to devise a racial theory 'explaining' why the Tutsi minority was indeed dominant even though the Hutus were in the majority. In the absence of any real cultural or linguistic differences, the description of apparently distinct physical features is presented as the main criterion for differentiation. The Hutus, described as short and stocky with heavy facial features, supposedly contrast with the tall and slim Tutsis with fine features: 'real negroes' as opposed to the 'Hamites'. These two 'races' are said to be of different origins: the Tutsis, a cattle-breeding people, were said to have arrived from Egypt and to have rapidly dominated the sedentary farmer Hutus; an affirmation that seems plausible since many Tutsis kept cattle.[30] But this highly schematic racial categorisation by agricultural activity did not in any way reflect the real (and high) numbers of poor Tutsis and higher-class Hutus. Till the early 1950s the Belgian colonial administration nevertheless legitimised such representations, relying on Tutsi royalty to help rule the country. It also favoured education of the Tutsis, considered to be more intelligent, with the support of the very influential Catholic Church. In the 1930s Belgium even went so far as to institute an identity card that specified the individual's 'origin': Hutu, Tutsi or Twa.[31]

However, some twenty years later, in the early days of decolonisation, the Belgians did an about-face: they chose to promote the social advancement of the Hutus. Among the better-educated Hutus a discourse emerged demanding rule over the country in the name of the majority population to bring an end to exploitation by the Tutsi minority. The result was, once again, another vision of the past claiming that the Hutus were the first to arrive in the hills of Rwanda, well before the Tutsis. The future first president of the Rwandan Republic, Grégoire Kayibanda, became the standard bearer for this discourse, which advocated in reality a radical social and political change.[32] Thus the young Rwandan state was built from the start on this sovereign proclamation of 'We, the Hutus', 'majority people'. In the very first book devoted to the genocide of 1994, Gérard Prunier showed that this cultural mythology constitutes a remote but nevertheless fundamental cause of this genocide.[33]

In each case we thus see an identity process being constructed on the basis of a rebirth or recomposition of 'us' as a collective response to a situation of crisis, trauma or intense upheaval. As the French political scientist Denis-Constant Martin points out, identity narratives are a means 'in modern situations of turmoil and rapid change, both in material and moral terms, to verbalise anxiety and at the same time to assuage it by restoring meaning to what no longer seems to have any, by use of familiar historical, territorial, cultural or religious references'.[34] It should be noted here, however, that it is far from being the case that construction of this identity always leads to confrontation and violence. By definition, identity is conceived through the perception of a difference, giving substance both to One and the Other. And this One can enter into peaceful relations with this Other: History provides enough examples. But it is also true that this identity 'open' to another can retreat and withdraw into itself by establishing a criterion of exclusion from this Other. The criterion can either be race or ethnicity, the idea of a nation, or even both at once. The idea of 'race', once championed by many scholars (ethnologists in the first place), is today totally untenable, even though it is still undeniably based on tenacious presuppositions. The idea of 'ethnic group' does not appear to be any clearer: having been used also by anthropologists, it is tending to be abandoned for lack of a pertinent definition. As for 'nation', largely accepted and vindicated by contemporary thinkers, the American anthropologist Benedict Anderson has demonstrated in a brilliant essay that it is also the product of an imaginary construct.[35] By the same token the English philosopher and anthropologist Ernest Gellner maintains: 'It is nationalism which engenders nations, and not the other way round.'[36]

The stigmatisation of 'minor' differences. But let us turn our attention beyond these critical considerations, for the point here is not to discuss racism, ethnicism or nationalism but the way in which such doctrines influence the course of history. And surely what matters primarily in this regard is what people believe to be true. Is it not first and foremost their imaginary representations of reality that count? In short, we are interested in the conditions that make the *imaginaire* in politics effective, when a large number of individuals—gathered together in a country and beyond its borders—believe or want to believe that they belong to one and the same 'race', 'ethnic group', or even 'nation'. They give themselves this identity-based criterion that they use as a 'safety shell' to get through a socially agitated period. When individuals tend to lose their own bearings, one of the most frequent responses is to withdraw into what they believe is their common identity in order to face the situation that disorients them. They then tend to abandon their own individuality to blend into what they perceive to be their common group of membership, their 'community'. They take what was given to them by birth and through education (language, religion, nationality)—the main-springs of their collective strength—to react to the crisis. In some respects they 'essentialise' what they are, or believe they are, in order to make it the very substance of their combat.

The community of 'us' will be constructed at the expense of rejection of some 'Other', perceived as a profoundly different 'Them': the Aryans as opposed to the Jews, the Hutus as opposed to the Tutsis, the Serbs as opposed to the Croats—called *Ustachis* and *Chetniks* (the names of their nationalist groups during the Second World War).[37] A classic social phenomenon, one group's identity is asserted in opposition to the stigmatised otherness of another group. This is how 'differences' are constructed.[38] But how can we understand how this antagonistic dynamic between identity and otherness in some cases becomes incandescent? It's as if symbolic barriers were erected between individuals who are nevertheless close. For the paradox is that this conflictual process does not operate against a distant other but rather one that is nearby: a neighbour. 'The best enemies, contrary to a commonly accepted idea, are not recruited out of difference but in resemblance and proximity.'[39]

Sigmund Freud explored this paradox in his study of the 'narcissism of minor differences'. He noted that human beings—all alike—seek to differentiate themselves from one another by highlighting minor differences. Since they exaggerate their importance, this emotional investment becomes a cause of hostility among men. It is basically a narcissistic inclination: attention is shifted toward the other only to distinguish oneself and reinforce one's own self-esteem. Freud noted that even long-standing emotional ties such as those among families are not shielded from such crises. In general, the closer the relations between human groups, the more hostile they may be towards one another. The same phenomenon can be observed between societies and nations: 'Of two neighbouring towns each is the other's most jealous rival; every little canton looks down upon the others with contempt. Closely related races keep one another at arm's length; the South German cannot endure the North German, the Englishman casts every kind of aspersion upon the Scot, the Spaniard despises the Portuguese.'[40]

Drawing inspiration from this study of Freud's, Michael Ignatieff believes that nationalism can be conceived as a form of narcissism. Nationalism takes differences that are minor in themselves and transforms them into major differences. The narcissistic outlook has the particular characteristic of approaching the other only to confirm his difference. In a crisis situation perception of this supposed difference becomes downright intolerable. 'In that Serbian bunker I heard reservists say that they disliked breathing the same air as Croats, disliked being in the same room with them. There was some threatening uncleanness about them. And this from the men who only two years before had not even thought that the air they breathed belonged to one group or the other!'[41] However, Sigmund Freud formulates an overall judgement that does not take context sufficiently into account. In fact, it is not so much the difference in itself that causes the conflict as the specific perception of this difference and the exploitation of it to reassure a group of individuals about its identity in a situation in which this group feels threatened. In times of peace and prosperity, this identity fixation does not occur. Differences in language and traditions can be fairly insignificant. A Serbian man can love a Croatian woman; Hutus and Tutsis can help each other out working in the fields. There are many individuals who hold identity criteria to be unimportant and even pay no attention to them.

In Germany before Hitler's rise to power, some people were not even aware of their 'Jewishness' till the Nazis forced them to be. The remarkable diary kept by the philologist Victor Klemperer bears witness to this evolution.[42] He gives a day-by-day account of the extraordinary social pressure that mounted against the Jews inside the country, to the extent that they lost any individuality, since this was dissolved into the overall notion of 'Jew'. Once this point had been reached, mixed marriages could founder, and inter-ethnic friendships or professional relations that were once 'normal' could be broken up. The identity criterion takes over everything and defines everything, crushing the individual, who is no longer known as Martin, Bogdan or Seraphin. He is first and foremost a Jew, a Serb or a Tutsi. People can always try to resist such pressure. In Germany many 'mixed' couples refused to divorce, although the regime strongly encouraged them to do so. This resistance of the heart was in fact a recurrent problem for the Nazis.

Figures of the enemy within. Identity pressures can gain ground and become all the more forceful as those encouraging them actually acquire the instruments of power. For the reductive force of this process lies certainly not only in the motives of group psychology. Its dynamic is basically political: those who believe that this 'identity solution' can lift their country out of a crisis fully intend to impose this belief on the entire social body. In short, they use the emotional power of identity to incite the people to support them and thus win or retain power, whether this manipulative device is called nationalism, racism or ethnicism. Such struggle for power is not so much led against a 'them' to be rejected as it is against segments of 'us' that resist this identitarian vision of their country's future. Here emerges another paradox regarding a possible upsurge in violence.

Indeed, the first hostile figure of the enemy that tends to constitute itself not only in people's minds but also in reality is not necessarily what one would believe. We shall recall, for instance, that Nazi concentration camps were first designed to imprison socialist and communist political opponents, and that Milosevic slowly consolidated his power by gradually dismissing all those in the Yugoslavian communist apparatus who were hostile to his nationalist ideology. Not to mention the insults and attacks Hutu moderates were subjected to well before the genocide undertaken by Hutu extremist supporters of President Habyarimana: the extremists used terms that made them out to be monsters, '*Ibihindugemb*': animals with no head or tail.

Thus the enemy is first of all that segment of 'us' that backs different political positions, that is opposed to marginalising the Jews or the Tutsis. Of course the political struggle against these opponents goes together with the banishment of 'them': the two go hand in

hand. But all things considered, I accord a decisive role to this preliminary political struggle that goes on within 'us': its outcome
indeed determines what turn the ensuing events will take, in other
words, whether the identitarian process will become radicalised or
not. Such political confrontation within the very confines of 'us' is
not all spelled out beforehand: everything depends on the outcome
of the power struggle. At stake is the power to dominate the other
members—all the members—of the group.

For partisans of an identitarian policy this enemy lurking within
'us' takes on the overall figure of the 'suspect', even the traitor. In
Rwanda it is called '*Icyitso*', meaning 'accomplice'. The fight against
this enemy can go well beyond the neutralisation or elimination of
declared opponents, be they political, labour or organisation leaders.
What is expected is the unfailing solidarity of all group members to
confront the designated enemy. The desire for control over all the
constituent members of 'us' thus tends to be total. The process is a
fairly logical one: if this identity-based mobilisation is founded on a
sense of collective threat to the afflicted 'us', then it is reasonable to
close ranks to confront the common danger. All members of a group
are called on to mobilise in this existential combat and, as an
important corollary, point their finger at, even reject, those who seek
to stand apart.

However, it is highly unlikely that a country, through its social,
professional and generational diversity, will manage to achieve the
degree of unanimity that characterises totalitarian regimes. Even in
such a case, thorough socio-historical studies show that the concept
of 'totalitarianism' as a vision of a totally levelled society does not
account for the capacity of such a society to maintain true diversity
in the system's interstices. Unanimity is merely on the surface. In the
case of the former Soviet Union it has been demonstrated that the
social sphere retained a certain 'autonomy' regarding official regime
policy: Soviet ideology ran up against the resistance of family and
social nuclei deep-rooted within the collective mentalities.[43]

In any event, even if this will for total control is only apparent, it
necessarily engenders attitudes of suspicion toward such individual
or group due to this requirement of loyalty toward the identitarian
ideal. The potential 'traitor' will, by definition, be the one who,
while a member of 'us', seeks to conceal his dissension. Even as a

member of the 'people', he turns out to be an 'enemy of the people'. He may have the same appearance, the same face, and the same blood as 'us'. But he does not want to be part of 'us'. The imaginary dynamic then becomes something altogether different: rather than being based on highlighting a 'minor difference', it is constructed on the basis of the recognition of a fundamental similarity but one that turns into betrayal. In other words, violence arises from the conflictual relationship between twins, one of which ends up declaring the other to be a 'traitor' to their common identity. The violence that can result from such a split can only be horrific. It can go from ostracism to imprisonment, even elimination, of 'traitors'. It is difficult to imagine for instance what happened in Nazi Germany during the period of 'peace' in the 1930s. The account given by Marie Kahle, an 'Aryan' who dared help a Jewish shopkeeper in Bonn to put his shop back in order after it had been ransacked by Nazi militants during *Kristallnacht* on November 9, 1938, helps us to some extent. This simple gesture of kindness earned her denunciation in the press; her husband, an academic, was increasingly harassed at work, not to mention the insults their children were subjected to at school. The few words anonymous hands scribbled in paint in front of their house say it all: 'Traitors to the people, friends of the Jews'.[44]

How can we understand this stupefying desire for coercion over individuals? Naturally the relationship between terror and ideology seems to be the determining factor and at the very foundation of the totalitarian system, as philosopher Hannah Arendt argues.[45] The dialectic is perfectly diabolical: an ideology (that is, the logic of an idea) sets out to impose itself on everyone through terror, and terror, in return, justifies all its crimes in the name of that ideology. However, this analysis, forged from a comparison between the case of Nazi Germany and Stalin's USSR, falls short of the mark. All in all, it proposes an instrumental explanation through the 'tools' of ideology and terror, when what really seems to be at issue is the inner workings of the *imaginaire*: an *imaginaire* of unity at all costs against a common enemy. Philosopher Claude Lefort moreover explored this theme of the fiction of totalitarian unity: the image of a 'people united' leads to the elimination of all those perceived as not being part of this unity, or as a threat to it. This quest for unity at all costs, necessarily illusory, does indeed have the capacity to shape social relations.[46] And therein is probably one of the powerful vectors for the rise in mass violence: the mad desire to build a world without conflict or enemies.

But why restrict ourselves to a totalitarian framework? An inquiry into the power of imaginary constructs offers a less restrictive approach, in tune with the analysis already proposed. For this identitarian quest, which is constructed on the rejection of a 'different' Other, after all expresses a regressive desire toward perfect 'unity'. The narcissistic fantasy of complete peace characteristic of an infant expelling the bad object, as described by Franco Fornari, is not far off. This identity reconstruction of the One against an Other attests to the fantastical desire to retrieve this 'one' without the other. The desire to bond One with One or Self with Self precludes any vague impulse to discuss or arrive at a compromise. It is impossible for an individual belonging to 'us' to voice his disagreement with the identitarian monad. Can it thus be any surprise that this dream of oneness, this rage of oneness, can draw into an infernal spiral of coercion and exclusion anyone inclined to show a desire to go against this fantasy of unity?

From the quest for purity to the figure of the Other in excess

This search for 'oneness' also very often goes along with a headlong quest for 'purity'. This is another theme of the *imaginaire* that 'toughens' the identitarian process and impels it more inexorably toward an episode of mass violence. To define oneself as 'pure' in fact implies categorizing some 'other' as impure. The accusation of impurity constitutes a universal accusation against the population one is going to massacre. Purity already implies a requirement of cleanliness as opposed to another catalogued as 'dirty', perceived as rubbish. Purity also contains an appeal to the sacred: the need for purification falls within the province of religion, and constitutes a powerful springboard for unleashing a purgative violence (cf. Chapter II). These clichés—pure-impure, cleanliness-dirtiness, whiteness-blackness—seem terribly crude to us. Their binary structures mirror however the elementary functioning of the human psyche in times of crisis. As soon as we feel seriously threatened, we immediately seek to find out who wishes us good or evil. That is the child's and the adult's completely understandable reflex in perfect accord with the structure of our basic emotions. Dichotomies such as good/evil, good-guy/bad-guy, etc. constitute the imaginary space within which to deposit ideologies that, however misguided, seem credible and reassuring.

The purity theme has been studied by anthropologists from the standpoint of bodily uncleanliness and more broadly the 'pollution' of the social body.[47] This metaphor can be extended to the need to defend the purity of civilisation against the corruption of modernity. The outcome is often an apologia of nature and particularly peasants, the true champions of tradition and the eternal soul of the people. Native peasants, those who have an intimate knowledge of the fatherland, embody the customs and spirit of the nation. But it is especially among racist or ethno-nationalist leaders and militants that historians see this myth of purity most clearly at work. In the Nazis' conception of race, the idea of purity goes along with that of health. The Nazis took up the hygienist medical theories circulating at the time in Germany as well as other European countries, including France and England.[48] This desire to strengthen the 'purity of German blood' led them to pass a law in September 1935 for the 'protection of German blood and honour'. This was soon translated into two major decrees legalising the banishment of German Jews: the first one made marriage, and more generally any sexual intercourse between Aryans and Jews, illegal and punishable by prison. The second terminated the equal rights acquired by the Jews in 1871.[49] This will to 'sanitise' the race however was not only directed at the country's Jews, for it was rooted in the worship of a healthy, attractive, clean body. 'The healthy, clean, hardworking, athletic Aryan man, married to a woman of the same race who produced many children for him, was set up as a model and a norm. Anything that deviated from this model was, by contrast, thrown into relief and soon became the object of measures of extirpation: Germans suffering from hereditary diseases (about 400,000 of them) were sterilised; tens of thousands of "asocial" individuals and homosexuals were sent to concentration camps; Gypsies were segregated, and so on.'[50]

In Yugoslavia the ethnologist Ivan Colovic has provided a remarkable demonstration of how deciphering a 'mythical imagination' provides an essential key to understanding the war in the early 1990s.[51] It has often been claimed, he writes, that the cause of war was the bellicose nationalist sentiments that managed to impose a cult of the past and urge the population to devote themselves to a nicely embellished national history, as it sought to make them to lose sight of their true needs. But this theory is only partly valid. In fact, the Serbs were less enjoined to return to the historical past than to 'leave real historical time', in other words 'return to the myths of heavenly and eternal Serbia', the cradle of which is supposedly in the sacred land of Kosovo'. Serbian political myths, he explains, constantly invite a 'return of the same', the cult of the 'ancestors' and the return to nature. This is why the Serbs' glorious ancestors are resurrected in today's leaders, such as the nationalist Radovan Karadzic who claims a genetic link with his famous namesake, reformer of the Serbian language, Vuk Karadzic (1787–1864). This permanence of the timeless 'Serbian soul' is allegedly due to the fact that the 'same eternal blood' runs through the veins of Serbian identity, wherever they may be. According to Colovic, the Serbs are affected by a 'type of insanity which is all too familiar', the insanity of ethnic purity. He illustrates this by quoting the words of the biologist Biljana Plavsic, also a Bosnian Serb political leader, who in reference to his scientific discipline unabashedly claims that 'the Serbians in Bosnia, and in the border regions in particular, have maintained and sharpened the ability to recognize danger for the nation early on and to develop the mechanisms for its defence. In my family it was said that the Serbians in Bosnia are much better than those in Serbia... I am a biologist, and therefore I know that those species which live next to others and are constantly threatened by others have the best possibility to adapt.'[52]

To characterise a people or a nation that sees itself as being a homogeneous entity, and almost a physical entity, the English sociologist Michael Mann has put forward the notion of 'organic purity'. He notes that most modern states refer to some idea of the people, which implies saying 'us' as though it were one and the same collective 'person'. The United States Constitution begins, for instance, with the words 'We, the people', and La Marseillaise, the French national anthem, begins 'Allons enfants de la patrie...' (Arise children of the fatherland). Michael Mann believes that if the population of a given territory invests in such a collective sovereignty, it is in danger of conceiving itself as an 'organic whole' at the expense of some Other, perceived as foreign. For the notion of 'people' combines two different meanings. The first refers to what the Greeks called '*demos*', the 'ordinary population', the mass of the citizenry. But in our modern times the 'people' also means the 'nation', through another Greek term, '*ethnos*', an ethnic group, a population that shares the same common heritage and differs from another people. Hence the constant risk, the author notes, of defining oneself as a 'pure people' with respect to another that is 'impure'. The French anthem in fact explicitly alludes to this in one of its couplets: '*Qu'un sang impur abreuve nos sillons!*' (Let impure blood water our furrows). The founding ideas of democracy can thus engender various forms of mass political violence or ethnic cleansing. 'The ideal of rule by the people began to entwine the *demos* with the dominant *ethnos*, generating organic conceptions of the nation and the state, writes Mann, that encouraged the cleansing of minorities.'[53] This tendency is the perverted product of the most sacred institution of Western modernity: democracy. A provocative theory? Over and above the way European nations overpowered indigenous peoples in what were to become their colonies, the author waxes ironic about the past of several American presidents who were at the same time 'great democrats' and 'great ethnic cleansers': against the Native American Indians. Comparing the Indians to wolves, George Washington gave orders to attack the Iroquois and 'lay waste all the settlements... that the country may not be merely overrun, but destroyed'. Thomas Jefferson repeated at will that the Indians had to be 'exterminated' and 'driven off the land', whereas Andrew Jackson encouraged his soldiers to slaughter women and children. And Theodore Roosevelt declared that the extermination of the Indians 'was as ultimately beneficial as it was inevitable'.[54] This past makes up the 'dark side of democracy' on the basis of which Mann constructs his entire analysis. His conclusion: authoritarian or totalitarian regimes cannot be said to have a monopoly on massacres. Ethnic cleansing is a modern phenomenon closely bound up with the formation of democracies.

His analysis leads to exploring another fundamental facet of 'organic purity'. According to Mann, the typically modern political forms of fascism and communism are also the warped legacies of the democratic project. In fascism the 'organic us' is embodied in the ideal of the nation, whereas in communism it takes root in the idea of the proletariat. For the former the enemies are ethnic, for the latter political. Mann thus establishes a sort of parallel between racial enemies and class enemies, thereby contributing to the debates on comparisons between Nazism and communism. This theory has also been developed by some French historians such as Stéphane Courtois and Jean-Louis Margolin in *The Black Book of Communism*: they view class genocide as the equivalent to racial genocide.[55] Mann however refuses to use the term 'genocide' to describe the crimes committed under communism. He prefers the terms 'fratricide' and 'classicide', a word he coined to refer to intentional mass killings of entire social classes.[56]

Putting the leftwing and rightwing 'organist conceptions' on the same footing seems debatable. Mann in fact does not perceive the differences between the two fundamental types of purity that can be deduced from his analyses: purity based on identity (of which Nazism is the most consummate expression) and a political type of purity (which reached paroxysmal proportions in Stalinist and Cambodian communism). Each engenders very different figures of the 'enemy', and so it is important not to confuse the dynamics of violence underlying their formation.

The identity-based purity described above in fact tends to result in the formation of a separate enemy figure. This 'them' perceived as basically different from 'us' becomes an 'other in excess'. This figure of the enemy proceeds from a magnified vision of a difference on to which 'our' anxiety will adhere to the point of wishing his destruction. This 'Other in excess' is of course different from 'us' from a qualitative standpoint: he does not have the same blood as we do, or the same customs; he does not have the same nose or the same body shape, he is taller or shorter, his skin is a different colour. In fact, did he not arrive in this land after we did? He thus has no right to remain here and his presence is literally unbearable: he spreads his stench over this territory that belonged to our ancestors, our nation, our God. This 'Other' can also be perceived as being too great in number, in addition to being in excess: as he tends to multiply, proliferate, pullulate, he may well submerge us if we are not careful. In Yugoslavia Serbian nationalists openly recommended a 'demographic solution' to the Kosovo question, which clearly implied reducing its Albanian population. In the early 1980s it was moreover the Serbs in Kosovo who began to talk about the 'ethnic cleansing' they might be subjected to if they did not react. This expression thus first serves to define oneself as victim. Against the real or imaginary backdrop of population growth, a sort of fantasy of disappearance is constructed which takes hold of a group that perceives itself as suffocating under the presence of an 'Other' in the process of contaminating the body of a healthy people. And it is a well-known fact: 'the Jews are everywhere; they want to take over the world and drive us to ruin.' Radical measures must therefore be taken to defend ourselves against these vile and perverse creatures.

Identitarian purity and political purity. Is this Other in excess even human, in fact? The 'bestialisation' of the enemy is a highly significant indicator of the potential unleashing of violence against him. We all use names of animals to demonstrate our affection for someone. But conversely, names of animals can also serve to indicate hostility toward a person. War moreover tends to produce such metaphors among soldiers who in this way convince themselves they are not actually killing people. Animalisation of the other can also develop against a group in conjunction with the upsurge in violence against this group. It is often said that a massacre ensues when the victims have been dehumanised. Is this always the case? Not so sure, as we will see further on. There is no doubt, however, that dehumanisation indeed takes place via this animalisation of the Other by placing him outside the realm of human relations. The killing starts with the use of words disqualifying his humanity. Since the Middle Ages the word 'massacre' in fact has meant putting an animal to death, for instance in the course of a hunt. And the boar's head, a trophy exhibited in the main room of the château, is called a '*massacre*' in French. Killing supposedly human 'animals' then becomes entirely possible. Even more, the metaphors used are those of animals perceived as harmful pests. For this 'supernumerary other' is certainly not endowed with the dignity of the European buck or African lion. No, the imaginary charge is far more hostile and perverse: The Nazis spoke of the Jews as mere 'rats' or 'lice', whereas Hutu extremists called the Tutsi invaders cockroaches ('*Inyenzi*').[57]

Don't we have the 'right' to get rid of vermin? It is a purely hygienic matter of housekeeping. Everyone can do it, everyone should do it. This notion also produces the metaphors of 'cleansing' associated with cleanliness and healthiness. In *Mein Kampf* Hitler constantly used metaphors such as 'Jewish germ' and 'Jewish cancer', or described Jews as 'social parasites'. And insects often arouse a certain degree of psychological revulsion: we want to stamp them out.

As for the theme of political purity, it can easily be identified in Lenin's rhetoric in the Soviet Union or Pol Pot's in Cambodia. Many writings of the father of the Bolshevik revolution testify to this quest for an ideal of purity, a 'cell with no slag' that the party should be. Lenin's expression is unambiguous: 'the Party grows stronger as it is purified' (*'ocistit'*), a method that, in his mind, should spread throughout the entire society.[58] Some of Pol Pot's declarations are along the same lines: 'we must give a pure and perfect depiction of the history of the Party.'[59] The logical conclusion: everything that is 'impure' should be cleaned out or eliminated. And Lenin himself animalises his enemies in many of his writings: 'The Russian land must be rid of its harmful insects,' he writes. 'Either the lice will defeat socialism, or socialism will defeat the lice!' To mobilise his partisans, he borrows metaphors from the struggle to control epidemics, claiming that 'parasites (and typhus) are the main scourges assailing socialism'. He is pleased that 'Russian cities have been cleansed of that whiteguard vermin'.[60] Pol Pot and his friends were generally less verbose than Lenin but their declarations are similar. Thus notes the Australian historian David Chandler, author of a remarkable study on the notorious Toul Sleng prison in Phnom Penh. Pol Pot believed that Cambodia's internal enemies were intrinsically impure. Duch, head of this prison (where over 14,000 detainees were tortured and killed) compares the enemies' strategy to the way in which woodworms bore through wood. He compared them to worms or germs from the CIA or from Vietnam out to eat away at the healthy revolutionary people. Once infected, an individual could infect others. Unless the counter-revolution was nipped in the bud, it could turn into an epidemic.[61]

Political purity is a requirement that anyone is in fact bound to. The enemy figure is not an 'Other in excess' perceived as fundamentally foreign, but indeed one's fellow man, who, it is feared, might be wrong-minded. David Chandler moreover shows to what extent the Khmer Rouge regime multiplied and diversified its enemies, both real and completely imaginary. No one is shielded from this permanent political inquisition. Once unmasked, the traitor must write his 'confession', a practice first used in the Soviet Union. Actually, his analysis of communist Cambodia brings to mind Nicolas Werth's work on the USSR under Stalin, in which a multitude of internal enemies follow in succession: 'the masked enemies' defined by their suspicious past, 'ex-nobles' or 'ex-Mensheviks', former Bolsheviks, the Kulaks, the cadres, the 'socially harmful elements', in other words delinquents and vagabonds, 'nationalist' peoples and so on.[62]

Political purity thus refers much more to the figure of the traitor described earlier, who has many forms and is hidden everywhere. The traitor by definition is two-faced and plays a double game. As Lenin once again says: 'Our worst enemy is among us.' He may have already betrayed us. He claims to be for the revolution but is actually a bourgeois. He says he is for the people, but in fact is a counter-revolutionary. It is impossible not to think back in time here to the period of the French Revolution. The rhetoric of Terror seems indeed close at hand, as Jean-Clément Martin remarks: 'the definition of the enemy, during the course of the year 1793, became more and more vague and increasingly broad, constantly taking in new groups.'[63] The terms of political confrontation can also be inverted by taking the viewpoint of a so-called rightwing conservative revolution.

Since both camps at first glance resemble each other, the primary criterion by which to differentiate them is ideology. But the verification of an individual's ideological conviction is open to interpretation: what does he really believe? Isn't he misleading us? The accusation can also be directed at an entire group for fear of missing the 'real' traitor. According to a Khmer Rouge dictum, 'It is better to arrest ten innocent people than to let one guilty one go free'.[64] Didn't these villagers help our enemy before we chased him out? They say they have nothing to do with him. But they must have hid him and given him weapons. And the women are certainly not innocent. So all these villagers are traitors and will receive the punishment they deserve. The distinction between combatants and non-combatants vanishes entirely, resulting in massive, indiscriminate violence.

So we note: even if identitarian purity and political purity are both associated with the animalisation of what is perceived as impure, the rationales of violence they give expression to are not identical. The perspective of identitarian purity tends to focus on a single enemy such as 'the Jew' or 'the Tutsi', whereas political purity sifts through the social body in search of alleged traitors. The former aims to eradicate the enemy perceived as an Other in excess, the second to subjugate society by eliminating suspected enemies. Of course, the same historical situation often displays a combination of these two dynamics of violence. We have seen earlier that as the identitarian process of 'Us' against 'Them' takes shape, the part of 'Us' that was hostile to demonising 'Them' had to be subjugated or eliminated. But simply noting that these two rationales interact does not settle the question of their respective importance in a given historical situation.

It is as if one or the other (but not both at the same time) constituted the original 'trademark' of a system of violence. The well-known examples of Nazi Germany and the USSR under Stalin illustrate this well. In the former case, radical Nazi anti-Semitism gives violence against the Jews a foundational role in the regime. In the second the Bolsheviks were so afraid of not remaining in power (they had in mind the short-lived Paris Commune) that they seemed to wage war against their entire society, having no qualms about killing again and again in order to endure. This is why the very foundations of the Bolshevik and Nazi systems, even if they are both presented as totalitarian, remain extremely different. They are the expression of two rationales of total violence, one systematically oriented toward the total subjugation of the group, the other more focused on eradicating one or more groups. I believe that I have identified here three fundamental interpretive frameworks for processes of violence that can lead to massacres. At the end of this book I will sketch them out more thoroughly.

From the security dilemma to the destruction of the enemy

A third theme remains to be examined in our attempt to explain how violence can multiply its destructive intensity. True, the reshaping of the identity of an afflicted 'us' against 'them' is decisive. True, the quest for purity to which this 'us' attests is also central and, frankly, tragic. But the main aspect must not be neglected, without which such a process could not develop: the need for security. Imaginary or real, authentic or manipulated, it gives material form to the rise to power for any process of violence.

For fear is indeed present, behind the scenes and at the front of the stage, at the root of it all. Fear of modernity, as many scholars have written? Of a world that moves too fast, in which the future seems a dead end? Most likely. But also fear of the Other, perceived as a hostile stranger or one's own fellow man, on which the anxiety of the unknown is catalysed. Fear in fact of oneself, of a collective self that has lost its bearings. The elites in power have probably not managed to make the right economic or political choices. They have failed in their modernisation of the country and do not seem prepared to admit it. Unless this country has just lost a war? Or is on the verge of losing one? In any event, society is 'falling apart' and fear overcomes people's minds.

It is normal to seek out the causes of fear. We believe that understanding the causes will give us the means to control, if not eliminate them. We can tell ourselves: 'If we have come to this point today, it is because our country's leaders have not made the right choices. We are ruled by a bunch of incompetents that we need to replace. In fact, I would be better off behaving differently myself. As we gradually gain control of the situation, we will empower ourselves to dissipate our fear'. But another response involves not questioning one's own motives, or those of one's group, and saying: 'If everything is going wrong, it's because of those people, it's because of THEM.' At that point, the fear that one cannot comprehend or channel finds an extremely convenient receptacle, so why call oneself into question? In short, the anxiety is transferred on to a 'them' that one begins to hate. The greater the hatred, the less the fear. For hatred is born out of fear and not the other way round. But fear nevertheless remains a necessary fuel for hatred. We might ponder these words penned by Georges Bernanos during the Spanish Civil War: 'Fear, true fear, is a mad delirium; of all the lunacies we are capable of, it is certainly the cruellest. Nothing equals its energy, nothing can withstand its blow. Anger, which it resembles, is merely a passing state, a vast dissipation of the forces of the soul. Moreover, it is blind. Fear, on the contrary, provided that you overcome the initial anxiety that goes with it, forms along with hatred one of the most stable psychological factors there is.'[65]

Now, there are people who help to structure this fear as hatred. These are the ones who were already saying: 'we are victims of History. If we are all victims, we certainly have the right to defend ourselves against Them! And besides, didn't they already slaughter us in the past? Remember those *Ustashis* (Croatian nationalists) who murdered thousands of Serbs during the last war! Remember those *Chetniks* (Serbian nationalists) who murdered thousands of Croats! And the '*Inyenzi*' (Tutsi combatants) who attacked our country in the 1960s, killing our women and children, now they're coming back to do the same thing all over again.' The awakening of painful memories and still vivid traumas is an effective way of stoking fear and developing hatred. This hatred can then be projected into action, armed with a desire for revenge. For the common perception of a mortal danger creates a sentiment of the tragic, as the anthropologist Véronique Nahoum-Grappe observes. A situation that is labelled tragic is an impasse; it compels people to take action, which is usually violent and has every chance of turning out badly. And fed on the agonizing memory of past massacres, this situation irresistibly arouses 'the desire, the obligation, the *duty toward the dead* to seek revenge'.[66]

Conspiracy and paranoia. The notion that an external enemy is threatening the country considerably reinforces this feeling of anxiety and death. So far, our analysis has only dealt with the various representations of an enemy within that must be unmasked. But this is not enough for the *imaginaire* of fear: it is also projected on a dangerous Other outside the nation. This enemy that threatens the borders calls up a bellicose vocabulary even more. It is the jumbling of these two enemy figures—internal and external—that lends these imaginary representations an absolutely explosive potential for violence, which, it is to be feared, could well materialise in reality.

This is what enables conspiracy rhetoric really to take off. It goes without saying: an enemy on the outside is aiding the enemy within. Both, in reality, are part of the same crowd seeking to ruin us. The

Jews had already been accused in Germany of having 'stabbed them in the back', precipitating defeat in the First World War. Nazi propaganda goes even further, associating them with the rise of the 'red peril' in Europe since the Russian communist revolution. Early in the 1920s Hitler thus pooled the Jewish and Bolshevik threats to construct the hideous amalgamation of 'Judeo-Bolshevism'. Before his manifesto, *Mein Kampf*, was even published in 1923, 'by autumn 1922 his conception of the absolutely pivotal relationship of anti-Semitism and anti-Bolshevism had reached the point of development which was to dominate his political mission to the end.'[67] The enemy was thus both outside and inside Germany. This dual threat was the great peril against which the people had to react.

The success of the *Protocols of the Elders of Zion* is also revealing of the indissociable nature of the perception of a common threat of both Jews and Bolsheviks. This document was a complete fabrication by the Tsar's police in the late nineteenth century: it presents a member of the Jewish government (the Elders of Zion) describing over the course of twenty-four secret meetings how to achieve world domination. The document remained virtually unknown till the 1917 Bolshevik revolution. The fear that the latter aroused throughout Europe lent 'credibility' to this preposterous document (it claims for instance that the Jews will use subway tunnels to blow up the European capitals). The presence of Jews among the Bolsheviks 'proves' the thesis of the Protocols, in other words the existence of 'a global Jewish conspiracy'. In Germany even, in the traumatic context of the defeat, it was to have a major impact, because it provided an 'explanation' for the country's misfortunes.[68] Did not the Spartacist League want to take power barely two months after the surrender? This was indeed proof of a Judeo-Bolshevik plot. In this way 'the *Protocols* exacerbated to the most extreme degree the paranoia prevalent in those years of crisis and disaster.'[69]

Paranoia: the word fits perfectly, since the structuring of these imaginary representations of the enemy is reminiscent of the descriptions psychiatry ascribes to paranoid personalities. The character traits of a paranoiac can be recognized in a combination of wariness (excessive aggression toward other people), inflexibility (the incapacity to question one's own value system), a hypertrophied

Ego (which can go as far as megalomania), flawed judgment. The last of these traits constitutes the essential trait of a paranoiac personality.[70] A paranoiac's logic is flawed by passion, which leads to a delusional interpretation of reality. Ideas are guided by a preconceived belief. Doubt is as foreign to the paranoiac as self-criticism. His apparently rational reasoning is actually hyper-affective in nature, and in the end only a justification for his emotional tendencies. The paranoiac reasons correctly on false premises. The starting point seems obvious to him because of a subjective preconception that he is unable to question. Due to this flaw in judgment, the paranoiac always skirts the real problems, seems out of tune with reality and is impervious to other people's opinions. Yet his intellectual faculties are intact. His discourse does draw on reality, but gives it an imaginary interpretation. The paranoiac attributes all his difficulties and all his failings to someone else. He can't call himself into question: the world is all wrong, or people are out to get him. But his interpretations are still plausible, and the paranoiac can enlist their support.

Delusional rationality. To what extent can we apply such a description of a psychological structure to a group or a whole society? Superimposing this kind of generalisation of the individual on to the group, reworking the psychological model on to the social, remains problematic. The few psychoanalytical essays on major figures in history such as Hitler and Stalin have been disappointing.[71] Although the psychological approach can sometimes construct a useful viewpoint on the phenomena of collective violence, it cannot replace historical or sociological inquiry. It is up to historians or political scientists to make precise and subtle use of it in order to lend greater relevance and depth to his own research. In this regard the work of the American historian Saul Friedlander is exemplary, particularly his remarkable essay, *Nazi Germany and the Jews.* Speaking specifically of the Nazis' 'paranoid discourse', he writes: 'We must face the social pathology of sects. It is unusual, however, for a sect to become a modern political party, and it is even more unusual for its leader and his followers to keep their original fanaticism once they have acceded to power.'[72] But the question remains: how can the world view of this 'sect' succeed in irrigating a broader social body to the extent of seeming commonly shared by all. The vector for such propagation indeed seems to be a paranoiac type of discourse that unites 'us' through its evil-minded perception of 'them'. In the eyes of an outside observer, such discourse seems positively mad, whereas among 'us' it elicits collective support. Seemingly irrational, it nevertheless hones to a logical argumentation.

I suggested the notion of 'delusional rationality' to describe this rhetorical core from which a process of violence radiates that can lead to massacre.[73] This rationality can if necessary draw on purportedly scientific discourse such as the scientism that leads to justifying racism. The Nazis for instance based their argumentation on Darwin's theory of evolution to defend what is called 'social Darwinism'. From the natural selection of animal species, it is easy to shift to the principle of a vital war between races, in this case a 'struggle for existence between the productive Germano-Aryan race and the parasitic Jewish race'. But the property of such delusional rationality is that it also claims to be 'instrumental', in Max Weber' sense of the term: it aims to endow itself with the actual means to achieve its ends. It must implement a plan, a strategy by which to translate words into deeds. This delusional rationality thus not only structures the figures of the enemy to be destroyed into a sufficiently elaborate ideological discourse. It also enables this discourse to precipitate destructive action. Here again is evidence of the permeability between the imaginary and the real.

Should those perpetrating such a discourse be described, however, as paranoiacs? Probably, as in the case of Stalin or Hitler. But doubt seeps in with respect to other leaders. Was it true, for example, of Milosevic? The paranoiac believes what he says. It is not certain that this can be said of Milosevic, when all studies point to his political opportunism in making the transition from communism to nationalism. But this is not the decisive point. Machiavelli amply showed that the art of politics is not so much to believe but to make believe. A leader's charisma can undoubtedly be a fundamental catalyst in the collective dynamics of a people, as it was in Nazi Germany. But many countries have been the theatre of mass violence without the instigation of a charismatic leader. This is why I accord more importance to the nature of the discourse offered up to the public in a crisis situation. It is the structure and themes of such discourse that will manage to win the people over or not.

If we now take any situation of serious crisis, a paranoiac discourse is decidedly attractive. It has the ability to tap into collective emotions, and channel them in to a largely (or totally) imaginary enemy figure. And the rational discourse that accompanies this psychological undertaking can not only arouse conviction, but can also spur the group into action, which is why delusional rationality is potentially so dangerous. Thus the *imaginaire* of fear, which takes root in reality but offers an imaginary interpretation of it, in a way 'returns' to reality... but in order to act.

Here we are touching on one of the keys to understanding the descent into violence. Convinced of an imminent threat born of the *imaginaire* of fear, men are driven to seek a rational means of eradicating this threat. Raymond Aron explored this point in a luminous passage on the extermination of the Jews: 'As for genocide, at the risk of causing an uproar, I would say that the apparent irrationality results from an error of perspective. Hitler had proclaimed a number of times, particularly in the early days of hostilities, that the Jews would not survive a war that in his opinion they had started. We didn't believe him, we didn't want to believe him, but as they say, "he meant it". If we would only admit that the liquidation of the Jews, the "Jewish poison", the "corrupting blood", was Hitler's primary objective, the industrial organisation of death becomes a rational means to an end: genocide.' But Raymond Aron immediately questions the basis for this rationality: 'In that the notion of rationality is not separate from reason and in that reason is the opposite of passions, such an aim excludes reason. A single passion unleashed or a repressed anxiety dictates such a decision.' Decisions and reason should go together, whereas this was obviously the product of a 'passion unleashed or a repressed anxiety'. He wonders: 'What impersonal force, what social function can be named? I see only one unsettling conclusion: the cause of genocide was the obsessive hatred (which may be a case for psychiatry) of a little group of men who arrived in power on the back of a national or social crisis. The detonator of an explosion is not necessarily proportionate to the explosion itself.'[74]

Thus the pressure of this *imaginaire* of fear as detonator (and, I would add, as 'fuel'), spurs men on inexorably toward rationally organised action. The 'us' must find the means to eliminate the 'them' that poses a threat both inside and out, henceforth perceived as a total enemy. Some scholars view this conflictual dynamic as a specific feature of totalitarian systems. Yet, this radical confrontation between 'us' and 'them' can be seen in other crisis situations. It is as if this imaginary conflict took on the configuration of an imperious security dilemma, according to the political scientist Barry Posen, a dilemma that can be likened to a war situation: it is either 'them' or 'us' who will get it.[75] This rhetoric of the survival of 'us' through the destruction of 'them' may have already been very present in the Nazi propaganda of the 1920s, but it could also be found in the period leading up to several conflicts that have been labelled 'ethnic' or 'religious', such as between the Serbs and Croats.[76] The neighbouring group's sense of identity is perceived as a deadly threat. So action becomes unavoidable: since they want to kill us, we must kill them first.

Destroy 'Them' to save 'Us'. The undertaking to destroy 'them' is thus analogous to an operation to save 'us', a 'war of self-defence' as some in Rwanda called it. In short, it is an undertaking to prevent violence against oneself! He who is about to commit murder presents himself as the victim. What could be more logical? Having already adopted the victim 'profile' in his accusatory discourse, he then maintains and further reinforces it as he launches into action. But first he presents himself as innocent of the crime he will be accused of.

Here we have reached the threshold of war. The radical nature of the friend–enemy antagonism brings to mind Carl Schmitt's concept of the political, in which he maintains that perception of an enemy to be destroyed is the very essence of politics: 'The specific political distinction to which political actions and motives can be reduced is that between friend and enemy.'[77] He detects the most perfect expression of this in Cromwell's speech against the Spanish or the fiery words Saint-Just used against the 'enemies of the people'. War will only be the ultimate actualisation of this enmity. It isn't surprising that Schmitt, who formulated his thought during the rise of Nazism, and who is furthermore anti-Semitic, winds up developing such a radical vision of politics. Reflections on violence are often the product of a context of extreme violence, as in, for example, Thomas Hobbes' work *Leviathan* written during the English Civil Wars. An opposite conception to Schmitt's can certainly be defended (for instance the quintessence of the political resides instead in the construction of the public sphere, in the conciliation of opposites, the search for consensus and cohabitation, etc.), but what he says about it nevertheless seems well-founded: in times of high social tension, any mediating third party ends up collapsing and the conflictual relationship is reduced to the radical confrontation between friends and enemies, as much imaginary as physical.

The representation of this 'totally other' total enemy then ties into the essentialisation of his difference. 'He' no longer has anything in common with 'us'. The symbolic barrier of THE difference simply cannot be crossed. The totally different other is already no longer really human. But more than an animal, is not this other in the process of reifying to amount to almost nothing, a mere thing? Simone Weil remarked this with brutal simplicity: 'force—it is that x that turns anybody who is subjected to it into a thing. Exercised to the limit, it turns man into a thing in the most literal sense: it makes a corpse out of him.'[78]

And so we've come full circle. We started with a construction of identity based on the stigmatisation of differences. We have seen that this identitarian process becomes radical by making claims of purity in reference to an 'other' perceived as dirty, foreign, corrupt and treacherous. But the fear aroused by the threat of his malevolent difference invites people to reject or even destroy him, for reasons of security. And this radical determination to destroy 'them' of course designates the death-defying 'us' as all-powerful. We must not however rest on the idea that these *imaginaires* of destruction and omnipotence are constructed in a linear fashion. These three themes are actually intertwined and mutually reinforce one another, looping in and around one another. Nor do they have the same function in this imaginary alchemy of the enemy. Identity supplies the framework within which the process of violence will take shape. The desire for purity toughens this identitarian framework by grafting on to it a theme of religion or secular sacredness, which is thereby absolute in nature. The need for security, in phase with the context of crisis that led to the development of this imaginary construct, makes it urgent to move into action. I will thus argue that this elemental psychological core, rooted in the *imaginaire* of early childhood, is at the basis of processes of violence that can lead to a massacre. We can suppose that this psychological core, precisely because it is elementary, is universal in nature. A common denominator of the human species, it transcends cultural differences. Of course its political realisation varies from one country or continent to another: processes of violence will always vary in intensity and have individual characteristics. However, I would not hesitate to resort to this explosive metaphor: manipulating this core *imaginaire* in a crisis situation can turn it into dynamite! For what is only for the moment 'psychic matter' will surely vent its full destructive power by entering into 'reaction' with an especially anxiety-laden social context.

How can we actually measure the praxological power of this *imaginaire* of the enemy? What concrete effects can it have on social and political events? Some scholarship provides fruitful paths of reflection. In history, Georges Lefebvre brilliantly showed how what he called the 'Great Fear' during the summer of 1789 played a decisive role in mobilising the peasants for the French Revolution. Rural areas had been swept up in a movement of panic that bred on itself: fear of a conspiracy by aristocrats who were supposedly going to send in 'bandits' to destroy the harvest and starve the people. It was against the backdrop of this huge collective terror (that had different origins depending on the region) that peasant agitation grew in scale against the designated enemy: the lords. The Great Fear was not an 'epiphenomenon', Lefebvre points out. 'The wave of panic was followed by a vigorous reaction in which the warring fervour of the revolution can be detected for the first time and gave national unity the opportunity to manifest and fortify itself.'[79]

In the domains of both economics and sociology, imaginary representations are considered to be capable of shaping reality. This is referred to as the 'self-fulfilling prophecy' elucidated by American sociologist Robert Merton: if men define situations as real, they are real in their consequences.[80] Merton studies several cases: the bankruptcy of a thriving bank in 1932 caused by a rumour of insolvency, the outbreak of a war made inevitable due to the belief in its inevitability. The economist J.M. Keynes had observed similar phenomena. The 'prophet' will use events as proof he was right: 'I told you so'. A false description of the situation provokes behaviour that makes it true.

Such a line of interpretation is easily applicable to ethnic conflicts and genocidal situations. Thus Jean-François Bayart states that 'in Rwanda and Burundi the ethnic description of political and social divisions now operates as a "self-fulfilling prophecy", each of the groups involved calculating that its adversary has planned its extermination and acting accordingly. These are extreme situations. Nevertheless, they remind us that the phantasm of conspiracy is a strong and universal form of political *imaginaire*.'[81] Must we then consider that this political *imaginaire* of destruction of an 'other', which is crystallised in a given public discourse, is enough to prompt people to take action? That boils down to posing the problem of intention in the carrying out of a massacre: this is the topic of the following chapter.

II

FROM INFLAMMATORY DISCOURSE
TO SACRIFICIAL VIOLENCE

How does this all-powerful and destructive *imaginaire* described above gradually affect a society, igniting a truly inflammatory discourse, and finally giving rise to increasingly destructive social effects? Two major contradictory theoretical explanations, drawn from European history, are available to us. The first of these was put forward by students of Norbert Elias: the idea of a 'process of de-civilisation' working in counter-current to that identified by the German sociologist as Europe's progress since the Middle Ages right up till the nineteenth century. Elias's overall hypothesis is that the formation of the state, by monopolising violence (and by controlling taxation), progressively gives rise to more 'civil' or civilised relationships between individuals, resulting in a reduction of all forms of violent behaviour, including state-instigated violence. With the passage of time, in the same way as we see individuals concealing themselves to defecate or urinate, hide their nudity and so on, we can also observe violence, as such, being compartmentalised, or kept from view.[1] Violence nevertheless remains present in this progressively pacified society, and can break out again subsequently. From this stems the idea of a possible de-civilisation process resulting ultimately in regression towards barbarism. According to Jonathan Fletcher, this was already observable in Germany, well before Hitler's rise to power, in the Weimar Republic.[2]

The second explanation argues the exact opposite of this thesis. Formulated by Zygmunt Bauman, this theory observes that it is precisely in the most civilised European society, in which culture and art had attained the height of refinement and intelligence, and where—what is more—the integration of Jews had progressed

52

furthest, that their fate of extermination would be sealed. For Bauman, then, the process that led to Auschwitz is typically an expression of modernity, as suggested explicitly in his book written in 1989.[3] Modern civilisation was certainly not a sufficient condition for the destruction of European Jews, but it was a necessary one. Without it, their mass murder would have been unimaginable. This monstrous event is no accident of history, but a product of the modern rationality of bureaucracy and technology. Can these two theories be reconciled by showing for instance, as the Dutch sociologist Abram de Swaan believes, that they both actually study the same phenomena, while adopting different analytical perspectives?[4]

It would seem that the two authors do not necessarily invest the term 'civilisation' with the same meaning. As for 'modernity', a term Bauman never defines very clearly, it can be used to characterise plenty of other nations that have not for all that turned to genocide. But my intention here is not to come out in favour of one or the other of these theories, but rather to suggest an *observation methodology* that enables us to trace within a given society the 'process' in question, whether or not it is approached from the standpoint of 'decivilisation' or 'modernity'. To this end, we need to arm ourselves with several planes for observation, in such a way as to be able to follow the internal development of a society, at least in these four key domains: intellectual, political, religious and social. In the life of a nation, each of these is of course separate and interlinked at the same time. However, for each of these domains a crucial question arises that will determine the growing risk of a group sliding into acts of mass violence. I shall formulate these questions in the following manner:

— To what extent do 'intellectuals' take up the themes of identity, purity and security, to fabricate ideological constructions of the enemy, starting from myths and fears peculiar to that society?
— Will these mythical ideological constructions find themselves 'projected' on to the political scene to the point of inspiring and founding a state policy?
— Is this political evolution reinforced, or even legitimised, in parallel by the nation's principal moral authorities, especially religious authorities?
— Finally, does the sum total of individuals, groups and communities of this country reveal themselves to be receptive to this policy,

and first of all, to its propaganda? As a result, will the social and inter-generational ties that link designated victims to the other members of the society hold good, or, on the contrary, will it snap?

These four questions make up the structural framework of this chapter. In effect, I shall reveal how events unfold as though con-vergence between these different registers—intellectual, political, religious and social—create optimal conditions for a process to flourish that results in a descent into the act of massacre. What this involves, in effect, is the warping of basic social mores so that they become oriented towards destructive practices. Let us attempt, then, to trace the way circumstances evolve step by step, slowly or rapidly, to create an environment conducive to the collective transgression of a founding social principle: the prohibition of murder.

The intellectual springboard

If massacre proceeds first and foremost from a mental process, it is clearly a priority to examine the 'intellectual framework' that pro-vides meaning to mass violence before it occurs. The genealogy of this framework of meaning is both difficult to reveal, and subject to multiple interpretations. Over and above the tangle of variables to be taken into account, a common trait nevertheless unites these dif-ferent scenarios from the standpoint of their ideological genesis. In the lead-up to the committing of a violent act as such, we can ob-serve that its framework of meaning will have invariably been con-structed by 'intellectuals' who, ostensibly working for the 'good' of their country, have articulated radical analyses of its situation. These analyses more often than not led in practice to the stigmatisation of a particular group. Their proposers are part of the actors mentioned in the last chapter, who generally try and come up with a 'new solu-tion' that could restore this afflicted 'we' to greatness. The term 'in-tellectual' is perhaps not always the most appropriate one to use in their case, but I use it for lack of a better alternative.[5] It would probably be more accurate to refer to them as 'identity entrepre-neurs', since their writings aim to show that the core of the pro-blem—and therefore its solution—resides in the affirmation of their group's identity in the face of a threat from another group. But one could equally describe them as 'political entrepreneurs' because, through this defence of their group's identity, they conduct a truly political campaign that aims to bring about recognition of its rights, or even of its 'superiority'.

Whatever the scenario, these intellectuals for the most part belong to professions of the mind, of education, knowledge or science. Teachers or professors, they have studied at university, sometimes without completing the academic course (and so perhaps harbouring feelings of failure). They are writers or journalists, academics, doctors or engineers; or they could be artists or men of the church. In the crisis situation their country is undergoing, and faced with frustrations that they themselves feel personally, it is often they who will first start formulating a 'solution' to resolve these problems, a solution that they will doggedly defend using the strength of their pen or their discourse. Their personal responsibility in the intellectual and spiritual rationalisation of an identitarian discourse is total. Depending on the individual historical situation concerned, their roles can be very different: they may have some kind of influential hold on a person expected to assume the role of political leader in their country, or they may play a direct role in the 'emotional awakening' of their people, or they may transform themselves into front rank politicians. By way of example, we can cite the cases of Alfred Rosenberg in Germany, Dobrica Cosic in Yugoslavia and of Grégoire Kayibanda in Rwanda, whose trajectories are characterised by these very qualities.

During the rise to power of national-socialism in Germany, there is no doubt that Adolf Hitler was the principal vector for its development, as both doctrinal authority and charismatic figure. At the start of the 1920s a few other people succeeded in enlarging his ideas and helped forge his ideological weapons. According to the historian Ian Kershaw, Alfred Rosenberg, the Baltic-born German, was one of these. He started out as a student of engineering and architecture, but having witnessed the 1917 Bolshevik revolution he fled from Russia and became very active in Germany in 'White Russian' circles. In 1919 he joined what was still an embryonic Nazi movement, a straightforward extremist group, in the newly emergent Weimar Republic. Rosenberg met Hitler there, and it seems that this meeting was to play a key role in the development of the future German leader's thinking. At the outset neither Russia nor

Bolshevism occupied a very central position in Nazi ideology, but through contact with Rosenberg, Hitler became familiar with the idea of an international Jewish conspiracy, expounded in the *Protocols of the Elders of Zion*. Indeed it was Rosenberg, together with another individual hailing from the Baltic, Max Erwin Scheubner-Richter, who persuaded Hitler that Bolshevism was essentially Jewish, an idea that very quickly became the cornerstone of his ideological edifice. As Kershaw notes: 'By the time we reach *Mein Kampf*, the extirpation of "Jewish Bolshevism" has become synonymous with the destruction of the Soviet Union in the German quest for "living space".'[6]

In the 1920s Rosenberg became a kind of guardian of the general doctrine (*Weltanschauung*) of National-Socialism, propagating through his writings profound personal convictions about the reality of a Judeo-Masonic world conspiracy. His masterwork *The Myth of the Twenthieth Century*, published in 1930 (thus three years before Hitler came to power), was to become the second Nazi 'bible' after *Mein Kampf*. This book, which had taken him years to prepare, is deeply inspired by the racist theories of the Count of Gobineau and Houston Chamberlain. The myths of Rosenberg are based above all else on the mystique of the purity of Aryan blood which, under the sign of the Swastika, sparked off a worldwide spiritual revolution: that of 'the awakening of the Aryan soul'. The arts, the sciences, laws and customs are all seen and analysed from the point of view of race, often in an obscure style. General world history is nothing other than the history of races. This work, the procurement of which was recommended as proof of Nazi commitment, was in reality difficult reading for most people. But Hitler gradually learnt how to reach these very masses through the sheer power of his discourse.

In Yugoslavia the career of the nationalist Serb writer Dobrica Cosic followed a different course. A former *protégé* of Marshal Tito, Dobrica Cosic rose to fame by publishing historical novels describing the suffering and uprooting of the Serbs during the two world wars.[7] A member of the Communist Party central committee, he was expelled in 1968 because of nationalism directed against the Kosovo Albanians. But this expulsion did not in any way lead to his renouncing his political convictions. When he entered the Serbian

Academy of Sciences and Arts in Belgrade in 1977, the writer drew attention to himself once again through his defence of the Serbian people. It was here that he made his infamous pronouncement 'The Serbs have always won at war and lost in peacetime.'[8] This was his way of exalting the myth of a martyred people, always ready to sacrifice themselves for freedom, but in the final analysis losing in peacetime because they fall under the domination of other peoples. Cosic made himself in this way quite openly the mouthpiece for the Serbian people who, according to him, were crushed in the Yugoslavian federation and physically under threat in Kosovo. A brilliant writer sometimes nicknamed the 'Serbian Tolstoy', he contributed to making the Academy of Sciences and Arts a bastion of renascent Serbian nationalism. In 1986 it was the ideas of Dobrica Cosic that led some of its members to draw up a memorandum that was to cause a considerable disturbance. In it members of the Academy denounced the 'physical, political, judicial and cultural genocide of the Serbian population in Kosovo'[9]—no less! Criticism was also hurled at neighbouring republics like Slovenia and Croatia, which were accused of politically dominating Serbia, and against Yugoslavia's federal system as a whole as being responsible for the 'discrimination' to which Serbs within the federation were subjected.

The memorandum was published on 24 September 1986 in a Belgrade newspaper, and was widely condemned by the political leaders of the time. But one segment of opinion saw some of its fears justified by the members of the prestigious institution. A politician still relatively unknown to the general public, Slobodan Milosevic, was to ascertain the interest that he could draw from theories defended by members of the Academy. Dobrica Cosic was soon to pick out Milosevic as being just the man Serbia needed. The role of the writer had effectively been to 'bewitch the nation', as one of his opponents, the former mayor of Belgrade Bogdan Bogdanovic, testified.

In Rwanda might one say likewise that the historical role of Grégoire Kayibanda, future first President of the Republic, was to 'bewitch' the Hutu people in the first years of independence experienced by his country? The personal and political trajectories of his life are very different. Nevertheless, the ideology he upheld produced just as inflammatory a discourse, the destructive effects of which

were soon to be unleashed on the Tutsi minority. He owed his intellectual training to the White Fathers of the Catholic Church, keen
to promote an anti-Hutu elite during the 1950s. Following a period
of study at the main Nyakibanda seminary, Grégoire Kayibanda
campaigned more and more in favour of Hutu emancipation,
denouncing Hutu oppression by the Tutsi monarchy. From 1948 to
1952 he was secretary of the Belgian-Rwandan association, and then
chief editor of *Kinyamateka*, the nation's mostly widely read Catholic
periodical.

In 1957 Kayibanda and a few other Hutu intellectuals wrote a
'Note on the social aspect of the indigenous racial issue', entitled
'The Bahutu Manifesto'. According to Gérard Prunier, this text represents the first political interiorisation by Rwandans of the racial
categorisation introduced by the colonizer. Indeed this text states:
'The problem is basically that of the political monopoly of one race,
the Mututsi. In the present circumstances this political monopoly is
turned into an economic and social monopoly. ... And given the *de
facto* selection in school, the political, economic and social mono-
polies turn into a cultural monopoly which condemns the desperate
Bahutu to be for ever subaltern workers...' Kayibanda and his colleagues moreover spotted the political interest of building on this
notion of 'race' to get in first with the pronouncement that the Hutu
are strongest because they represent the majority of the population.
'In order to monitor this race monopoly we are strongly opposed,
at least for the time being, to removing the labels "Mututsi",
"Muhutu" and "Mutwa" from identity papers. Their suppression
would create a risk of *preventing the statistical law from establishing the
reality of facts.*'[10] In other words, democracy understood to be rule by
the greatest number was to be confused with rule by the racial
majority, that is the Hutu. The presentiment is there: with these
kinds of ideas circulating, the future was becoming alarming, even
threatening, for those Tutsi who were still in power.

The creation of scientific myths. These three different personal trajectories show how an ideological essay writer, a nationalist novelist,
and a Partisan teacher played vital roles in forming a framework of
interpretation from which new political dynamics were thrown into
gear. The success of their reading of a crisis situation depended, then,

on the way their ideology (racist, nationalist etc.) could graft itself on to imaginary representations and myths peculiar to the society concerned. Because all these intellectuals homed in on this kind of alchemy of the imaginary overlaid on reality, through which different faces of the enemy took shape, and invested it with meaning. Their principal role in this respect was to forge—or to recreate—a new reference vocabulary harking back to ideas as much as to symbols and myths. The writer Dobrica Cosic was especially brilliant at this, to some extent replacing the communist fraternity's class struggle vocabulary with that of the ethnic Serb and his transcendence in history. This is how, at the end of the twentieth century, he rekindled a story—from a collection of images and Serbian nationalist myths—that had originated in his country at the beginning of the nineteenth century, as in most of the Balkan states, under Ottoman or Austro-Hungarian rule. The province of Kosovo, where in terms of sheer numbers the Albanians dominated in the middle of the 1980s, and where such powerful and explosive myths circulated, provided the perfect example for application and demonstration of these nationalist theses.[11]

In other situations the function of the intellectual will be rather to distribute and adapt an ideology hailing from the exterior by grafting it on to the individual cultural context of the country concerned. Such an operation can only succeed if it manages to articulate this ideology with the history, myths and symbols peculiar to each country. In an interesting comparative study of the cases of Rwanda, Bosnia and Cambodia, the American political scientist René Lemarchand, having first assessed the weighting of ideological factors (Marxism-Leninism, nationalism or a perverted vision of democracy), rightly stresses that the impact of these ideologies on the masses is rarely very deep, above all when they are of foreign extraction; unless, he stipulates, their language is radically transformed and adapted to the local culture. It is the re-interpretation and even the fabrication of myths peculiar to the history of these countries that allows this ideological graft on to local culture to succeed.[12] It is therefore important to study the fairy tales, myths, rumours, and memories specific to a culture in order to understand massacres that have been committed within it. It is this plunge into the imaginary that will give historical and emotional resonance to the ideological discourse. In a way the intellectual's job is to make something new out of something old, that is to transpose ancient themes on to a new ideological grid. This seems to be the only really effective way for this ideology to 'speak' to the people. A mythical narrative is constructed in this way, identity-bound, and likely to contain a strong mobilising power over peoples' minds. Studies undertaken by anthropologists and ethnologists can be of great interest here for understanding the symbolic dynamics leading to massacre. In this way artists, poets, doctors, scientists, men of the church, all kinds of people serving as the representatives of know-ledge or faith can come together to forge a mythical narrative anchored in the notion of identity. All of them, in their own way, help to make this more appealing to an even wider audience than just circles of the converted, striking chords that resonate in their particular branch of activity, and using language familiar to their discipline.

If the discourses of Rosenberg, Cosic and Kayibanda could have an impact in their our countries, it is because the themes they evoke found a perceptible echo among wider circles. In Germany doctors with eugenicist leanings in favour of 'improving the race' were a well-known phenomenon, like the openly racist anatomist Eduard Pernkopf.[13] In the former Yugoslavia the role of members of the prestigious Serbian Academy who worked to defend nationalist themes has been remarked upon. We should also note that psychia-trists such as Jovan Raskovic and Radovan Karadzic discovered in the Serbian nationalist cause the opportunity to ally ideological fantasy to their psychological know-how.[14] In Rwanda *The Bahutu Manifesto*, written in collaboration with two White Fathers, bene-fited from extensive church support favouring the promotion of the Hutus.

Warmongering intellectuals? Should we really be surprised to find that men of knowledge or faith participate in the formation of identitarian ideals that may engender violence? A little historical hindsight can in this instance prove useful, and the way persecution in Europe from the Middle Ages onwards evolved is especially illu-minating. The American historian Robert Moore has examined the essential role played by scholars and men of the church in justifying and implementing forms of persecution dating from the eleventh and twelfth centuries. These men learnedly determined who the 'enemy' is (the term 'enemy' is used by Moore), principally the heretics, Jews, lepers and later witches. Through these different periods of exclusion, banishment, torture, putting to death, knowledge and faith were used to impose various forms of political or religious power over the population as a whole. The development of these groups of scholars is associated with the development of systems of punishment and persecution, which in turn reinforce regal and religious power.[15] We can note in passing that, in the crusade against the Cathars in the 12th century, metaphors for purity (and the struggle to control the plague) are already used to justify massacres in the southwest of France, such as those perpetrated in Béziers and Albi.

This should make us particularly cautious when evaluating the emancipating role of culture as a means of raising mankind through instruction. True, enlightenment philosophers defended the idea that culture constituted the authentic route to individual fulfilment and freedom, but this conviction needs, at the very least, careful conditioning. Education is, of course, for man the means to overcome human misery, widening horizons by opening the door to knowledge of the world and providing the means to act more effectively through knowledge of its laws. However, culture does not in itself have the faculty to lead man to free himself from violence. It is rather the contrary, that culture can supply him with the means to be more intelligent in exercising violence, and in resorting to cruelty.

As one survivor of the Rwanda genocide commented, learning 'does not make man better, it makes him more efficient. He who wishes to inspire evil will be at an advantage if he knows of man's quirks, if he learns morality, if he studies sociology. If the educated man's heart is ill conceived, if he spills over with hatred, he will be more capable of evil-doing.'[16] I therefore fail to see why people are still surprised to find that barbarism could flourish in a European nation as cultivated as Germany. Culture in itself is no safeguard against barbarity. On the contrary, it provides an armoury for anyone seeking a rational justification for his emotions and passions.

Are these intellectuals, the figures of which differ from one country to another, directly responsible for the massacres of the future? Let us beware once again of falling into the trap of drawing a straight line between ideas and deeds. Everything will depend in fact on how the political situation develops, on whether or not the economy is in decline, to what extent there is social instability, the state of the inter-national environment, etc. The more this context is deteriorating, with the threat of destabilisation, the more the identity discourse risks being accepted as the mental framework of collective reas-surance. Unless, that is, a competing intellectual discourse—one de-fended by other intellectuals—manages effectively to counter the identity subtext by revealing it as aberrant. In short, the course of events is undetermined. Moreover, those same thinkers who con-tributed to the construction of ideologies of fear and hatred do not as a general rule become perpetrators of the violence to come. They may sometimes even regret the turn of events, for example the sava-gery of certain fighting units or militia who belong to their camp.

It is undeniably the case, however, that at a key moment in the history of their country these intellectuals devise ideological tools that, if applied, are capable of detonating mass violence. The 'solu-tion' they propose does not in effect offer any perspective of com-promise. Their analyses, founded on a radical affirmation of identity, really consist of 'essentialising' differences: Aryan-Jews, Hutu-Tutsi, etc. They legitimise an existential confrontation between 'them' and 'us'. It is the identity of this 'them' posed by 'us' that is perceived as being, by nature, threatening. Negotiation is therefore impossible because the difference is presented as intangible. But this identity framework still needs to translate into a significant political force; and this in itself is still far from being an automatic process.

Reaching political legitimacy

In history there is nothing more dangerous than interpreting events in the light of their aftermath. Every historian risks being ensnared by the temptation to pre-determine the logic of a historical event because of being himself in the comfortable position of knowing the outcome. This is a major source of error as regards perceptions of mentality and behaviour on the part of actors. On this point Arlette Farge takes to task historians studying France in 1750 who claim to be able to foresee the coming of the 1789 Revolution: 'I have learnt at least one thing,' she remarks, 'and that is that history is totally unpredictable.' The conclusion she draws from consulting the archives is that 'no fact or event leads to another fact or event without other types of posturing, position taking, or contrivance, possibly being present at the same time'.[17]

To write history is to open up the field of possibility, while mistrusting any simplistic and deterministic causal interpretation of the past. This commitment to representing the past faithfully, an exacting job at the very least, is expressed in a position like: 'I am going to study the eighteenth century not knowing that the Revolution took place.' Applied to this book's subject matter, this cautious approach becomes 'I will study the persecution of the Jews in Germany in the 1930s, unaware of Auschwitz.' This therefore represents a move in the right direction to the extent that otherwise the sum of events might prompt one to believe that an inexorable causality leads from the virulent 1920s anti-Semitism expressed in *Mein Kampf* to the organised persecution of German Jews during the 1930s, and culminated in their extermination at the start of the 1940s. Moreover, it is on this irrefutable chronology that the so-called 'intentionalist' thesis was based, according to which the intention to destroy the Jews was already explicitly contained in Hitler's writings before he himself had even come to power. The realisation of the project would have subsequently only been a question of time and opportunism. No historian would ever try to defend such a position today. Not only is there no direct path leading from idea to action, but nor is there any direct causality from one historical action to another. No one today, then, would maintain that the economic, professional, administrative, civil or any other type of marginalisation of Jews residing in Germany, instituted from the start of the Nazi regime, had necessarily to entail their extermination, *a fortiori* to the genocide of all European Jews, if not the Jewish people worldwide.

Hitler's rise to power. Nor was it written into Germany's history that this democratically elected leader hailing from the backrooms of bars and cafés in Munich in the 1920s was to come to power some ten years later. As the English historian Ian Kershaw points out, the nomination of Adolf Hitler to the position of Chancellor on 30 January 1933 was 'the result of a combination of fortuitous circumstances and an error in the calculations of the conservatives (the German right-wing)'.[18] In the 1924 elections his party (the NSDAP) had obtained less than 3 per cent, and in 1928 only 2.6 per cent of the vote. But the national crisis (instability of the Weimar republic) coupled with an economic and social crisis (the 1929 crash, the full impact of which hit Germany in 1930–1, causing millions to become unemployed) saw German opinion being pulled in different directions towards opposite and extreme poles (Communist and Nazi). Hitler, then, with his political flair and unerring aim targeted the three groups suffering most from this situation: the unemployed, the farmers, and the middle classes. In other respects, in the face of growing worker agitation, his special force known as the Storm Troops (SA) led by Ernst Röhm, a war hero (and commander of the Bavarian infantry regiment in 1919), were brought in to replace the police force in order to re-establish order, all at the price of bloody confrontations all round. This provided necessary reassurance to those fearing that the Bolshevik revolution, recently sweeping through the newly formed Soviet Union, would reach Germany. This crackdown afforded a leap forward for the Nazis in the September 1930 election. Their party obtained 18.3 per cent of the vote. From this point on, they were there among the 'greats', and this in turn qualified them to broadcast on national radio. Still swept forward by the crisis and climate of violence that reigned across the nation, the NSDAP made another leap forward in the Reichstag elections of July 1932, obtaining 37.3 per cent of the total votes cast (13,779,000).

Hitler knew exactly how to profit in this way from the crisis in which the country was plunged. With the support of a journalist, Joseph Goebbels, he devised a hard-hitting political communication strategy, combining the latest techniques but relying nonetheless on the appeal to traditional German values. The Nazi party electors recruited their numbers mostly among craftsmen, farmers, shopkeepers, civil servants and white-collar workers. These people voted for the Nazis primarily because they believed that their party would bring about a return to order and stability. For their part, right-wing conservative circles believed themselves capable of holding Hitler hostage so that he would continue to serve their political ends. Did they not recognise themselves in these values Hitler emphasised: nationalism, militarism, anti-Bolshevism? They thought they could 'domesticate' Hitler. But leaders of these conservative elites grossly misjudged the personality and ambitions of this extraordinary individual—unpredictable, fanatical, violent—and he was rapidly to extricate himself from their grasp.

Milosevic and the dream of a 'Greater Serbia'.   In the case of Yugoslavia, Milosevic's rise to power was not inevitable either. One might even have thought that this country, non-aligned on the Eastern and Western blocs and already open to the West, was in a good position to embark truly on political and economic democratisation, aided and abetted by the fall of the Berlin wall. This transition seemed even to be taking shape at the beginning of 1990, thanks to measures put in place by the Federal Prime Minister Ante Markovic, a Croat, who

'set in motion a programme of highly successful economic reforms, stifling the country's galloping inflation so the rate dropped from 26 per cent to 0 per cent in only a matter of months.... Markovic acquired great popularity throughout the country. During this brief period, it seemed as though Yugoslavia experienced a breath of fresh air and had a chance of surviving as an ordinary state. Respected for his liberal ideas and tangible economic achievements, Markovic represented ... the opportunity to side-step the path of destruction to which they were already committed, enabling them to turn instead towards the future, modernisation and European integration.'[19]

But this did not take into account the crisis of legitimacy that had infiltrated the federal system since the death of Tito. Likewise the nationalist clamour coming from the Serbian minority in Kosovo, who from the middle of the 1980s began to make themselves heard through their 'meetings' (term used to sound modern) bringing together an ever greater number of sympathisers. With the support of the writer Dobrica Cosic, the key issue for their movement was the advent of the people: the Serbian people, of course. It was never, therefore, a question of ethnic cleansing, but rather a rallying of all Serbs to the objective of a 'Greater Serbia'. It did not take into account, either, the development of other nationalist fires, in the first place in neighbouring Croatia, stoked by their Serbian counterparts and for whom the intellectual Franjo Tudjman, knight in shining armour for the official history of Tito and the 1960s, became the leading figure. Finally, it did not take into account either the political opportunism of a man born of the Communist political apparatus, the Serb Slobodan Milosevic, who had spotted how rallying to this nationalist cause would further his objective of seizing power.

Citing Ivan Stambolic (then president of the Serbian presidium), John Allcock recounts that in the early stages Milosevic was not particularly enthusiastic about the actions of the Serbian nationalists. They 'took him in hand', and this he did not appreciate. But Milosevic understood the political interest of rallying their cause. 'Consequently, through the narrowness and the lack of imagination of his political vision and those of the circle who surrounded him (rather than the manifest greatness of his native political talent), the Socialist Party of Serbia, Serbia itself and ultimately Yugoslavia were pushed away from the one track that might have saved them all—the relegitimation of both party and state based upon democratisation.'[20] This mutation from communism to nationalism in fact almost instantly won over other members of the Yugoslavian federation, and in the first place Slovenia and Croatia. Numerous polls ensuing during the 1990s bear witness to this evolution, the chronology for these ballots moving from north to south through Yugoslavia: Slovenia (April), Croatia (April–May), Bosnia (November), Serbia (December). The Federalist path that Markovic was still offering could not compete with the increasing strength of the identitarian retreats that were finding expression in these electoral consultations. Creating his party very late (in July 1990) Markovic was beaten at the December elections, while Milosevic's party triumphed. The latter was, then, at the peak of his popularity—in the very name of the political legitimacy he had just acquired, Milosevic could from this point on embark on the 'Greater Serbia' project, if necessary going to war.

Kayibanda and the formation of the Rwandan state. Moving on to Rwanda, it was no more a certainty that Grégoire Kayibanda, formerly a student at the Nyakibanda seminary, would become in 1961 the first President of the Rwandan Republic. At the end of the 1950s his ideas extolling Hutu power from an almost racist standpoint, as expressed in *The Bahutu Manifesto,* were only shared by a minority of Hutus, both 'educated' and closely aligned with the

Church. If he succeeded in coming to power, it was precisely because the Church, and with it the Belgian administration, from that point onwards supported this movement for emancipation of the new Hutu elite. On 3 November 1959, at Gitamara in the northwest of Rwanda, a series of violent confrontations broke out, and quickly spread to other places. This 'Rwandan All Saints day',[21] a straightforward jacquerie of Hutu peasants against the Tutsi, resulted in hundreds of deaths, numerous homes being destroyed by fire, and the first exile of thousands of Tutsi. In fact, this 1959–60 'revolution' that was 'aided' by the Belgian administration paved the way for the eviction of both the monarchy and the entire Tutsi political-administrative structure on which Belgium had based its indirect political administration for decades. Confirmation of this was forthcoming in the various electoral polls organised in 1961, won largely by the Kayibandan party or Parmehutu (Party for the Hutu emancipation movement). The Republic was proclaimed on 28 January 1961, and Rwanda officially became independent on 1 July 1962.

The post-colonial Rwandan republican state in this way founded its legitimacy on victory over the Tutsi feudal system. 'The Hutu victory was total', asserts Claudine Vidal. 'Meanwhile, the victors continued to act, not just as though former Tutsi leaders were still a threat to the Republic, but as though all Tutsis were hereditary enemies, and had become a foreign body within the country.'[22] Repressive practices exercised against the Tutsis from these very first years of the Rwandan Republic explain their mass departure.[23] Some of those exiled in Uganda reacted during these 1960s years by organising armed raids into Rwandan territory to attack representatives of the Hutu authorities. Such incursions almost systematically provoked reprisals against Tutsis still living in Rwanda. So, for example, the raid carried out at the end of December 1963 resulted by way of retaliation in several massacres of Tutsis, the best known of these being that in Gikongoro in January 1964, which resulted in between 7,000 and 10,000 deaths.[24]

Meanwhile, the second Republic inaugurated on 5 July 1973 through the coup d'état of Juvénal Habyarimana apparently wanted to make a break with the past. The role of the new president was, in effect, 'to calm things down, act as moderator, being the only person capable of controlling the extremists'.[25] His regime intended to promote Rwandan *unity*, not to protect the Hutus against the Tutsis.

So the country experienced a period of calm, noticeable from the arrival of a Tutsi to the government (André Katabarwa), without in the meantime abandoning the slogan: 'The government of the majority is tantamount to democracy.' In addition, the economic climate improved considerably, above all at the start of the 1980s. Infant mortality fell, and the percentage of children in school rose from less than 50 per cent in 1978 to nearly 62 per cent in 1986. Who would have thought then that this country would become the stage, nearly ten years later, for one of the most horrific genocides of the twentieth century?

Unfortunately, this economic resurgence was not to last. Famine reappeared, and the price of coffee on world markets fell by 50 per cent in 1989. Inequality ravaged the country to a dangerous level, with the vast majority of Rwandan peasants being the main victims, as amply documented by André Guichaoua.[26] Rwanda plunged once more into crisis, along with other African states. In 1990 the IMF imposed a 57 per cent devaluation of its currency. The Habyarimana regime became increasingly corrupt, and with the heightened paucity of wealth, competition between the elites stiffened. Yet at the time, western aid agencies considered Rwanda to be a model of development that emerging countries throughout the world should follow. Was this not a pure illusion? Peter Uvin has no doubt about it: the development ideology promoted by the West paradoxically contributed to increasing poverty and inequality in the country. This development enterprise (*amajyambere*) espoused by the elites of the second Rwandan republic reinforced the state of structural violence in the country. Instead of decreasing poverty among the ranks of peasants, it contributed to increasing tensions and frustration of the destitute masses. According to Uvin, in early 1990s Rwanda, economic and political crises combined with this substratum of structural violence to tip society into destruction.[27] Worse, the exiled Tutsi diaspora in Uganda unleashed another armed attack clearly aimed at regaining power. This assault carried out by the RPF (Rwandan Patriotic Front) on 1 October 1990 rekindled old political reflexes seen thirty years earlier, namely fear that a Tutsi attack from without would be sanctioned by Tutsi massacres within.

Prophets of chaos. In each of these three cases it is difficult to identify what actually stemmed from the actors' will to seize power, and what was simply the outcome of a set of circumstances conducive to their achieving their aim. But in any event, we can see that their political rise occurred above all through stigmatisation of a minority group. However, this analysis needs to be qualified somewhat in the German case: while Hitler played the anti-Semitic chord to excess, it is by no means certain that this theme had played a decisive role in his electoral success. It is much more likely that his militarism seduced the German people. The fact remains that hatred of the Jews was one of the fundamental character traits of the new master of the Reich, and that he used this as the cornerstone of his regime; and against this the Germans did not protest.

With the accession of this type of leader to the highest responsibility in the nation, a crucial step was taken: from that point on there was in effect political legitimisation of what had hitherto been only a dialogue of protest (grafting on to social fears and frustrations)—it now became government strategy. What had till then been only an extreme political discourse, propagated by some intellectuals, a handful of organisations, a party, underwent a transformation into national policy. Such ideas might just have remained at the level of inflammatory debate, sparking off sporadic violence here and there from time to time, but now, with the support of the state, things were on a different scale. Doubtless such a development, whether it matured slowly or rapidly, was likely to bring about profound change in any country, at the heart of institutions as well as in daily life. One could expect a veritable 'reshaping of identities' for the society, heavy with the violence to come, and in perfect coherence with the discourse that had brought it about. But how would the population, through the various groups and networks composing it, react? And what would be the modalities and intensity of this violence? When and under what circumstances? No one really knew.

The prime instigators of these upheavals will always be the leaders who embody such policies. It is conceivable that, once in power, a Hitler, a Milosevic or a Kayibanda might have forgone the ideas that brought them to the top as head of state. It would not be the first time in history that a political leader, having achieved his end, would abandon the more excessive or demagogic aspects of his programme, but in the cases we are concerned with, it was not to be. Such an 'oversight' would seem inconceivable, since their rise to power was based to such an extent on an emotional relationship with the 'people' whom they claimed to be setting out to protect. These leaders found themselves constrained to become what they had wanted to be: champions of 'us' against 'them'. Whether or not their audiences believed in their discourse, partly or totally, they themselves believed they had a vocation. They awarded themselves the title of 'prophet' and the obligation to accomplish their self-assigned tasks. It was as though they had been singled out to detect the threat, predict it, fabricate it as required, and finally destroy it. It was always from chaos that they drew their legitimacy as protectors of 'us'.

While these situations always seem to stem, more or less, from the same psycho-affective chords (fear, resentment, frustration), Hitler certainly stands out as the one who exploited them with the most astonishing efficiency. Firstly, because of his personality: a great orator, he had an exceptional talent, a 'charismatic power', Ian Kershaw shows,[28] to drive crowds who came to listen to him into a kind of ecstasy. He was literally a creator of public emotion. He had the capacity to react, and also to improvise: he took advantage, for example, of shockwaves reverberating in public opinion about the Reichstag fire on 27 February 1933 to promulgate the very next day a decree for 'protection of the people and of the state', that inaugurated the first legal foundation for the Nazi dictatorship. Changes then came about at an alarming speed: mass arrests of communists, creation of the first concentration camps for their internment, suppression of unions, dissolution of all political organisations (except the Nazi party). While taking great care to reconcile the ruling elites, Hitler used violence in this way from the very first months of his reign, even against his former friends: during the 'Night of the Long Knives' (29–30 June 1934) he had Röhm and the principal SA leaders murdered to eliminate any potential political rivals. So it was that in scarcely a year and a half he managed to install a fully-fledged regime of personal dictatorship and an all-embracing system of command over the population. The Weimar Republic was well and truly dead.

The political conduct of a Milosevic is a pale imitation by comparison. He certainly had a less colourful, if tortured, personality, his personal history being overshadowed by death.[29] But he also exploited, in his very own way, the emotions of fear and resentment. When reproducing Serbian Academy memorandum texts for his speeches, he regularly employed the word 'genocide' to suggest what might happen to the Serbs if he didn't defend them. In his speeches the Croats are systematically likened to the Ustashis, and the Germans to the Nazis. Even in 2004, during his trial at The Hague, he alluded to the similarity between the foreign policy of Hitler in the Balkans and that of Chancellor Kohl in 1990: 'a million Serbs were wiped out, over half of them being expelled and then driven to their death amid the most grievous sufferings. This monstrous activity was certainly contributed to by the directive of Joseph Goebbels, which remained alive and topical in German practice, political practice, to toady up to the Croats in order to work against the Serbs, and this is evident in the German relationship to the Balkans in the twentieth century, the late twentieth century.'[30]

Playing with emotions therefore remained for him the ideal means of appealing to a patriotic reflex, to muzzle his opponents if not eliminate them. Because the population was in danger, anybody unwilling to take the necessary defensive measures immediately became suspect. Unlike Hitler, Milosevic was already in the power apparatus. In the guise of a good communist apparatchik, he tried little to take control, finally succeeding in September 1987 during the 8th session of the League of Communists of Serbia (LCS). From that point on, he sidelined, ousted or replaced all those who appeared too moderate, in the army, the police and the media (and above all in television broadcasting).

In Rwanda President Kayibanda's style was probably more paternalistic, but no less ruthless. His regime was fuelled by revenge against the Tutsis and the idea that the Hutu majority embodied democracy. The relationships of domination were reversed, with the dominated of yesterday becoming the dominant group within the first Rwandan republic, the new power at Kigali instigating a single party system. During the regional elections of August 1963, the president's party (the Parmehutu) took 140 of the 141 'burgomasters' or town seats. Classic procedure: the Parmehutu had used obsessive fear of the Tutsi danger from without as a political lever to increase his authority. Following the attack in December 1963 by the exiled Tutsis and the reprisals that followed (nearly 10,000 Tutsis murdered in January 1964), President Kayibanda was himself to use the word 'genocide' in his speech of 11 March 1964. It was probably the first time that this term was publicly used in Kinyarwandese.

A few voices were raised then in Europe describing as genocide the massacres that had just been carried out in Rwanda. But Kayibanda retorted with: 'Who is making themselves guilty of genocide?', 'Who is searching for genocide?' 'Who wants genocide?' Using this word six times in a speech lasting only minutes, the Rwandan president was in fact stigmatising the actions of armed Tutsi factions on the outside, levelling at them accusations of partaking in 'subversive' and 'terrorist' activities. His extremely violent words contain an extraordinary and terrifying prophesy: 'Assuming that you achieve the impossible, in taking the town of Kigali, describe how you imagine the chaos that would result from this glorious feat to be, and of which you would be the first victims? ... It would be the total and precipitous end of the Tutsi race.'[31] It is a rare historical event when a head of state forewarns of genocide. In Germany, Hitler did the same on 30 January 1939 at the Reichstag. Yet nothing had been decided and organised at that date for the mass destruction of the Jews of Europe; I will return to this later. What took place in Rwanda on 11 March 1964, was similar and yet such words uttered in public are far from harmless: simple words, a few short phrases, pronounced in a context of threat and fear, open the future of a country to the apocalypse of mass murder. Perhaps it will happen, perhaps not. But if...., then.... the prophecy will come true.

Feeding fear and resentment: the role of the media. Manipulating emotions thus occupies a central position in the instigation of such powers. But it is propaganda that will be used to maintain and develop this emotional state. It is the necessary accompaniment and consolidating element in the establishment of such political systems. Propaganda is often seen as a set of techniques employed to demonise the enemy, and this is indeed what it involves. But this 'technical' approach does not touch on what propaganda provides above all: a new universe of meaning for all. What had previously been articulated by a few intellectuals, relayed and then developed by political leaders, is then offered up in its entirety to a whole country as soon as these leaders come to power. The press, radio, and television are 'invited' or in some cases even obliged to be the ongoing vectors of this vision of the world. Propaganda becomes in this way a general system of 'envelopment' for the population. How does it actually operate?

The basic principle is always the same: to manufacture emotion. In other words, arouse fear, mistrust, and resentment and then provoke a reaction of vigilance, pride and revenge. The propaganda machine is first and foremost a device for fabricating public emotion as dictated by political leaders whose words it relays and amplifies. It is by working on emotion that it sets out to hold sway over the public: 'no choice, it says; WE have all got to defend ourselves against those people there. It is a question of identity: our survival depends on it.' And it is via this route that propaganda makes its assault on our minds: 'Faced with this common threat, we must show ourselves to be stronger and affirm the power of our identity.' Propaganda sets out to impose an interpretation of the world presented as being 'vital' for the principal group of belonging. So it is that the emotional envelopment of the public is immediately expanded to ideological envelopment. The two cannot be separated: they each contribute in a combined attempt to invade minds. It is by cultivating fear and suspicion that propaganda tries to 'engrave' its vision of the world on each individual. It says to everyone: 'This is what you must think from now on, here are your new guidelines, whether you like them or not.' So 'are you for or against us?'

Does this necessarily mean, then, that a system of totalitarian pressure is in the process of coming into being? Each historical situation is different. As soon as the Nazis came to power, they took over the media almost totally, starting with the radio, having ascertained early on its strategic interest as an instrument of mass communication. Professions involved in publishing were subjected to government control through the creation of a professional chamber of journalists, writers etc. Each was therefore placed under state tutelage: censorship became superfluous. Goebbels, in his new position as minister of propaganda, could declare: 'Let everyone play their own instrument, so long as they play the same music.' Any journalist accused of betraying the 'German people' very quickly found himself in prison, with or without trial. The totalitarian propaganda system was set up in this way.

The same analysis cannot be applied to Yugoslavia, in the period at the end of the 1980s that would see the crumbling of the federal system and the rise of nationalism in the principal republics. After the death of Tito, in Serbia, it was above all the prestigious news-paper *Politika* that became the spearhead of Serbian nationalism, while television steadfastly maintained a federal line. But from 1987 onwards this same television in Belgrade increasingly supported the Milosevic campaign, relaying for example in real time the vast nationalist demonstration of the 28 June 1989, commemorating the 600th anniversary of the battle of Kosovo. It would nevertheless be a mistake to believe that all the state media followed suit, because the public radio did not in any way demonstrate the same nationalist zeal.[32] An even more remarkable development, as compared with Nazi Germany, was that in Yugoslavia in 1990 freedom of the press and the end of the single party system were decreed in principle. The result: it became possible in law for anybody to express an opinion and communicate it freely. Independent press organs came into being, like the opposition paper Vreme. The same thing hap-pened in radio and television, with the launching of Studio B. There is a wide divergence, however, between the principle and its appli-cation. For example, the papers may have enjoyed freedom of expression, but they barely had the means to reach their readers due to a lack of available distribution networks in the provinces. Tele-vision, the only medium to reach the more distant corners of the country, remained well and truly under the control of the new master of Belgrade.

Rwanda underwent a similar development during the same period. Indeed, at the beginning of the 1990s the Habyarimana regime accepted some opening up of the media, and decreed the end of the single party system in 1991. As a result, a veritable 'springtime for the press' took place, characterised by the creation of new newspapers.[33] But this move towards liberalisation paradox-ically played into the hands of the extremists who enjoyed support from personnel even within the regime itself, then had the facilities they needed to fuel their own media for propagating their ideas. In 1990 the bi-monthly *Kangura* came out, launching campaigns to encourage informers among the public to denounce Tutsis, and notably publishing the famous 'Ten Hutu commandments' a ver-itable call to hatred and apartheid regarding the Tutsi. In July 1993 a private station was set up, the Radio-Television Libre des Milles Collines (RTLM). The tone of the RTLM was 'young', relaxed, and with very catchy Zairian music discernible in the background. This was a real innovation for this country, because the official national station, Radio Rwanda, was often boring. In the interval between two music tracks on Radio RTLM, the standard commentary would be a deluge of words denouncing Tutsi 'cockroaches' and glorifying the greatness of the Hutu.

The Ten Commandments of the Bahutu*

In December 1990 the extremist monthly publication *Kangura* ('Wake up!') published a highly significant text appealing to the 'conscience of the Bahutu' and laying out for them a code of conduct: this was the 'Ten Commandments', a total misappropriation of the Biblical text:

1. Every Muhutu should know that Umututsikazi, wherever she may be, is working for the profit of her Tutsi clan. As a result, any Muhutu who marries a Mututsikazi or makes an Umututsikazi his concubine or his secretary or protégée is a traitor.

2. Every Muhutu should know that our Bahutukazi daughters are more worthy and more conscious in their role as women, wives and mothers. Are they not pretty, good secretaries, and more honest!

3. Bahutukazi, be vigilant and bring back your husbands, brothers and your sons to good reason.

4. All Muhutu should know that all Mututsi are dishonest in their business dealings. Their only ambition is to achieve racial supremacy. It follows that a Muhutu is a traitor if he

— forms business alliances with the Batutsi;
— invests his money or the state's money in a Mututsi business enterprise;
— grants the Batutsi business favours (import licences, bank loans, building plots, public contracts, etc.)

5. Bahutu must be appointed to all strategic positions whether political, administrative, economic, military and security.

* Refer to note 10 on page 397 for explanations of the terms used in this text.

6. The teaching sector (pupils, students, teachers) must be predominantly Hutu.
7. The Rwandan Armed Forces must be exclusively Hutu.
The experience of the October 1990 war taught us this. Military personnel may not marry a Mututsikazi.
8. The Bahutu must cease to have any pity for the Batutsi.
9. The Bahutu, wherever they may be, must be united, responsible and concerned for the wellbeing of their Bahutu
brothers. The Bahutu from both inside and outside Rwanda
must constantly seek out friends and allies for the Hutu cause,
starting with their Bantu brothers. They must constantly oppose Tutsi propaganda. The Bahutu must be firm and vigilant
against the Hutu cause, starting with their Bantu brothers.
10. The Social Revolution of 1959, the Referendum of 1961,
and the Hutu ideology must be taught to all Muhutu and at
every level. All Muhutu must broadcast this ideology to as
wide an audience as possible. Any Muhutu who persecutes his
Muhutu brother for having read, distributed and preached this
ideology is a traitor.

Quoted by Jean-Pierre Chrétien (ed.), *Rwanda: Les medias du genocide*, Paris,
Karthala, 1995, pp. 141–2.

This brief analysis of the media gives us a better perception of
how media development would be specific to each country. As far as
Nazi Germany was concerned, we see a 'classic' case of the demise of
an unstable republic leading to the abolition of the parliamentary
regime and the abrupt instigation of a system of total control over
every means of communication. When we look at former Yugoslavia and Rwanda, we see rather the 'exit' of a dictatorship, which
authorises a relative form of freedom of political expression, taking
the form of multipartyism, that those at the extremes knew exactly
how to turn to their advantage. To some extent, then, their histories
on this point are reflected in the vocabulary used by researchers:
some speak about the founding of a 'democrature' in Serbia, and of a
'controlled democratisation' in Rwanda.[34] In other words, while the
German case shows that violence arises logically from a process of
'dictatorisation' of the state, the developments in Serbia and Rwanda
illustrate, conversely and paradoxically, that violence is engendered

in the presence of a political democratisation process that is limited, but not framed by the rule of law. There is food for thought here as regards the supposedly always positive virtues of what we call, in common parlance, the 'democratic transition'.

Depending on these different political configurations, the propaganda machine will then be more or less powerful, and more or less total. And the language of this propagandas will be different, reflecting specific cultural traits. But its themes and procedures, from the point of view of its imaginary structure, often remain very closely related. That is because propaganda tends to resort to the same types of operators who in this regard appear as constants, over and above cultural differences. The function of these operators is to give form to the *imaginaire*, and to express it in concrete reality through words and images that generate emotion. And it is through these operators—real poles of transformation of the *imaginaire* into ideology—that the figures of the enemy described in Chapter I are constructed.

The pernicious tree of propaganda

I propose to summarise the above using as metaphor a poisonous tree, the branches and leaves of which are like the principal operators of this propaganda:

The first of these operators, the one we could identify as being the main vehicle for everything else, is the instrumentalisation of a common past of suffering, of a collective trauma: that of the First World War for the Nazis, of the Second World War for the Serb nationalists, of the domination of Tutsi royalty for the Hutu extremists. It is one of the most effective triggers for awakening resentment and fear in a people through manipulation of their collective memory. It is in this fertile ground of misery that the pernicious propaganda tree flourishes. It sprouts two large branches that together make up its entire stature: the almost eternal principle of grandeur and purity of our people who, it goes without saying, will not put up with such humiliations again: 'We are not going to be had again, are we?' Parallel to this branch runs the other, the demonisation of this 'other', the source of all of our people's unhappiness: 'It is from THEM that all our suffering arises. We cannot trust them. Those people are not like US.'

From these two large branches sprout new, very threatening off-shoots. One of these levels accusations of treachery against those who, in our own ranks, refuse to follow us. These are the anti-patriots, traitors in power. Beware, these traitors may be operating in disguise among our neighbours. The other bears the terrible accusation of a 'plot' against this 'other' so different from 'us'. In fact, 'these people are preparing our downfall. We might not realise it but, as you know, they are extremely powerful. Whether it is at home or abroad, their objective is without doubt to destroy us.'

Next come the leaves that clothe the branches, a multiplicity of emotional overlays that work to make this double threat a little more credible. One particularly dense variant of such foliage progresses through the manipulation of rumours: 'Did you know that in Kosovo, the Albanians think nothing of raping our women and van-dalising our cemeteries?' But this was just a rumour, and the type of rumour that always circulates in any society against a group per-ceived to be a threat. But the special trick of propaganda is to draw on this pool of rumours (or even invent some more) and create 'new' ones. In this way, from one day to the next, these rumours can find themselves being selected as newspaper headlines, and broadcast on the television evening news. It is no coincidence that they always relate to sexuality, the sacred, and family ties, namely what we hold to be most intimate.

Another type of foliage, horribly effective when it comes to raising anxiety levels, is that of levelling accusations that might well prepare the ground for a mirrored answer: 'You know that these are veritable assassins who do not hesitate to commit the most ferocious crimes, and even to burn our babies.' What crimes could be more odious than those aimed at the most innocent among us? 'Sooner or later, we will take revenge!' Somewhere in this tree, perhaps at the top, we will find yet another kind of foliage: animalisation. People accused of such crimes are beyond being considered human. They are animals, no longer deserving of our respect. And here, there and everywhere, as though enveloping the whole tree, spreads yet another foliage of crude and vulgar words and images used to depict the enemy. This is vulgarity in both the true and figurative sense: here we enter the realms of outrage, excess, and pornography. The use of caricature in the newspapers like the *Sturmer* in Germany or the

Kangura in Rwanda is very revealing of this lifting of taboos. As though suggesting that things had already reached the point of overflowing into the excess of violence.

Let us make no mistake: this tree will bear fruit, but it will be poisonous. These fruits of hatred, all of them repugnant, are the different faces of the enemy. Here the Jews, there the Reds but also the drains on the economy or the degenerate (handicapped, asocial, homosexual); there the Albanians, the Croatian Ustashis, the Muslims (or 'Turks') and even the Vatican or Europe that has understood absolutely nothing. Yet further the Tutsi, who in any case are unsalvageable but also the 'bad Hutu' because they are friends with the Tutsi or too moderate. What is one to do with all this noxious and evil fruit? Sort it? Crush it all? The most poisonous leave us with no choice: if we spare it, it will proliferate and pollute our territory. So we need to get rid of it. But how? Make it disappear? Exterminate it? The vocabulary hesitates. The tree will have to be cropped, purged or purified. The words are still vague. They are still not a part of any political programme as such. This propaganda tree constitutes 'simply' the semantic matrix from which massacre can come about.

Do individuals exposed to such a machine of hatred really believe in it? Too often research on propaganda postulates that it is all-powerful over the human spirit. The sociology of media reception shows, however, that this is a far too simplistic and caricature-like view. I will return to this idea later. The development of such a propaganda system, conjugated with the establishment of a political apparatus that sustains it, must nonetheless have considerable influence both in public life and in the day-to-day life of a nation.

This propaganda provides the wherewithal for the powers that be to legitimise their actions, and justifies the first measures taken against its enemies from within. The Nazis rapidly took action in this way against the Jews, taking away their German citizenship, eliminating them from any public function and from numerous professional and socio-cultural associations. The Nuremberg laws of 1935 for 'the protection of German blood and honour', over and above the prohibition of any sexual relationship between Jews and Aryans (because of the risk of 'sullying' the race), put an end to the equality of law acquired by the Jews since 1871, by distinguishing between nationality and citizenship (the latter only being recognised for individuals of 'German blood'). Then, in the name of the Aryanisation of the nation, the Jews were excluded from economic activity and relieved of their personal wealth. In Rwanda measures were also taken to limit the influence of the Tutsis, for example within the administration (a maximum quota of 9 per cent Tutsis was imposed). For his part, Milosevic in 1989 did away with the autonomy of the Kosovo government and parliament, a decision that on its own signified the end of Yugoslavia. In just a few months, 90 per cent of all Albanians were sacked from their jobs in the health sector, the media, culture and education. In 1991 some 450,000 Albanian school children and students found themselves outside the education system, refusing its exclusive control by the Serbs.

It falls also to the role of propaganda to create a deleterious climate: it propagates the tone of violence via slogans and images. It voices in public that violence is possible, without explicitly saying it is authorised, against the enemy within. As the French political scientist Philippe Braud has remarked, 'the discourse of hatred, the exhibition of arrogant titles of superiority set up, with time, an 'authorisation' of violence against victims designated as scapegoats'.[35] It is as though the new regime not only tolerates, but also encourages violence against its enemies. For the rest, in most cases it is the state itself that is the initiator of violence through its police force or via the intermediary of armed groups that are either more or less unofficial (criminal organisations and *ad hoc* militias). The political context becomes very favourable to the formation of such groups in the shadow of power: Arkan's Tigers in Serbia, *Interahamwe* militias in Rwanda. These groups will then operate with total impunity. In Kayibanda's Rwanda and in the last years of Habyarimana some Tutsis were massacred in this way. And in Kosovo in the 1990s some Albanians were also arrested and tortured. In Nazi Germany in the 1930s, the physical abuses committed against the Jews and the number of murders that took place cannot even begin to be counted.

From this point on, the way these societies evolved bears out that mass violence can and will happen. In effect, what happened was nothing less than the overturning of a fundamental political rule uniting all individuals who agree to live together: the murder taboo. If this taboo is removed with regard to a particular group, where will this transgression lead? In principle, the role of the state is to protect its citizens, as a large number of social scientists have explained. In return for the allegiance of individual citizens—who therefore defer to its authority—the state ensures their security. But in the cases examined here, the state is no longer the protector of all citizens. It is the state that becomes murderous, and the protector of murderers. Who, then, is left to restrain its violence?

From the religious to the sacrificial

Is it not, above all, down to the religious community to reaffirm the murder taboo as a principle underpinning any human community? Restating this fundamental law is an absolute priority as moral sign-posting goes for any society plunged into torment. In each of the three cases examined, the Christian religion is largely dominant: mostly Protestant in Germany, Orthodox in Serbia, and Catholic in Rwanda. And one of the basic tenets of Christianity is respect for one's neighbour: we can cite here the sixth commandment in the Bible, 'Thou shalt not kill' and Jesus' rather exacting invitations to 'love thy enemy' or 'love one another as I have loved you' (John 15:12). Will the Christian church then approve or deplore the violent impulses of political bodies against such or such a group?

The question needs looking at first of all on a general level, through examination of structural relationships that tend to become established between Church and State. At first sight the convergence is striking: we can observe a quasi-institutional collaboration between the religious and the political. In Germany the Protestant and Catholic Churches supported or sanctioned the new Nazi power. In Rwanda the Catholic Church itself participated in Kayibanda's accession to power. In Yugoslavia, on the other hand, the dignitaries of the Orthodox Church were officially hostile to Milosevic, whom they perceived to be a Communist ruler. But as the nationalist politics of the latter came to converge with the aspirations of this Church, the Church in turn offered its support, if only partly. When certain official events were held or public stands taken in each of these countries, there was a perceptible closing of ranks, or sometimes even collusion, between Church and State. Foreign policy is another aspect that should be taken into account, in the first place for Catholics subject to the Vatican's authority. For example, the signing of the Concordat in 1934 between the Holy See and Berlin was certainly aimed at preserving German Catholic institutions, but it came at the price of the Pope's recognition of the Nazi regime, which amounted to asking the bishops and their following to obey the new power. To be sure, within these Churches, voices with greater or less authority could offer an opinion about such a development. As a general rule, there will always be one or two. But what could they hope to achieve in the face of the institutional rapprochement with the new authorities?

Taking this one stage further, it is useful to observe what statements are made by the Church and how they react when violence is actually committed against state-designated enemies 'within'. In effect, they might accept the new government's overall policies, while reserving for themselves a margin for judgement as to such or such an aspect of this policy. Their reactions—or absence of them— in the face of violent acts constitute then a crucial test of their capacity to state the law, even from the point of view of their religious legitimacy. Will they remind the state of what the limits are? Will they, still more, wield their moral influence in order to call the body politic to order, that is to say, call on the state to protect everyone within it?

Germany: Dietrich Bonhoeffer's solitary crusade. In Germany, when Hitler had only just come to power, a young Lutheran pastor called Dietrich Bonhoeffer realised that the current situation was a 'crucial test' for German Protestantism. He explained in a manuscript completed on the 15 April 1933 that the responsibility of the Church vis-à-vis the state was directly challenged as regards the manner in which the 'Jewish question' was handled. Following on from Luther's direct line of thought, Bonhoeffer recognised that 'it is not the role of the Church to instruct the state directly about any action that is specifically political. The Church should not praise or blame state laws ... and should recognise its work as the giver of orders.' It is the state that makes History, he insisted, not the Church.

Bonhoeffer seemed, then, to make a heavy concession to the new regime: 'There is no doubt that one of the historic problems that the state must resolve is the Jewish question, and no doubt either that the state has the right on this point to embark on new paths of action'. But to this was immediately added: 'This does not mean, however, that the Church should allow political action to take place before its very eyes without doing anything, on the contrary, it can and should … request the state whether it is willing to take full responsibility for (*verantworten*) its action as a legitimately national action, that is to say an action that will provide law and order, and not the absence of law and order. It will be beholden to ask this question with insistence in situations where the state will appear justifiably threatened in its being (*Staatlichkeit*), that is to say, precisely, compromised in its function of provider of law and order, by dint of the power it is invested with. The Church must, today, pose the question fair and square with regard to the Jewish question. And in so doing, it is in no way interfering with the responsibility that is the state's alone, but on the contrary reassigning the state its heavy responsibility vis-à-vis its own prerogatives.'

In other words, Bonhoeffer reaffirmed the respective responsibilities of state and Church: of course, the state is acting within its role when it legislates, but it also falls to the Church to react if it perceives the law of the state to be unjust. Bonhoeffer is even more precise on this point: 'There are three possible ways in which the church can act toward the state: in the first place … it can ask the state whether its actions are legitimate and in accordance with its character as state, i.e., it can throw the state back on its responsibilities. Second, it can aid the victims of state action. The church has an unconditional obligation to the victims of any ordering of society, even if they do not belong to the Christian community. 'Do good to all people.'[36] In both these courses of action, the church serves the free state in its free way, and at times when laws are changed the church may in no way withdraw itself from these two tasks. The third possibility is not just to bandage the victims under the wheel, but to jam a spoke in the wheel itself. Such action would be direct political action (*unmittelbar*), and is only possible and desirable when the church sees the state fail in its function of creating law and order, i.e. when it sees the state unrestrainedly bring about too much or too little law and order. In both these cases, it must see the existence of the state, and with it its own existence, threatened.'[37]

Putting thought and action together, Bonhoeffer did everything to convince his own Church to mobilise help for the Jews, finishing this text barely one week after the 'Law for the Restoration of a Professional Civil Service' was promulgated, banning Jews from all public service institutions. But he was not to win his case. He did, of course, find himself once more among the minority opposed to the 'German Christians' trend (Protestant pro-Nazis) and participated in founding the Confessing Church. But these very people who created this new Church did not share his steadfastness, because they accepted the introduction of the 'Aryan paragraph',[38] which amounted to exclusion of apostate Jews (Jews converted to Christianity), of which Bonhoeffer totally disapproved. In this way, for him even the Confessing Church was failing in its historical responsibilities even though it incarnated a kernel of resistance to the regime, on religious foundations. Some thirty-five years later the great theologian Karl Barth, himself a figure of Protestant opposition to Nazism, would pay homage to the clear-sightedness of Bonhoeffer, remarking that he 'had been in 1933 the first, and almost the only person to have perceived the Jewish question to be so central, and to have fought for the cause with so much energy'.[39]

Another pastor of the Lutheran Church, Hermann Umfried, dared to protest openly in March 1933 against the violence numerous Jews were subjected to. 'When the attacks against Pastor Umfried started, no local, regional or national church institution dared to come to his support or to express even the mildest opposition to violence against Jews.'[40] Driven to resign by his hierarchy, he committed suicide in January 1934. The Protestant and Catholic Churches also kept silent at the moment the discriminatory Nuremberg laws were published, with the exception of the Catholic region of Aachen and some protests from evangelical pastors in Speyer. The most forceful institutional speech against Nazism expressed by the Christian Church was pronounced in March 1937 in Pius XI's encyclical, *Mit Brennender Sorge*, published directly in German and read from the pulpit in every German Catholic parish. In it the Pope firmly condemned the pseudo-religion of Nazism and the regime's racial theories, without, however, making any direct reference to the fate of the Jews.

The pogrom of 9 November 1938, referred to as *Kristallnacht*, marks the peak of Jewish persecution in Germany five years after Hitler's coming to power. Preceded the day before by a radio broadcast in which Goebbels sent out over the airwaves a clear call for murder and pillage, this party-orchestrated action resulted in as yet unprecedented levels of violence: more than 100 Jews were murdered, numerous synagogues were burnt, and Jewish-owned shops were looted. Thousands of Jews were incarcerated in concentration camps. However, not a single official voice from the religious hierarchy was raised in protest against what had happened, either from the Protestant or from the Catholic side. True, Pope Pius XI wanted then to break off relations with Berlin; but his pro-German future successor Eugenio Pacelli, dissuaded him from doing so. And the Concordat continued to silence the tongues of the German bishops, who were nevertheless not anti-Semitic.[41] Bonhoeffer certainly must have taken the non-reaction of the Churches to this event as proof that they were compromised considerably in their evangelical foundation. Their silence in 1938 bears witness to a collapsing of religion: religion was no longer capable of calling the population to order by reminding them that murder is prohibited, while the state, via the mouthpiece of its propaganda minister, had just openly incited the Germans to commit murder against the Jews. If politicians were inciting people to violence while the religious community no longer dared to exercise its traditional role of condemning such action, who could say what would happen next?

The Orthodox Church and the 'Serbian martyr'. In Yugoslavia the Orthodox Church was fully in favour of the renaissance of Serbian nationalism. If the fundamental interests of the Serbs were threatened, as its hierarchy thought they were, the Church could not be expected to try and restrain the violent impulses of the political leadership. In fact, the separation between nation and religion did not really have any meaning in this country. For the Church, definition of the state was not a political problem, but one pertaining to religion. In the Byzantine spiritual world Church and state went together. As Radmila Radic points out, national belonging came first even in the name of the 'Serbian Orthodox Church'.[42] During the 1980s the latter reappeared at the forefront of the public stage defending forcefully and loudly the cause of the Serbian people. From 1982, twenty-one priests (among them three eminent theologians) signed an 'appeal' addressed to the highest political and religious authorities to emphasize the value of 'the spiritual and biological essence of the Serbian people in Kosovo-Metohija'. The same year the journal *Orthodoxie* published an article in which the author upheld that the 'message of the irredentist Albanian' reveals 'their true final objective: the extermination of the Serbian people on Kosovo territory. This message hailing from the Albanian Nazis has been repeatedly expressed... for several decades.'

Even before Milosevic had employed the term in his own speeches, it was the Orthodox Church that first used the word 'genocide', during its 1987 synod, to describe the suffering endured by the Serbs in Kosovo. A religious rhetoric borrowed from Christianity was grafted on to this attitude of total victimhood. It was precisely these experiences of suffering, both those of the present and, even more so, of the past that, like those borne by Christ, transfigured the story of Serbia. 'Serbian martyrdom' in this way led eminent Church representatives, for instance, to take up the theme of 'Heavenly Serbia'. In itself this theme did not necessarily promise that revenge would simply fall from the sky. It borrowed from Christian theology, and asserted that despite its suffering Serbia, an eminently spiritual nation, could and would one day rise again, like Jesus Christ. But it is the context in which this religious rhetoric was used that gave it such ferociously destructive potential.[43]

The words of Bishop Jovan of Sabac-Valjevo, delivered in his 1988 pastoral letter on the arrival of the holy relic of Prince Lazar in Kosovo, are a good example of this rhetoric: 'The Serbs are creating above all a heavenly Serbia, he declared, which has to this day without any doubt become the greatest heavenly state. If we take only the innocent victims of the last war, millions and millions of Serbs, men and women, children and old people alike, killed or horribly tortured, or even thrown into ditches and caves by the criminal Ustashis, we could imagine the Serbian empire extending throughout the heavens today.' So, since Serbs were today threatened with a new 'genocide', the Church would be there to defend them, in Kosovo, or elsewhere. Because the threat weighing against them was also to be found in Croatia, in Bosnia–Herzegovina, etc....

When it came to the Kosovo question, then, religion contributed greatly to reawakening and amplifying the Serbian nationalist cause. The Bosnian Serb leader Radovan Karadzic was to repeat on several occasions: nothing can be done without the Church. The 'Love one another as I have loved you' can only apply between Serbs, and certainly not with regard to the Albanians against whom the situation of legitimate defence prevails. It is hard to see, therefore, how the Orthodox Church could protest in any way against the abuses and humiliations the Albanians were subjected to with ever greater frequency at the hand of the Serbs. The taboo of violence regarding the Albanians had already been lifted, and a war of 'self-defence' seemed possible. Some priests or Orthodox theologians refused nonetheless such a perspective, like Father Sava at Kosovo, who appealed for true dialogue with the Albanians, and Professor Ignatije Midic, who was opposed to the war as much from a human standpoint as a religious one. But the Church hierarchy did not understand it in this way, justifying its position by referring also to biblical texts. So the original murder of Abel by Cain was used explicitly by the Patriarch Pavle to justify the war: 'Evil always attacks, and good must defend itself, he declared. Cain always tries to kill Abel, and Abel has to defend himself. Defending oneself against attacks by wrongdoers, defending one's life, life and the peace of one's nearest and dearest against the criminals. These are the limits that define a just war.'[44]

The Rwandan Catholic Church: between support for the regime and internal contradictions

In Rwanda the strong institutional ties binding the Catholic Church to the state greatly restricted the Church's scope when it came to wielding its power to exercise free and critical speech. We know of the personal ties binding Archbishop André Perraudin (a White Father from Switzerland) to the first President of the Republic, Grégoire Kayibanda. In February 1959 this new leader of the Rwandan Catholic Church clearly legitimised the political aspirations of the former in a pastoral letter affirming that 'in our Rwanda there are several quite clearly distinguishable races' and that 'social inequalities are to a large extent linked to racial differences'.[45] Such a public stance, close in spirit to 'The Bahutu Manifesto', thus constituted a fundamental shift for the Church as compared with former years when its dignitaries had upheld the domination of the Tutsi royalty.

Subsequently it was the Hutu Archbishop Vincent Nsengiyumva, Perraudin's successor, who was to befriend the second President of the Republic, Juvenal Habyarimana. In addition, Nsengiyumva was to remain a member of the central committee of the Presidential party right up till he was persuaded in 1990 formally to abandon such membership. So it is not surprising to find that the hierarchy of the Church abstained from condemning the quotas policy instituted by the regime against the Tutsis, and was generally rather silent on the subject of the violence perpetrated against them. However, some of the Vatican's stands on the issue did not fail to condemn killings quite forcefully whoever perpetrated them, if one can believe an analysis of press releases and articles published in FIDES, the Vatican press agency.[46] To what extent were these 'external' positions reported locally?

Whatever the answer, despite silence from the hierarchy, the Churches served nevertheless as places of refuge for the Tutsis till the 1960s, when episodes of massacre occurred: the assailants did not then dare to violate these sanctuaries. These religious spaces remained safe regarding the prohibition on murder, even though violence increasingly threatened to break out, at least up till 1994. Later, however, the churches were to become a trap for anyone taking refuge in them. As for the different Protestant Churches representing 18 per cent of the population, although they had no unified position vis-à-vis the regime, the high Anglican clergy and the Baptist Church generally supported it. Effectively 'both Catholic and Protestant clergy cooperated with officials by passing on state announcements from the pulpit.'[47]

Relations between the Rwandan state and the Roman Catholic Church have nevertheless known periods of crisis. The make-up of the Catholic Church has a lot to do with this, even if this factor is not the only cause of tension. Indeed, while still being directed by Hutu bishops (seven out of nine at the start of the 1990s) the clergy were mostly Tutsi (about 65 per cent). As a result a considerable gap existed between the pomp and magnificence visible in the higher echelons, and the down-to-earth realities of life in the parishes, where many Tutsi religious men and women were very committed. Moreover, it was this presence which they upheld at grassroots level that often facilitated the reception of the Tutsi population in churches when their lives were under threat (even though some Hutu priests might have been equally accommodating in the event). This paradoxical situation—a predominantly Hutu hierarchy dominating a predominantly Tutsi clergy within a predominantly Hutu population—could partly explain the silence of the Rwandan church on the most sensitive questions: it found arriving at any consensus of opinion impossible. But dialogue was no more forthcoming between Hutu bishops and Hutu priests. The rift between the hierarchy and the base was in fact very deep, not only because of compromises made by Archbishop Perraudin over the regime, but also because of the enrichment of religious leaders or indeed the fact that often they were simply feeble. It was rare therefore for joint decisions or for any clear position to be taken. Linked to this state of affairs, certain problems that were deep-rooted in Rwandan society (and in its Church) were never (or only very rarely) tackled, as when it came to racial problems.'[48]

This considerable gap between the Church's base and its summit had, in part, favoured some independent speaking out, as the regime became progressively more blameworthy and corrupt. Protests were expressed elsewhere in publications issued by the Catholic Church itself, like the bi-monthly *Kinyamateka*, directed by Abbot André Sibomana. This notorious opponent of the regime notably defended imprisoned and tortured journalists, and became president of the Rwandan Association for Human Rights and Public Freedoms. The visit of Pope John Paul II to Rwanda on September 7–9 1990 also created, to some extent, the possibility of a forum for discussion. In 1991 a letter from Archbishop Thaddée Nsengiyumva (known as 'from the Presbytery of Kabgayi'), had some repercussions, denouncing the flagrant discrimination being exercised against the Tutsis.

Other initiatives were also undertaken during this period by both the Catholic and Protestant churches, to favour dialogue between the main political opponents (cf. Chapter III). But the impact of these attempts remained limited. They did not enable the regime to cast off its original ethnic logic, since it felt under threat from the war started by the RPF. As though responding in their 'traditional' manner, the authorities were to resume their practice of massacring the Tutsis from the 1990s onwards, in the same way as massacres were undertaken during the very first years of the regime.

The sacrificial regeneration of 'We'. These different situations are thus characterised by the lifting of the ban on murder: religion encouraged this with the aim of legitimate defence (Yugoslavia), or did not succeed in opposing it, and may even have condoned it (Germany), and could in some extreme cases provide places of refuge that were subsequently to disappear (Rwanda). Probably a threshold was in the process of being crossed, or risked being crossed, in the eruption of violence. While institutional religion (through the Christian Church) was no longer, could no longer, or no longer wanted to be the spiritual guarantor for the prohibition of murder, a new logic was tending to develop: one that put the perpetration of murder at the centre of religion, or rather at the centre of another kind of sacred entity—a sacred entity which, depending on the instance, assigned itself as a common object of veneration, whether race, the nation or ethnicity. This sanctification of the 'elected' majority presupposes the building of a sacrificial altar on which to burn all those designated as that 'other', the dangerous outsider. Sacrificial exclusion is necessarily constitutive of this movement of the veneration of oneself, of 'us'.

The relationship to violence has thus been completely reversed: murder is no longer a taboo to be observed but becomes, on the contrary, a foundational practice—not of a new religion, but of a different conception of collective transcendence, that draws on instituted religious practices, or even recycles them. In short, it is violence—and this includes violence perpetrated through murder—that regenerates the group through the sacrifice of those designated as being responsible for the crisis.

The development of this sacrificial social dynamic does not cancel out the presence of religion as represented by the Church. But it does end up being in a sort of competition with this logic of the sacred through murder, which tends to overwhelm or even replace it. In the case of Germany, it was as though religion was paralysed or annihilated by the unfurling of an incredible sacrificial wave of which *Kristallnacht* marked the spectacular climax. In Yugoslavia, it is religion that, of itself and through itself, stirred up the embers of an identity crisis, setting up the 'Heavenly Serbia' as a common object for Serbs to worship: in a way, religion is offering in this way a sacrificial future to its flock. Following the RPF's attack in Rwanda, the sacrificial dynamic was to gain ground increasingly within the institutional framework of religion, remaining silent as at the time following massacres of Tutsis in Bagogwe and Bugesera.

Such analyses are inspired by René Girard's central thesis, which upholds the notion that 'violence is the heart and secret soul of the sacred'.[49] The Girardian vocabulary does indeed help to some extent to conceptualise all that we have been looking at in the death-laden evolution of the countries examined. In referring to the biblical custom of the 'scapegoat',[50] René Girard has offered an interpretative model of violence that, in communities in a state of crisis, befell any victim declared to be guilty. The murder of the surrogate victim allows this violence to be purged, and the group to be appeased. Whether in Germany, in Yugoslavia or in Rwanda, are we not in effect witnessing the enactment of what can be described in real terms as a sacrificial crisis, the designated victims of which literally pay the price with their lives? Historical and cultural factors preside over the appointing of the victims: it could be anyone having a marginalised social status, against whom longstanding rancour has accumulated over the years, in short, people already cast in the role of victim within a society. The magnitude of their numbers or their precise influence within the society in question have very little to do with the process of designation as surrogate victim: they are representations of hostile faces starting to show up in a society in crisis searching for an explanation for its misery. This reading corresponds to the figures of the Jews, the Tutsis or the Albanians, for all of whom social marginalisation was liable to worsen. A certain language and particular attitudes then appear or develop around them, targeted to disqualify them as human beings (abuse, vulgarity, attribution of animal characteristics, brutality, etc.). And the deeper the crisis afflicting the society, the higher the risk that it will slide into purgative violence against these victims. But under what conditions will such a plunge into violence produce something sacred that is of the right nature genuinely to reconcile the group with itself?

Girard's work makes uncomfortable reading for anyone with a preference for adhering closely to social and historical fact. His theory is constructed on a temptingly attractive hypothesis of mimesis at the root of all human relationships ('I always desire the object of another's desire'), from which point he sets out to explain amorous conflict just as much as war. But while his thesis comes across convincingly when analysing the psychology of heroes from Shakespeare or Dostoyevsky, he remains allusive or silent on the subject of contemporary conflict. His thinking is never subject to the test of historical contextualisation and, as he always places at its centre this 'mimetic hypothesis', he inevitably falls prey to systematising his idea. Another difficulty derives from the fact that he theorises relationships between violence and the sacred starting out from a mythical narrative of a supposed sacrificial murder by which the primitive community would have arbitrarily killed one of its members, primarily to appease tensions. As men are incapable of understanding the reasons for their reconciliation, he remarks, they will subsequently worship substitutes for this victim through rites and myths that will recall this story to mind.

But the narrating of this foundational murder, which lends itself to a similar interpretation to that expounded by Sigmund Freud in *Totem and Taboo* (the murder of the father by primitive hordes), is just as speculative: you either believe in it or you do not. This dimension of belief again can be seen in the central position that Girard gives to Jesus Christ, who as innocent victim supposedly came to reveal the sacrificial mechanism by which men descend into violence only to be reconciled at a later date. Thus there is supposedly a before and an after in the history of humanity from the fact of the death of Christ: an affirmation that a Christian like Girard would certainly have supported. But how can the pertinence and universality of this notion be verified from the perspective of the social sciences? Demonstrating its veracity would not seem to be an easy task.

However, what I will retain of René Girard's theory is his notion of a sacrificial violence that aims to 'regenerate' the group at the expense of an 'other' to be excluded or banished. This regeneration aims as much to reshape its identity as it does to redeem it through purification. Moreover, it is not by chance that we find here once again the themes of identity and purity touched on in Chapter I. Sacrificial violence prospers on groups' respective *imaginaires*. In an uncertain world, violence crystallises identity: it creates certainty there where uncertainty reigned, erecting insurmountable barriers between 'us' and 'them'. It is a way of refounding the way 'us' lives together by sacrificing 'them'. In so doing, sacrificial violence resembles a purification ritual. It is in this way that it penetrates the universe of the sacred, and itself becomes sacred. It is like an act of purification destined to purge that which is perceived to be foreign, even diabolic. In so doing, it grafts itself on to cultural frameworks of religious belief or magic specific to each country. For it is often the case that visions of the devil are associated with representations of the enemy: to kill the enemy is to chase away the devil and overwhelm evil. And it is via this route that the group believes it can in one action cleanse itself and achieve salvation. Sacrificial massacre becomes the condition of its safety. But is it such an easy thing for the individuals belonging to this society to join in this macabre dance?

Societies torn between adhesion, consent and resistance

If political power is no longer custodian of the prohibition of murder, and if religion no longer represents a spiritual restraint to violence, what is left to pose any obstacle if not the very individuals making up that society? Politics and religion do not mechanically imprint their myths and ideologies on passive individuals or down-trodden communities. The idea that a society can be completely monolithic and uniform is pure abstraction: it negates the faculty the human spirit has to defy strategies of domination and belief. The classical historian Paul Veyne ponders the question: 'Did the Greeks believe their myths?'[51]

This pertinent question can be usefully applied to each of the cases studied. *A priori*, we can reply: it is not true that all Hutus detested the Tutsis, or that all Serbs became nationalists and that all Germans felt themselves to be 'Aryan' as soon as Hitler seized power. Many historical or anthropological works bear witness to this differential between what is experienced on the scale of individuals or groups, and what arises out of collective mythical and ideological representations.[52] Consequently we can postulate a potential capacity for resistance in what is social, a social resistance to the development of identity-based violence. But appearances would suggest on the contrary that nothing significant went on in this respect. Violence appears to have known no limits, and kept being ratcheted up a notch. But can we be so sure? Isn't an invisible kind of resistance there somewhere to be found?

At first sight, repression seems able to stifle and crush everything. Let us, however, dispense with a simplistic notion of phantasmal powers tyrannising innocent people. For these despotic powers have a history: they actually derive from their own societies, and are the product of them. If political leaders like Hitler or Milosevic arrive in the higher echelons of the state apparatus it is because they are perceived to be legitimate by a large segment of the population. They fulfil a popular expectation at a particular moment in the history of their country. Many analyses have thus described the Führer as the 'saviour' the Germans were waiting for to put their ailing country to rights and restore its greatness. In another context the same was said of Milosevic, with whom many Serbs identified at the end of the 1980s because he aroused hope of a 'new Serbia' which, freed from the tutelage of bureaucracy, would recover the place it deserved in history.

All the reasoning suggested in this chapter is based on this line of interpretation. If extremist intellectuals succeeded in propagating their ideas, if political leaders relayed them successfully, it is because these ideas were planted in a fertile social environment. How can we avoid calling to mind here Etienne de La Boétie's *Discourse of Voluntary Servitude*?[53] This text indeed contains flashes of intuition about this enigma: individuals do in fact consent to obey a tyrannical power. But beware! A 'fertile' environment does not equal 'completely won over and subjected to power'. Historical and sociological surveys bring to light a variety of social and individual conduct. The range is wide, from a minority adhering unambiguously to the dominant ideology, numerous types of behaviour whereby people consent or adjust to the system, and more or less tangible forms of dissension, even resistance. The historiography of German society under Nazism thus shows that, over and above its overall support for the Führer, manifestations of defiance or even rejection are discernible in daily life, referred to by Martin Broszat as '*resistenz*'. This author has shown the undeniable usefulness of local studies to evaluate in real terms the ways in which Germans accepted or rejected, on a day-to-day basis, Nazi norms of conduct. He establishes, for example, that wherever Catholics were strongly represented, signs of defiance towards the regime were more frequent. Pursuing this line of inquiry, Pierre Aycoberry[54] for his part applied himself to the task of assessing attitudes of cooperation or rejection according to social class and age group.

In the case of Rwanda, André Guichaoua speaks of an art of appearances that went hand in hand with the 'ethnic peace' of the 1980s. Whether they supported the ethnicist dialogue or not, the Rwandans at first adjusted to the Tutsis who successfully integrated the system, made their way into trading circles, within the Catholic Church, in international networks etc. At the same time, Hutu or Tutsi peasants could spontaneously develop a form of passive resistance in the face of intrusion from a central power perceived to be arrogant and incompetent. Another noteworthy phenomenon is the persistence of the initiation rite into the *Kubandwa* cult, practised clandestinely, and considered by Claudine Vidal to be a form of resistance to religious colonisation.

In the same way, the idea that individuals are 'crushed' by a political propaganda system conditioning their thoughts is largely exaggerated. To be sure, propaganda distils the framework of meaning
defining the ideological universe of authority. Notes taken daily in
Nazi Germany by the philologist Victor Klemperer are fascinating
in this regard: by closely analysing the 'language' of Nazism he
reveals in it the 'lexical poison' that enables killing to happen in
advance by using words. But to what extent does the public exposed
to this propaganda fully adhere to it? Nobody can really say with any
precision or qualification. The sociology of media reception in any
event provides sufficient proof that we have a tendency to overes-
timate the media's general impact.

Individuals do indeed maintain a certain critical capacity for deciphering propaganda and reinterpreting its messages as a function of
their personal experience and entourage. If propaganda is in fact
effective, it does not rely on content alone. It depends also, and
perhaps primarily, on the *receptivity* of those exposed to it, and
whether they really want to believe in it. It is the reception context
of this propaganda that makes it even more credible: a context of
crisis and collective fear. From which point on, even if the information is not credible, it can be believed. In this regard, fear and propaganda find themselves positioned in a dialectical relationship.
Sentiments of fear and apprehension about the future provide excellent conditions for receptivity to propaganda, even a very crude
form of it. Fear of a threat perceived to be deadly can make credible
an irrational line of thinking that is apparently (and really) setting
out to eradicate the said threat. Conversely, the propaganda itself,
through repeated transmission of anxiety-producing messages, contributes to increasing fear within a population that is already worried. Propaganda has then the effect of mobilising the group that is
feeling under threat, and of developing hatred within it against the
group perceived to be a mortal danger.

'The spiral of silence.' Another fear-related phenomenon is that of the
spiral of silence described by the German sociologist Elisabeth
Noelle-Neumann: individuals have a fear, not of being destroyed,
but of finding themselves isolated from the group they normally
belong to. The author starts from the idea that to avoid experiencing

isolation or, worse, banishment, individuals may go so far as to renounce their freedom to exercise their personal judgement altogether. This tendency to conform is in fact one of the conditions for their social integration. It proves crucial in a situation of instability within which individuals, witnessing a struggle between opposing positions, are obliged to take sides. They may, of course, find themselves in agreement with the dominant point of view; this turn can bolster self-confidence sufficiently to enable them to express themselves without reticence, and without any risk of setting themselves apart from others maintaining totally opposite points of view. But they may, on the contrary, realise that their convictions are losing ground: and the more this happens, the less sure of themselves they will be. The less also will they be inclined to divulge their opinions. The tendency for outward expression in the one instance, and to maintain silence in the other thus gives rise to a spiral that gradually establishes a dominant opinion. Alexis de Tocqueville has admirably described this process in *The Old Regime and the Revolution*, when he describes how mistrust of religion developed into a widely held attitude during the eighteenth century in France. He comments as follows: 'The men who kept the old faith feared to be the only ones who remained faithful, and dreading isolation more than error, they went along with the crowd, without thinking like it. What was still the feeling of only part of the nation thus appeared as everyone's opinion, and therefore seemed irresistible in the very eyes of those who gave it that false appearance.'[55]

Using this 'spiral of silence' as starting point, Noelle-Neumann defines public opinion as 'the opinion which can be voiced in public without fear of sanctions and upon which action in public can be based'.[56] Public opinion will therefore include saying 'Jews are worthless', 'Bosnian Muslims are Turks', 'the Tutsi are the former invaders and oppressors of Rwanda'. In parallel, this public opinion can be shored up by public policies aiming to achieve exactly what that opinion is calling for. Noelle-Neumann never once suggests that individuals really believe in this majority opinion. This would doubtless be the case for those with the strongest conviction, but, according to her, most would rally to the opinion through conformity and fear of isolation. To sum up, divergent opinions really do exist, but they are kept silent. The opinion displayed and hammered home is that 'one is not supposed to like Jews'.

But is this injunction confirmed every time a non-Jewish person meets a Jew? It probably is, because Noelle-Neumann's model reposes on the submission of individuals to a majority viewpoint because of their fear of sanction and isolation. But sometimes it is not, because her theory firmly maintains the distinction between public rallying and personal conviction. A resistance to majority opinion therefore always remains possible, provided that the individuals taking this initiative would have the courage to brave the fear of being marginalised: 'the active role of starting a process of public opinion formation', she says, 'is reserved to the one who does not allow himself to be threatened with isolation'.[57]

Who, therefore, is going to be able to endure non-conformity in order to stand up against the exclusion of this other depicted as the enemy? Here we have arrived at the crucial point in this chapter. The stakes for such an individual amount to an existential choice between two possible forms of isolation: one already afflicting the designated victims, and another waiting to dog anyone wanting to help them in some way. The web of this crisis focuses on what the sociologists call the 'social tie', that is the stuff that binds individuals of a single society together, letting them see themselves as belonging to the same community. Is this social tie in the process of 'coming undone' or does it still hold good? This is the main question underpinning the drama discussed here. Will the problem not spread to afflict even inter-generational bonds, somewhere along the line shattering relationships between parents and children? The Nazi power certainly intended to attack these relationships. On this point the historian Omer Bartov cites several examples showing how the Hitler regime not only organised a mass indoctrination of German youth, but went so far as to encourage children to denounce their parents as 'enemies of the Nation', using them as informers on the family circle.[58]

For the American sociologist Helen Fein, one of the pioneers of comparative studies on genocide, the social tie is based on something she calls 'the universe of obligations'. This she defines as 'that circle of people with reciprocal obligations to protect each other whose bonds arose from their relation to a deity or sacred source of authority (the state constituting one of the current forms of this authority to which individuals swear allegiance)'.[59] But, she says, to make the inhumanity of these victims perceptible, you only have to place them outside this universe of obligations. This 'other' enemy therefore becomes completely 'other', that is to say disengaged totally from any reciprocal relationship of identification. It is in effect a process of de-identification (or even of deculturation, as psychologists might say) that expels individuals from the community to which they belong.

In this sense the conflict seems to be much more radical than in the context of a civil war, because in this case the actors in conflict still recognise each other as being part of the same political or national community. In the Spanish civil war, for example, Franco supporters and Republicans continued, even while fighting each other ferociously, to recognise each other as Spaniards. Here we are moving towards something completely different. The development of the persecution of Jews in Nazi Germany appears, from the end of the 1930s, to present an extreme example: a series of steps taking persecution further each time and, more powerfully, constraining the Jews to an exclusion that was in turn judicial, political, economic, physical. So they found themselves effectively outside the 'universe of obligations', and projected outside the national community. To say that social relations decayed in this case falls short of the mark: here we are faced purely and simply with the destruction of the social fabric in every respect.

To get some idea of this disaster, let us turn again to Victor Klemperer's journal; he describes, for example, the way in which his former university colleagues showed no solidarity with him to the point that he found himself becoming more and more isolated. In his memoirs the former Jewish resistance fighter Jean Améry records his feelings that seem to go way beyond abandonment: 'The Jew without positive determinants, the Catastrophe Jew, as we will unhesitatingly call him, must get along without trust in the world. My neighbor greets me in a friendly fashion, *Bonjour, Monsieur*; I doff my hat, *Bonjour, Madame*. But Madame and Monsieur are separated by interstellar distances; for yesterday a Madame looked away when they led away a Monsieur, and through the barred windows of the departing car a Monsieur viewed a Madame as if she were a stone angel from a bright and stern heaven, which is forever closed for the Jew.'[60]

The breakdown of social relations. There are many ways in which social relations can collapse. In Yugoslavia this process of disassociation was very different from that in Germany. Many authors have drawn attention to the burden of the wounds and traumas the massacres perpetrated during the Second World War engraved in people's memories. For instance, years later feelings of distrust and resentment that had never been completely extinguished were able to persist among each of the populations making up the Yugoslavian federation Tito sought to create. This traumatic heritage should not, however, eclipse that left by Yugoslavian communism itself. It was indeed the case that during the epoch of autocratic communism, anyone seeking to oppose Tito and his 'brotherhood of peoples' ideology could only do so on a nationalistic footing.

Transgression of this basic taboo for the regime seemed necessary in order to assert the right to freedom of expression. To the extent that, in the years just after Tito's death, aspirations for liberty and democracy were increasingly confounded with the quest for nationalism. Elections held successively in 1990, 1991, and 1992 were nearly always based on the same scenario of 'freedom': to vote for democracy was to vote for the party representing 'their' nation. But in fact this scenario harboured a major contradiction because it was based on a fundamental opposition between party and democracy: since the party was mono-ethnic, it could not tolerate any other forms of expression. This is why the federal system so to speak imploded because of its internal contradictions. In real terms each person was forced to ask himself a question that generally he had not hitherto had to consider. Who am I? And Who is this 'other'? Serb, Croat, Bosnian? Up to that point, very few would ever have worried over the issue. Now this criterion of ethnicity existed in people's minds. The result was therefore an ethnicisation that has as much of a political basis as a personal one.[61] However, this process by no means had the same intensity everywhere. The question didn't arise in Slovenia where 92 per cent of Slovenes saw themselves as Slovenes, and so felt themselves to be safe. In most Croatian towns the inhabitants saw themselves as being Croats, and so throughout two-thirds of the Croatian territory nobody feared having his throat slit by a neighbour, except in the case of military attack from the outside. It was only really in Bosnia that this feeling of insecurity assumed such tragic dimensions.

In this sense Xavier Bougarel has shown how this crisis of citizenship undermined the federal system from the inside, and how this has notably had the effect of once more bringing under scrutiny the rules governing good behaviour between neighbouring communities, rules that have been in operation ever since *komsiluk*, inherited from the Ottoman Empire. This term of Turkish origin designates neighbourly relationships in their entirety—peaceful co-existence between different communities (exchanges in work and daily life, invitations to religious ceremonies, association to family events).[62] The importance of *komsiluk* derives from the fact that Bosnian society is a post-Ottoman society, still marked by the *millet* system (non-sovereign and non-territorial religious communities), which enabled co-existence within a single territory. Without reference to any written law or formal code, *komsiluk* is more a social practice endowed with its own rituals. This practice in no way implies social hybridity, but is based on an assumption that two people from different communities live in two different houses, while a mixed marriage implies that two people from different communities live under the same roof. It is a system by which everyone remains at home but enjoys a system of inter-community exchange for which the guarantor is ultimately the state.

In effect 'this reassurance on a daily basis of the stable and peaceful character of relationships between communities functions because the state is in a position to guarantee this stable and peaceful character at the political level. Should the state cease to assume this role, or if the state were to set communities against one another, *komsiluk*—the search for security through reciprocity and peace—could then turn to crime, the search for security through exclusion and war.'[63] This is precisely what seemed likely to happen at the start of the 1990s, with the increasing fragmentation of Bosnian society and the ethnicisation of the political struggle. The immediate consequence of this was the decline of good neighbourly practice. In the same way the frequentation of common places of sociability (bars and cafés) or participation in the same activities (folk dancing) tended to decrease. Each side was inclined or invited to stay in 'its' group.[64]

This ethnic development in Bosnia-Herzegovina is nevertheless not uniform. For example, the town of Tuzla and its region resisted nationalistic pressures. Without doubt because the town was an industrial and mining city with a strong social identity, it managed to preserve the equilibrium and modes of operation associated with the old Yugoslav system while these were corrupted, or had simply collapsed, elsewhere. Rather than assuming that ethnicism became generalised in Bosnia, we need to examine situations case by case: only by doing a local and regional history would the complexity of these relationships be revealed.

The same remark is valid in other respects for Rwanda. While the ethnicist dialogue is dominant, the stigmatisation of the Tutsis is very unequally distributed in the country. The ethnic antagonism follows different contours depending on the region, and, within individual regions, depending on the social groups and political networks. In the region of Butare for example, in the south of the country, the Hutu-Tutsi categorisation has very little impact on social relations. In this case, as at Tuzla, the social tie seemed to hold good despite a political environment that was trying to tear it apart. But for how long?

It is in any case essential to examine the same phenomenon from every possible side—what relates to the destruction and to the preservation more or less of social ties. With regard to Yugoslavia, the sociologist Antony Oberschall questions the interpretive models offered by way of explanation for the plunging of the country into ethnic war. He concludes rightly that the major difficulty is managing to devise simultaneously two contradictory 'cognitive frameworks' for social relations—those of cooperation and of hatred—either one of these being capable of activation depending on the economic and political circumstances of the moment.[65]

Along the same lines, the anthropologist Danielle de Lame conducted a remarkable study of the life on a hillside in the south of Rwanda between 1988 and 1990, and so before civil war broke out. She explores all aspects of life there, including production, consumption, monetary flow, social relationships, networks of influence, conflicts and so on. It would be hard to detect in her analyses the first stirrings of what was to happen scarcely four years later. It really was still 'the calm before the storm'.[66] If Rwandan culture can effectively legitimise vengeance in some cases (out of loyalty to ancestors, a murder committed within a given lineage can legitimately be avenged through the murder of any male of the murderer's lineage), goodness and nobility of heart are also a part of this. In Danielle de Lame's view the universe of meaning that gave coherence to this culture's system of representation collapsed abruptly due to the economic and political crisis at the end of the 1980s. As soon as the threat of chaos was perceived, it called on a new form of order, and the triggering of serial murder could be seen as such an attempt. However, this sacrificial dynamic did not cancel out gestures of solidarity, even during the crisis.

The role of the third party

Too often, when the situation in a country descends into 'ethnic violence', journalists are inclined to see nothing but violence. This spontaneous attitude is understandable enough. The violent action being easily identifiable, it lends itself more readily to journalistic treatment. But such media coverage is deceptive. Who can say that at the same moment other actors, discreetly and without making any waves, are not in the process of deploying considerable efforts to save victims under threat of being carried away by the storm? Many years after the event, the work of the historian is often able to show just this, even if these gestures of solidarity remain modest ones. Spectacular and tragic though the act of violence may be, it should under no circumstances allow us to overlook humanistic and often anonymous gestures of mutual aid.

When analysing these different situations, we need to be extremely careful about how we view events. An analytical grid would be helpful to take into account this fluctuating complexity. Right here and now I would uphold this point, which is in my view fundamental: if changes in social ties play a decisive role in the development of violence, then it does not boil down to a binary persecutor-victim relationship. This would be too Manichean and reductive a vision of the complexity of their relationship. Between these two terms there always exists a 'witness', a 'third party', a 'bystander'. Even if the word 'bystander' is not entirely satisfactory: as its construction suggests, it designates a third party who is 'standing to one side' and, as a result, not really taking part in events as they unfold.

Now, in such situations the opposite is actually true: this third party is well and truly implicated in the social dynamic that may or may not lead to the increasing marginalisation of the designated victims. In reality, as Jean Améry remarks, in the daily exchanges between Jews and non-Jews, as we have also seen for Bosnia, this third party is the neighbour. Is he himself going to howl with the wolves? Will he just close his eyes? Will he openly or covertly express friendship or solidarity? This neighbour-third party is not necessarily an enemy of the new regime. He can adhere to the new authority's politics of 'restoring order' while still being at odds with one or other aspect of the measures taken. In this way he may consider that as regards persecution and marginalisation of a particular group they are 'going too far'. This does not necessarily prevent him from recognising, in phase with the propaganda that he hears every day, that 'yes, there is a problem with the Jews'. However, towards the Jewish person or persons making up his immediate entourage, or the Jew he meets by chance, he might prove solicitous in every way. In other words, he can adhere to an abstract opinion, known as anti-Semitism, but conduct himself into contradiction with this idea in order to help someone he knows to be Jewish.

The role of this third party is therefore particularly important where the development of the persecutor-victim relationship is concerned. This role is never just a binary and antagonistic relationship, but rather evolves according to a triangular structure. If the third party actually demonstrates solidarity with the victims, his intervention may curb the development of violence. Better still, these reactions of solidarity 'at a grassroots level' may even be expressed through the formation of a new public opinion, resistant this time, as Noelle-Neumann's model suggests. But if this third party remains globally indifferent to the persecution of victims, then the way forward is open to the development of even more intense violence.

Regarding the persecution of the Jews, the historian Léon Poliakov intuited, very early on, the importance of this third party. As early as 1951 he maintained that the Nazis had taken into account the reactions of German public opinion.[67] For example, the attempt to boycott Jewish shops in 1933 and 1934, an event of which many Germans were unaware, was not pursued. But when another discriminatory measure was instigated without arousing any hostile reactions, this effectively enabled the persecution to be notched up a grade. This basic model has not been contradicted by subsequent research, even if it has been made more complex. We know, for example, that German opinion disapproved of the '*Kristallnacht*' in 1938. As noted by the Israeli historian David Bankier, the Germans were no longer 'accustomed to seeing Jews'. And suddenly the pogrom brutally reminded them of their existence, and shocked them by such an unleashing of violence.[68] Did the Nazis draw from this the conclusion that they should demonstrate more clemency with regard to the Jews? Certainly not. They deduced from it that the Jews should be even more thoroughly cut off from the rest of the population to encourage their departure. Such, moreover, was the immediate effect of this pogrom: the terror it provoked increased the applications for exile. At the end of 1939 more than 250,000 Jews had left the Reich. The message was perfectly clear: they were totally undesirable, their situation having continually worsened since 1933. One could, in other ways, find it somewhat astonishing that 200,000 chose to stay. For once again, following the outbursts of violence, nobody had protested. The Churches were silent. They had not played the part a protesting third party might have done, in an attempt to sway the authorities.

Could this utterance of protest, so dramatically absent within Germany, not have been forthcoming from the outside? Could a supporting third party not have emerged on the international scene, as it were by proxy? This question in fact opens a whole new field for analysis: trying to understand a process of violence leading to massacre not just from the point of view of a nation's internal development, but also in its international context. The confines of this book prevent these two dimensions from being treated at the same time, but it is clear that the domestic and the international constantly interact, and so it is towards the international sphere of the crisis that we now turn our attention, the situations under scrutiny in the mean time taking ever more tragic turns. Since what will ultimately radicalise people's minds even further and make the actors involved even more brutal is the transformation of this process of violence into an act of war.

Kristallnacht, 9–10 November 1938

'On the evening of 9 November, the propaganda minister Goebbels delivered a furious speech, a skilful blend of denial, reality and a call to murder. He added that 'the [Nazi] Party had neither planned nor organised these actions; but because they had spontaneously erupted, they were not to be repressed.' (…) A clear call to murder, acted upon throughout Germany by dozens of SS and SA and ordinary citizens. The following day in Berlin, the damage, destruction and pillage of 3,767 houses and shops belonging to Jews was deplored, as was the destruction by fire of nine of the town's fourteen public synagogues. Five remained just about intact, and among them was the largest and most beautiful, whose position would have made its survival seem impossible, at the intersection of the great Humboldt University, which contained a huge swarm of young Nazis, and the 'warehouse district', home to many Jews from the East ('*Ostjude*'), on whom were heaped the most violent forms of anti-Semitic hatred. Why then was this synagogue spared?

The story is both short and straightforward. Nothing to do with great heroism, but a matter of a routine gesture. Police precinct no. 16 in Berlin was at that time in charge of the warehouse district. At its head was Wilhelm Krützfeld, born near the Danish border in 1880, a Berlin policemen who had been appointed to this district in September 1932, some months before Hitler was named Chancellor. Under Hitler, in 1937, a little before *Kristallnacht*, he was appointed police chief. On the evening of 9 November 1938 he was at home with his wife and two children when he received the call of a colleague on duty: the SA, completely out of control, were pillaging shops, destroying the valuables in the synagogue and putting bales of straw around the building with the intention of setting fire to it. Krützfeld made some telephone calls, armed himself with a gun and his briefcase, and went with several other officers to the site. On the Oranienburgerstrasse, he positioned his men around the synagogue, chased off the pillagers who were hanging around, called the fire brigade, who he ordered to extinguish the first flames in the treasury, and protected in his briefcase several precious documents. And so the synagogue was saved. Not a single SA or SS member, nobody else of rank or out of pure rebelliousness opposed him. He sent other policemen to protect the Jewish school behind the synagogue, a few metres away. It also survived the flames. A few policemen sufficed in this instance, through the determination of one man, to stem the course of what everywhere else was to be designated as the inexorable course of history and destiny.

Narratives describing the days that followed this event help us to understand what this gesture owes to temerity or recklessness. Indeed the next day, and entirely logically in these remarkable circumstances, the Chief of German security and Himmler's right-hand man Reinhard Heydrich, sent an official letter to the Attorney General requesting that he 'make no prosecutions with regard to the 'Jewish action' (*Judenaktion*)'. Without being charged or tried, therefore, 10,000 Jews were sent to concentration camps. The police did not follow up the case, and nothing was discussed in judicial circles. Already in 1938, then, the regime was no longer even trying to keep up appearances as far as justice was concerned. Chief of Police Krützeld alerted the tailor on the corner of the street, Herr Hirschberg, and also saved once again with a simple telephone call the Rabbi of the great synagogue, who was later to escape to Stuttgart, and then to Britain. On 11 November Krützfeld was ordered to appear before the Berlin Prefect of Police, the SA-Obersgruppenführer Wolf Heinrich, Graf von Helldorf. ... He owed his glittering career in the police force under Hitler to his nationalist exploits. However, from 1938 onwards he started to participate in various military conspiracies against Hitler, such as that of 20 July 1944, the failed coup that almost cost the dictator his life: on 20 July, he had completely demobilised the Berlin police, and had in this way enabled many conspirators to escape the SS. He was executed on 15 August 1944. In other ways he was also to permit Jews to escape from Germany by trafficking false passports. But this was for rich Jews only, who could put together the 250,000 Reichsmarks that he demanded for this service.'

Extract from Fabien Jobard, 'Au nom de l'ordre. Policiers en résistance lors de la nuit de Cristal', *Alternatives Non-violentes*, no. 118, Spring 2001, p. 40.

III

INTERNATIONAL CONTEXT, WAR AND THE MEDIA

Too many studies of genocide limit themselves to analysing factors at work inside a country, such as the character of the dominant ideology or state apparatus and its mutation into murderer of its own population. Such research contents itself with circumscribing the aberrant development within a given society disregarding its immediate outside environment (neighbouring countries) or more general environment (the world space). This kind of closed cell analysis is untenable. It is impossible to understand the course of events in Germany, Yugoslavia, or Rwanda in isolation from the outside world. These nations and societies are necessarily the products of regional history and, in a wider sense, of a particular constellation of international relations. The difficulty is therefore to conjecture the pathways that allow a progression towards crossing the threshold into massacre, while taking into account both local and global contexts, as we also have to do when embarking on similar analyses of the outbreak of war.[1]

However, there is no standard explanatory framework that we can propose. Trying to arrive at an understanding of relationships between 'massacres' and the 'international system' would, in short, appear well-nigh impossible. Nevertheless I will take the step of distinguishing between two types of interpretation. The first looks closely at the foundations of the international system itself, particularly the history of a region, to show in what ways certain types of observable facts (state sovereignty, former massacres, movements of refugees, rivalries between powers-that-be) are likely to be propitious to outbreaks of violence. The second shows how this esca-

lation into violence—within a particular country—can always go
further because, on an international scale, there is no braking system,
no serious obstacle to its ineluctable progression. These two approaches are clearly complementary, the one being rather of the structural type (because it is founded on the state of a system or region),
and the other more functional (being based on the conflict dynamic). But this labelling is only very approximate because, as we shall
see, the structural data influence the conflict dynamic and vice versa.

A dynamic, but towards what? Towards war. Even if war hadn't
appeared to be imminent, it could in fact have been predicted more
often than not. But this plunge into war would bring with it devastating consequences, as much for the actors in conflict as for the
groups already designated as victims. A state of war can, from its
point of inception, provide a ready justification for persecution or
even elimination of the said victims: the process of violence, hitherto
in gestation, can now 'detonate'. But where will it end? Is there
nothing left to stop the massacre? Who can testify to the events
unfolding? Might one hope, for example, that the media would play
an all-seeing role to alert what is currently referred to as 'international public opinion'—and that armed intervention could then be
mobilised in the name of the law? How fervently those already
facing danger would long for this last-minute scenario! But unfortunately such interventions 'before it is too late' do not even present
themselves for us to examine. In the pages that follow, everything
just goes from bad to worse. We shall endeavour to understand why
this should be.

A structure of political opportunities

The 'structural' approach consists of looking first of all at the very
nature of the legal principles governing the international system. Is
this system not conceived in such a way as to allow massacre to take
place, even in a way that makes state-perpetrated massacres per-
missible? According to the principle of the sovereign territorial state
arising from the 1648 Treaty of Westphalia, the state can do whatever it deems right within its borders. For the American sociologist
Leo Kuper, a pioneer of comparative studies of genocide, there is no
doubt 'that a sovereign territorial state claims, as an integral part of

its sovereignty, the right to commit genocide, or engage in genocidal massacres, against people under its rule, and that the United Nations, for all practical purposes, defends this right. To be sure', he adds, 'no state *explicitly* claims this right to commit genocide—this would not be morally acceptable even in international circles—but the right is exercised under other more acceptable rubrics, notably the duty to maintain law and order, or the seemingly sacred mission to preserve the territorial integrity of the state.'[2] And he goes on to cite as examples the massacres of the Ache Indians in Paraguay and those perpetrated by Idi Amin Dada in Uganda, and by Pol Pot in Cambodia.

The United Nations Charter is the mirror image of this state of affairs. True, the preamble expounds the faith of the contracting parties in basic human rights, in the dignity and value of the human person. But the charter also stipulates in article 2 that no clause within the Charter authorises the United Nations to intervene in matters that are essentially 'within the domestic jurisdiction of any state'. As a result, the latter can be democratic just as much as dictatorial, despotic as totalitarian, to the extent that it pleases, and so can treat its population as it sees fit. Because of this fact, nation-states can effectively, without any major legal impediments, commit mass murder.

The tragic history of the twentieth century attests dramatically to this: according to the American researcher Rudolf Rummel, 164 million people were killed by their own governments during the twentieth century, this figure being well above that of the 35 million deaths caused by wars during the same period (including, of course, the two world wars).[3] Rummel therefore denounces the 'democidal' capacity of the state, in the sense that nations have at their disposal the means to destroy 'their' people.[4] For him the greatest democidal heads of state were Mao Zedong, Stalin, Hitler, Chiang Kai-shek, Lenin, Deki (Japan), Pol Pot, Yahya Khan (Pakistan) and Tito. However, the principle of sovereignty would not seem to be something we should reject out of hand, because it legally protects smaller states from the appetites of their neighbours. It is in this sense one of the formal means of putting all states on the same footing, however unequal their levels of power may be. It is not so much the principle of sovereignty that in itself causes the violence, as the way in which states can use it, either to legitimise policies that infringe human rights or to remain indifferent to such infringements. In both cases state sovereignty merely constitutes a legal argument to justify its action or inaction. This is why so many experts have tried to make the case for this principle being regulated, structured or curbed, but not abandoned. In this perspective some, like Mario Bettati, have campaigned in favour of a right and even of a duty to intervene.[5] Meanwhile, other legal experts have criticised this expression, pointing out that governments of countries formerly under colonial rule perceive this right to intervene as a disguised means of enabling major powers to continue to interfere in their domestic affairs. They also prefer to talk, like Robert Badinter, of a responsibility to protect civilians in danger just as there already exists a responsibility, in French law, to assist a person in danger.[6] Everyone agrees, ultimately, that we need to work towards developing an authentic international penal code, one that is equipped to punish mass atrocities, as the Polish legal scholar Raphael Lemkin recommended in the 1930s.[7]

Modern states and massacres. Another structural approach to the relationships between massacres and international relations, more sociopolitical than legal, is offered by Michael Mann in his wide-ranging study of ethnic cleansing. Central to his thesis is the question of a conflictual structure, potentially violent, stemming from the issues linked to territory and sovereignty. Starting from this classic problem that features in war theories, Mann puts forward the following hypothesis: when two rival ethno-nationalist movements lay sovereign claim to a state within a single territory, then the conflict reaches a 'danger zone'. Their confrontation risks becoming embittered to such an extent that either the weaker actor decides to fight rather than submit because he benefits from some external support, or the dominant party reckons that it can deploy a force capable of instantly crushing the adversary. Elsewhere external pressures such as war will provoke the radicalisation and 'factionalisation' of the state. The author does not say that this type of conflict will always lead to the outbreak of violence and massacre: compromises may occur, and even ethnic cleansing may take place without overt conflict (for example of the type where population exchanges occur). But there nevertheless remains a high risk that ethnic cleansing through murder will also take place. The author provides as proof a number of examples of ethnic wars, in the Balkans and other regions in the world. Still, he points out that his theory does not really apply to the extermination of the Jews by Nazi Germany because the Jews did not lay claim to any territory in Europe. In so doing he is then forced to abandon this model in order to give due weight to the paranoiac Nazi representation of the Judeo-Bolshevik enemy.

An additional problem posed by Mann's theory is that he re-peatedly insists on attaching this type of conflict to the construction of a democratic nation because, according to him, ethnic cleansing results from the initial overlap between *ethnos* and *demos* (cf. Chapter I of this book). But as some commentators have remarked, in many cases of ethnic cleansing there is *ethnos* without *demos*.[8] No one, for instance, would describe as 'democratic' all the 'ethnic nations' like Serbia, Romania, Bulgaria and Greece that emerged in the nine-teenth century when they extricated themselves from Ottoman tutelage. This would amount then to saying that the phenomena researched by Mann are not really consubstantial with the birth of democracies, but rather, in a more general way, with the formation of nation-states, be they democratic, authoritarian, fascist etc. To sum up, the title of his book is misleading: it is less a comparative analysis of 'the dark side of democracy' than of 'the dark side of the nation-state' in the democratic age.

Working from this perspective as well, the English historian Marc Levene has explored in minute detail the relationships between nation-state and genocide (a term he uses in his writing equivalent to Mann's 'murderous ethnic cleansing'). Both authors agree on the need to see twentieth-century mass violence within the context of a long-term historical timescale going back at least as far as the era of the Western revolutions in the eighteenth century. But where Mann sees rather a structure of conflicts between ethno-nationalistic ac-tors, Levene focuses primarily, through the formation of the first nation-states, on the birth of an international system at the political and economic level. In the race for progress, the first fruits of what today we refer to as globalisation, genocide would necessarily occur only when certain states, bent on rapid modernisation, would take as targets populations perceived to be a threat or obstacle to their desire for power.[9]

'Genocide' would in this way also be linked to the steps taken by these nations to restructure indigenous or traditional societies hastily, often making 'great leaps forward' of a seemingly revolutionary kind. For Marc Levene it is therefore not by chance that the first authentically modern 'genocides' actually date back to the seventeenth and eighteenth centuries, in countries that were at the forefront of the movement to form nation-states. In this way revolutionary France (Vendée massacres), the United States (the slaughter of Indians) and England (massacres in Ireland and then in the 'colonies') have inaugurated modern prototypical procedures of genocide. Overall, what we call 'progress towards modernity' would combine the foundation of nations with the perpetration of massacres with the aim of 'dividing up' and exploiting the society to the perpetrators' convenience. As this model of modernity spreads through continents, other builders of nation-states sought to imitate the pioneers of this movement, which had become worldwide. There would then allegedly be a link of sorts between the great massacres throughout the world, whether they had taken place in Germany, Indonesia, Burundi, Iraq or Guatemala.

Such reasoning is based on an overgeneralisation, since many modern states have not been built through massacre. This is why the question still stands: why is mass murder perpetrated here and not there? On what specific historical and geopolitical context would it depend? If a global approach is useful, it only really becomes relevant to the extent that the analysis becomes regional, that is circumscribed within a precise space, with its particular territories and traditions. To focus our attention on those regions of Europe and Africa of greatest interest to us, let us first raise this question: did the practices of ethnic violence that developed in Germany, Yugoslavia and Rwanda already have a history in one or several neighbouring countries? Is there not a *habitus* of extreme violence? In cases where practices of massacre have been implemented in the recent past, there exists a serious risk of 'transfer' of this technology of destruction. To understand fully each individual case of massacre, we need to ask if it is really 'new' in the country in question, or if it falls within an already identified repertoire of collective action specific to the region in question (to use the vocabulary of the sociologist Charles Tilly), if it is innovatory in some way as compared with previous forms, and so on. Of course, just because one massacre has happened does not mean that another will necessarily happen also. Everything depends on the current constellation of political factors, and whether these would favour massacre or not, in a context that is already propitious.

A legacy of ethnic violence. European history is singularly blighted as regards 'ethnic cleansing' programmes of all kinds, even though this expression only began to be widely used in the 1990s. The American historian Norman Naimark has devoted an interesting comparative study to the different cases of ethnic cleansing in Europe during the twentieth century: exchanges of populations between Greeks from Anatolia and Turks, the Stalinist deportations of the Chechens, Ingush and Crimean Tatars, expulsion of the Germans from Poland and from Czechoslovakia.[10] In fact, from the nineteenth century onwards the propagation of West European nationalist ideas contributed to the decline of the Austro-Hungarian and Ottoman empires and to the formation of the young nation-states in the South-East of Europe. But since Serbia became independent in 1878 right up to the Balkan wars at the start of the twentieth century, these young states were constructed through violence, and with the massacre of part of an undesirable population, forcing people into exile or assimilation. 'The burning of villages and the exodus of the vanquished populations are normal and habitual events of wars and insurrections in the Balkans,' the Carnegie Commission had already noted in its 1914 report.[11] The acme was reached during the First World War with the Ottoman Empire's mass murder of Armenians, perpetrated by the Young Turk government then in power in Istanbul and rapidly corroborated by the Englishman Arnold Toynbee's report.[12]

If one of the overall consequences of the First World War was the destruction of the former multinational empires, from this also stemmed the accelerated flight of minorities. President Woodrow Wilson's doctrine of national self-determination, put forward by the victors, largely inspired the Treaty of Versailles of 1918. Scarcely a year after Lenin came to power in Moscow, the Allies played the Wilsonian 'national card' against the 'internationalist card' of the Bolshevik revolution. But the English historian Eric Hobsbawm judiciously observes that the realities of all populations living in Europe reveal the totally inapplicable aspect of the Wilsonian principle, according to which state borders should coincide with national and language boundaries. 'The logical implication of trying to create a continent neatly divided into coherent territorial states each inhabited by a separate ethnically and linguistically homogeneous population was the mass expulsion or extermination of minorities. Such was and is the murderous *reductio ad absurdum* of nationalism in its territorial version. ... Mass expulsion and even genocide began to made their appearance.'[13]

The consequences of this general trend: while 60 million Europeans were governed by a foreign power before the First World War, this number was reduced after it ended to 20–25 million, and moreover in 1926 the number of refugees in Europe had risen to some 20 million. The dispersion and breaking up of populations who had lived before the First World War within multi-ethnic empires thus constitutes an important factor of destabilisation of the European continent. In 1920 two-thirds of Hungary's territory and three-fifths of its population were amputated: three million Magyars in neighbouring nations suddenly became minorities. In the same way 4–5 million Germans from the Austro-Hungarian Habsburg Empire and the Eastern confines of the German empire lost their dominant nationality status ('*staatsvolk*') to become minorities in countries in the sway of nationalism, like Poland, Czechoslovakia or Italy. After 1918, 6 million Germans became national minorities, starting with 3 million of these living in Sudetenland, in Czechoslovakia.[14] There was a multiplicity of nodes of tension in Europe that nationalist authorities could stir up as and when they liked, and at the top of the list were the rightwing and extreme right movements in Germany itself.

However, did the new European nations fulfil the Wilsonian criteria? Certainly not, when one looks at 'multiethnic' nations such as Poland, Romania and the new Yugoslavia. The 1918 victors' diplomacy set out to arouse, support and encourage these attempts at national homogenisation, going so far as to ratify expulsions of populations, as happened after the 1921–2 war between Greece and Turkey. In this way the Lausanne treaty of 24 July 1923 recognised the expulsion by Turkey of 1,200,000 Anatolian Greeks (who had been living there since the age of Homer), while 700,000 Turks were forced to leave Greece. For the first time international law contributed to the organisation of a form of ethnic cleansing that had been mutually consented to by the nations involved. All this came about well before Hitler's rise to power, causing Eric Hobsbawm to remark with an acidic humorous footnote that he was a 'logical Wilsonian nationalist', because he 'arranged to transfer Germans not living within the territory of the fatherland, such as those of Italian South Tyrol, to Germany itself, as he also arranged for the permanent elimination of the Jews'.[15] So how can we be surprised that from 1937 the Serb Vasa Cubrilovic went ahead and published a monograph recommending the expulsion of Kosovo Albanians to Turkey, to bolster the national identity of Serbia?[16]

Massacres and population flows. In the case of Rwanda the answer to the previous question is also, unfortunately, positive: it is certainly not the only country in this region of the Great African Lakes to have known 'ethnic massacres'. We know too little of the history of neighbouring Burundi, a small country of some 3.5 million inhabitants situated to the south of Rwanda, also made up of Hutu, Tutsi and Twa. When it became independent in 1962, this other former kingdom of the Great African Lakes experienced from the outset an evolution very different from its neighbour's. On the initiative of Louis Rwagasore, one of King Mwanbutsa's sons, the party called the Union for National Progress (UPRONA) formed a government bringing together the nation's various ethnic strands. However, Rwagasore was assassinated in October 1961, an ominous augury for the country's future. But progressively, and notably in reaction to the events that were unfolding in Rwanda, political life in Burundi proceeded to 'ethnicise'. In the middle of the 1960s, UPRONA split between Hutus and Tutsis. In 1965 a putsch organised by the Hutu, Antoine Serukwavu, resulted in some Tutsi peasants being massacred at Muramvya, in the centre of the country. By way of reprisal, eighty Hutu personalities were executed; thousands of Hutus were imprisoned or executed by firing squads. From that point on, Burundi was to fall into a build-up of ethnic violence.[17]

The most dramatic episode occurred in 1972, when the violence peaked at a level hitherto unknown to Rwanda. The government of President Michel Micombero found itself faced with a Hutu insurrection in the south of the country, triggered on 29 April 1972 by rebel groups, some of which had come in from neighbouring Tanzania. The assailants used machetes to execute dozens, if not hundreds, of Tutsi civilians. This attack was immediately interpreted by Micombero partisans as being a deliberate attempt to destabilise the regime, and so aroused on their part a totally disproportionate response. Between April and June 1972 not a single region of Burundi escaped mass repression. The army and town and country police forces, supported by the Jeunesses Révolutionnaires Rwagasore (JRR), all launched into a Hutu hunt throughout the country. In Bujumbura (the capital) between 5,000 and 10,000 Hutus were summarily executed, including members of the government and civil servants of Hutu origin working for public services. With the exception of those who managed to flee to Rwanda, Tanzania or the Congo, almost all the country's Hutu elites were annihilated, including most of the students at the University of Bujumbura. In all, about 100,000 Hutus were killed.

René Lemarchand reported that these murders were accompanied by unbelievable atrocities. But here we need to beware, as he himself insists, of making any ethnicist reading of these events: it was not the Tutsi 'ethnic group' that was responsible for these massacres, but some of its most radical elements.[18] But the most essential fact to isolate in all this is that neither Burundi nor Rwanda had known such episodes of massacre and on such a large scale before their independence. Not that these countries had hitherto been havens of peace; they had also gone through periods of war. But never had such systematic massacres between Hutu and Tutsi been perpetrated as from 1960–70 onwards, during the formation phase of the Rwandan and Burundian nations.

Such political transformations generally have considerable effects on population flows and, as a consequence, on a region's demographic equilibrium. And this gives rise to another question, also of the 'structural' type: could these population movements, whereby peoples intermingle and then re-divide into groups, not in themselves create focal points of instability that could in the short or medium term turn into focal points for violence? Rwandan history provides an illustration of precisely this; the flight abroad of numerous Tutsis following the first massacres of 1959–61 (these were the first refugees of independent black Africa) had long-term consequences, of which most observers were not conscious at the time. The same scenario occurred following the massacres of 1963, 1966 and later. In all, several hundred thousand Rwandan Tutsis fled from their country (no one knew at the time the exact number) and lived in exile mainly in Uganda, Burundi, Tanzania and Zaire. It was above all the north of Rwanda (Ruhengeri, Gisenyi, Byumba) that was emptied of its Tutsi population, some finding refuge also in the Bugesra (still at the time mainly bush and marshland). In Kigali no one really cared about their fate: they belonged to those former 'feudals', defeated once and for all.

But with time this dispersion of exiled people, combined with assimilation difficulties in the asylum countries, became a serious problem in the region, the importance of which the Rwandan authorities did not properly gauge. In the 1960s refugees were treated decently by their host countries. The context of decolonisation was helpful in this respect: Africa was opening up and looking ahead to the future; it needed the skills and expertise it lacked to go forward. And the exiled Rwandan elite was, as it happened, relatively well qualified. But some ten years later the situation started to deteriorate. In 1981 Zaire started to scrutinise the legitimacy of the nationality that had previously been granted to Rwandan refugees, while in Uganda also the 'Banyarwanda' seemed to be no longer wanted. In October 1982, pushed out by the Ugandan president Milton Obote, some tens of thousands of them had to flee to Rwanda, which did not want to take in any more. The situation became grotesque for all those who found themselves trapped between the two frontiers (others left for Tanzania).

The feeling of insecurity born of this Ugandan experience contributed to the politicisation of some of these refugees, who felt they had been left by the wayside. From all sides the answer would reverberate: 'You are not in your native country.' These integration difficulties in this part of Africa (Uganda, Zaire) repeatedly put under the spotlight the question of their right to their new nationality. At the end of the 1980s between 600,000 and 700,000 Rwandans lived in exile in this way. Among this second generation (the children of those exiled in 1959) there grew a demand for the right to return, if necessary by armed force. It is in this context that in 1987 the Rwandan Patriotic Front (RPF—Front Patriotique Rwandais) was created, and launched an attack on Rwanda on 1 October 1990, seeking to take advantage of the weakness the Kigali government was experiencing at the time. Directed at the outset by Fred Rwigema, who died in 1990, the RPF was then commanded by Paul Kagamé. A problem, then, that had remained unresolved for thirty years—the status of a population that had dispersed to live in several different countries—can be seen to be at the origin of the civil war that was gradually spreading to Rwanda.[19]

State collapse and outbursts of extreme violence. In Europe might we also find that there is a relationship between the risk of violence, even of massacre, and the demographic structure of populations? Recent research by the historian Omer Bartov and his team draws our attention to those geographic zones situated at the crossroads of empires. It is indeed true, he points out, that the most extensive and the most frequent massacres on the old continent were perpetrated in the area referred to as the '*borderlands region*', reaching from central and Baltic Europe to the south-eastern part of Europe, and as far as Asia Minor. All these territories, diverse in so many respects, nevertheless have two traits in common: they were the meeting point between four empires—Germanic, Russian, Austro-Hungarian and Ottoman—and were peopled by a multitude of ethnic, religious or national groups.[20] These buffer zones between two worlds, between two or more empires, would indeed appear fragile, if not uncontrollable. The melting-pot situation whereby populations mix and mingle constitutes a factor of uncertainty and of potential risk of violence, whether on the part of some community groups or of neighbouring nations.

In the same way 'the Ottoman and Austrian Balkans at the start of the nineteenth century are an inextricable mix of different populations, languages, and religions living alongside one another within the same territories.'[21] A remarkable illustration of this is provided by Ivo Andric's historical novel, in which the protagonist is the bridge across the Drina, this bridge seeming to link together the East with the West symbolically at that precise place.[22] The author relates the upheavals lived over nearly four centuries by different generations of inhabitants of the town of Visegrad living near the bridge, on the border between Serbia and Bosnia. In the nineteenth century, and during the time the nation-states were being formed, the ensuing wars and massacres caused some peoples to leave. The inhabitants of Visegrad thus watched Muslims crossing the bridge as they left Serbia to find refuge in Sarajevo, while others, passing in the opposite direction, attempted to return to Turkey. Later, after the assassination of Archduke Franz Ferdinand on 28 June 1914, it was the turn of the Serbs to be dangerously worried because the Austro-Hungarian army considered them to be enemies and persecuted them, at Visegrad and throughout the region. This historic fresco thus shows how a territory where diverse communities had hitherto succeeded in cohabiting was one of the very first to be subjected to the violent shake-ups born in the surrounding states.

Meanwhile, whether in Europe or in Africa, neither the identifiable historical data (former massacres) nor the individual demographic data (intermingling of populations) can, in themselves, explain the outbreak of violence at a given point in time. We need also to take into account geopolitical data to assess the balance or imbalance of the forces at work in the area concerned. In the border regions of Europe the situation of dominance or decline of an imperial power plays a vital role in the general destiny of peoples. In this regard the massacre of one part of the population residing in this region can result from two opposing scenarios.

The first of these scenarios features an increasingly powerful state that imposes what is in reality an imperial will over these frontier zones. For example, the formation of the Soviet state in 1917 and then the Nazi state in 1933 *de facto* put intermediate countries in Central and Baltic Europe in an unfavourable position. The internationalising dynamic driving the Bolshevik revolution could legitimately make them fear the totalitarian grip of Moscow. Among other peoples, the Ukrainians dramatically paid the price at the time of the mass famine Stalin orchestrated in 1933–4 to crush any stray impulse to resist. Poland as neighbour was in an equally vulnerable position. Its fate was to be rapidly sealed in the framework of the German-Soviet Non-Aggression Pact of 23 August 1939, which contained a secret clause anticipating its being divided in two between Germany and the USSR. In Berlin certain experts were already reflecting on a full reshaping of this block that was Eastern Europe, perceived to be archaic, and an immense zone of territories ripe for colonisation to the profit of the 'vital space' the Reich would require.

The second scenario—the reverse of the first—arises from the crumbling of an empire (or multinational state) that had previously been dominant. So long as this political entity was largely respected within it, the region could experience a certain degree of stability. Such was the case of the Ottoman Empire in south-eastern Europe right up to the start of the nineteenth century, and of Tito's Yugoslavia between the end of the 1940s and the start of the 1980s. But if this empire or this multinational state came to be contested from the inside, due to the rise of nationalist aspirations, then the system became increasingly fragile, the communities of which it consisted tended to cut the ties of their old allegiances, and the outbreak of violence became probable. This is exactly what happened in the former Yugoslavia at the end of the 1980s.

Rwanda-Burundi: false ethnic twins. In the case of Rwanda we can also refer to a scenario of a crumbling imperial power in the general context of the decolonisation of Africa during the 1960s, which manifested itself in Kigali with Belgium's retreat. But the context was entirely different at the end of the 1980s at the time when the RPF was preparing to invade the country. In this period France became so to speak a tutelary power for Rwanda, most likely because President François Mitterrand saw a strategic interest in reinforcing the French presence in this region in order to curb the Anglophone influence. This support from a major actor on the international scene represented a considerable asset for President Habyarimana. True, the injunction issued to African heads of state at the La Baule summit (20 June 1990) by the French President to democratise their countries was not to his liking; Paris intended to make its economic aid to developing countries contingent on progress made in internal political democratisation. This was all against a background of euphoria in the wake of the fall of the Berlin wall, which raised hopes of a global democratising movement, with some already predicting the 'end of History'. In Rwanda it was rather a new history that was in the process of starting up… or rather, of erupting.

The forced establishment of multipartism had the effect of permitting Hutu opposition to develop, and this was mainly expressed in the Mouvement Démocratique Républicain (MDR) or the Parti Social Démocrate (PSD). These opponents were set on disregarding the ethnic division with a view to constructing a Rwanda that was truly democratic; what can we conclude from this? Politics in that country was not simply, between 1990 and 1994, a face-to-face confrontation between the 'Hutu block' majority rising up against the Tutsi minority.[23] Hutu extremists also knew how to exploit the situation and to mobilise. In the new monthly publication *Kangura* they were soon presenting François Mitterrand as their 'true friend'. In actual fact the RPF's attack in October 1990 was halted thanks to the intervention of a contingent of the French military protecting the capital.[24] From 1990 to 1993 France was to play a pivotal role in keeping Habyarimana in power, and this without any real awareness on the part of French public opinion.[25]

However, Paris supported attempts to mediate that sought to set up negotiations between the RPF, the Rwandan government and the opposition. The Organisation of African Unity played an active role in this respect, with Tanzania leading the negotiations. These efforts were to lead to the Arusha agreements (4 August 1993) that Habyarimana was forced to sign, with France threatening to cut off aid if he refused. These agreements seemed to establish a political compromise between all protagonists, to the great regret of the Hutu extremists who didn't want it. To ensure they were applied, the United Nations decided to send in a peacekeeping force, the UNA-MIR (United Nations Assistance Mission in Rwanda), made up in part of Belgian Blue Helmets, and of which the Canadian Major-General Roméo Dallaire, took charge. Despite these attempts at peacemaking, the internal situation nevertheless rapidly deteriorated.

What is there that could explain the development of violence in Rwanda at the start of the 1990s? How can we understand that all these attempts to mediate proved futile in the end? In fact, there is indeed something missing from all the explanations presented so far: an additional 'something', or essential ingredient that in a way tips the whole system into a rejection of the 'other'. This ingredient, that multiplies by sprouting up anywhere and everywhere, overpowering the minds of a majority of actors, something impossible to grasp but in the end enveloping everything, is fear. It is like the oil needed to grease the gears of a machine, and in this case an infernal machine.

We have already seen how fear operates in constructing one or several enemies on the inside. Now we can see how it arrives also from the outside, as a threat of destruction. It is this two-way—internal/external—movement of fear that risks pushing the conflict over the edge into tragedy.

In Rwanda, Alison Des Forges dwells on this propagation of fear, and the way people are mobilised by it. At the start of the 1990s, she set about defending both ethnic camps: 'Rwandans—Tutsi as well as Hutu—were frightened by the RPF attack. Tutsi recalled the reprisal killings at the time of invasions by refugee groups in the 1960s and feared they would be targeted again. Hutu remembered the slaughter of tens of thousands of Hutu by Tutsi in neighbouring Burundi in 1972, 1988 and 1991 and dreaded killings on a similar scale by the RPF'.[26] We must therefore pause and examine the role played by this fear that spreads from one country to another: without taking fear into account, an analysis of the background situation cannot throw any light on the nature of this conflictual dynamic that puts the other elements, hitherto identified, into motion.

At this point in our enquiry, should not each of us wonder how best to assess the real meaning of these words uttered by one of the most eminent analysts of Rwanda quoted above? What is my experience of this fear she talks about? Am I really in a position to understand the phenomenon taking place in this country, never having been faced with the terrifying hold fear can have? I can hardly claim to do so. The sociologist reflex makes me think that fear does not overcome everybody, and that there are probably nodes of resistance to it, depending on the regions and individuals concerned. The historian reflex orients my attention to the fact that this fear flourishes on the memory of massacre, as we have already remarked. The political scientist reflex makes me note that this fear is constructed in mirror image in relation to another country: in this case, Burundi.

This is the most striking thing about this instant in the drama: to discover the narrative of events from another point in time, of the story peculiar to this strange pair that is Rwanda-Burundi. Had they not both since their 'independence' been like false twins, each one's particular history interacting with the other's? They share the same 'ethnic map' give or take a few minor differences, while remaining totally tied to their own 'national' identity. When an 'ethnic crisis' occurs in one country, it inevitably has consequences for the other. In the 1960s fear spread through Burundi, originating in Rwanda following the massacres of Tutsis in December 1963 and January 1964. Conversely, at the beginning of the 1970s, fear arrived in Rwanda from Burundi following the massacre of some 100,000 Burundian Hutu in 1972. This event then provided fertile ground for the anti-Tutsi riots that followed in Rwanda in 1973, these being instrumentalised by President Kayibanda to ensure he remained in power; not, however, that this prevented the rise of Habyarimana in July the same year. All this happened, then, as though the mirrored relationships Rwanda had with Burundi had encouraged this outbreak of violence through increasingly radical identitarian mobilisations.

This comment seems to me an essential part of analytical methodology: to establish the relationship between the intertwining histories of Rwanda and Burundi is effectively to tap into an understanding of how, through shared fears, escalating violence can be geared up. Of course the variables internal to each country remain decisive. But it is their interaction, along with local external factors, that may make the conflict much more extreme.

Serbia/Croatia: a fratricidal duo. Elsewhere, in Yugoslavia, the fratricidal duo of Serbia-Croatia presents a similar kind of configuration. But this example presented a different turn of events since the respective nationalist propagandas for the two countries provides us with an unmistakable glimpse of the possibility of direct armed confrontation. At the end of the 1980s one might have expected tension to mount even higher between Milosevic's Serbia and the Kosovo Albanians. But the latter did not respond with armed resistance, against which the Serbs could have immediately fought back. On the contrary, their leader, Ibrahim Rugova, clandestinely elected President of the Republic on 24 May 1992, came out in favour of peaceful resistance, since he was convinced that recourse to armed conflict would be a trap Milosevic could use to crush the Kosovars even more. The conflict between the Serbs and the Kosovo Albanians was therefore to remain during the early 1990s at a very low level of intensity.

It is rather between the two nations that 'made' the Yugoslav state that the risk of violence escalated. It was from their *entente* that the first Yugoslavia was born in 1918, as was the second in 1945. And it was through their confrontation that the federal state had every chance of collapsing. But, as we saw earlier, the rise of nationalism in the region is associated with the rise of fear and vice versa. Serbian and Croatian nationalist propaganda bear witness precisely to these reciprocal accusations that could only increase tension, stemming from the revival of massacres committed in the Second World War. Given the overlapping of minorities, this determination to construct territorial national states could only lead to an open crisis. Croatia, for example, was home to some 600,000 Serbs, of whom nearly half resided in Krajina and Slavonia. From the end of the 1980s, Belgrade and Zagreb began to find themselves in opposition to one another due to this Croatian Serb minority. Terrified by the rise in Tudjman's Croat nationalism, the latter was supported by Belgrade, and pressured to armed rebellion so as to come back into the fold of the Serbian national state. Unless a last-minute agreement could be reached, war was not far off.

What happened in fact was that on 25 March 1991 Tudjman and Milosevic met secretly at Karadjordjevo, not to make peace but to agree on how to divide up Bosnia-Herzegovina, where large numbers of Croats and Serbs also lived. 'They did not have identical interpretations of this agreement', insisted the Yugoslav Prime Minister at that time, Ante Markovic. 'Milosevic said that Bosnia and Herzegovina was an artificial entity created by Tito, [and that] most of the Muslims were in fact Orthodox who had been forced to change their religion [...] He said that they had envisioned an enclave for the Muslims. [As for Tudjman] he said that Europe would not allow a Muslim state in its heart [and] that the Muslims were anyway Catholics who had been forced to adopt Islam.'[27] In any event, the two most powerful nations of Yugoslavia prepared to 'swallow up' the bulk of these territories. In this respect, too, war was close.

Nazi Germany/the Soviet Union: two totalitarianisms clash. If the identification of these conflictual pairs—Rwanda-Burundi, Serbia-Croatia—has any meaning, then it would seem interesting to explore the strategic importance of the explosive potential of the Nazi Germany-Soviet Union pair. The German historian Ernst Nolte has been severely criticised for defending the idea that Nazism was built primarily in reaction to the formation of the Soviet Union. All the right conditions were present, according to him, for the development of a vast European civil war, born out of the confrontation between Bolshevism and Nazism.[28] Nolte draws from this a moral conclusion: the crimes of Communism are more reprehensible than those of Nazism, because the latter constitute a reaction to the former. This reasoning also leads him to obscure the causes of Nazism that were strictly internal to Germany, namely the German anti-Semitism on which Hitler's fanaticism had flourished. From this duplicitous point of view, his reasoning is not acceptable. Both internal *and* external causes of the rise of Nazism need to be viewed in perspective, without trying to rank one in relation to the other.

However, one has to admit that he is right in identifying the relationship between Germany and the Soviet Union as being the strategic pair from which a major European confrontation could result. He is also right to ascribe great importance to fear, which he considers to be the principal internal machinery of Nazism: fear of seeing a traditional Germany disappear, threatened by Communism, and a fear that was all the more comprehensible since several Bolshevik leaders had declared their intention to exterminate their enemies, and that the Communists might well seize power in Germany itself one day. Here too there therefore a major antagonism in the relationship between the double rivals. Nolte moreover devotes a chapter of his book to the study of their reciprocal propagandas.[29] The German-Soviet Non-Aggression Pact of 1939 would appear incomprehensible if it hadn't allowed the two powers to reach agreement on how Poland should be divided.[30] This agreement, according to Kershaw, was for Hitler just a 'strategically necessary but no more than temporary arrangement' and so one that did not in any way represent a solution likely to change completely his racial and imperialist vision.[31]

The passivity of the 'international community'. In this way, however you look at it, each of the regions examined is characterised by a high potential for violence, contained, or already expressing itself. At this point an important question arises: what can be done by what is labelled the 'international community'? On what terms and with what means could it intervene in the crisis? Even though everyone agrees to use the term, it is a strange one: it is actually a wonderful example of an oxymoron. That which is international is in fact anything but a 'community', such is the degree to which the interests of several nations can be contradictory. When we speak about the 'international community' it evokes above all the role of the great powers, that, precisely because they are powerful, can impose their law on smaller nations, or join forces against a nation posing a threat to make it see reason through pressure or force as required by armed might. Over and above this point of vocabulary, the question is absolutely crucial to the outcome of the crisis: could the said international community in some way put the brakes on, stifle, or contain the process of violence that is gaining ground? Once again, this would require on the part of the international community a clear perception of the issues and, using this analysis as a starting-point, a strong will to do something about it. But in the crises examined in these pages it is singularly passive. How can we qualify this almost generalised passivity: indifference, ignorance, hypocrisy, cowardice? All these words fit—despite the moral connotations that apply to some of them—since we can observe for each crisis a more or less complex combination of these diverse attitudes.

It must be said that more often than not the so-called international community does not seem to see the crisis coming, or behaves as though it doesn't see it coming. Here the case of Yugoslavia is exemplary. At the end of the 1980s the world was living through the *Glasnost* that Mikhaïl Gorbachev had set in motion in Moscow. The fall of the Berlin Wall on 9 November 1989 was an event of world significance, far more sensational that any expert believed possible without so much as a single shot being fired. But what was to happen from then on? How would relations between the Germans develop? And would the USSR itself start to fall apart? Taken up with these upheavals, the Europeans and Americans did not worry themselves about Yugoslavia, which, in any case, was theoretically one of the 'well-disposed' countries that had been open to the West for years, and belonged to the non-aligned camp. Who, then, noticed the explosive charge contained in Milosevic's speech delivered at the huge rally on 28 June 1989 in Kosovo? Who would be worried about his decision, one year later, to cancel the province's autonomy? The world had its mind on other things, and this eminently suited both the Serbian and Croatian nationalists. The Yugoslav army, of which Milosevic had managed to gain control, was preparing for action in 1991. The Moscow putsch, even though it failed, contributed further to focusing international attention on the USSR, but Yugoslavia escaped attention. Then came Iraq's attack on Kuwait on 2 August 1990, and this turned all eyes once and for all away from Eastern Europe to the Middle East.

Meanwhile, the Serb minority in Croatia was preparing to secede, and receiving weapons from Serbia. In Belgrade the army declared itself ready to act, but feared that the Western countries just emerging from the Gulf war would not try to intervene in Yugoslavia, a fear that was to be quickly proved unfounded. A comparative study of the diplomatic archives of the major powers will no doubt one day enable us to formulate a more accurate picture of the ways they expressed their apprehension in 1990 and 1991 about the future of Yugoslavia. But whether or not their diplomats posted in Belgrade did seriously send any warning signals as to how the situation was evolving, they apparently did not react to them.[32]

In the case of Rwanda there was not even the excuse of lack of visibility as regards the crisis to come. In effect, following the Arusha Peace Agreement, the international community was already in place, because of the presence of the UNAMIR armed forces, led by the Canadian Major-General Roméo Dallaire. But he did quickly realise that there was an increasing risk of massacres on a large scale occurring. In a telegram addressed to the United Nations dated 11 January 1994, he wrote: 'We have no reason to believe that such occurrences could not and will not be repeated again in any part of this country where arms are prolific and ethnic tensions are prevalent.'[33] This telegram is only one of the warning signals transmitted in 1993–4: to it we should add a Belgian information service report, several human rights organisations reports, plus the discovery of weapons caches and racist remarks floating on the airwaves from the brand new Radio Télévision Libre des Milles Collines centre. 'It was therefore impossible to believe that the Western partners were unaware of what was afoot,' wrote Jean-Pierre Chrétien.[34]

What stands out, in diplomatic circles, is therefore not the ignorance, but the refusal to take action. Rwanda, a small African nation without any great strategic interest and without natural resources, was of no interest to the major powers, except France or the United States, who saw in it an asset by which to back their presence in the region. But once the Arusha agreement had been signed, Paris tended progressively to disengage itself, having noted the nation's deteriorating internal situation. The UN's arrival on the scene gave France the pretext. But the UN did nothing, despite Dallaire's repeated requests for more resources.

This kind of indifference is nothing new. Whether one looks at the massacres that have scarred Rwandan history since its independence or those perpetrated in Burundi, the major powers were hardly very dynamic in putting a stop to them. Conflicts flaring up on the African continent are perceived to be of secondary importance as compared to those affecting the Middle East region, and more globally the East-West confrontation in Europe. The French intervention in Burundi in October 1993 following the assassination of Melchior Ndadaye, the first Hutu President in that country, is probably an exception to the rule, although that point of view is disputed. Nonetheless, for journalist Stephen Smith it allegedly limited the massacres perpetrated by Hutus coming down from the hills to avenge 'their' President, and to put the brakes on the excesses of the repression. The net result of these massacres (80,000 deaths primarily of Tutsis, but also Hutus) could have been even worse.[35] And yet, in this region anyone committing massacre had nothing to fear as regards reprisals from the international community. From here to the notion that this international passivity was opening the way to further potential massacre, in Rwanda or anywhere else, there is only a very fine line, soon to be crossed through subsequent events.

As for Nazi Germany, it is scarcely tenable that the world was not aware of what was going on. The plea of ignorance can still less be put forward by one of the largest European nations as by any other country. But information is only one of the elements that leads to action. Everything depends on the context for reception of such information and on the categories of analysis used to interpret it. But during the 1930s the great powers at the time, still marked by the trauma of the First World War, were reluctant properly to assess the reality of the Hitler threat. Here the list of missed opportunities for demonstrating any firmness is a lengthy one. We can cite the withdrawal of Germany from the League of Nations in 1933 or even the announcement in 1935 of the reinstatement of obligatory military service and the constitution of a new German army, in flagrant violation of the Versailles Treaty. But what can be said about the reoccupation of the Rhineland on 7 March 1936, that negated *de facto* a clause in the Treaty of Versailles? At the last moment, Hitler had hesitated to make this '*coup*' that his diplomats had advised against. But very quickly it became apparent that his audacity had paid off. Hitler was jubilant, and Goebbels was able to record in his journal: 'The Führer is beaming. England remains passive. France takes no action on its own, Italy is disappointed, and America uninterested.'[36] No need, either, to go back over the signing of the Munich agreements on 29 and 30 September 1938 that allowed Hitler to annexe the Sudetenland with the consent of France and Britain. With public approval in both countries, these agreements remain the symbol of the capitulation of Western democracies in the face of the devastating diplomacy shown on the part of a totalitarian state that no one wanted to notice was preparing for war.

Still more interesting for our purposes is the attention the Nazis devoted to the possible international protests following the increasing persecution of the Jewish minority. The tactical considerations of Martin Bormann at the moment of the organisation of the 1936 Olympic Games shows clearly that their reasoning took account of this variable: 'Due to external political imperatives, he wrote, we must in our combat against Judaism act a little more discreetly, while knowing fundamentally that the aim of the NSDAP is irrevocably fixed: to exclude Judaism from every domain of life in the German nation.'[37] In the same way, the killing of the principal Swiss Nazi leader, Gustloff, in February 1936, did not give rise to reprisals in this same period of preparation for the Games. On the other hand the murder in Paris on 7 November 1938 of Ernst von Rath, the first secretary of the German Embassy, served as a pretext for triggering the *Kristallnacht*.

Thus the context is very different, because the famous Munich agreements had just been signed; the Nazis therefore gambled once more on the passivity of the great powers, and they were not mistaken. Protest was sometimes quite heated in some countries, for example among public opinion in the Netherlands and Britain. But governments, for their part, did not budge: they remained 'onlooker states'.[38] Certainly the United States recalled its ambassador immediately to Washington, but Under Secretary of State George Messersmith downplayed the significance of this gesture: 'Calling back our Ambassador "for consultation" cannot interfere in any way with our relations, political or commercial, with Germany and our interests in Germany will not suffer.'[39] The White House's gesture aimed to startle German public opinion, but still more to retain control of American public opinion, incensed as it was by *Kristallnacht*.

The passivity of governments towards the persecution of Jews in Germany must be viewed in relation to their refusal to accommodate Jewish refugees fleeing from Germany and Austria. The attitude of the Swiss is well known, being illustrated as early as 1938 by their policy of stamping German Jews' passports with a 'J', and later the decision in the summer of 1942 to close Swiss borders to any refugee persecuted for reasons of 'race' alone. At that time the Swiss authorities were perfectly aware of the fate awaiting the Jews. This is the reason why the Bergier Commission report found that they 'really contributed to achieving the National Socialists objectives'.[40] But in reality it was all of Europe, the United States and even Australia that did not want the Jews. The international conference in Evian that took place from 6 to 15 July 1938 on the initiative of President Roosevelt had shown clearly that this closed attitude was shared by all governments. While most countries expressed sympathy for the persecuted Jews, they nevertheless declared that their countries' social and economic situations would not allow them to increase their immigration quotas. This conference, the outcome of which was inconsequential, provided the Nazi leaders with new proof that governments, despite their protestations of indignation, would do nothing for the German and Austrian Jewish refugees. The Protestant writer Jochen Klemmer noted in his journal on 23 August 1938: 'After it was revealed at the Evian Conference that the German Jews could not expect help from abroad, everything became far more tragic.'[41]

Wherever we turn, once violence has already been unleashed in a region or country, it will not run up against any obstacles or prohibitions in the international arena capable of restraining it. Local actors can even sometimes be protected, or believe themselves to be protected, by a major power that in some ways provides them with top-ranking international 'coverage'. Such protection contributes to their feeling of impunity, and also dissuades other countries from intervening directly in the crisis. Some such tutelary relationships developed between France and Rwanda, and to a certain extent between the Soviet and Yugoslav armies.[42] Other instances of this come to mind, for example the relations between Pol Pot's Cambodia in 1975 and Communist China, the government of the Young Turks in 1915 and imperial Germany, or Chile and Argentina in the middle of the 1970s and the United States. But this scenario does not operate for Nazi Germany, which was not under the tutelage of any other power. So it would seem wiser to seek an even wider framework of interpretation.

In the sociology of social movements, Sidney Tarrow put forward a theory of the 'structure of political opportunities'. According to him, the success or failure of a social movement depends on a conjunction of contextual factors that may or may not favour its development.[43] I would say the same of a process of violence potentially leading to massacre. Here there is also a structure of favourable opportunities that can facilitate the slide into violence. The trigger mechanism is conditioned by a certain number of internal factors (explored in Chapter II) and external factors (explored here). Certainly the actors will keep some room for manoeuvre to be able to bring this process to a halt: we shouldn't go as far as to resort to fatalistic determinism; anybody studying the history of man knows that it is full of unexpected turns of fate and events that are totally unheralded but move things forward, changing the course of history as they occur, and leaving the future open. It is nevertheless clear that the more those actors capable of intervening with any effect in the crisis delay in doing so, the more their margin for manoeuvre diminishes. If they persist in remaining passive, the conflictual dynamic has every chance of rising in power and finally spilling over into war.

Spilling into war

War also has a history. To what extent does this history have a bearing on what is being acted out in Berlin, Belgrade, or Kigali?

The history of war is often recounted like an epic, as by Homer the Greek, or it can be thought through strategically as it was in equally ancient times, by the Chinese author Sun Tzu. To put it more provocatively, we can speak about the enduring appeal war holds for men. Whether we like it or not, men—at least some of them—are fascinated by war and love waging it. It is futile to try and deny this tendency in human beings to seek in war as much glory as death. 'Nor should it be overlooked', writes the military historian Martin Van Creveld, 'that combat itself has very often been treated not just as a spectacle but as the greatest spectacle of all.'[44] But this fascination with the grandiose spectacle of war obscures the horrors of the battlefield. This is why I will approach the war phenomenon here through its darkest face, that which military narratives tend to obscure, but which historians like Joanna Bourke, Annette Becker and Stéphane Audoin-Rouzeau have sought to bring to light: the aspect of battlefield violence and, finally, of massacre.[45]

For war is obviously something that by its very nature will 'produce' massacre. Certainly, massacre is not always perpetrated in a situation of war (*Kristallnacht* in 1938 being the example of a pogrom executed 'in cold blood', in peacetime); in Ukraine the Kulak famine was instigated by Stalin while the Soviet Union was not at war, and not all wars result ineluctably in massacre, particularly when war defines itself as an organised and violent activity mainly involving the intervention of soldiers—more or less motivated and paid to fight—and not that of the non-combatant civilian population.

But since the dawn of time, and certainly as far back as ancient Greece, war and massacre have married well. We tend to idealise its civilisation because it left us its legacy of democracy. But the Greeks had their barbarians whom they treated mercilessly. Thucydides, chronicler of the Peloponnesian war, devotes several pages to a narrative describing the massacre of the inhabitants of Melos by Athens 416 years before Jesus Christ,[46] an episode that some authors consider to be one of the first 'genocides' known in human history.[47] We can also read or reread the Bible, pausing to reflect on the Old Testament decree: 'And you shall destroy all the peoples that the Lord your God will give over to you, your eye shall not pity them' (Deuteronomy, 7, 16), and again: 'But in the cities of these peoples that the Lord your God gives you for an inheritance, you shall save alive nothing that breathes, but you shall utterly destroy them, the Hittites, the Amorites, the Canaanites, the Per'izzites, the Hivites and the Jeb'usites, as the Lord your God has commanded, that they may not teach you to do according to all their abominable practices which they have done in the service of their gods, and so to sin against the Lord your God' (Deuteronomy 20, 16–18). These texts are certainly subject to interpretation depending on the context in which they were written. They tell us something very profound, however, about the history of humanity and its relationship to violence.

Massacre often accompanies war, then, and above all when the victors permit themselves to exercise vengeance against the vanquished, or when they kill the enemy's soldiers once they have disarmed. In his *Mémoires d'outre-tombe*, Chateaubriand amply criticized Napoleon for acts against 'the rights of humanity', for example the order he gave on 10 March 1799 to execute soldiers conquered during the Syrian campaign.[48] Massacre also provides a means for rapid material gain by pillaging the goods of populations killed or forced to flee. One might say that from the wars of Antiquity through to modern warfare, and including also colonial wars, massacre is almost always there, not as an 'excess' of warfare but as one of its true dimensions.

However, let us attempt to be more precise. The crises seen in Germany, Yugoslavia, and Rwanda plunge us into the history of the twentieth century, a century that is characterised by an extraordinary rise in the number of non-combatant victims. The figures are indeed impressive: it is estimated that in warring conflicts the proportion of civilians among the victims overall rose from 10 per cent at the start of the twentieth century to nearly 90 per cent a century later. This trend is due to increasingly powerful means and techniques of destruction being invented, starting with the invention of dynamite in 1866 by Alfred Nobel. Moreover, the advances brought through industrialisation have considerably improved the firepower of modern weaponry, increasing the number of potential civilian victims, but this technological trend only provides part of the explanation. In parallel, since the end of the eighteenth century, the whole attitude to war has profoundly changed.

According to the English historian John Horne, the model of a 'nation in arms' inherited from the French Revolution engendered what he calls the 'politicisation of war': the doctrine of national sovereignty enlisting each citizen under the auspices of unprecedented terms and conditions. In this way the heritage of the '*levée en masse*' or mass conscription, that is the forced enrolment of 'male citizens' in armies, disturbs representations of self and of the enemy.

The politicisation of war. Mass conscription has the effect, first, of engaging total mobilisation of the population for war, a notion that reached its peak during the First World War. At the same time as all young men were called up to serve in the army, the remainder of the population was also invited to participate in the war effort. The government expresses in this way its intention to mobilise all the country's resources, not just the military ones, but also human, economic and ideological resources. In 1793 women and children were called upon to manufacture weapons, as old people were to denounce tyrants.[49] From this moment onwards, war involved the mobilisation of an entire country. Because of this, any formal distinction between combatant (armed or not) and non-combatant tends to disappear. The blurring of the distinction between military and civilian, between combatant and non-combatant, can be found at the heart of almost all contemporary conflicts.

The main consequence of such changes is that they alter people's representations of the enemy. In effect, the doctrine of total mobilisation logically leads to making the entire adversary population a military target. Each segment of the nation is perceived as potentially hostile, because it constitutes part of the political, economic and cultural resources of the same. In this way, from the start of the First World War, the German army invading Belgium and France imagined they were about to face a civilian uprising in a war of snipers.[50] In general, perhaps, we could say that all warmongers tend to have dehumanised representations of the enemy, who are accused of having committed the worst possible atrocities, whether or not this can be proved to be true. Given that the authors of these atrocities could equally be civilians, they will not be spared when it comes to reprisals (or indeed other measures applied in an attempt to discourage such acts).

In a combat mobilising all kinds of resources (including propaganda) the victorious nation will be the one that first breaks the material and moral resistance of the enemy. The distinction between

the 'front' and 'rear' tends to disappear in the context of what becomes total war, as theorised in the early 1930s by Erich Ludendorff.
For this German strategist total war, requiring absolute cohesion on
the part of the people, aims to annihilate the adversary by striking
intensively at the rear quarters, destroying economic infrastructures
and civilian populations.[51] How do you strike at the rear quarters?
Using, of course, newly available aviation, declared General Giulio
Douhet. War in our time is total, he writes (*'guerra integrale'*). Over
and above the mobilisation for the war effort, civilians became the
true subjects of the war. And airborne weaponry became the only
decisive factor: according to him, devastation must henceforward be
made to reign behind enemy lines, by striking vulnerable targets, or
industrial, energy, military or even human agglomerations.[52]

The politicisation of war explains how violence aimed at civilians
developed under another banner: that of political and cultural mobilisation against national minorities or foreign elements, presented as
enemies within. In this regard 'the September 1792 massacres in
Paris, capital of the Revolution, where the fear of invasion was combined with the dread of a counter-revolutionary conspiracy, were a
key event in the elaboration of the concept of the enemy within in
its modern form. The most extreme violence against civilians during the First World War was of this type.'[53] In August 1914 a wave of
xenophobia against the imagined spy or secret invader took over.
Minorities suspected of being agents or sympathisers of the enemy
were marginalised, or worse, excluded from the process of mobilisation. Forced deportations and pogroms caused by the Russian
army during its retreat in 1915 targeted frontier populations, many
of whom where Russian. This is even clearer in the instance of the
mass murder of Armenians already mentioned. These were not only
defined by the Young Turks as an obstacle to the construction of a
modern state, they were also perceived, in the context of war, as allies
to the Turks' Russian opponents, and so as traitors to the Turkish
nation. In Germany itself, in 1916, the census of the Jews, accused in
nationalist circles of being 'shirkers', contributed to a demonology
of the enemy within, of which anti-Semitism was to become a central element.

In short, the figure of the enemy without tends to link up with the
enemy within. A state of war provokes precisely this kind of over-

lapping. In peacetime, propaganda had already helped construct the figure of the enemy within. Now wartime could in some way validate the arguments it had put forward. War facilitates 'self-ful-filment' of the prophecy: 'There is an enemy within who seeks to harm us. And this enemy within tends to be the same as our enemy without.' The obvious consequence of going to war is to enable in this way a 'closing of ranks' against this double enemy. The under-lying identity crisis that in peacetime had already given rise to a sac-rificial discourse against an 'other' to be excluded, proceeds to find in war a 'solution'. Such is the modern legacy afflicting in one way or another the participants in war, whether in Germany, Yugoslavia or Rwanda. But it goes without saying that depending on the par-ticular context in which they find themselves, and according to the means at their disposal as regards force, they will 'invent' their own ways of making war against the enemy within/without.

Conquering 'living space'. When Hitler attacked Poland on 1 Sep-tember 1939 he intended to take over the share of territory that he had secretly agreed with Stalin was to be his. The German aggress-ion triggered the Soviet occupation of the Eastern part of the country, east of the Vistula. Poland of course lacked the strength to do anything about this. It had to trust in its alliance with France and England. But neither country came to Poland's rescue. Once more, Hitler had gambled on their passivity and won. Would he stop there? Scarcely had the operation against Poland been realised than he ordered his commanders to prepare an attack against Northern Europe (Denmark, Norway), and also on Belgium and France, oper-ations that took place in stages between April and June 1940. Europe was plunged fully into a war it had not wanted to see coming.

The lead-up to what would become the Second World War had immediate and significant consequences for civilian populations. In Germany itself the first to suffer were the mentally ill. On the pre-tence of cleansing the 'race', those afflicted had already undergone measures such as sterilisation, discrimination, exclusion and aban-don. The acceleration of the march towards war led to the secret preparation during the summer of 1939 of their collective murder in a 'euthanasia' programme that went into operation that autumn. In Poland the German invasion was accompanied by the immediate elimination of Polish elites in accordance with Hitler's orders. At the same time the Germanisation of territories began (notably in Silesia): the forced departure of the population towards the East enabled settlers 'of German race' to take their place. A decision was also taken on 21 September to create ghettos to contain the 2 million Jews living in Poland. Then, from 12 to 30 October, the first deportations of Austrian and Czechoslovak Jews to Poland were organised. On the Soviet side the picture was equally bleak: some months after their partial occupation of this country, the Soviets proceeded to massacre Polish officers in the Katyn forest (April 1940), and organise deportations of Polish, Ukrainian and Belarusian Jews.

On the military front Hitler meanwhile had no intention of calling a halt having accomplished these early victories. The blitzkrieg strategy that had enabled him to reap such incredibly rapid successes (above all against France) gave him reason to be ever more ambitious. Following his failure to invade England, he convinced his commanders to prepare the conquest of the Soviet Union. In this decision strategic considerations were uppermost (appropriation of vast resources in the USSR before turning back to attack England). Intent on conquering their 'vital space' the Nazis set off also to the East, wielding a kind of colonialist *imaginaire* to reduce the Slav populations who would fall beneath their dominion there to slavery. The fact that Operation Barbarossa was led by the largest army ever formed in Europe was immediately to have enormous consequences for the destiny of these civilian populations. While this invasion amply fulfilled strategic imperatives, it was also a political-racial war against 'Judeo-Bolshevism'. German aggression against the Soviet Union enabled the full conjunction of the enemy without and the enemy within to come about. On the military side, Red Army soldiers were to pay the price, because the Wehrmacht let them die of hunger by the million. At the beginning of 1942, 2 million Soviet prisoners had already died.[54] As for civilian populations, the Jews were to be the main victims: under the auspices of war, they were diabolised by virtue of a double threat, internal and external. So it was that the *Einsatzgruppen*, armed groups specially assigned to the task of exterminating Jews, operated right from the start of the invasion of the Soviet Union at the rear of the German divisions, and with the participation of the Wehrmacht.

War against civilians. Slovenia's and Croatia's declarations of independence on 25 June 1991 provoked the final crisis of the collapse of Yugoslavia. Markovic's federal government tried to keep Slovenia in the Union, but there was nothing to be done. In any case there were hardly any Serbs in Slovenia, and Milosevic remained indifferent to its loss. This was not true of Croatia, where he deemed it wise to support the Serb minority who demanded protection from Belgrade. And so in July 1991 the first ethnic purification operations began in Croatia. People who had lived alongside one another for years without so much as thinking about their ethnic ancestry or religious affiliations suddenly became 'enemies' to be hunted down; unless they decided of their own free will to leave, suddenly feeling themselves to be in a position of considerable insecurity. More than 100,000 Serbs then lived in Zagreb and its environs, mixed in with the population at large. But the context of war made the situation difficult for them, and shattered numerous mixed-race married couples. More than half of them left Croatia. Then began a full-scale war against a threatened population, according to the expression coined by Mirko Grmek, of 'memoricide': the aim being not only to get rid of those deemed undesirable on the territory to be 'purified', but to annihilate any trace that might recall their erstwhile presence (schools, religious buildings and so on).[55]

Ill prepared for war, Croatia declared a general mobilisation on 26 August 1991. In Belgrade, for the benefit of the major powers, Milosevic displayed an apparent desire to preserve Yugoslavia's unity against secessionist forces. But in practice the Yugoslav army, the JNA, of which he had seized control despite internal opposition, did exactly the opposite. On 27 August 1991 it attacked the Croatian town of Vukovar and then, on 17 October, Dubrovnik. The siege of Vukovar ended on 17 November with the massacre of several hundred hospital patients, these criminal deeds being the work of the militias, and particularly of Arkan's Tigers (cf. Chapter IV). In some of the neighbouring villages, other missions of ethnic cleansing took place at the same time. For their part, the Croats tried to take control of Krajina. International attempts to mediate barely managed to bring the crisis to a halt, while both Serbs and Croats sought to gain as much territory as possible. The major European nations did nothing to rally resources that could have put a stop to the war.

Croatia was supported by Germany and Italy, while France, England, and Spain proved well disposed towards Serbia if not complicit with it.

Some months later, Bosnia–Hercogovina's declaration of independence on 15 October 1991, soon recognised by the European Union, provoked the outbreak of war in the region.[56] From 6 April the JNA began the siege of Sarajevo while ethnic cleansing operations were undertaken along the whole length of the Drina valley in Eastern Bosnia. At the beginning of 1993 the Croats proceeded to penetrate central Bosnia using the same methods as the Serbs, burning houses, killing their inhabitants and so on. Forced likewise to defend themselves, the Bosnian Muslims, rallied by Alija Izetbegovic, in turn committed atrocities against Serbs and Croatians. The massacres seemed in this way to have been propagated by mimicry, in a 'macabre round dance'[57] in which all the protagonists ended up resembling each other. History repeating itself? This land of Bosnia, which had been the stage for unspeakable acts of cruelty during the Second World War, was experiencing horror once more, with slaughter sometimes occurring in the same villages as it had fifty years earlier.

Towards the destruction of the Inyenzi.   In Rwanda the Arusha agreements of August 1993 had permitted a glimpse of a real hope of peace after three years of war. A consensual equilibrium seemed finally to be established between the main actors: President Habyarimana and his group, his internal opponents, and the RPF. In the streets of Kigali the crowd welcomed the compromise joyfully, relieved to see the end of the conflict that had left several thousand dead and hundreds of thousands displaced. In the throes of such public expressions of joy and relief, who could have imagined that nine months later the blood would flow again on all sides? History holds in store some astonishing reversals. In reality hardly had the agreements been signed than radicals from the opposing factions were already seeking to disqualify them. A large number of Habyarimana's soldiers were frustrated at his decision to accept the agreements when the army had not in fact been beaten. Officers and various government officials also feared the consequences of their application, in finding themselves obliged in some cases to give up their positions to compatriots returning from exile. Politicians too feared coming under scrutiny for their involvement in the commission of various crimes.

Finally, political events in neighbouring Burundi were once again to have dramatic repercussions on Rwanda. On 21 October 1993 a putsch of Tutsi officers put an end to the attempt to democratise power undertaken by President Melchior Ndadaye: he was assassinated, and Burundi plunged once more into a horrendous episode of massacres, to which the international community was totally indifferent. In Rwanda, with mirror image symmetry, these events immediately sparked political radicalisation that would further compromise the Arusha agreements. Indeed, the Rwandan Hutu extremists read into events taking place in Burundi the urgent need to defend themselves against the Tutsi enemy, threatening them not just from the outside (RPF) but also from the inside. Hadn't they been saying all along 'you can't trust the "*Inyenzi*"' (cockroaches)? And Hutu opponents of the regime who refused this ethnic line could no longer make themselves heard, or even began to acknowledge that there was indeed a Tutsi threat.

In short, a new threshold had just been crossed: the number of Rwandans still hoping that national reconciliation was possible was dwindling, while many simply no longer believed in it. The extremists were galvanised. Two days after Ndadaye's assassination, the first public meeting of Hutu Power was held at Kigali, this group bringing together Hutu radicals in an attempt to overcome all political divisions between Hutus. The keynote policy of Hutu Power was clear: to dispose physically of the Tutsi menace. Had its leaders already decided, then, to launch an attack in the near future?

Whether they had or not, the assassination some months later of the Rwandan President Habyarimana, whose plane was shot down as it landed at Kigali airport on 6 April 1994, gave them the pretext they needed. It has never been clearly established who was responsible for this attack, and the issue has caused deep controversy ever since.[58] Whatever accusations were made, the immediate effects of this event are well known. As in Burundi some months earlier, the death of the President immediately provoked massacres. From 7 April hundreds of Tutsis were killed in the streets of Kigali, along with some Hutus, among them the Prime Minister Agathe Uwilingiyimana. The same day ten UNAMIR Belgian Blue Helmets were also murdered. On 8 April a provisional government was set up in Kigali, made up of political representatives who, within each of the principal political parties, were hostile to national reconciliation, and of which Jean Kambanda became Prime Minister. Even though his name did not appear on the list of members, the Defence Minister's former cabinet director, Colonel Théoneste Bagosora, appeared to be its mastermind.

The new authorities from then on repeatedly called upon the population to defend itself against the Tutsi danger and the Hutu opposition, summoning the public at large to participate actively in their elimination. But no one could yet imagine the scale on which these massacres would occur. For Gérard Prunier, those organising them had above all planned an event along the lines of 'a sort of political Saint Bartholomew's Day'.[59] A massacre of some thousands of people, seeking out primarily elites and senior management, in short what James Gow described in the case of Yugoslavia as an 'elitocide'. But in Rwanda this process did not stop, gaining in scope from elimination to extermination: the process accelerated with staggering momentum over the course of three months, rising from several thousand victims to a figure somewhere between 500,000 and 800,000 deaths.[60] The massacres thus took on an unprecedented scale, even as compared with Burundi, which itself had seen an episode of mass killing in 1972 on a scale hitherto unknown in the region. Between 10 and 22 April the massacres gained a foothold in other regions of Rwanda, namely Kivungo, Cyangugu and Kibuye. On 18 April they reached Butare in the south of the country.

This war against the enemy within did not, however, hinder the progression of the RPF towards the capital. The Rwandan army was regularly defeated by Paul Kagamé's Tutsi soldiers. On the way the latter committed atrocities, mainly against Hutus but also against Tutsis. According to Abdul Ruzibiza, a former lieutenant in Kagamé's army, the Armée Nationale du Rwanda (ANR) purposely slaughtered civilian populations, as much to pillage their belongings and subjugate them as to make them flee, with the aim of enabling Tutsis from abroad who wanted to return to Rwanda to take possession of their land.[61] He qualifies these massacres of Hutus committed by Kagamé's men as 'genocide'. By Ruzibiza's account, these atrocities certainly helped to radicalise Hutu extremists between 1990 and 1993. He thus deems that Kagamé to some extent 'provoked' the mass killing of Tutsis and thus bears partial responsibility for the unleashing of the genocide. This is one of the bases for the theory of the 'double genocide' of Hutus against Tutsis as well as RPF Tutsis against Hutus.[62]

The violence perpetrated by RPF soldiers against civilian populations does not, however, appear to have been of the same nature as that committed by Hutu extremists against the Tutsi minority. Although the latter seem indeed to have set off a genocidal process to get rid of the Rwandan Tutsis for good, the RPF soldiers instead used systematic techniques to terrorise civilians to seize power once and for all. And so the two camps engaged in total combat, both resorting to extreme methods of violence but having different dynamics. As in many armed conflicts, a distinction must be made between practices of massacre that aim to subjugate or eradicate the enemy group (cf. Chapter 6). But it was Kagamé's strategy that ended up paying off. At the end of April the RPF soldiers already controlled the east of the country. On 4 July they took control of Kigali.

Refusing the spiral of mass murder. These three succinct narratives tell us almost nothing about what really goes on in time of war, what the real underlying issues are that might explain how things can overflow into massacre. From one day to the next, war transforms the fate of individuals, turning some into fighters and some into victims. In both the literal and figurative' senses, the war will crush them: it will annihilate them under its bombs or bullets just as it crushes them psychologically. War reifies personalities: each individual is reduced to the status of patriot, traitor or enemy. Whether for or against war, individuals are recruited into a role or function. Do they have any room left for manoeuvre, to refuse to participate? Several examples confirm that indeed they do.

In Germany thousands of young people refused to enrol in the Wehrmacht, and were imprisoned in concentration camps. In Serbia more than 100,000 young people refused to join the army to take part in Milososvic's war, while nearly 40,000 others deserted.[63] In Rwanda some officers refused to participate in Colonel Bagosora's hunting down of the Tutsis. These examples of refusal, even disobedience, prove that some individuals are capable of saying no to violence, despite the risk of marginalisation or punishment. But they swim against the tide. So while the political circumstances of the moment should impose compliance on the group, their moral or political resistance, even if limited, shows just to what extent human beings remain able to fly in the face of any social determinism. As the American psychologist Ervin Staub has noted, 'the courage needed [to limit violence] is not necessarily a willingness to put one's life on the line. It may be the courage to oppose the group and endanger one's status or career.'[64]

Nevertheless, these oppositions rarely succeed in halting the dynamic of collective and state-organised violence. War's peculiarity is to push the mobilisation of the group to extreme limits, pitting the cohesion of the self against the enemy 'them'. The figures of the enemy constructed in peacetime become realities in wartime: the prophecy can, in the end, materialise. This is unfortunate for all those who have already been depicted as enemies! War rapidly destroys old solidarities, annihilating any remaining community or social links with the previously designated victims. The documentary film made by the Norwegian anthropologist Tone Bringa during the Bosnian war clearly shows how friendly relations between neighbours within the same village can be totally destroyed by the outbreak of war (see box).

When war turns neighbours into enemies

The Norwegian anthropologist Tone Bringa's film *We Are All Neighbours*, is set in January 1993 against a background of war in Bosnia between Croats and Muslims. Over the course of several visits to the region, Bringa observes how relationships evolved between inhabitants of one village. Two thirds of the inhabitants there were Muslim, and the other third were Catholic. Conversions between religions had taken place in both directions. At the start of the film we meet a relatively old woman who is visiting her oldest friend in the village, a Catholic. They have been neighbours and known each other for forty years: they are like sisters. 'Whatever happens, we will always have our coffee together,' they say. In the distance we can hear gunfire.

A man we have previously watched cutting wood has just left for the front. The war is getting closer: fighting had broken out the previous night in a nearby village. It was Croats attacking Muslims. In the village fear starts to spread. The two old friends can no longer be seen chatting together. Some houses belonging to Muslims are burning somewhere nearby. Some of the inhabitants have been massacred. This happens just 4 kilometres away from the two women's homes. Someone shouts 'I am afraid: afraid that the same thing will happen here.'

People are afraid to go to their local market in the neighbouring village as they are used to doing. The whole area seems completely disrupted: refugees can be seen passing in the street in both directions, not knowing where to go to find safety. Everyone is terrified. A young Muslim woman remarks 'People have withdrawn inside themselves. They can't relax. They are suffocating inside. Whatever our nationality, we all feel fear and panic.'

Neighbours start distrusting each other. Croatian inhabitants are nowhere to be seen. Muslim men keep watch in patrols. The old Muslim woman interviewed at the start of the film affirms: 'We thought it all came from the Chetniks (Serb nationalists) but not from our Croatian neighbours. Before, we shared the good times and the bad. We never imagined it would be like this. We've got to go beyond this. We hardly wish anyone good-day or good-evening any more. Suddenly people have a different look about them, their faces have changed. For me it all happened in one day. It is indescribable.' She tries to call her old friend, sure that she is at home. But her friend does not come out. From then on, the two old women who were like sisters no longer converse. At night the Muslim men take turns standing guard. Nobody really sleeps any more in the village.

The Croatian fighters finally arrive one day. They burn the Muslims' houses and kill some of them. The others are forced to flee. The scene is one of desolation, but the Croat houses are spared. And the survivors are forced to flee.

Tone Bringa, *We Are All Neighbours*, 1993. See also her book *Being Muslim the Bosnian Way: Identity and Community in a Central Bosnian Village*, Princeton University Press, 1995.

The new universe of war. More generally, the state of war disturbs not only relationships to others, but also to space and time. Space can be synonymous with insecurity (places that can no longer be frequented) or refuge (trying to find shelter). Time becomes uncertainty: no one really knows what tomorrow will bring. Whole populations can in this way be taken over by various depressive states, or can exhibit hyper-vigilance (of which the most obvious symptom is insomnia). Time seems suspended, and yet life continues, despite death that is constantly stalking, taking one by surprise, whether or not one is at 'the front'.

Going to war in reality is to penetrate another universe in which human behaviour is completely transformed. Can anyone having known only peace really understand the inner workings of war? War's special trick is to push to incandescence the *imaginaire* of fear (described in Chapter I): it is 'them' or 'us'. In the name of this security dilemma, everything becomes justifiable. War is thus a formidable lever of inhibition and prohibition. However trite it may seem to recall, it is staggering to consider how, in just a few hours or a few days, a man who just before had lived a peaceful existence, respectful of everyone around, becomes a killer. Killing his fellow man is no longer a crime, but has become a duty or mission.

The lifting of the prohibition on murder brings with it, and authorises, other transgressions: breaking into houses, taking someone else's food and belongings, raping women (sometimes men too), etc. This other that one can so easily defile, rape, kill, is in fact no longer one's fellow man, but a 'barbarian' to be exterminated. Propaganda has already done its work in the lead-up to war. Or is it in fact wartime that produces a hideous construction of the other to be destroyed, making it easier to accept the practices aiming to annihilate him? Propaganda is not only a factor that always precedes war, it is a dynamic construction that evolves with circumstances, maintaining all the while certain constants, once it has started, the state of war 'regenerates' the propaganda itself. The more horrible war becomes, the more it requires propaganda to rationalise such practices.

And it is in this way that massacre, whether perpetrated on the battlefield or not, becomes an integral part of war. In fact, war masks the realities of massacre in at least two ways. First, through rhetoric. Massacre takes on the appearance of an act of war. During the Polish campaign in 1939, shootings of civilians were justified in the name of the fight against 'snipers', a security obsession directly traceable to practices used by the German army at the beginning of the invasion of Belgium in 1914.[65] More than a year later, as war raged between Germany and the Soviet Union, Himmler noted in his personal diary (dated 18 December 1941) on the subject of the Jews: 'Jewish question. Exterminate like partisans.'[66] To what extent was he convinced by what he was writing? Nobody can say. These few words scrawled in his diary after a meeting with Hitler could express his personal conviction as much as an order to be transmitted to his subordinates. In any event, the massacre of the Jews, which had already claimed some tens of thousands of lives through shooting in Soviet territory, was envisaged as a war tactic to be deployed against supposed 'partisans'.

In the second place, the conditions in which war is conducted make acts of massacre 'disappear' from the field of vision of the outside observer. In the name of security, the territory becomes a no-go zone, with access to journalists forbidden. But who knows what could happen there? War masks massacre because it is often conducted 'behind closed doors'. By keeping any third party that might otherwise present itself at arm's length, it favours face-to-face confrontation between bully and victims. In such a confined space, massacre can occur more easily.[67]

However, let us not claim that war camouflages all ongoing massacres. The position of any external observer itself needs to be scrutinised. To what extent does such an observer really want to 'see' what is happening? It is true that the Nazis did everything they could to dissemble the reality of the extermination of the Jews, if only so as not to frighten the victims. But the same does not hold true for Rwanda, where massacres were perpetrated openly, in the streets of Kigali and elsewhere. In this case the 'behind closed doors' scenario does not exist: massacre is a public activity in which the population is invited to participate. And yet those who did perceive the gravity of ensuing events were not heard. Are we forced to conclude that we refuse to see the horror of a situation in a country that we feel does not concern us? There are none so deaf as those who will not hear.

But as we have seen, the passivity of the third party generally constitutes an aggravating factor of the victims' fate. Who, then, is left to shatter the wall of silence and indifference? Who is left to become this third party that could, as a last resort and despite the tragedy foretold, alert the world?

Telling the world: a last resort?

This ultimate third party is first a witness that has survived the massacre. More often than not, and whatever the method for mass murder chosen, there is someone who makes a chance escape, through luck, complicity or strategy. If still capable of talking, he will want to tell the world what has happened to him, to those who have died and with whom he was to have been killed, and to all the others still in danger. Another possible witness is someone who has been a bystander in the massacre. The 'bystander' is not just a spectator: he can decide to speak, even to act. By virtue of his profession—diplomat or engineer, doctor or nurse—he is close to the theatre of operations. He is present when the condemned pass by, he hears gunfire, he sees the corpses. And he finds this 'spectacle' so unbearable that he wishes to speak, even if this entails overstepping his professional duty to remain silent. Over and above his function—and in some cases, *because* of his function (for example when he is a member of a humanitarian organisation) the main thing is to bear witness, to tell people as quickly as possible so that 'something' can be done to stop the carnage. The witness's narrative is paramount in bringing the massacre to a halt, when there is still time. But will anyone believe him?

The extermination of the Jews: discovering the horror...and then doing nothing about it. News of the massacres of Jews in Europe posed this type of problem. Hitler wanted to keep the mass murder of Jews a secret. But his extermination programme quickly reached several European capitals, particularly in neutral countries (Geneva, Stockholm and Istanbul). From these cities the news reached London and Washington. So in spite of the war, Nazi-occupied territories in central Europe were not, in fact, hermetically sealed. Witnesses of mass extermination included German military personnel, representatives of satellite states of the Reich, and even survivors. Information about the massacres perpetrated by the *Einsatzgruppen* was the first to spread. Then news started to circulate about killings using gas. The first distribution networks for this news were Jewish organisations like the Bund in Poland, which sent an important document to London in May 1942. This described notably that in 'November and December 1941 massacres of Jews had begun in Polish territories annexed by the Reich. Executions were perpetrated using gas in the village of Chemlo.'[68]

The second network was the Polish resistance itself, which transmitted firsthand reports quite regularly to the Polish government in exile in Britain. One of their best agents, Jan Karski, brought his own personal testimony to London in November 1942, having managed to gain entry to the Warsaw ghetto and the Belzec extermination camp. But those receiving the information didn't believe it. These reports that arrived one after the other, and started to accumulate from 1942 onwards only aroused incredulity, even among Jewish circles in Jerusalem, London and New York.

Walter Laqueur underscores this phenomenon: a credible piece of information is not necessarily given credence. When Jan Karski was received in London by Justice Frankfurter, and reported that mass executions were taking place in Poland, the latter told him 'that he did not believe him. When Karski protested, Frankfurter explained that he did not imply that Karski had in any way not told the truth, he simply meant that he could not believe him—there was a difference.'[69] Meanwhile, Thomas Mann had already claimed over the BBC airwaves in December 1941 and January 1942 that the Jews were being killed *en masse*. The same was true of the *Daily Telegraph* newspaper, which announced on 25 June that 'more than 700,000 Polish Jews had been assassinated by the Germans in one of the most extensive massacres in world history' and then on 30 June suggested a figure of 1 million victims. These articles represent a turning point, the newspaper considering that the Jewish massacres were not 'traditional' pogroms, but that it was the Nazis' plan to eliminate the Jewish 'race' from the European continent. On 30 June and 2 July the *New York Times* fell into line, but published the information on the inside pages, which may seem surprising. 'The editors quite obviously did not know what to make of [these reports],' remarks Laqueur. If it was true that a million people had been killed, this clearly should have been front page news; it did not, after all, happen every day. If it was not true, the story should not have been published at all. Since they were not certain they opted for a compromise; to publish it, but not in a conspicuous place. Thus it was implied that the paper had reservations about the report: quite likely the stories contained some truth, but probably were exaggerated'.[70]

The gap between credibility and belief poses the particularly complex problem of the different ways an item of information may be received. By what tortuous route can individuals finally manage to 'integrate' a piece of news that has so far escaped their field of consciousness? I will outline in this regard three phases of unequal duration, the length of each phase depending on the individual crisis concerned. The first of these is that of *resistance to the information*. In the case of the extermination of the Jews, this is expressed as an attitude of pure incredulity: the unprecedented nature of the massacre makes it simply incredible. The information is taken to be exaggerated, so that for example it is recognised that while the Jews were certainly being mistreated by the Nazis, they were probably only being subjected to hard labour. In this refractory stage, inherited modes of information reception play a major role. An example of this occurred during the First World War when in 1916 the British press propagated the 'news' that the Germans were burning corpses of soldiers to produce lubricants such as glycerine or soap. Even a respectable newspaper like the *Financial Times* hawked stories about how the Kaiser himself had ordered the torture of three-year-old children, while the *Daily Telegraph* reported that the Austrians and the Bulgarians had killed 700,000 Serbs using asphyxiating gas. But all this proved to be untrue, and was recognised as such after the war. We swear we will never again be taken in by such ineptitudes. In other instances this phase of resistance to the news item is based on an ideological defence: thus, over the years Western intellectuals did not want to see the mass repression imposed by Communist regimes because they thought that their leaders were necessarily on the side of 'right', and were for the progress of mankind. Resistance can also be based on indifference, which might also have its roots in representations of the past, such as the seemingly universal each of interest in something happening in another part of the world, whether in Africa or elsewhere.

In a second phase the news item begins to make a groove in the vast interchange of information and rumours borne by a state of war.

It is in this phase of a *power struggle* that the news item ends up commanding the attention of a growing number of individuals. The information increasingly gets a hold of the imagination in a quantitative sense, being the direct result of an accumulation of eyewitness accounts. In the case of the extermination of Jews, Renée Poznanski shows clearly how successive reports, even when these are sometimes mutually contradictory, gradually reinforce the same idea: the Jews were killed *en masse* on Polish territory. In this way the news item is virtually constructed by a cumulative process, in a series of brushstrokes. For example, she remarks, The 'Bund's letter certainly did not succeed in imposing reality on those who refused to see it, but it nevertheless created a climate in which people receiving the reports that followed had already had their eyes opened to some extent.'[71] In assimilating a truly 'new' piece of information, it is actually a psychological process that is set in motion: the information 'incubates' in individuals' consciousness, thus fully erasing prior modes of reception.

The third phase that finally ensues is that of actually *becoming aware*, during the course of which previously intact defence mechanisms start to break down so the present reality can be absorbed. At this stage, a curious phenomenon often occurs: a report or narrative, or an event that very often only confirms what is already known, serves nevertheless as a 'revelatory' event. It is as if for realisation actually to burst out into the open a cathartic moment is required for it to assert itself. For example, in Jewish circles in America the fundamental step towards realising that Jews were being exterminated occurred when a cable was received from Dr Gerhard Riegner, the World Jewish Congress representative in Geneva. In this telegram he conveyed information of a report he had been given by a German industrialist of a plan to exterminate all European Jews, who had been rounded up to this end in Eastern Europe in 1942; the report talked of the use of prussic acid.

However, while this piece of news aroused strong feeling(s) in the World Jewish Congress, it still only prompted incredulity among American and British leaders. In fact, the moment of realisation of course varies according to whether individuals are directly concerned or not by the news, and more generally according to their social background and what countries are involved. For each instance one could write an entire work of international cultural sociology about how information is received. The process of realisation is thus a building of awareness that is gradually propagated, encountering resistance here and there, before finally appearing as an incontestable fact. The common declaration signed by eleven allied governments and the Committee for Free France on 17 December 1942 bears witness to just such growing awareness. In it we read that the attention of these governments had been drawn to 'numerous reports from Europe that the German authorities, not content with denying to persons of Jewish race in all the territories over which their barbarous rule has been extended the most elementary human rights, are now carrying into effect Hitler's oft-repeated intention to exterminate the Jewish people in Europe. From all the occupied countries Jews are being transported, in conditions of appalling horror and brutality, to Eastern Europe. ... None of those taken away are ever heard of again. The able-bodied are slowly worked to death in labour camps. The infirm are left to die of exposure and starvation, or are deliberately massacred in mass executions. The number of victims of these bloody cruelties is reckoned in many hundreds of thousands of entirely innocent men, women, and children.'[72]

This statement was given wide publicity. But as things turned out, the allies did not take any specific action aimed at halting the Nazi action, even though other reports arrived in 1943 and 1944, including one about the operations at Auschwitz. For Jewish organisations, the aim was no longer to inform, but to incite to action. When the Nazis took direct control of Hungary in 1944, there could no longer be any doubt as to the fate of the Jews in that country. The Jewish Agency in Jerusalem therefore asked London to bombard the railways leading to Auschwitz. But the Royal Air Force replied that this operation was technically impossible. And yet documentation confirms that British planes came to bomb an armaments factory situated not far from the camp.[73] This morally shocking passivity of the Allies prompted much controversy, in the United States also, about the reasons for the 'abandonment' of the Jews.[74] The only 'explanation' of any worth is a strategic one: the allies were engaged in 1942 in a total war against the Axis powers which they were not sure they would win. Their main aim was therefore to gather as many troops as they could to destroy the German and Japanese war machines. In the context of total war Auschwitz did not, in their eyes, have any strategic value.

Some have stated after the event that, had it been feasible to smuggle television cameras into Auschwitz, 'the world' would have understood earlier, and acted as a result. It is true that information about the extermination of the Jews, while it was known about from 1942 onwards, remained 'abstract'. It was an accepted idea, but not a tangible reality. It is also maintained that images making the tragedy in progress visible would have been necessary actually to trigger the emotion required to make people react. In the case of the Jews these images came when it was too late, that is, just as the war was ending, when on 15 April 1945 British troops discovered the camp at Bergen-Belsen. In the days that followed, news of the horrors at Belsen spread through the entire world: hundreds of journalists and photographers then visited the camp. But the tragic paradox of this is that Belsen had nothing to do with the destruction of Jews! It was not an extermination camp, and not even a concentration camp, but a 'krankenlager', a so-called camp for the sick who were left to die of hunger and cold.

Bosnia: knowing… and pretending. Since then we have learnt to put in perspective any belief we may have held as to the power attributed to images of the suffering and death of the other: it is certainly not the case that it will always trigger a realisation working in favour of the victims. The idea of the 'global village', in which the prodigious explosion of the media at the end of the twentieth century should enable warnings of any imminent massacre to be broadcast, thanks to a television camera constantly on hand to record and denounce the horror, is pure illusion. Consider the case of Bosnia. Here we can also observe a phase during which resistance to the information about 'ethnic cleansing' predominated.[75] Here again, in the short term, interpretative templates of the past obstructed any comprehension of events. Hadn't the Serbs consistently been on the side of France since the First World War? President François Mitterrand undertook to remind them of this, thus showing a degree of solidarity and seemingly remaining unmoved by the news coming in of their horrific deeds. The Sarajevo siege was soon to place 'proof' before the eyes of the entire world. The television cameras were right there. The Bosnian television could continue to broadcast from a bomb shelter. This is an absolutely exceptional case in the history of all sieges of towns, in that we could view 'live coverage' from the inside of the very town being besieged.

So the television in this case played the leading third party role, as witness of the tragedy unfolding. Televiewers the world over were able to cohabit for over three years with Sarajevo inhabitants, under threat day and night from Serbian cannons and automatic rifles positioned at high points around the town. We witnessed the terrible living conditions and daily suffering, and the constant risk ordinary people ran of being killed by snipers who shot at random at any passers-by brave enough to cross a street within range of their bullets. These images of violence and death did not, however, provoke any general response from the major powers to force the Serbs to lift the siege. The prevailing discourse of experts and journalists then was that the conflict was difficult to read, that each of the actors had its share of responsibility for the crisis, and that any external intervention risked finding itself enmeshed in a fatal dynamic of which the Balkan region alone knew the secret, etc.

And so the world 'got used to' the Sarajevo siege. In time these repetitive images ended up, paradoxically, creating a smokescreen, and so in effect masking what was happening elsewhere. Instead of revealing issues pertinent to the conflict, focussing the media on the town under siege did nothing but dissemble a deeper dynamic. On the one hand, hardly any journalists took any interest in the situation in Kosovo, even though a crisis had started in this province and the situation there was becoming increasingly tense. But the peaceful resistance of Albanians, prey increasingly to an ever more openly expressed Serbian aggression, was of interest to no one, except via a few rare newspaper articles. 'We will go to Kosovo when the blood starts flowing', one French television journalist told me. The leader of the Albanian resistance, Ibrahim Rugova, who sought to alert the Western capitals to the gravity of the situation in Kosovo, barely obtained an audience in Paris, London or Washington.

On the other hand, the media's focussing on Sarajevo obscured what was happening inside Bosnia itself. From 1991 NGOs like Helsinki Watch and Médecins sans Frontières (MSF) had already begun collecting information attesting that serious human rights violations were taking place. But the journalists who actually set out to investigate in 'deep Bosnia' were extremely rare. Roy Gutman, a reporter from the American daily *Newsday*, is one of these exceptions.[76] He explained that since journalists were not allowed in (between April and July 1992), the only means of reconstructing events was to interview refugees fleeing *en masse* from Bosnia. Gutman did not rely on images, but instead worked with the testimony of witnesses escaping from a zone where he could not go. Since he could speak Serbian, he was able to collect these narratives and discard whatever he deemed to be rumour or pure exaggeration. He also made use of NGOs, through which he was able to gather information and meet victims. He attributed great importance to the unravelling of messages emanating through propaganda and official statements. Finally, on 19 July 1992, he published his first article revealing the existence of 'death camps' set up by the Serbs, primarily the one in Omarska, located on the site of a former iron mine north of Banja Luka (a town of some 200,000 inhabitants of which the Serbs had taken control).

Two weeks later he reported that massacres of Muslims had been carried out in the region. Then came the discovery of practices of systematic rape in the regions of Split and Tuzla. In short, his research on the ground, like that of his colleague David Rieff,[77] revealed the basic facts of what was starting to be referred to as 'ethnic cleansing'. Roy Gutman and David Rieff embody, in the case of the war in Bosnia, the faces of witness-journalism that, by taking the victims' side, calls for international mobilisation to halt the aggression to which they are being subjected. In the wake of their reporting, Channel 4 and ITN (International Television Network) television camera teams were to broadcast the first images of these camps. On 26 July 1992 the Bosnian government published a list of 100 detention camps that it handed over to the United Nations Security Council. Some journalists and human rights activists likened them then to Nazi concentration camps, even though the similarity is debatable. Here again, we find ourselves reading the present with spectacles from the past. Their aim was also to confirm, as Gutman and Rieff maintain, that a genocide was being committed in Bosnia in order to force the 'international community' to intervene.

But despite their efforts, and the televised reporting that followed these revelations, the major powers had no wish to risk engaging in military combat in a war they did not consider to be their own, and which they were sure was going to escalate.[78] However, the 'international community' was beyond reproach as regards not having taken an interest in the Bosnian crisis. The UN intervened on several occasions, designating the Serbs as aggressors, imposing economic sanctions on them, decreeing an embargo on weapons, and sending in armed peacekeeping forces (Unprofor), etc. But the deployment of Unprofor (of which France took command in 1992) was not sufficient in itself to check the conflict: its mandate, which never explicitly included protection of civilians, depended on a consensual rationale of concerted action between the protagonists, and not on a rationale of confrontation. The setting up by the UN of the so-called 'safe zones' around the towns where many Bosnian Muslims sought refuge (Srebrenica, Zepa) made no fundamental change to this logic.[79]

The creation by the UN of an International Criminal Tribunal on 22 February 1993 is revealing of this same state of mind: the international community couldn't find the means to intervene in any decisive way in the crisis. In fact, by setting up this tribunal—which was indeed an important step in the development of an international justice—the United Nations were arming themselves with a new instrument for judging crimes that had been, and would subsequently be, committed in Yugoslavia, but not for preventing them from taking place.[80] The result: on the ground, the Blue Helmets were powerless witnesses of atrocities perpetrated against the civilian population, as their mission did not authorise them to intervene. The film *Warriors* by the English director Peter Kosminsky demonstrates with stark realism the dramatic and poignant character of the situations lived on the ground by the Blue Helmets. It is the same rationale of passive presence that allowed the Srebrenica massacre to happen (13–15 July 1995) in the proximity of a platoon of Dutch Blue Helmets. Perpetrated by General Mladic's Bosnian Serb troops, the slaughter of around 7,500 Muslims (the largest slaughter in Europe since the end of the Second World War) remains symbolic of the passivity of the international community in this war.[81]

Is this to say that the media coverage of the Bosnian crisis had no influence? Such a judgement must be discussed. While they did not force the major powers fundamentally to change their stance, the media did force them into some gesticulation. As one diplomat commented with rare frankness: 'We would have preferred to do nothing. But public opinion, sensitised by the media, would not have permitted this. ... We were therefore condemned to doing some-thing, but something ineffective.'[82] The dramatisation of certain events probably provided new impetus, as for example following the explosion of a mortar shell in the teemingly populated Sarajevo market place on 5 February 1994 (causing sixty-eight deaths and some 200 wounded). Filmed images of this event were immediately dispatched around the world. The consequences of the bombard-ment, of which the identity of its authors aroused lively debate,[83] were significant, starting with the first armed involvement of NATO in Europe (and not only of the UN) leading to the first American strikes against Bosnian Serb positions.[84] There also ensued a coali-tion of Muslim Bosnians and Croatian forces as part of the US ini-tiative (agreement in Washington on 1 March 1994) and a new international peace initiative. But were these decisions not already being prepared? Maybe one day research into the archives of the ministries involved will tell us—in which case the role of the media will have been above all to 'crystallise' measures that were already being arranged.

Rwanda: knowing... and leaving. The media's treatment of events in 1994 in Rwanda appear very different. While there was indeed resistance to understanding the violence that broke out following the attack on the president's plane, this was mostly due to ignorance of the realities of this country. Who then knew of the existence of Rwanda before this date, besides the Belgians and some experts in their field? In what part of Africa is Rwanda located? Analysis of the early television reports shows that journalists seemed to know nothing of the history of this country and France's support for the late President's regime.[85] The kind of explanation most often put forward revolved around the tribal hatred thought to be so typical of the African continent, a refrain taken up by journalists and political leaders alike.

Resisting comprehension of the event, we immediately insert it within Western representations of Africa, these always being presented on the level of natural and social calamities: drought, famine, AIDS, ethnic strife, etc. The dominant tone is therefore one of fatalism. Once again television plays on the heartstrings of emotion and compassion. To the viewer TV hardly offers the analytical tools needed to understand the issues surrounding bloodshed that is taking place in the country concerned, although it may be suggested that the violence is of the utmost gravity. Resistance to the event manifests itself again in the conscious refusal to explain 'conflict between Blacks'. One journalist from the French public channel *France 2 Television* bore this out when he claimed that his hierarchical superior, on sending him to Rwanda, clearly explained that his assignment was to 'cover' the departure of the French in the context of the Amaryllis operation, and to leave the Rwandan conflict alone.[86] The Amaryllis operation was being led by the French army which, over and above the evacuation of Western nationals, included the discreet departure of the deceased president's family.[87]

Nonetheless, the force of the event rapidly became apparent, not so much through television as through printed press coverage, which soon devoted a relatively large amount of space to Rwanda, un-usually large, anyway, in the context of wars and other events occurr-ing in Africa. Several special envoys from mainstream European papers were witnesses to the tragedy. The massacres did not occur behind closed doors, so it was possible, at great risk and peril to themselves, for these witnesses to realise quickly what was going on. Through their reporting, descriptions of massacres were plentiful, and the event thus began to assume considerable importance.[88] To start with, articles appearing in the press referred to massacres at Kigali, and then from 19 April onwards in the provinces. These first testimonials, while they all gave full coverage to the gravity of the violence, nevertheless differ in the manner in which they regard the relationship between war and massacre.

There were two opposing ways of reading the situation: either the journalist would emphasise the war between the RPF and govern-ment forces, and massacre tended to 'disappear' or take second place to the rationale of political and military confrontation; or the jour-nalist drew attention to the massacres *as* massacres, an atrocious prac-tice against a defenceless population.[89] Their writings differ again according to whether or not they take up the theme of 'ancestral hatred' or the official explanation offered by the authorities, which claimed the massacres were a spontaneous reaction of the population to the Tutsi military threat. In spite of these conflicting interpretations, Marc Le Pape observed: 'The immediate story of the massacres could be undertaken: by journalists from the printed press when these were working as witnesses, as eye-witnesses of the event where massacres had gone on for several months.'[90] These different accounts have some features in common: the massacres were all committed by groups obeying orders from their chiefs; among these chiefs were local authorities (burgomasters and local political leaders). Machetes and knives were mainly used in the killing, but rifles and grenades were used too. In several instances, both gendarmes and the army participated. Whole families were brutally executed. Not a single witness reported seeing a killing that appeared to be spontaneous and disorderly.

Johanna Siméant's research, which examines the way in which the televised French evening news referred to events in Rwanda, complements that of Marc Le Pape. 'The French televised news coverage was roughly the same as American news programmes: a coverage that focussed almost entirely on the evacuation of Western nationals following the coup that had claimed the lives of the Rwandan and Burundian presidents. It then practically abandoned Rwanda till the second week in May 1994, after which it increased again till the end of May.'[91] Very probably influenced by the reporting in the printed press, the television gradually changed its view of events. Having at their disposal very few images of massacres as such[92] and apparently not seeking to obtain any, it meanwhile gave voice on occasion to the experts on hand, like Philippe Gaillard of the International Committee of the Red Cross (ICRC), who declared that they were witnessing a 'manhunt for ethnic and political reasons'. Note that this account was not transmitted in image form, but delivered via telephone: television acting like radio.

Everything happened then as if this accumulation of accounts of massacres under way was changing the qualitative perception of the event. During the month of May, the realisation took hold that these systematic massacres were nothing less than genocide. The word was used at first randomly but then with increasing regularity. Here again the printed press was at the forefront; the Belgian daily *Le Soir* employed the word 'genocide' for the first time in its 13 April edition, and then the French daily *Libération* on 26 April. Some NGOs like Oxfam and Médecins sans Frontières also claimed that genocide was taking place in Rwanda, and called for international intervention. Television stations also began to invite personalities who used the word 'genocide' on their daily news programmes.

For instance, Bernard Kouchner on French TV channel TFI: 'It is close to being genocide and fascist methods' (26 April 1994). Philippe Douste-Blazy, Minister Delegate for Health, on France 2: 'We must stop the massacre, it is terrifying and terrible, the largest genocide of the end of the century' (14 May 1994). But even so, the major powers did not move. 'Is the world too tired to intervene?' asked journalist Ted Koppel, on 4 May, at the start of his interview with Boutros Boutros-Ghali, UN general secretary, on America's leading television channel ABC.[93] Rwanda and Bosnia were thus relegated to second place in the news line-up because of the deaths of automobile driver Ayrton Senna and of Jackie Kennedy. Even though the massacres had been going on for nearly four weeks, the UN Security Council had still not had any meaningful discussion about the situation in Rwanda.

Major-General Dallaire nevertheless sent several messages from Kigali to say that a force of 5,000 well-armed troops would suffice to halt the mass killings. According to him, because operations were centralised, halting the massacre in the capital would rapidly bring an end to the violence throughout the country.[94] The United States in particular opposed such a plan, but it was nonetheless well informed about the situation on the ground, as the remarkable research survey undertaken by Samantha Power has shown.[95] In December 1993 a CIA report revealed the import of 40 tons of small-sized arms. American intelligence announced in January 1994 that if the violence were rekindled, 'the worst case scenario would involve one half million people dying.'[96] But having been badly stung by its disastrous intervention in Somalia, the United States pleaded for non-intervention. And Washington forbade its diplomats to utter the word 'genocide' in relation to Rwanda: such a qualification of events would have obliged them to intervene in accordance with the 1948 Convention. In other respects, the Security Council hardly paid any attention to the Rwandan situation, since it was already preoccupied with the crises in Bosnia and in Haiti.

For Dallaire the decision made on 21 April to reduce the Unamir staff, because of the departure of the Belgian population, constituted the worst possible scenario: the perpetrators of the genocide could not have hoped for any better situation than being able to continue their task of 'pacification' unhindered. Faced with the UN's immobilism, Dallaire realised that only journalists were left to alert opinion. He helped them as much as he could, reckoning that one Western correspondent was worth a battalion on the ground.[97] Dallaire asked the United States once more to neutralise the propaganda station Radio Télévision Libre des Milles Collines by jamming the airwaves or destroying the whole installation with missile fire. Nothing was done, and a Pentagon official argued: 'Radios don't kill people, people kill people.'[98] Finally on 17 May, even though the massacres had been going on for more than six weeks, the Security Council voted in principle for the constitution of a Unamir 2 on the basis of Dallaire's plan, without knowing who would provide the men and the finance necessary for such an operation. In his press conference on 25 May, Boutros Boutros-Ghali was already assessing the damage: 'It is a failure not only for the United Nations; it is a failure for the international community. And all of us are responsible for this failure. Not only the great powers but the African powers, the nongovernmental organisations, all the international community. It is a genocide which has been committed. More than 200,000 people have been killed and the international community is still discussing what ought to be done.... Unfortunately, let us say with great humility, I failed. It is a scandal. I am the first one to say it.'[99]

It was the very first time that the world had lived through the perpetration of genocide 'with live coverage' as it were. It was impossible to say in this case: 'We didn't know.' However, accounts coming from Rwanda were not enough to mobilise the major powers to do anything to stop it.[100] True, there was France's intervention at the end of June 1994, which itself benefited from wide media coverage, including by television. Ten years later, the then Prime Minister, Edouard Balladur, strongly defended this operation, declaring that his objective was 'strictly humanitarian', and that France had moreover been alone in wanting to do something, while the other states were content to remain spectators of the drama.[101] But Operation

Turquoise, authorised by the UN and legitimate in its eyes, arrived too late: several hundred thousand people had already been killed. It appeared in addition to be highly ambiguous, in view of the support Paris was widely known to have given to President Habyarimana's regime.

So at the precise moment when French troops arrived in Rwanda, the RPF had practically won the war. While their intervention enabled some Tutsis to be saved, it also facilitated the hasty departure of about 2 million Hutus fleeing the country in fear of reprisals by the RPF. The confusion seemed to be total at this point since those who yesterday were in the bullying camp today appeared to be victims, and the more so because they were struck by a severe cholera epidemic. And the images finally coming out of Rwanda show not so much the victims of genocidal violence, but those who had participated as perpetrators or accomplices of that genocide!

The so-called 'CNN effect' and state indifference. In the three instances we have looked at so far, reports of massacres occurring have never managed to influence political and military decision-makers of the most powerful countries sufficiently for these to mobilise and put a stop to them; they have always come up with the same response, or rather the same non-response: either they have continued to wage war without making an effort to limit the destruction (as in the case of the Jews), or they rejected any idea of trying to conduct a timely and effective intervention (as in the case of Rwanda), or they become involved in the crisis but only take half-measures (as in the case of Bosnia). Their reactions thus pursue the passive or indifferent attitude they had shown before the crisis actually broke out.

An important fact sets the 1990s apart, however, from the 1940s: by the late twentieth century the NGOs and the media had acquired a strong capacity to enable reporting to have repercussions on the 'world scene'. NGOs and the media operated to some extent in tandem, a complex but complementary duo capable of arousing transnational public pressure likely to influence political and military decision-makers. But should we, for all that, conclude that there now exists what has been called the 'CNN effect', as if the invitation to political powers-that-be to intervene is being delivered *through media coverage* of a given crisis?

An in-depth survey conducted on the media-political conditions for the American intervention in Somalia would lead us to doubt such an assertion or in any case to put it in perspective.[102] Better, surely, to reverse the terms of this question, as Johanna Siméant rightly remarked: 'Rather than wondering whether better journalistic coverage would have brought about a more effective political response, shouldn't we ask instead to what extent a political response apt to qualify the situation would not have provided the structure for better media coverage'.[103] In the case of the Yugoslav crisis, pressure exerted by the media seems to have had, laboriously, some impact in 1995, and then again with NATO's air strikes in the Kosovo war in 1999. But while countries are doubtless taking the 'communication' factor into account much more today in their defence strategy and political mobilisation, this still does not mean that the development of the media has fundamentally modified their behaviour.

It is true, as Pierre Hassner remarked, that 'protestations and gestures of solidarity nowadays accompany more and more instances of famine and genocide where indifference can no longer hide behind ignorance. But whether this will result in a moral and objective consensus, and a legitimacy capable of bringing about or imposing cohesion between nations and groups in conflict, to arbitrate their differences, to judge and punish their aggressions and their crimes, … this must be an illusion and a mystification.'[104]

In the 1990s this passivity of spectator-nations was often explained by the fact that public opinion in Western countries would have been refractory to the idea that soldiers of these countries were killed in conflicts that did not concern them. This argument is mostly without foundation. And it does not enable comprehension of the passivity manifested by the allied forces with regard to the extermination of the Jews. The only way of explaining the indifference generally demonstrated by governments in such circumstances is simply to declare that their leaders do not have the political will to intervene, an inertia perfectly consistent with the dominant conception of their role in the international system. What are, in effect, the first missions devolved to modern states, if not to defend their own interests, their territory, their wealth, their economy, their culture, and in general, their own population?

To defend their interests and to make them prosper, countries could work together and form coalitions in all manner of multilateral cooperation deals. International law also recognises their right to resort to deploying armed forces for legitimate defensive purposes. Such are the basic principles of their *modus operandi* in the current world system. So at any moment protection of 'foreign' populations, that is those not under their direct authority, cannot be considered to be part of their principal mission. In this regard, inventing the 'right to intervene' amounts to seeking to impose on governments a responsibility to protect that goes against their 'political nature'.

For example, in a crisis situation such as the one in Rwanda, the first reflex of Western countries is not to try and cut off the warmongering party or put a stop to the massacre, but to save their own nationals from slaughter. If states intervene in this type of crisis, as happened in Kosovo in 1999, it is usually because they perceive there a direct or indirect interest. The prime motives for what we therefore call a 'military-humanitarian' intervention can be extremely varied: to gain a foothold in the region in question, to provide a strategic presence (control of part of the zone and/or access to its wealth), to halt the gearing up of a crisis to preclude their getting involved despite themselves or to stabilise the population on the ground to avoid a possible flow of refugees towards northern countries. This is why one of the basic questions posed by this type of operation is that of its *legitimacy* as shown by Nicholas Wheeler's interesting comparative study.[105]

Let us note again that American public opinion was only really prepared for the United States to stop the war in Bosnia when its television networks gave wide coverage to the accidental death of three senior civil servants near Sarajevo on 19 August 1995. As Richard Holbrook pointed out, the Bosnian war had just arrived in the United States, which itself determined President Clinton to go to war with the Serbs, having the feeling that he had the support of the American people.[106] It is also true that France, under President Chirac, was then resolved to show greater intransigence following the 'media humiliation' created by images of French soldiers held as prisoners of war by the Serbs. NATO's intervention that resulted from this in September 1995 was to be decisive for the lifting of the

Sarajevo siege. What had been deemed impossible or too risky over a period of more than three years of beating about the bush had just been accomplished in three weeks.

It is therefore rare that a 'humanitarian-military' intervention can be considered as disinterested on the part of governments, that is to say, as having as sole objective the saving of lives. This is what leads Samantha Power to conclude that the United States has always shown indifference to genocides and mass murders in the twentieth century, whatever the administration in power at the time. From Washington's point of view, 'the U.S. record is not one of failure. It is one of success.'[107] Such a statement applies not only to the United States but to all the other members of the UN Security Council and to the majority of governments. We are forced to conclude, then, that eyewitness accounts of massacres taking place have not played the role hoped for, of signalling distress to prevent the worst from happening. These accounts cannot claim to work in the present: they will be set down in history as reminders of the tragedy that was being acted out in the hurly-burly of the world.

IV

THE DYNAMICS OF MASS MURDER

As demonstrated earlier, massacre is the outcome both of a country's internal evolution and a favourable set of circumstances making up a particular regional and international context. But how, in real terms, does it take off? How does it gain in stature to become a full mass murder, to the tune of tens or hundreds or even thousands of separate spates of killing on both a small and larger scale? There is no longer any possible doubt that an organised policy of destruction of a particular group has been set in motion. We should note here also that this process of annihilation often goes hand in hand with the appropriation of wealth by this group: mass murder and mass theft often go together. We are moving inexorably, then, into the eye of a storm that is ravaging a country, if not an entire region. We are right in the time span—an instant or a longer spell—in which a group crosses the threshold and commits mass murder.

The collective dynamics of this process of extreme violence are certainly multiple: each event has its own story, depending on the country concerned.[1] At first glance the great country of Germany, already heavily industrialised, differs in every way from the much smaller and largely rural Rwanda. However, the diversity of the disparate historical trajectories does not mean that problems common to both countries cannot be singled out which are highly illuminating in an effort to construct a political sociology of mass murder. This chapter examines the dynamics of such phenomena from the standpoint of these collective rationales and from four points of view:

The core impulse. In the cases studied it stands out that the way massacres multiply is clearly not a random process generated of some

unknown tribal hatred or ancestral ethnicity, but a deliberate mobilisation launched to implement a policy of destruction. The question
then arises as to the origin of this core impulse that induces a change
in the massacre's scope: from being episodic, it becomes systematic.
In the instances examined here this decisive impetus emanates from
the very people at the height of power.

State and para-state actors. These mobilise the main perpetrators of
state-controlled violence (army and police) and may even go so far
as to designate specific actors to propel and perpetrate massacres
(militias and other groups of specialised killers). The first type may
be diverted from their primary tasks, the second are specially trained
for this type of mission. Both types may be put in charge of organising and carrying out most mass murders.

Public opinion and participation. Are the public aware of the massacres
in progress or about to happen? Do they approve? I have already discussed briefly the question of public opinion. This question should
be asked repeatedly for the entire period during which mass killings
are carried out to assess to what extent public opinion is for or
against, whether it turns a blind eye, or shows signs of dissent. For it is
one thing to launch a mass murder, and quite another to succeed in
gaining society's approval for this kind of violent interlude.

The morphologies of extreme violence. The convergence of these three
factors culminate in forms of extreme violence, of which massacre is
the most spectacular expression. These 'morphologies' of massacre
take various forms (for example killing on the spot or following
deportation) and vary according to the techniques used (fire, shooting, gas, etc.). Other variables should also be considered, such as territorial features or geography, spontaneous participation by local
actors, the scale of a war in progress, and so on.

These scenarios are not scripted ahead of time. The drive coming
from those who decide and organise massacre may not be con-
tinuous, allowing room for manoeuvre or respite, only to be followed by sudden accelerations as a function of an evolving war
situation or international context. A degree of leeway may also result
as designated actors refuse to participate in the killing, or on the

contrary act before receiving orders, and some latitude can also result from public opinion showing its censure. Similarly, on the ground things never turn out quite as intended: perhaps the victims' reactions are not those expected, etc. In short, although the process of destruction gains momentum, it is never fully predetermined. It has not really been finally accomplished till the moment the appointed victims die. But the further the process advances without meeting any kind of restraint, the more difficult it becomes to stop it in its tracks.

The decision-making process and the decision-makers

Massacre can only spread on a grand scale if a central authority more or less overtly encourages it. While it may be claimed that a pogrom, a riot, or a lynching results from spontaneous forms of violence in a group or a crowd, empirical surveys on such phenomena often establish that they were in fact planned by their leaders.[2] The idea of 'spontaneous outbreaks of mass violence' is more often than not mere propaganda, wielded by the powers-that-be in seeking to mask their primary responsibility in the outbreak of violence. There is no doubt that in the cases studied here, there is a *core determination* that is progressively established to destroy partly or totally one or more populations defined as being hostile, useless, a nuisance, etc.

Who is the instigator of this enterprise of mass murder? A small group of men (there are rarely any women among them) of whom it can be asserted that they are at the heart of an undertaking to put a group to death. They often describe their task as 'historic' and so find it to be both necessary and exalting, in the name of their people or 'race', and their political vision of their country's future. For Nazi Germany, apart from Adolf Hitler, we can cite the names of Hermann Goering, Heinrich Himmler, Reinhard Heydrich, and for former Yugoslavia those of Slobodan Milosevic, Vojslav Seselj, Radovan Karadjic and Biljana Plavsic (Bosnian Serb leaders), Matte Boban. In Rwanda we are less familiar with the names of Theodore Sindikubwabo, President of the interim government,[3] Jean Kambanda, Prime Minister of this same government, and Colonels Theoneste Bagosora and Augustin Bizimungu.

How, then, does it happen that these men cooperate to devise what we might call a massacre policy? How do they get involved in implementing such a policy in practical terms? Painstaking research on the subject (and notably biographies) bear witness to the attempts made to understand, although hazy areas often persist in each of these actors' stories. Independently of their respective roles, what is vital is that the first of these cited is generally perceived as being legitimate in the eyes of the population. Indeed the legitimacy of the power of a Hitler or a Milosevic is not contested in the countries concerned at the time events unfold; no more, for example, than was the provisional Rwandan government put together following the death of President Habyarimana, that none of the major powers questioned at the time. It is because these leaders bear the hallmarks of legitimacy that their subordinates within the state apparatus itself agree to put themselves at their service, even to the extent of mobilising this murderous enterprise (even though some resistant to this policy might come forward).[4] Is this to say that majority support for their authority is enough to lead a massacre, always and everywhere, in the manner in which a general might command an army? Certainly not. The dynamics by which mass murder develops are extremely varied: they stem from a large number of factors, as this chapter sets out to demonstrate.

Nazi Germany: the pre-eminence of Hitler. Nevertheless, without this central and legitimate authority that gives impulse to, and organises, the massacre, it is difficult to see how it could gather any significant momentum. The most recent research on Nazi Germany says nothing to contradict this, while it throws into relief the pre-eminence of the role the Führer played in the application of progressively radical measures taken against the Jews. However, the Nazi state should not be seen as a rigidly hierarchical machine ranging from dictator to the lowest rank of individual. The Nazi regime, far from being a perfectly coherent system, was like a confused and unstable conglomerate of proliferating administrations. Refusing to get involved in administrative management, the Führer constantly delegated power, and most often by means of verbally delivered orders, couched in rather vague terms that left plenty of scope for interpretation or initiative by his subordinates. At the same time Hitler asserted a cruel determination to flout any law, whether state legislation or his own party rule. Many administrations in this way found themselves pitted against one another, with conflicting briefs they had to fulfil as best they could to satisfy the Führer's 'wishes', Hitler being ultimately the keystone of the whole system. So it was that up till 1939 the regime's anti-Semitic policy zigzagged along under the influence of the interplay of various centres of power. The direction the regime was taking, nevertheless, was perfectly clear: to make the Jews leave and appropriate their wealth. As the English historian Mark Roseman pointed out, it was undoubtedly Hitler who, through his sporadic interventions, set the pace of the persecution.[5]

With the occupation of Poland, this anti-Semitic policy was suddenly exacerbated. Moreover, it was only one of the ways the brutality of Hitler's power expressed itself, as it was also directed at victims other than the Jews. In effect the context of war provided new possibilities to the most determined Nazis to implement their deepest aspirations, whether this was for the purpose of improving the 'race' or conquering a *lebensraum* or 'living space' to the East. In both instances Hitler was still the one who gave the impetus and authorisation for the most extreme measures taken.

As regards the improvement of the 'race' he secretly ordered the murder of the mentally ill and the crippled (a resolution he had already proclaimed in *Mein Kampf*), his personal doctor, Karl Brandt, being one of the instigators of this plan, along with Philip Bouhler, the director of his chancellery and *Reichleiter* of the party. Very uncharacteristically, Hitler gave written instruction to this effect dated 1 September 1939, the very day Poland was attacked, as though the war was from that point onwards opening up wide to the possibility of massacre. For the first time the Nazi regime granted itself the right to kill, in a 'rational' manner, a specific segment of its own population. After various trials, gassing by carbon monoxide was the method chosen, the first conclusive experiment being carried out in January 1940 on some fifteen patients in the old prison of Brandenburg.

As regards the conquest of living space, it was the Polish population, both Jewish and non-Jewish, who immediately paid the price. On 22 August Hitler declared unambiguously to his generals that 'the aim (of the Polish campaign) was to liquidate the lifeblood of the country, and not to reach a given line'.[6] The Polish occupation, cruelly repressive from the outset, led some German officers to denounce abuses committed by some of their men. It probably would still have been possible to limit the escalation of violence against civilians by ordering the invading forces to act with greater restraint. But once alerted, Hitler reacted by pardoning those guilty of the worst excesses, and withdrew administration of the country from the army. Higher-ranking officers, like Colonel General von Küchler, who was fiercely opposed to the abuses, were obliged to fall into line. In other words it was the head of state in person who himself guaranteed the military's impunity, which inevitably resulted in the Wehrmacht becoming more and more involved in the perpetration of massacres. This attitude of the Führer is revealing of his personal disposition: whenever he found himself faced with a conflict that had to be settled, he opted for the most extreme solution, that is to say the most brutal.

It was as though the Führer's impulses were to keep pushing back the limits, always ratcheting up the assault at each stage, and shattering the most fundamental of prohibitions. He encouraged in this way what we might call a climate of *impunity of thought*, a climate shown by the German historians Götz Aly and Suzanne Heim to be characteristic of the prevailing thinking among various experts and technocrats within the regime.[7] In effect economists, demographers and statisticians did not hesitate to devise grandiose plans for constructing a German and 'modern' Europe, advocating mass displacement of populations, and even their total extinction. These experts were all the more encouraged to put forward such projects since Hitler was convinced that in order to establish the supremacy of the Aryan race, the 'ethnographic ratios' in Europe had to be radically altered.

So it was that on 7 October 1939 he nominated Heinrich Himmler as Commander of the Reich to strengthen the German race. His role was to repatriate Germans living outside the Reich to newly conquered Polish territories, which in itself involved regrouping or expelling undesirable populations residing in these territories, starting with the Jews. The idea of deporting them to a 'reservation' near Lublin was quickly abandoned. Ghettos were therefore created as a temporary measure to isolate them from the rest of the population, the first of these being formed near Lodz on 28 September 1939. They also began deporting Jews by train from the Great Reich to these Polish territories, conceived as a kind of human depot. At the very same moment, Himmler was bringing the new German settlers into Poland. Sooner or later, a problem of overpopulation was bound to arise. On 12 March 1940 Hitler declared that the Jewish question was an issue of space, and that there wasn't enough of it to go around. In fact, by 15 November 1940 'only' 5,000 Jews from Prague and Vienna as well as 2,800 gypsies had been deported.

If Poland was not even capable of 'absorbing' the German Jews and, even less so, its own, what was to be done? What fate lay in store for these 2 million Jews suddenly falling under Nazi domination? The extravagant plan to send them to Madagascar was seriously contemplated by the Himmler administration in 1940 after the fall of France, but the impossibility of gaining military control of Britain (thereby securing control of the seas) made this scheme even more unrealistic. It was this impasse that led to the prolongation of the ghettos scenario, conceived as a temporary solution, with the result that the death rate there escalated as living conditions became more and more intolerable. It became imperative to end this situation, more especially as the ghettos were becoming major centres for the propagation of typhus, a disease much feared by the Germans. Even more radical measures began to be envisaged, although war had not yet been declared against the Soviet Union.

Rwanda, a public call to genocide. In Rwanda, several events and documents bear out that the massacres of April 1994 were prepared in the preceding months by a small group close to President Habyarimana. Was he himself part of it? Or just his wife and several members of *Akazu*?[8] In any event, in 1991–2 a group consisting of soldiers, political leaders, intellectuals and a few businessmen began to believe that the only way of preventing the RPF's total victory was to mobilise the population on a grand scale in the task of killing the Tutsis. In 1992 some had identified a 'zero network' that was operating under cover and in the shadow of the presidency, taking decisions to assassinate political opponents, and even to give orders for massacres.[9] And had not Colonel Deogratias Nsabimana, chief of staff, already sent a secret memorandum to his subordinates on 21 September 1992 in which the Tutsis were defined as the enemy within? This text was a part of the report of some ten officers who in December 1991 had been assigned the task of researching the means to conquer the enemy on the military, media and political levels.[10]

In this document the military constructed their propaganda, distilled by Hutu extremists. So at the end of 1992 lists of Tutsi 'suspects' and Hutu opponents were drawn up: they were to be among the very first enemies to be arrested (and exterminated?), and this was a priority in the event of a crisis.

Over and above the need to combat the enemy within militarily, some also perceived the advantage of linking in the civilian population so they were more directly involved in the hostilities. In a radio address a few days after the RPF attack, President Habyarimana had himself advocated the creation of a self-defence force armed with traditional weapons rather than with guns.[11]

Other voices had come out in favour of this civilian self-defence force, one of which was that of the intellectual Ferdinand Nahimana who was teaching at the University of Butare, shortly to become an eminent propagandist on the *Radio des Mille Collines* airwaves. Another intellectual, Leon Mugesera, also spoke out during this period in a speech that was to become notorious. On 21 November 1992, during a gathering of the President's party, the MNRD, he announced that the only possible action to be taken in the face of the threat of an invasion by the RPF was to throw the Tutsi in the Nyabarongo River. In appealing to the population to rise up, he offered his own interpretation of the oft-quoted words from the Gospels: 'If someone slaps you on one cheek, slap them twice in return', and finished by comparing the Tutsis to vermin or snakes; 'Know that the person whose throat you do not cut now will be the one who will cut yours.'[12] It remains to be established exactly when the partisans of this civilian self-defence force started their preparations.

Colonel Theoneste Bagosora, head of the Defence Minister's cabinet, made a diary entry for 1 February 1993 outlining what can only be described as a serious programme for training civilians to this end—he specified that it was to consist, preferably, of 'married men' (who had 'something to defend')—lead by the military. He even specified the nature of the weapons to be issued to these men.[13] But we are not told at what moment this plan was to be put into action.

Just at this time the Arusha negotiations were starting, which aimed at reaching a peace settlement between the RPF and the Rwandan government. Of the two solutions to the problem that

presented themselves—resolving the crisis politically through negotiation, or the other approach of arming people against the Tutsi
threat—which would carry the day? During 1993 Bagosora and his
friends were preparing their own 'popular-military' scenario. Their
resolve was the greater given that the RPF had resumed hostilities
in February 1993, killing several hundred civilians in and around
Ruhengeri.[14] Human rights organisations then brought credible
accusations against the RPF claiming that it had assassinated at least
eight Rwandan government leaders and their families during this
period, killed by members of the President's political party, and at
least 200 other civilians.[15] Hutu extremists then had a strong hand in
being able to say that the RPF had no intention of negotiating peace,
but in reality sought to seize power for itself alone. In their eyes it was
becoming even more urgent to prepare a popular resistance movement. Considering firearms to be far too expensive for wide-scale
distribution, they advocated a bulk purchase of machetes, the most
widely used agricultural tool for cutting trees and scrub. The figures
confirm that in 1993, the number of these machetes imported was
abnormally high. Between January 1993 and March 1994 some
581,000 arrived in Rwanda, double the number usually ordered
each year. By the end of 1993 the stock of new machetes had
probably already been distributed throughout the country: there was
one available to one in three men. In other respects, 85 tons of
ammunition (grenades, for example) had also been distributed across
the country.[16] In the same period an exceptional rise in the number
of radio sets and batteries was also recorded.

The Arusha agreements signed in August 1993 could nonetheless
have brought about peace, to the extent that they were based upon
power-sharing between all the parties involved in the conflict. But
these agreements remained very fragile (cf. Chapter III). Some
months later the assassination of Rwanda's Hutu President on 6
April 1994 was the event proving the need for action. But would the
people do as they were told? Would the Hutus really set about eliminating not only the Tutsis but also those who, even if they were
Hutus, had shown moderation?

This was the core of the historical tragedy that Rwanda experienced in the wake of the assassination of the President on 7 April.
The massacres had certainly been prepared centrally by a group close

to power, and it is also certain that this group benefited from numerous complicities in the state apparatus. But the group lacked the
political legitimacy that would enable it to enlist the people's
support. Would it have been ready to act—and if so, when?—if the
Rwandan President had not been assassinated? In any case this group
seized the opportunity provided by the President's death to snatch
the power it lacked, immediately setting up an interim government
with two notorious Hutu extremists at its head—Theodore Sindikubwabo as President and Jean Kambanda as Prime Minister.
Exploiting the emotional shock that followed the assassination, these
two leaders called the population to defend itself against the '*Inyenzi*'.
A symbol: Mbonyumutwa Kayibanda, son of the former Rwandan
President, personally issued a statement over the radio using extraordinarily harsh language, and accusing the Tutsis of seeking to commit genocide against the Hutus: 'They are going to exterminate,
exterminate, exterminate. They are going to exterminate till they
alone remain in this country, so that the power their fathers have
kept for four hundred years they themselves can keep for one thousand years!'[17]

The majority of Rwandans had no reason to doubt that these
people represented the new official voice of authority, all the more
so given that the main media, and in the first place the *Radio
Télévision Libre des Milles Collines*, were calling directly for a hunt to
the death of the Tutsis. In a way, the new political authorities had
decreed a general armed mobilisation of the people to defend the
regime against the '*Inyenzi*'. In actual fact this call to mobilise to the
Hutus was nothing other than an extraordinary appeal to the public
to commit mass murder against a minority and its allies, cast in the
role of mortal enemy.

Yugoslavia: the dismemberment of the federal system. In Yugoslavia it was
a completely different scenario. Nevertheless, there is no doubt that
Slobodan Milosevic played a pre-eminent role in the lead-up to the
war in forcing undesirable populations to flee. Should we, however,
consider him to be alone responsible for the ethnic cleansing operations of the 1990s? This would be too simplistic a vision. An international political actor, even head of state, always evolves within a
complex environment that can never be fully orchestrated by the
individual himself. To what extent were Milosevic's policies the

product of constraints over which he barely had any control? Or on the other hand was he powerful enough to make historical contingency work in his favour? Certainly Adolf Hitler had succeeded in just a few years in 'forcing history' to go his way in making Germany the master power of Europe, even to the extent of plunging the whole world into war. But for Slobodan Milosevic such a verdict is certainly debatable.

At the end of the 1980s the Serbian nationalists were not the only ones moving in the direction of dismembering Yugoslavia. It was also the case that the Slovenes and Croats wanted their independence. One could say, then, that there was a 'system effect', centrifugal in character, and tending towards its disintegration, as various writers have theorised.[18] Against the background of communism collapsing in Europe, it was the Yugoslav federal system itself, as constructed by Tito, that could not withstand nationalist pressure. After all, the first to manifest their national aspirations, once Tito had gone, were the Kosovo Albanians in 1981, which engendered, in reaction and in parallel, the increasing mobilisation of the Serbs in the province.[19] To consider Milosevic as someone controlling remotely from the wings the expressions of desire for change that took place in Ljubljana, Zagreb or Pristina would amount, then, to considering him as a megalomaniac. I don't think we should cast him as the all-powerful dictator directing all of Serbia's plus other nations' political forces with a magic wand. It is true that he inherited structures from Tito's dictatorship and wielded them skilfully, like a good communist apparatchik. But numerous reports, even during his trial in The Hague, confirm that he exercised his power in a rather solitary manner, in the company and under the influence of his wife. To achieve his ends 'Milosevic appeared above all as a grand manipulator, allowing himself to be carried by the prevailing currents, and knowing how to make use of people at the opportune moment, to the sole end of strengthening his power.'[20]

In other respects, when Milosevic took control of the League of Communists of Serbia in 1987, his intention was still to act in the framework of Yugoslav unity. But very quickly the radically changed international background led him to implement a new political line, one that was not premeditated. For Joseph Krulic everything then happened as though the Yugoslav political system had been incapable of managing this cascade of upsets. He invokes David Easton's theory that a political system over-burdened by demand ('input') can no longer provide appropriate responses ('output'). This 'letting go' was all the more possible in the case of Serbia since 'the inherited political culture did not provide categories to make the change legible and bearable, and also because one part of the population felt threatened by this change.'[21] As a result the conflicts between Serbs, Slovenes and Croats had probably become irreconcilable by 1990, and the break-up of Yugoslavia therefore inevitable. But was war really an essential part of this equation?

After all, Slovenia and Croatia could have withdrawn from the federation relatively painlessly since their frontiers were not challenged. It was not impossible to achieve these separations by peaceful negotiation. But matters could no longer proceed in the same way now that Milosevic, exploiting the nationalist Serb demands, was seeking to redraw the frontiers to enable all Serbs to live within the same territory. The result was that what should have been a political transition turned into a confrontational one, as Marina Glamocak has commented.[22] So Milosevic, in fact, contributed to transforming the political crisis into war, and a war of 'ethnic regrouping' of territories. But in 1990 did he actually have a fully operational strategy? The political scientist James Gow prefers rather to speak of a flexible and adaptable plan, but not of a unique, detailed strategy of how to achieve set objectives, namely the seizing of various territories for the purpose of annexing them to Serbia, reuniting all Serbs within them, and emptying territories like Kosovo of non-Serbian elements: 'The plans came and went, depending on need and opportunity, but the project continued.'[23] Thus Milosevic deemed it important to support the nationalist Croatian Serb rebellion in 1990 against Tudjman. The historian Tim Judah interprets the dealings in Belgrade in this way, which translated in real terms into the supply of weapons to the secessionist leaders.[24] But Judah makes an interesting point: Milosevic may not really have wanted his plan to succeed, perhaps believing that the Croats would be frightened into staying in the federation. What is certain is that Milosevic considered arming the Serbs living outside Serbia to be a good idea, with a view to constructing an enlarged Serbian nation.

For his part Franjo Tudjman was at that moment seeking to set up his own military and police forces, with the very aim of forming a

Croatian state. According to Marina Glamocak, consignments of weapons coming into the country from Spain via Austria to be subsequently funnelled into Slovenia and Croatia (via Opus Dei networks) started in July 1990.[25] She also notes that paramilitary drafts by Tudjman's Croatian Democratic Union (HDZ) party became active during the same period. Was he also preparing for war? In any event it was Zagreb's declaration of independence on 25 June 1991 that radicalised the growing agitation of nationalist Serbs in the course of the summer, and above all in Krajina. In the town of Knin, for example, the police refused to wear the new Croatian uniform, and the Serbs perceived Croatia's adoption of the red-and-white chequered flag as its national symbol, with the gloomy memories associated with it, as a real provocation.[26] The clashes between Serbs and Croats continued to multiply in this way. War was not far away.

Pinpointing THE decision?

To sum up, in a context where nationalism in one faction feeds the nationalism in another, is it really possible to isolate the exact moment the decision is taken, through which the crisis breaks out into war and massacre? The joint refusal of two factions to compromise precipitates the transition into action. The closely woven interplay of the actors' trajectories is such that they end up resembling one another. And ultimately it is this conflictual duo that gives rise to violence, even when one of the two parties is demonstrably more prepared to attack than the other.

All this bears out the difficulty of defining, even among those who themselves are primarily responsible, the decisive moment for moving in on the act of massacre. Of all the measures Hitler took against the Jews throughout his years in power constantly to stimulate and 'recharge' the violence of his men, which was the most determining? Was it on 31 July 1941 when Goering ordered Heydrich to 'take every preparatory measure necessary … to obtain a total solution to the Jewish question in the German zone of influence in Europe'? Or was it on 18 October 1941, from which point all Jewish emigration from the Reich was prohibited? Was it, rather, mid-December 1941, just after America entered the war Or 20 January 1942 when Heydrich brought together in Berlin, in the Wannsee district, fifteen high-level Nazi officials to decide on the fate of European Jews and mixed couples? Was it still later? Historians put forward significantly different interpretations (and to this point we will return in a moment). The Rwandan case prompts the same debate. Should the turning point towards the massacres of 1944 be considered, for instance, to have already occurred at the end of 1992, due to political restructuring on the part of those who would constitute Hutu Power? Or should it be considered instead that it was preparation of a civilian strategy for self-defence in the spring of 1993 that more concretely constitutes such a turning point? Or was it rather just before October 1993, following the assassination of the President of Burundi?[27]

To remove such ambiguities, we can of course refer back to speeches made in public by key leaders. Their words indeed carried considerable weight when they called openly for violence to be launched against a group, and the more so since they were legitimate leaders. But it would be wrong to take such public debates as an indicator that the decision to massacre had been taken. When the leader of the Bosnian Serbs, Radovan Karadzic, declared before the Bosnian Parliament in October 1991 that the Muslims, by opting for independence, would be risking disappearance, he was clearly referring to some kind of ethnic cleansing operation, if not genocide. But this in no way means that such an operation was ready to be implemented at that precise moment. One could say the same of Adolf Hitler's famous speech to the Reichstag on 30 January 1939, during which he prophesied 'the annihilation of the Jewish race in Europe'. To deduce that the 'final solution' was already being implemented, even programmed, would be a gross error of historical interpretation. At the precise moment they were expressed, such declarations cannot be taken literally: the intention they formulate publicly has no tangible translation in actual fact at the time.

Resorting to the notion of 'intent', so familiar to the legal expert, poses a problem for the historian and the sociologist. To qualify the crime, the judge will always seek to establish what the criminal's intent was: did he really have murder in mind? Was the crime premeditated?[28] We can of course speak of a person's intent in describing his frame of mind in relation to a particular action, at a given moment in time. But to apply this notion to the workings of a power structure is problematical.[29] It amounts to 'psychologising' its operation, while in fact it is always better to analyse a political stance and describe the organisational means implemented to attain it. Moreover the notion of 'intent' implies a simplistic vision of the slide into violence: there would be a thought/action sequence extending from the plan to destroy a group to its implementation in concrete terms; as if it were a question of formulating the idea, constructing a plan to achieve the stated goal, and then putting it all into practice. Such an approach obscures straight away the fundamental enigma that mass murder poses: that of its actual realisation. To approach the question of the implementation of the processes of destruction of a civilian population through the idea of intent therefore risks completely bypassing the complexity of the development of such phenomena.

Better then, one might concede, to stick to archives, notes and documents that prove without any doubt that decisions have been taken, instructions given, and so on. But this kind of investigation is far from always being possible. In many instances of massacre, written documents that might permit dating and unambiguous authentication of the decision to shift into action are rare, even non-existent. And the reason: those responsible hardly wish to leave proof. Following a massacre, they will in all likelihood seek to eliminate any trace of their crime, as in the case of the Srebrenica massacre. Time and again debate ensues about the 'real' intention of the decision-makers, about the presumed date of the decision, and of course, about the *a posteriori* negation of the reality of the facts. The case of the massacre of Armenians in 1915–16 is exemplary in this regard.[30] Nevertheless, the study of the archives proved particularly fruitful in the analysis of the extermination of European Jews, the German administration having produced numerous notes and documents relating to the 'final solution'. Raul Hilberg was one of the very first to exploit these, and produced a remarkable work on the subject.[31] Nevertheless, this profusion of documents did not enable identification of *the very instant* that genocide was decided upon, in as much as nobody to date has ever found a written order from Hitler to this effect.

Christopher Browning has suggested in his more recent work that the key moment for the 'final solution' decision was just at the start of the war against the Soviet Union, so falling exactly within the period from July to October 1941. In this period Hitler seemed to have reached a kind of 'euphoria of victory', fuelled by the successes of the Wehrmacht, which was rapidly advancing into Soviet territory.[32] It is argued that while carried away by the success of this 'military-racial war of destruction', the Fürher ordered Himmler and Heydrich to conduct what one might call a 'feasibility study' for an operation to exterminate the Jews (31 July). At the beginning of October, after the fall of Kiev (19 September) their proposals were approved and there followed a cascade of measures, among them the halting of all Jewish emigration (18 October), the first deportations of Jews from the Reich, the choice of the sites Chemlo and Belzec (for extermination by gas), etc. Browning asserts that during November 1941 to March 1942 the 'final solution' was progressively implemented.

However, on the basis of those same dates, the Swiss historian Philippe Burrin suggested another interpretation that traces the process of the 'final decision' not in victory, but rather in the perspective of a possible defeat of the German army, which since mid-October 1941 had been becoming ever more likely on the Russian front. As Hitler had always held the Jews to be responsible for the war, they would now have to pay a heavy price for German blood spilt. In deciding to exterminate them, the Führer would have been making the Jews pay in advance for the disaster of a possible military defeat. Through the 'quasisacrificial death of the Jews', says Burrin, 'Hitler braced himself fanatically so as to bring about victory or fight till annihilated.'[33]

But the German historian Christian Gerlach offered yet another reading of this period, enlightened by the discovery of new documents in Soviet archives. While he agrees with Browning and Burrin in considering that the fate of Soviet Jews was sealed in the autumn of 1941, he also felt that it remained to be explained at which moment the decision was actually taken to kill all Jews in Europe. For Gerlach it was just after the United States entered the war following the Japanese attack on Pearl Harbor (6 December). In the context of a war that had truly become a world war, Hitler would have been at that point determined to realise fully his 'prophecy' of 1939. Gerlach followed this line of enquiry in focussing on a note in Himmler's diary under the entry for 18 December 1941, and offers a penetrating analysis of the protocol drafted during the famous Wannsee conference, the historiographic value of which is indeed exceptional (one of the rare written documents from the Nazi administration confirming the existence of a pan-European plan to 'resolve' the 'Jewish question', and including also Jews residing in England).[34]

But for the French historian Florent Brayard, the decision process was not yet over by the time of the Wannsee conference. Referring to Peter Longerish's research, he estimates that in reality it was well into May or even June 1942 before the destiny of European Jews was decided on. Brayard refers to one of Himmler's speeches, delivered on 9 June (at the funeral of Heydrich, who had been assassinated several days earlier in Prague), to confirm that Hitler had just decided on the eradication of all Jews over the length and breadth of the continent. Moreover, Himmler set a timescale: the 'programme' must be accomplished in one year.[35] In fact, by the end of the summer of 1943 the objective of the Nazi leaders was almost accomplished, at least in the major territory of Europe that had fallen under the direct jurisdiction of Berlin.

These researchers provide erudite readings of the speeches, notes and reports produced by the German administration (of which we have clearly only reproduced a summary presentation here). But in the end they arrive at significantly different and even divergent conclusions, and in no way point to a single 'moment' in the decisional process. In researching this precise instant when THE decision would have been taken, their analyses seem to be markedly influenced by the value they ascribe to a document (for example, for Gerlach, Himmler's diary entry for 18 December 1941; for Brayard, Himmler's speech on 9 June 1942, etc.). The substance of the text weighs heavily on the construction of their reasoning.

But isn't this type of exercise completely vacuous? In any event it seems rather artificial to want to isolate completely just one moment, an event, as the decisive turning point. Rather than a single decision, surely it is better to speak of a *decision process* and a succession of measures that evolve against a background of changing circumstances, moving towards a 'solution' that is more and more brutal. In short, one decision eventually brings into play another one, and this new decision taken in the new context appears 'natural' in relation to the previous one, with one thing leading to another in a kind of domino effect, one decision leading to the taking of yet another measure even more radical than the last. In this way the dynamic that leads towards mass murder gathers force cumulatively, without the different stages necessarily being planned.

The sociologist Michael Mann has suggested a fairly similar approach, because for him also the genocidal process builds up in stages, through complex interactions between actors, at the same time from the top and bottom of society, and as a function of a war context. Not that he denies that what he calls 'ethnic cleansing' could be really accidental. This phenomenon is 'eventually perpetrated deliberately', he writes, 'but the route to deliberation is usually a circuitous one.'[36] And while the rightful political leader remains well and truly the pivotal point for this dynamic, he is certainly not its only driving force. Many other actors have to be taken into account, and at the top of the list will be those responsible for organising and executing the killings.

The organisation of mass murder and the actors involved

Here, in fact, is another line of enquiry for researching massacre routines. Indeed, while it is difficult to identify the moment the decision was taken, it remains possible to turn to the study of the ensuing organisation on a practical level. Surely the best evidence of the will of those deciding to massacre is the deployment of the means set up on the ground for the purpose of perpetrating the massacre. Here we can see the importance of a historical method of enquiry: *to describe how in order to understand why.* Even if a written order cannot be found, we can deduce that such an order was given. If, for example, in a region of Bosnia, on the same day at the same time, in villages a few kilometres apart from one another, all Muslim houses were burned by several different units of Serbian or Croatian fighters, it goes without saying that these attacks did not occur by chance: the facts observed reveal the link between these concerted operations. It is therefore important to look closely at the identity of the troops deployed to this end, and the nature of their command.

Comparative scrutiny of this kind enables us to identify in each instance two types of violent actors, at the same time distinct and complementary, involved in the execution of massacres. The first come under the state apparatus *per se*: the army and the police. These so-called sovereign powers of the state, pledged in principle to defend the nation and protect its citizens, can thus find themselves diverted from their missions. More specifically, their hierarchical command ends up espousing the idea that to destroy a particular a group of civilians is really part of their brief to defend order and security. Instructions are then given along these lines to their men. Simultaneously, a second type of actor is constructed: specialised battalions of killers, created more or less in the government orbit. The task of the latter is not only to give impulse to the massacre on the ground, but also to carry out the task in an organised and systematic fashion: this is the *rasion d'être* that is given to them as a group.

While the military and the police come to participate directly in organising and perpetrating massacres, they may express at some moment or other a degree of reticence on the grounds that such an activity does not fall within their usual brief. In this respect, instances of refusal to participate, and even disobedience, may occur. On the other hand, the battalions of killers and all manner of militias appear to be *ad hoc* groups, formed expressly to carry out the killings. Sometimes a semblance of officialdom is assigned to them, via the creation of a new government body. Even when these militias have a para-governmental or even private status, they still have definite informal or secret links with leaders themselves occupying positions within the state apparatus.

The constitution and subsequent activation in the field of what can only be called organised death squads will of course depend on the existence of a network of determined leaders, occupying positions of responsibility within ministries or operations divisions. Such personal networks, attached directly to the head of state, depend on transversal modes of communication that operate generally between three types of leader: political, military and police. Some of these will be particularly visible by being more actively engaged than others, and come to symbolise the process of mass murder, from the point of view of its practical organisation. This is true of Heydrich in Nazi Germany, Stanisic in Milosevic's Serbia, and Bagosora in Rwanda. Convinced of the importance of their mission, these determined men know how to work state structures, but also how to short-circuit their operations, not hesitating then to exit from the framework of legality to achieve their own ends. By instrumentalising the state apparatus, they are able to implement their policy of destruction.

But the existence of these networks does not signify that they control the whole destruction process. Once it has been 'dynamised' a bureaucratic apparatus is self-propelled, and individuals within it can take initiatives in the desired direction. The case of Nazi Germany is symptomatic of such a phenomenon. On the whole, by exploiting power structures in this way, leaders end up sucking the lifeblood out of the state like a vampire, so it becomes murderous of its own population or other populations falling under its control through acts of war. This vampirical hold on power gives rise, in the state apparatus itself or in its orbit, to new 'creatures' conceived especially to dole out death, these sadly famous *Einsatzgruppen*, the *Interahamwe* militias, or Arkan's Tigers.

Raul Hilberg has shown how adept Nazi leaders were in using all the services of the German bureaucracy to put their racial theories into practice in the Third Reich and beyond. 'The destruction process was a step-by-step operation,' he wrote, 'and the administrator could seldom see more than one step ahead. The steps of the destruction process were introduced in the following order: At first the concept of *Jew* was defined; then the expropriatory operations were inaugurated; third, the Jews were concentrated in ghetto; finally the decision was made to annihilate the European Jewry.'[37] Hilberg sets out in detail how the functioning of a modern state, such as already described by Max Weber, can be totally diverted into serving the objective of mass murder. This is what has led authors such as Zygmunt Bauman to speak of the genocide of the Jews as a sociological phenomenon truly linked to our modernity.[38]

Nonetheless, the immensity of this bureaucratic machine risked eclipsing the weight of these radical Nazis that the German historian Dietrich Pohl calls '*ideological warriors*'. Occupying key administrative positions, they did not just wait for orders from above, but acted by themselves. These fanatical leaders sought to dynamise the bureaucratic apparatus, the better to achieve the objectives of the Nazi party. To fulfil their Führer's wishes, they could if necessary bypass the sluggishness of this administration by forming more flexible structures outside the state administration. It was thus that Himmler, between 1934 and 1936, managed to delink the entire police force from the control of the Ministry of the Interior: the Gestapo and the SS were to appear to be state organs, but would escape state control, being in actual fact placed under Hitler's direct authority. According to the French historian Edouard Husson, Heydrich's mode of operation—Heydrich having been recruited by Himmler first to run his intelligence department, and having then become his deputy—provides a typical example of this scheme to short-circuit administrative routines from the top down and from the bottom up, in order to implement an effective and coherent racial policy.[39] Taking control in 1939 of the Reichssicherheits-hauptamt (RSHA), the new central Reich Security Main Office, Heydrich spoke of it as a 'combat administration'. It was these men, recruited from the RSHA, who would become organisers and executors of the first genocidal operations at the time of the invasion of the Soviet Union.

Nazi Germany: ideological warriors. The apparatus of terror conceived by Heydrich culminated with the formation of the *Einsatzgruppen* (mobile killing units), opportunely reconstituted before the attack on the USSR.[40] Made up entirely of volunteers, the *Einsatzgruppen*—3,000 men in all, organised in groups of 500 to 1,000—reveal Heydrich's capacity to translate into action Hitler's special conception of war and politics. Their principal mission was in effect to eliminate Judeo-Bolshevik enemies, that is to say, to destroy Jews residing in territories that had only just been conquered. For Hitler the enemies of the Reich must above all be prevented from 'stabbing Germany in the back, as they did in 1918'. Heydrich's units were also obliged to 'stick' to the advance of the Wehrmacht towards Moscow. So the massacres begun in June had by August become widespread. No attempt was made to keep them secret, in contrast to the scrupulous care taken subsequently. The Jewish population captured in towns and villages were usually shot on the spot (including women and children). The most notorious massacre of this period was that of Babi Yar in Ukraine on 29 and 30 September 1941: ten days after Kiev was taken, the *Einsatzgruppen C* commandos shot 33,771 Jews in two days.

Regular German army units also found themselves repeatedly carried along in the wake of this mass killing dynamic. The instructions given by Hitler to his highest command were to launch a battle to the death against the Judeo-Bolshevik enemy. As Field Marshal

von Reichenau, Commander-in-Chief of the German 6th army on
the Eastern front, emphasised on 10 October 1941 'The most essential aim of war against the Jewish–Bolshevistic system is a complete
destruction of their means of power and the elimination of Asiatic
influence from the European culture. In this connection the troops
are facing tasks which exceed the one-sided routine of soldiering.
The soldier in the Eastern Territories is not merely a fighter according to the rules of the art of war, but also a bearer of ruthless national
ideology and the avenger of bestialities which have been inflicted
upon German and racially related nations. Therefore, the soldier
must have full understanding of the necessity of a severe but just
revenge on subhuman Jewry.'[41] We can understand better, then, why
the Wehrmacht found itself involved in the perpetration of numerous massacres of Jewish populations, in the role of logistical support
or direct actor, whether in Ukraine, Belarus, Russia or Serbia.

But the Jews were certainly not the only target. Aiming persis-
tently to eliminate the so-called Asian influence, the German army
were to leave millions of captured Soviet soldiers to die of hunger.
What could be more logical? In both instances the army contributed
to the destruction of a total enemy, the face of which was both
Jewish and Bolshevik. Omer Bartov's research on the subject is one
of the most outstanding works when it comes to understanding how
the Wehrmacht thus found itself implicated in this fight to the death
against the total enemy, and how the troops absorbed this ideology
through their collective apprenticeship of violence.[42]

Rwanda: 'Going to work'.   In Rwanda the opposite of this situation
prevailed. The Nazis were, in the case of Germany, the installed
power base with control of all state services when they undertook
the elimination of the mentally ill and the Jews. In Rwanda, on the
other hand, massacres prepared by Hutu extremists before they took
power were perpetrated in the very phase of constitution and con-
solidation of their new power when the war was starting up again
with the RPF. The success of their enterprise therefore depended on
ensuring complicity and collaboration at all levels of the state,
whenever they ran into pockets of resistance. To achieve their ends,
they depended as much on their armed forces, ready to combat the
enemies within, as on their 'civilian forces', all equally essential for

'pushing' the Hutu population to massacre in the name of collective security. During his trial in Arusha, conducted by the International Criminal Tribunal for Rwanda, Jean Kambanda, the former Prime Minister of the interim government, gave a fairly precise idea of the different hierarchical structures that had driven the massacres after 7 April. He describes five levels of command: the army's crisis committee (endowed, according to him, with a 'phantom structure' to which Bagosora belonged), the official military hierarchy, the political leaders under the influence of the military, the interim government, and the 'civilian self-defence' program.[43]

No sooner had the President of the Republic been assassinated than Colonel Bagosora endeavoured to secure the support—or at least the consent—of all the army commanders at the very moment when his men were starting the slaughter in the streets of Kigali. While General Dallaire wanted the Prime Minister to broadcast an appeal over the radio for calm, Bagosora sought to profit from the situation to form a military government under his own authority. But he came up against the refusal of several high-ranking officers. Following the assassination of the Prime Minister, Bagosora proposed the formation of a civilian government made up of Hutu extremists. This suggestion being finally accepted, some officers who remained hostile to him appealed to the international community. But the diplomats posted to Kigali were taken up with evacuating their nationals as quickly as possible, not with preventing the killings. Bagosora could count on some 2,000 elite soldiers (in the first place, those of the Presidential guard) as well as on some units of gendarmes. The military, gendarmes and the police were to play an important role in the incitement to massacre, principally with the aim of conquering the province. Before 6 April soldiers and gendarmes had already been discreetly distributing weapons to the Hutu population; after that date they did so overtly. In parallel the military put pressure on the civilian authorities who were still manifestly reluctant to engage in the slaughter.

The other armed force, at the disposal of those preparing the massacres, was made up of the militias, created by those political parties close to the deceased President. In 1992 the MNRD had created the *Interahamwe* militia (literally, 'those who are together') and the CDR the '*Impuzamugambi*' ('those having the same aim'). The formation of these militias always proceeded from the same idea: to arm civilians so that they could combat the RPF and hunt down the Tutsis, who were assumed to be allied with them. They were mainly made up of young refugees and unemployed. Using these militias presented the advantage of not involving the administrative authorities, the official armed forces or the gendarmes directly in the perpetration of the mass killings. So in March 1992 the *Interahamwe* were deployed for the first time to slaughter Tutsis in the region of Bugesera. They numbered less than 2,000 men before April 1994, but subsequently their ranks swelled to 20,000 or 30,000 because of the substantial material gains these militiamen could reap from their violent acts.

Right from the start of the massacres, political leaders had put their militias at the disposal of the military. For example, in the wide-scale massacres—like the attack on the church at Gikondo on 9 April—the militiamen by all accounts took orders from the soldiers present on the ground. And to meet the needs of the authorities, militia leaders moved their men around from one region to another, a fact that amply bears witness to the fact that killing operations were both centralised and coordinated.

But the number of soldiers and militiamen was still not large enough to kill Tutsis in the desired quantity, that is, on a grand scale and in a very short period of time. The new government party line was that the responsibility of defending one's country fell to everyone, and this amounted in effect to inciting the entire population to kill. To this end the organisers reinstated the former colonial practice, that had already in fact been revived by the Rwandan administration, of enforced community tasking (*umuganda*). This consisted of civilians undertaking jobs that needed doing in the community in the general interest, for example clearing scrubland, repairing roads, digging drainage ditches, etc. The *umuganda* were coordinated by the *nyumbakumi* (chief of the district, responsible for a group of ten households) who kept a register of those present, and had the power to fine anyone not participating in the group work sessions. In the present instance, this community service task, this national cause of great urgency, became the elimination of the Tutsi enemy, neighbours included.

The political and administrative authorities had organised this kind of rallying operation in the past up in the hills to provoke the

first massacres of Tutsis. Reinstating such a practice, Calixte Kali-
manzira, Interior Ministry chief of staff, was supported by bureau-
crats used to carrying out orders fully and promptly. So, from the
Prefecture to the town authorities, the organisation of the massacres
depended in this way on the bureaucracy and hierarchy of the young
Rwandan state—something that gave this mass murder a very
'modern' character. Generally it was the burgomasters (the mayors)
who were in charge of organising the population on the ground, and
of inciting people to denounce 'suspects'. They sent subordinates
from house to house to enlist the male population, and to inform
them of the appointed time when they would be obliged to 'work',
work being synonymous at this point with the words kill and steal.
Statements made by Jean Kambanda during his trial in Arusha are
revealing of the ambiguous use of this word. When his interrogator
asked him what the word 'work' meant, he replied: 'There were two
meanings…. during this period people weren't working at all.
People just got together in the morning and listened to the radio to
see what was happening. So 'work' could mean to make one's living
… but in the historic context in the past 'work' meant 'kill Tutsi'. In
1959 when people said that they were going to 'work' this meant we
are going to massacre…going to eliminate the Tutsi…so there was a
confusion.'[44]

This general mobilisation to 'work' meant that the collective
killing dynamic, borne along in turn through administrative and
political channels, was not, for all that, a prisoner to bureaucratic
routine. It was in fact the opposite, remarked Alison Des Forges:
'The organization that ran the campaign was flexible: primacy depended more on commitment to the killing than on formal position
in the hierarchy. Thus within the administrative system sub-prefects
could eclipse prefects, as they did in Gikongoro and Gitarama, and in
the military domain lieutenants could ignore colonels, as happened
in Butare.'[45] In this exceptional situation the actors could overstep
the legal limits of their functions: military personnel could move
freely into the civilian domain, while civilians, who had no power,
could procure the support of the military whenever they wanted to
attack the Tutsis.

Another actor gave the perpetration of these massacres a very
modern character: the *Radio Télévision Libre des Mille Collines*

(RTLM). This radio station, that for months had distilled a virulent hatred against the Tutsis, was calling openly now for their liquidation. Radio presenters called themselves 'the high command of the word', a phrase that spelt out their self-appointed role only too clearly. It lavished encouragement on those manning barricades, denounced soldiers who deserted the war front and reprimanded the militiamen who were apparently more interested in pillaging than in killing, pressed the army to distribute rifles and drugs to young people coming forward in response to its calls for mass mobilisation, and promised a decoration of the highest rank for all who had taken the risk of staying in the capital to cleanse the city of Tutsis and to prevent it from falling into the hands of the enemy.[46] In this way RTLM unequivocally set about making itself the voice of the Hutu people's resistance.

In so doing it assumed some of the functions undertaken by radio that I have already identified in other political crises.[47] RTLM assigned itself the role of messenger, for instance giving precise instructions and even orders to the militiamen to rendezvous at particular places. It acted out a prescriptive role also in giving Hutu listeners instructions ostensibly relating to vigilance and self-defence which in reality were public calls to murder, and even murder of close neighbours. 'People have to look at who is next to them, look to see if they are not plotting against them. Because those plotters are the worst. The people must rise up, so that the plotters will be exposed, it is not hard to see if someone is plotting against you.'[48] It invited listeners who would like to check out suspicious persons, whose names had been given to the radio station to contact it for more information. This was the first time in history that a radio station openly incited its listeners to participate actively in a slaughter, one soon to be recognised as genocide.

Serbia: alternative armed forces. In Yugoslavia the political situation of those preparing for war can be situated roughly midway between that of the Nazis in 1940 and that of the Hutu extremists at the beginning of 1994. Milosevic had indeed been in power in Belgrade since 1987, but his power remained limited: he was President of Serbia and the Communist League of Serbia. In this way his wish to impose his authority on the Yugoslav army, the JNA, ran up against resistance within the military institution itself, which was federal by definition. Up till 1991, even though effectively under Serbian command, the Yugoslav army had been 'multiethnic', all the while remaining authentically communist and so opposed to any secessionist movement. Milosevic set out, first, progressively to increase the hold he had over the institutionalised military, and second, to gather together an alternative armed force for his practical, political, and personal needs.[49] But control over the JNA was apparently not as easily obtained as Milosevic had predicted, as James Gow reports in his study of the '*Serbianisation*' of the army. General Eljko Kadijevic, then federal Minister of Defence, did not much approve of the line taken by Milosevic, even though he later resolved to rally to it. For his part, Milosevic found Kadijevic much too 'Yugoslav'. To destroy this state of mind within the army, little by little he appointed to its head those Serbian officers on whose loyalty he could count, like General Bozidar Stevanovic. The JNA was thereby to find itself more and more involved in ethnic cleansing operations.

The political circumstances also served Milosevic's designs. Indeed, the departure of Slovenia, Croatia and then of the other Republics considerably bolstered the Serbian presence in what remained of the Yugoslav army: in March 1992 no more than 5 per cent of non-Serbs remained.[50] At the start of the war in Bosnia, the JNA, formally dissolved on 19 May 1992,[51] gave birth to two distinct entities: the Bosnian Serb Army (VRS) and the army that was still referred to as the Yugoslav army (VJ). This decision was pursuant to the UN resolution imposing sanctions on Yugoslavia, designated as being the principal aggressor against Sarajevo. So that Belgrade would not be formally accused of having invaded Bosnia, Milosevic replied by provoking the dissolution of the JNA: he could then maintain that it was no longer the Serbs who were fighting on Bosnian territory, but the Bosnian Serbs under General Ratko Mladic, over whom he claimed no longer to have control. Pure fiction, of course, even though it was true that General Mladic's army did enjoy plenty of room for manoeuvre on the ground, and that the Bosnian Serbs sought autonomy on the political level. In fact, the Bosnian war enabled Milosevic gradually to build up his hold over the military. According to James Gow, he could be considered to control the army after the Supreme Defence Council meeting of 25–26 August 1993, marked by the forced departure of forty generals. Nevertheless, he suggests that the 'ghost' of the federal army appeared never to have been eliminated, and this meant that Milosevic could never have full trust in the military.[52]

It was within the Interior Ministry that the men most faithful to his cause were to be found, starting with Radmilo Bogdanovic, the ringleader of the 'anti-bureaucracy revolution' who brought him to power. Bogdanovic was to become Interior Minister, succeeding then to make of the Serbian police the 'Praetorian guard' for the regime.[53] Well equipped and highly paid, the police force units, 5,000 men strong (without counting reservists), constituted a veritable tool for coercion in the hands of Milosevic. From this one ministry alone a network of loyal adherents grew outwards to reach other milieus involved with the army and politics, as well as crime. This network was mainly run by Jovica Stanisic, who had joined the Serbian secret service just after finishing his university degree in political science. In 1990 Stanisic became the head of the 'military line' for the Ministry of the Interior (Vojna Linija).[54] This network, which included Serbian officers loyal to Milosevic (like Ratko Mladic), drew up the RAM plan (an acronym inspired by the word 'manager' in Serbian) in 1990. The Hungarian Mihajl Kertes, sometimes referred to as the Minister of Ethnic Cleansing, also belonged to it. This network's mission was to organise resistance among Croatian and Bosnian Serbs, and included the job of supplying them with weapons.[55]

Links still existed with the various paramilitary groups that emerged at the start of the 1990s. As in Rwanda, Serbian extremists had, in effect, armed militiamen who enjoyed the goodwill of the ruling powers. One of the best known of these was the White Eagles led by Vojslav Seselj, head of the Serbian extreme right wing party. Professing openly to be 'Chetniks', they joined in any operations aimed at redefining the frontiers of 'Greater Serbia'. In other respects it was men from Seselj who were to commit one of the first massacres in this war, at Borovo Selo, against the Croatian police.[56] Another notorious militia was that of the Serbian Volunteer Guard, known as 'Arkan's Tigers', led by Zeljko Raznjatovic, a man with a criminal past. To swell the ranks of the militias, the authorities set about freeing common prisoners, requesting in exchange that they go to fight in Croatia or Bosnia. These militias pillaged, raped and killed, and clearly constituted the spearhead of the ethnic cleansing operation: news of their arrival often sufficed to cause an entire village to flee.

Their overall numbers were assessed to be approximately 12,000 in 1991–2. In neighbouring Croatia militias of the same type were formed during the same period.

The use of these paramilitary groups, over and above the fact of their compensating for widespread desertions (*inter alia* of Serbian Serbs during the autumn 1991 offensive) in the ranks of the army, presented the great political advantage for Belgrade of masking the role of Serbia in such operations in the eyes of foreign countries. But in fact these groups were commanded by men from the Ministry of the Interior, and could not operate without the support of the army, because they needed cover from artillery fire before being able to move into action, and various other logistical support (at the top of this list being their need for fuel). This presence at the front of armed bands unfettered by any military discipline aroused indignation and abhorrence among many officers. But the growing control Milo-sevic wielded over the army led to strengthening the complement-ariness of these two types of armed forces on the ground. And so the same scenario tended to repeat itself: the army began by bombarding a town or a village, and then the paramilitary contingent moved in on the scene to kill or hunt down the non-Serbian inhabitants. In November 1991 the attack on Vukovar followed this pattern, with the paramilitaries going so far as to kill patients inside the hospital. These killing operations were to continue, one massacre after another, progressively forcing the Croat to flee, while Tudjman's forces in turn started to mobilise and organise in order to resist the advance of the Serbs, using the same expeditious methods.

Organised practices and local initiatives. So while massacre clearly requires a degree of organisation, we should beware of assigning it too rigid a representation. Some authors tend to encourage us to believe, for the purpose of demonstrating premeditation, that everything was calculated in advance by criminal minds. This vision is inspired by the legalistic approach that sets out to prove a slaughter was really the result of a concerted and coordinated plan. Thus journalists and historians naturally tend to assume the role of public prosecutors. While the process of destruction does indeed have a dynamic, and one that is triggered by a centralised impulse (issuing from those deciding to 'do' it and then organising it), it also depends on a degree of improvisation as regards men's actions. We know, for example, that during the first campaign to exterminate the mentally ill in Germany, incredible errors and blunders were made in informing the families. For example, a death certificate sent to a family might mention appendicitis as the cause of death, when the deceased had already had his appendix removed; some families might even received two urns of ashes instead of just one. In the same vein, 'in September and October 1941, transports [of deported Jews] were dispatched without a clear idea of what would happen to them, and to areas where there was no clear policy of what was to happen. Regional officials felt their way and did some of the center's thinking for it, though always in close liaison with Berlin.'[57]

Rather than approaching the issue as though everything emanated from the one central power system, we also need to look closely at its *periphery*, and in particular at those local actors capable of taking decisive initiatives. Several regional studies—like that of the German historian Dieter Pohl on Eastern Galicia (South East Poland)—show how actors at the periphery anticipated what was being sought by those at the centre of the system, the latter going only so far as to endorse what had already been accomplished... and urging them to go even further.[58] In this region, with the largest concentration of Jews (with the exception of the Warsaw area), the actors designed killing methods—in a dynamic between centre and periphery—that varied according to the individual contexts in which they periodically took place: pogroms, shootings, organised famine, gassing, and then shootings once again followed in sequence over a period of less than three years. In total, of the 545,000 Jews living in the area in 1939, only 10–15,000 remained in 1945. By the same token, when the new Commander-in-Chief of the German armed forces, Hans-Joachim Böhme, arrived in Serbia in September 1941, some of the officers suggested he should rapidly take radical measures (probably deportation) against the Jews. He had already received orders to institute a radically new policy of reprisals against Partisan attacks: for each German soldier killed, 100 male Jewish hostages were to be executed. But his superiors had not given him any particular instructions to persecute the Jews as such. It was on his own initiative that he took such measures. At the end of 1941 there were practically no male Jewish adults left in Serbia. At the start of 1942, with the extermination of women and children, Serbia was one of the first countries 'free of Jews' (*Judenfrei*).

Local leaders on the ground could thus acquire very real autonomy in implementing mass execution policies. And this autonomy was all the more possible as individuals moved precisely in the direction sought by the centre. Such observations seem verified also in the case of Rwanda. While operations were indeed coordinated, a large degree of autonomy was left to the actors. With the general instruction to kill Tutsis being repeated everywhere, it became relatively unimportant who actually carried out the deed. 'At every level, the superposing of those issuing commands compensated for any weaknesses that might exist at the level of individuals, or of one or other of the various structures. Even better, it brought an ever greater raising of the stakes, and increasingly indiscriminate violence by lower and middle ranks of command attempting to keep control amidst growing chaos; or trying to divert on to others any threat presented to themselves.'[59]

Concerning Bosnia the anthropologist Cornelia Sorabji speaks of a 'frank' organisation of massacres, in the old sense of the term 'franchise'. She points out that 'mayors and local military commanders could incite and facilitate violence in their own regions with impunity, deploying their own groups and 'hired guns'—sharp-shooters—to inject their own methods and sadistic inventions.'[60] The Bosnian example thus seems relatively non-bureaucratic and decentralised.

Such apparent disorganisation of violence should not, however, allow us to conclude that isolated acts of violence perpetrated by irresponsible extremists were involved. This type of explanation is often put forward by the authorities in power once the press reveals that some of their henchmen had committed atrocities on their victims. In reality 'these are rather the predictable results of an organisation enjoying absolute impunity, and the general aims of which are set by the chiefs, while the specific details of their implication are left to local initiative.'[61] And so a mass murder unfolds, through a kind of dynamic and interactive co-construction between those giving orders at the system's centre, and its actors, both regional and local, at the periphery.

The symbol of Srebrenica. Why don't we carry this reasoning through to its logical conclusion? If local actors can acquire a certain degree of autonomy in mass murder, will they not sometimes go beyond what is expected of them? The climate of impunity created by those very people who gave the massacres their thrust would make such 'excesses' not only possible but still more probable by actors who, on the very ground where the operations were unfolding, were intoxicated by their power. The massacre at Srebrenica, from 11 to 16 July 1995, by the Bosnian Serb forces commanded by General Mladic, elicits this kind of enquiry. Following the fall of this enclave, approximately 8,000 men (including adolescents and the elderly) were executed on the spot, while the women and children were forced to move to zones controlled by the Bosnian forces.[62] This tragedy has been analysed mainly in the context of the passivity of the Dutch UN peacekeepers who were supposed to be defending this town declared by the UN to be a 'safe area'. Moreover, a report by the UN Secretary-General Kofi Annan in November 1999 recognised the international organisation's failure over this tragedy.[63] Investigation commissions set up by the Netherlands and by France have also tried to assess their own responsibilities.[64]

However, the event has undergone very little scrutiny from another viewpoint, namely that of Srebrenica's history. It is naturally impossible to understand the 1995 massacre without taking into account the violent conflict that pitted Serbs against Muslims there in the first place, and more generally the conflictual history of myths and memories specific to this region. In the context of the Dutch report, the anthropologist Ger Duizjings achieved in this regard an interesting piece of work.[65] In 1992, at the very start of the war, the town fell into the hands of Serb paramilitary groups, but they were driven out again by Muslims led by Nazer Oric, a young policeman from the neighbouring village of Potocari whose 'sackers' (the 'Torbari') freely pillaged and burned the surrounding Serbian villages. Once the town had been reconquered, it then hosted a growing influx of Muslim refugees who had been the victims of ethnic cleansing in the neighbouring regions. Consequently, living conditions in Srebrenica became increasingly difficult due to critical shortages of food and other essentials. To procure food, Nazer Oric's men regularly carried out pillaging forays in nearby Serbian villages, one of them even taking place on the Orthodox Christmas Day on 7 January 1993 in the village of Kravica.

Among the Serbs, the rumour spread that during one such attack, a senior citizen called Nego Eric tried to fight back by shooting from the window of his house with an old rifle. He finally killed his wife and then himself. His house was burnt. This man became for the Serbs the symbol of resistance and passionate desire for vengeance against the 'Bosniaks' of Srebrenica.[66] This revenge might already have taken place in February 1993 when Mladic exerted even more pressure on the town. But the creation by the UN in April 1993 of 'safe areas' (including Srebrenica) prevented a bloodbath.

Nevertheless, Mladic did not abandon his projects, because in 1994 he openly expressed his desire to eliminate Muslims from this part of north-eastern Bosnia, 'to make them pay the price for their collaboration with the Turks', a reference to the suffering endured by the Serbs under Ottoman rule. From a strategic point of view the control of the region of Srebrenica was in fact indispensable for creating a monolithic Serbian political entity that was coherent and viable. Over and above the business of vengeance, the taking of this town was therefore an absolute necessity for the Bosnian Serb leaders. In fact, over the course of Spring of 1995, during the talks that were to lead to the Dayton Accords, Milosovic made it clear that he would never agree to a peace plan that preserved the enclaves in the east of Bosnia, even if the United Nations had declared them 'safe areas'. The permanent members of the UN Security Council, starting with the United States, agreed to this demand from Belgrade. Thus, Richard Holbrooke stated ten years later, 'I was given initial instructions to sacrifice Srebrenica, Gorajde and Zepa. And I felt it was wrong.'[67] But could the international negotiators, although they were perfectly aware of ethnic cleansing operations from the start of the war in 1991, imagine the scale of the massacres that would be perpetrated in Srebrenica? Carla del Ponte, chief prosecutor for the ICTY, said that she did not think the international community believed a genocide would take place in Srebrenica.[68] Questions remain for the researcher to elucidate better to understand what happened that Spring of 1995. For instance, as regards the Bosnia Muslims, what exactly were the relations between Sarajevo and Srebrenica during that period? Why did Naser Oric leave Srebrenica in April 1995 just when Mladic was posing an ever greater threat to the city? However, at the beginning of July 1995, when Mladic's army was preparing to attack, his initial goal still seemed to be to reduce the enclave to the boundaries of the town of Srebrenica itself, and to turn it into one gigantic open-air refugee camp. The idea was thus to force the United Nations to evacuate the area.[69]

But noticing the virtual lack of resistance on the part of the UN in the days preceding the attack, Mladic probably took the decision to strike much harder, realising that he had a clear playing field. Certainly his men remained under the control of Belgrade:—the taking of Srebrenica was definitely the subject of a top-level consultation with Milosevic. According to Carla del Ponte, there is no doubt that Milosevic, Maldic and Karadzic had organised the attack and that large-scale massacres would occur.[70] But was Milosevic aware of the preparations for the massacre? And if he was, did he sanction them? These questions are also clouded in obscurity. It is possible that Belgrade had given prior approval to Mladic's project, and it is also possible that Mladic, intoxicated by his victory and spurred on by a desire for revenge, took advantage of the situation to settle his quarrel with the inhabitants of Srebrenica, thereby presenting Milosevic with a *fait accompli*. Taking control of the town on 11 July, Mladic seems in effect to have been convinced he was going to accomplish a historic feat that he situates within the secular lineage of wars between Serbs and Turks: 'On the eve of yet another great Serbian holiday', Mladic said, 'we present this city to the Serbian people as a gift. Finally, after the rebellion of the Dahijas, the time has come to take revenge on the Turks in this region'.[71] There are many questions here that could doubtless have been clarified by his trial at The Hague and through historical research (assuming Serbian archives exist and are accessible).[72] This is why I believe a certain mystery still surrounds the Srebrenica massacre.

In any event, it is clearly inadequate to analyse the dynamics of mass murder simply from the point of view of those who decide upon and organise it. Here we would risk deploying too functional a view, even if care were taken to explore the complex interactions between the loci of decision-making and actors situated at the periphery of the process of destruction. A much more sociological (and anthropological) view will allow us to try and understand how a society could be led to participate in the development of a murderous dynamics.

From collective indifference to popular participation in massacres

What, then, becomes of local populations in nations perpetrating massacre, or populations falling under such nations' dominion? Do they fully go along with what is happening? I shall now take up the thread of my analysis of the third party role *before the threshold into mass violence is crossed*, i.e. consider those close at hand or further afield who might come to the designated victims' aid (Chapter II).

Once the point of mass murder has been reached, it is well and truly the case that the third party has collapsed. In one of the very first books devoted to the Srebrenica massacre, two Dutch authors highlighted this phrase of Tacitus: 'The worst crime was dared by a few, willed by more and tolerated by all.'[73] What an astonishing echo to the content of these pages! Certainly the authors have the failings of the 'international community' in Bosnia uppermost in their minds, but Tacitus' phrase can just as well be applied, even at the very outset, to the drama unfolding on the domestic stage. It is the passivity of Everyman, more or less complicit, that makes the escalation of violence possible. Protest becomes the more difficult as, with the country engaged in war, each individual is summoned to show solidarity in the face of the enemy. But perhaps the worst is still to come, because the outbreak of war can radicalise human behaviour even further. One can't help thinking of Franz Kafka's words about war: 'It is an inundation. War has opened the floodgates of Evil. The props supporting human existence are caving in.'[74] Sometimes massacre is actually carried out, not only by soldiers or policemen but also by civilians enrolled in one way or another by the new authorities. Between collective indifference and popular participation in massacre, the instances examined here display wide variations.

The fate of the Jews: between hostility and indifference. While anti-Semitism was widespread in Germany, this did not mean that all Germans wanted Jews to die. On this point the sociologist Daniel Goldhagen's thesis has aroused strong objections.[75] His work certainly poses the important question of the personal responsibility of 'ordinary' Germans, and not merely the Nazi leaders, in the persecution and elimination of the Jews. Goldhagen seeks to go further than Raul Hilberg, not content with just answering the 'how' of genocide, but also explaining 'why'. His undertaking is therefore particularly ambitious. What answer does he provide? It has the advantage of being simple: if Nazi Germany killed the Jews, it is because the Germans wanted that. And why did they want it? Because the project was there, not only at the top of Nazi authority, but also at the base, the society in question being infested with an 'eliminationist' anti-Semitism.

This claim is made with a surprising degree of self-assurance. It reminds one of similar assertions made by seventeenth century doctors mocked by Molière as follows: 'Why does opium make one sleep? Because it has dormitive properties'. Why did the Germans kill the Jews? Because such a plan was part of their culture of hatred for them. They all really wanted to get rid of them, and were heartily glad it was happening: this was borne out by the photos the soldiers brought back from the Eastern front as evidence of the killings.[76] The argument is therefore fundamentally culturalist, because it postulates a destructive trend peculiar to the German people. In so doing, it minimised the virulence of anti-Semitism in other countries during the same period, whether this was in Poland, Romania or France. Why, then, did the Germans have the will actually to commit these acts any more than other countries? Even more questionably, the argument is based on a single causality: everything stemmed from ideology, and this flies in the face of the basic tenets of historiographic research, that works to reveal the multiplicity of variables to be taken into account, a complexity that inspires this book. It is hardly surprising that Goldhagen's book aroused lively debate among many historians.[77]

Although most Germans may have been anti-Semitic, they did, for all that, disapprove of the openly aggressive actions undertaken by the regime against the Jews during the 1930s. In fact, the majority of Reich citizens would have been content with legal and orderly anti-Semitic measures, such as those instigated by the Nuremburg laws of 1935. But Nazi leaders certainly were not. They incessantly relaunched the 'charge' against the Jews. We know, for example, that following 'Kristallnacht' on 9 November 1939 large segments of the population were shocked by this unleashing of violence. However, spontaneous reactions against government policy could only possibly influence such policy if they were expressed by a public voice that would dare openly to convey disagreement. In fact, no spiritual or moral authority inside Germany openly echoed this popular emotion. This incredible outbreak of hatred was therefore followed by a deafening silence that could be interpreted as a kind of assent, or even satisfaction.

But leaders like Himmler and Heydrich, having ascertained from reports noting reactions of disapproval on the part of the people, argued to Hitler that there was much to be gained by employing more 'rational' methods that would no longer depend on resorting to the rather visible violence of the pogrom. War would give them the opportunity to take action, since in this new context the majority of Germans were primarily preoccupied with the fate of soldiers sent to fight, and problems to do with daily life which 'made them forget' the fate of the Jewish minority. From the diary of Victor Klemperer it is obvious that German public employees had no idea whatsoever of the miserable condition to which the Jews had been reduced. Were the 'Aryans' unaware of the plight of the Jews, or did they choose not to see, as suggested by Daniel Bankier?[78] It was still the case that the dominant attitude towards the Jews was a mixture of hostility and indifference. It was this ongoing absence of openly hostile reactions to their persecution, exclusion and deportation that facilitated their destruction, the terrible outcome of repeated abdications of responsibility.

Clearly, any individual daring to protest under Nazi dictatorship would have required exceptional political courage. Any dissident would have risked being singled out as a traitor more than ever once the country was at war. They would have risked arrest and execution by a regime that had withdrawn any kind of right to opposition from 1933. The execution on 24 February 1943 of Hans and Sophie Scholl, student members of the White Rose organisation who dared to protest in Munich against the regime, became after the war the symbol of a resistance apparently impossible within the Reich. However, another affair in which one faction of the Catholic Church opposed the euthanasia practised on the mentally ill bears out that there was still, even after war had been declared, a public space in which the regime could be contested. But this story shows the extent to which this opposition had been laboured and partial. First of all, several months after the start of the programme, in the autumn of 1939, queries marked 'confidential' were sent to the authorities by some pastors to convey the suffering, even stupefaction, of families having experienced the disappearance of their loved ones. But the Nazi leaders only equivocated, and the extermination programme continued. It was only one year later, in the spring of 1941, that some bishops decided to take the plunge and protest publicly in their sermons: Von Preysing, on 9 March 1941 in Berlin, and above all Clement-August von Galen in Münster, on 3 August 1941. The latter denounced the murder of the mentally ill, noting that he had complained to the court against crimes committed in his diocese, quoting article 139 of the penal code that stipulated that 'anyone with certain knowledge of an intention to murder, and omitting to alert either the authorities, or the person under threat, in good time, will be punished'.[79]

This event was remarkable: for the first time, a religious leader publicly reaffirmed the prohibition of murder under a regime whose main characteristic was to have constantly poured scorn on this prohibition from the start. This moral intervention was strong enough for Hitler to gauge it wise to interrupt the programme, which had nevertheless already claimed 80,000 victims. German society thus succeeded, via the protests of some of its religious dignitaries, in checking the first mass murder organised by the Nazi state. It seems to have been the context of the war being fought against the Soviet Union that led Nazi leaders to arrive at this decision. While on the one hand Martin Bormann spoke out in favour of eliminating von Galen, Josef Goebbels protested that if the Bishop of Münster happened to disappear, Westphalia would be lost for the entire duration of the war. Indeed, he feared that the bishop's disappearance would be a cause for major dissent in this region at a time when the offensive against the Soviet Union demanded rather a high degree of cohesion in the German nation. In other words, the international context that, as we have seen, could facilitate massacre in this instance furthered the success of an act of moral protest which might at first have appeared hopeless.

On the other hand, it must be said that neither the Protestant clergy nor the bishops were to mobilise in the same way to denounce publicly anti-Semitic aggressions. Another mark of this silence? On 1 September 1941, at the same time as the programme of eliminating the mentally ill was halted, it became obligatory for Jews to wear the yellow star throughout the Reich. There are several indications that this measure came as a new shock to a large part of the population. But the Church authorities said nothing. Their silence is all the more tragic since in this same period the personnel responsible for conducting the programme of euthanasia on the mentally ill were transferred to Poland to construct more gas chambers there. Thus prevailing mood in German public opinion at the time continued to be an attitude of passivity towards anti-Semitic policies, observable since the beginnings of the regime. Ian Kershaw, in his research on Bavaria, sums up this attitude thus: 'The road to Auschwitz was built by hate, but paved with indifference.'[80] However, some variations in the attitudes can be observed from one region to another. Thus in the Rhineland, a bastion of Catholicism, there were signs of resistance, or at least of dissidence,[81] while in Lower Saxony, at Göttingen, a very anti-Jewish community, the population eagerly participated in the pillaging of Jewish property even before they were killed.

Another important fact was that the Germans had access to information about the fate of Jews in Poland and in the Soviet Union. Daniel Bankier provides convincing indications on this point. Even though the Nazi leaders meant to keep it secret, Germans residing in the Reich could not ignore that the Jews were doomed to die; Klemperer's entry in his diary for 12 March 1942 mentions the name of Auschwitz as a place where one is doomed to die. But the Germans did nothing with this stupefying information, which in fact also aroused the incredulity of the Jews themselves, in the Reich and elsewhere. To be convinced of this, one need only listen to an account given by a certain 'Ruth', interviewed by the historian Michael Pollak: when she hears Thomas Mann announce over BBC radio in 1941 (even though she lived in Berlin) that the Jews were being massacred in Poland, she simply couldn't believe it.[82]

A paradox? The general passivity of the population despite this harrowing news nevertheless did not prevent some Germans from discretely demonstrating their sympathy towards the Jews. Let us turn once more to Klemperer's diary. For example, in the entry for 8 May 1942 he notes some very anti-Semitic reactions to himself ('Jewish sow' for example) and at the same time, the reaction of a lady who risked standing up for him in the street out of sympathy. And he notes: 'Such demonstrations (dangerous for both parties!) are said to happen frequently.'[83] Elsewhere he again mentions the party official who showed him understanding (26 April 1942) or some workers in Dresden who manifested a spirit of camaraderie towards the Jews: 'Again and again I observe the comradely, easy-going, often really warm behavior of the male and female workers toward the Jews; there will always be an informer or traitor somewhere among them, but that does nothing to alter the fact that as a whole they are certainly not Jew-haters. Despite that, some of us cling to the idea that *all* Germans, including the workers, are, without exception, anti-Semites' (4 June 1943).[84] So many indications confirm that on an individual level a bit of humanity towards the Jews still managed to survive this system that was so cunningly contrived to ensure its obliteration.

Taken overall, everything happened as though the capacity for collective reaction on the part of the people had been progressively bulldozed. German society had been sucked into a rationale of destruction it had allowed to happen, in the absence of any reaction from within. The less it armed itself with any means of protest, the more it found itself locked into a process, and with no control, in which it was more and more called upon to get even more involved—because this generalised *laissez-faire*, and passive ratcheting up of involvement, simultaneously turned into—let us not forget—an active gearing up of all kinds of sectors of activity collaborating with the 'final solution'. The crescendo of this incorporation of German society into the process of destruction of the Jews is certainly marked by the introduction of camps for extermination by gas at the end of 1941, and above all during 1942. In effect the mass killings perpetrated by the *Einsatzgruppen*, SS battalions and other police forces and military groups remained the business of professionals of repression, with civilians only intervening around the periphery, in putting the victims to death.

With the development of gas chambers, the process of destruction became 'civilised' because it involved an ever larger proportion of the economic and industrial tissue of German society: railways (the *Reichsbahn*), the automobile industry (for the first gas transporting lorries), the chemical industry (for the production of Zyklon B), the textile industry (for the recycling of clothes), the metallurgical industry (for transforming stolen gold), the banking sector (for the closure of accounts), etc. A figurehead was provided by the President of the Administrative Council of the IG Farbenindustrie, Carl Krauch, who chose the site of Auschwitz. And the slogan displayed at the camp entrance, '*Arbeit macht frei*', figured before the war in all the factories of the group. The process of destruction was in this way grafted on the heart even of the German economic apparatus. 'Crime cannot be considered to be something apart from the ordinary world: it interpenetrates even the most banal interstices of daily life.'[85] This was indeed the direction Himmler and Heydrich wished society to take.

Rwanda: towards mass involvement in mass murder. In Rwanda we are plunged into a universe that was poles apart from German industrialised society. Could it not still be maintained that the unequivocal efficiency of the massacring operations was due to their organisers' partial success, as they moved from place to place, in involving large segments of the rural population? That was, at the outset at least, the objective of the so-called 'civilian defence': to achieve massive participation of the Hutu population in the 'resistance'. If we listen to one RTLM broadcast dating from just a few days before the attack on the Presidential plane: 'The people, there is the real shield, it is the true army that is strong... the armed forces [i.e. the regular Rwandan army] fight, but the people, they say: we protect your rear, we are your shield. The day when the people rise up and want no more of you, when they hate you all together and from the bottom of their hearts, when you make them sick to their stomachs, I... I wonder then where you will escape to. Where will you go?'[86] A terrible threat uttered against the Tutsis: the radio was actually announcing in public that the *'people'* were going to annihilate them where they stood.

However, the realisation of this terrible 'prophecy' by mobilising the Hutus proceeded from a wager. True, the President of the Republic's assassination instantly created a political vacuum and public emotion that made violent reactions even more probable. Some thought the immediate public intervention of the Prime Minister in office could also strangle such an eruption. Major-General Dallaire was of this opinion, convinced that if Agathe Uwilingiyimana could address the nation on the radio, her appeal for calm could lower the tension, and demonstrate in this way that she was capable of assuring the continuity of power.[87] But this possibility vanished immediately after she was assassinated. At that point the Hutu extremists had free rein to form a new government.

A different call for restraint on the rising violence could still have come from the nation's church leaders. But four days after the death of the President the Catholic bishops were pledging their support for the new government. They asked all Rwandans to 'respond favorably to calls' from the new authorities and to 'help them realize the goals they had set', including in this the restoration of peace and security. It is true that one week later they issued another statement requesting a halt to the bloodshed; but this had scarcely any impact, while for his part the Anglican Archbishop who was also present in Rwanda at the time, far from condemning the killings, declared his support for the new government. By refraining from immediately issuing a condemnation of the massacre, the religious authorities left the way clear for civil servants, who claimed the killings actually met with God's favour.[88]

If then, for various reasons, these possible restraints on the violence did not function, the way was obviously wide open for it to spread throughout the country. But did this mean the farmers' participation was guaranteed? Not really, argues André Guichaoua: 'It is one thing to prepare massacres at the height of power, and quite another to succeed in enlisting the hillside agricultural population in the killings'.[89] After 7 April, the borders and roads were closed. Clearly the aim was no longer to allow the Tutsis to leave, but to eradicate them. However, nobody yet knew how many of the hundreds of thousands of people influenced by the ideas of Hutu Power, were really prepared to answer the movement's call to kill, rape, wound, burn or pillage. Public enquiries conducted by the African Rights organisation claim that the violence broke out in nearly all prefectures of the country on the morning of 7 April,[90] but during his trial Jean Kambanda admitted that in areas where the President's party had less of a following, it was harder to get the massacres going.[91]

RTLM radio was assuredly one of the most formidable vectors of the scheme to incite mass murder, but its importance should not be overestimated. Some authors support the theory of quasi-automatic obedience on the part of the largely uncultivated Hutu population on receiving RTLM's instructions, but this kind of explanation is totally superficial. Of course this radio, which started broadcasting just a few months before the assassination of President Habyarimana, came to impose a framework of meaning on an entire country that was profoundly traumatized by four years of war. With the talent of its presenters, the newness of its style, its songs, it had managed to become a part of the daily lives of a large number of Rwandans, eventually setting the tempo for this mind-boggling period of genocide. Yet for all that, we cannot claim that this radio manipulated its listeners like simple puppets. As Darryl Li's interesting metaphor suggested, these broadcasts would rather 'reverberate' in the thoughts and actions of the Rwandan people, some of whom would interact with its programmes while others would not. More than simple passive vectors of its propaganda, these were 'active receivers' interpreting these messages, and contributing or not to channelling them each in his own way, deciding or not whether to 'work' in the direction stipulated by the radio show hosts.[92]

The sociology of media reception has, moreover, already taught us: it is one thing to broadcast programmes destined for different audiences, but the way in which these audiences interpret and decode these messages is quite another.[93] While the propaganda certainly gives a framework of meaning, it is by no means certain that this would be accepted by all individuals. In any case, it would be subject to reinterpretations and adjustments depending on age, social group, affiliations, etc. Taking this one step further, how were the RTLM programmes received, commented on, believed, in the different regions of Rwanda? We can only follow the advice of anthropologist Danielle de Lame when she writes 'if we want to understand the role of the media from the Rwandans' point of view, we need to approach it from within the contexts of the different local sub-cultures.'[94]

The idea that all massacres were perpetrated by gangs of youths holding a radio in one hand, and a machete in the other is pure cliché. On the hills the encouragement to participate in hunting down Tutsis derived much more from the local authorities, the mayor and his deputies, local political party leaders, local businessmen, religious leaders, the military, gendarmes, police and militiamen, who all recruited the population at large to this end. The African specialist Timothy Longman's research on two adjacent Protestant parishes, Kirinda and Biguhu (the Prefecture of Kibuye), for example, showed convincingly the pre-eminent role these local elites played in involving farmers in the killing. But, he insists, their motivation was much more political than ethnic. Massacres were organised and supported by a local elite fearing loss of privilege, who focussed the people's resentment on the Tutsi minority in their attempts to hold on to power in their area.[95]

In fact, seen from the 'bottom' of society, this tipping over depended on multiple factors, in a context where the consequences of war had seriously altered people's behaviour. First, the soldiers of the Rwandan army returning to their villages wounded or mutilated in the war against the RPF were key vectors for the rise in ethnic tension. From 8–10,000 in 1991, their numbers swelled to 40,000 in

1994, and their were presence in the hills—many of them crippled, or missing limbs—bore witness to the tragic realities of civil war. Assigned to work for the local tax office or the police force, they could describe to anyone willing to listen how the Tutsi in the RPF behaved. They thus became, well before April 1994, powerful propagators in the mobilisation of the population against the 'Inyenzi'.

The rise in violence, remarked André Guichaoua, was also due in part to a change of heart among personnel in charge of keeping civil peace in the hills: headmasters of primary schools, teachers, priests, health centre managers. In daily contact with the population, these were the 'opinion makers', because what they said was 'true',[96] and their role was therefore even more important in a crisis situation. But the RPF offensives in 1992, and particularly in February 1993, provoked massive displacement of people fleeing the fighting. Their numbers were estimated at nearly one million at the start of 1994. These Hutu populations, fleeing the advancing RPF, lived in camps, most of which were in the north of Rwanda, in a general movement southwards. In passing from north to south, they recounted the atrocities committed by the RPF and spread all kinds of rumours. The 'opinion makers' referred to by Guichaoua were of course directly in contact with these displaced populations, for whom they often provided transport and lodging. They were to repeat these horror-laden narratives, and spread them in turn to the hills and their inhabitants. Such stories, of course, did nothing but confirm the RTLM propaganda, and so could only reinforce the Hutus' fear of an impending RPF victory. And thus fear, little by little, spread through the hills well before April 1994, with each Hutu being afraid that the arrival of the RPF could only mean death for themselves and their families.

The ethnic composition of each prefecture, even of each township, should also be taken into account in order to understand the slide into violence. For example, a large number of Tutsis lived in the Kibungo Prefecture, even though the President's party was well established there and the militias were also present in quantity. In April 1994 a kind of osmotic pressure built up between the authorities and the population that rapidly led to a slaughter of Tutsis. This was in stark contrast to the Cyangugu Prefecture in the Burundi and Congo borderlands, where the Hutus were split: inciting them to massacre Tutsis was a more difficult task, especially because in this

southern prefecture there was undying political hostility towards those from the north (those close to the President). In this instance the population cannot therefore be said to have participated in massacre till two or three weeks later, once Hutu opponents were eliminated themselves. Even in the Gitamara Prefecture, a bastion for the 1959 revolution, the plunge into violence only resulted from the fact of the army's intervention, the dismissal of the former Prefect, and the arrival of the provisional government fleeing Kigali, which had been attacked by the RPF.

The situation was completely different again in the Butare Prefecture, where there was the highest number of Hutu-Tutsi mixed marriages. The Prefect, Jean-Baptiste Habyalimana, adamantly refused to follow the new government line imposed by Bagosora and his friends. For nearly two weeks the local population was in no way involved in the massacres, except in one town located near to the Burundi Hutu refugee camps, these refugees being wielders of terror. Violence did not break out in the other towns till 19 April. André Guichaoua devoted an in-depth local study that attempts to understand the genocidal policy in this rebel prefecture of Butare, which did not slide into the massacres till it came under direct pressure from the self-proclaimed interim government.[97] And this did not happen till the recalcitrant Prefect was ousted (and finally murdered) and other members of his administration were dismissed, militiamen called in from the outside, etc. Was ethnic origin really the cause of these massacres? Another enquiry on the ground carried out in the Butare region suggests that it was at least not the sole cause. The widespread violence that had reached the area 'created the ideal conditions for the settling of former rivalries or tensions anchored in local life', which therefore had nothing to do with one's being Hutu or Tutsi. Other motives must also be taken into account, like jealousy or desire for profit. Yet it was above all the Tutsis who remained the main target of its assaults, in that the authorities encouraged their slaughter. In other words 'Many Butare farmers did not kill their own neighbours, or complete strangers, because they were Tutsi, but rather because it was possible to kill them as Tutsis. The choice of victims by peasants therefore revealed a multiplicity of local and personal factors'.[98]

All this suggests that popular participation in massacres, region by region, remains to be documented. The role of intermediary regional elites in involving peasants in the killings seems to warrant particular scrutiny. But what does this word 'participation' really mean? Most witnesses claim that it was not spontaneous but organised. The function of 'organisers' in the hills was not just to indicate who the enemy was, but also regularly to galvanise the 'killing spirit' among farmers, negatively through threats, and positively through rewards. To this end an *ad hoc* and flexible organisation was set up, with regular meetings taking place in the hills, and in cabarets (bars), restaurants, etc, in liaison with the authorities. Did villagers then follow the militiamen and gendarmes leading the massacre, or did they participate actively in the killings? In other words, was the population auxiliary to the slaughters or a whole-hearted actor?

In his book *Machete Season* the French journalist Jean Hatzfeld reports that the Hutu villagers in the town of Nyamata in the Bugesera region became perpetrators of the massacres in progress.[99] But was this the case everywhere? The idea that the entire Hutu population had participated in the massacres is not tenable. Of some 6 million Hutus living in Rwanda, how many really came actually to kill? While it is impossible to give a precise figure, Scott Straus has attempted an interesting estimation. He came to the conclusion that the number of Hutu killers in 1994 could be estimated at between 175,000 and 210,000, or between 7 and 8 per cent of Rwanda's active population, but more accurately, between 14 and 17 per cent of the male adult population.

Another essential point: Scott Straus observed that around 75 per cent of these individuals can be considered responsible for 25 per cent of the murders, which means in turn that between 20 and 25 per cent of Hutu killers carried out nearly 75 per cent of the massacring. Following on from this, 'even if mass participation characterizes the Rwandan genocide, a small number of armed perpetrators and especially zealous ones probably did the lion's share of the killing.'[100] Another key aspect of the slaughters, however, was that the more the rural population were involved, the more efficient they seemed to have been: only local people could know who the Tutsis were, and where they might be hiding. In this sense identity cards stating ethnic origin were not always necessary to identify an 'enemy'. Thus the complex articulation must be taken into consideration between the hard core of individuals who kill, the wider circle of those who occasionally lent a hand, denouncing those in hiding, and the larger mass of Hutus who passively allowed the massacres perpetrated in their names to be committed.

'They thumped left, right and centre, they chopped randomly'

'The day the killing began at Nyamata, in the street where the big market was held, we ran to the parish church. A large crowd had already assembled there, because when massacres begin it is Rwandan custom to take refuge in houses of God. Time granted us two peaceful days, then the soldiers and the local police came to patrol around the church, yelling that we would all soon be killed. I remember that you would think twice about breathing and speaking. The *interahamwe* arrived before midday, singing; they lobbed grenades, they tore down the railings, then they rushed into the church and started chopping people up with machetes and spears. They wore manioc leaves in their hair, they yelled with all their might, laughing scornfully from the throat. They thumped left, right and centre, they chopped randomly.

'People who were not flowing in their own blood flowed in the blood of the others, it was totally awful. Then they began to die without any more protesting. There was a great din and great silence at the same time. In the middle of the afternoon, the *interahamwe* burned little children before the front door. With my own eyes, I saw them writhing from the burns completely alive. There was a strong smell of meat, and of petrol.

'I no long had any news of my big sister, I was all at sea. At the end of the afternoon, I got knocked on the head with a hammer, I fell, but I managed to slide away and hide with some boys behind a railing. When the *interahamwe* had finished working for the day, young people from our area, still brave enough to escape into the bush, carried me off on their backs.

'The *interahamwe* finished off the killing in the church in two days; and immediately afterwards they set off into the forest with machetes and clubs to track us down. With dogs in the lead, they searched to catch runaways hidden beneath cut branches. It was here that I was caught. I heard a shout, I saw a machete, I got a blow on my head and I fell into a hollow.

'First, I ought to have been dead, then I insisted on going on living.'

The narrative of Cassius Niyonsaba, excerpted from Jean Hatzfeld, *Into the Quick of Life: The Rwandan Genocide: The Survivors Speak*, trans. Gerry Feehily, London, Serpent's Tail, 2005, pp. 4–5.

'The attackers in Musebeya wore banana leaves, especially around their heads like a kind of crown, and carried spears, but the people in Karambo wore banana leaf belts and other leaves tied around their shoulders and chests. They carried wooden clubs studded with nails. I saw National Police who shot at the houses that were made of durable material, because the walls were not so easily broken as walls of mud and packed earth. I saw the houses doused with gasoline to make them burn more easily.

The attackers made lots of noise and blew on whistles. And they shouted: 'We must exterminate them all.' Even if people were hiding, the attackers could find them in the night and then they blew on whistles to call the rest of the group to come. Sometimes they seemed intoxicated on marijuana. Women came behind the attackers to pillage. They also did a kind of security detail to see who was hiding. For example, they would keep track of who was in a house by the kind of laundry that was put out to dry.

During that time there were also barriers. They stopped everyone at the barriers to see if they were from my family and if they were, they would be killed. Those who were fleeing at night accidentally ran into barriers. When I was leaving the forest, I passed at Gasenyi and saw a fire. The fire showed that there was a barrier. If there had been no fire, I would have walked into the barrier.'

Excerpted from Alison Des Forges, *Leave None to Tell the Story: Genocide in Rwanda*, New York, Human Rights Watch, 1999, pp. 326–7.

The autism of the Serbian population. In former Yugoslavia this process does not seem to have gone quite so far. Indeed the Serbian population were never directly confronted with the massacres perpetrated in Croatia, Bosnia and later Kosovo. The war was going on outside Serbian territory, a situation reminiscent of that of the Germans in the Reich. But it is precisely because the population were at a distance from the theatre of operations that it was all the more possible for them to support what was unfolding, or to remain coldly indifferent to it. Their apparent insensitivity to the news of atrocities committed by the Serbs raises a number of questions. Indeed, while the regime used threads of propaganda, the population had access to additional sources of information via the foreign and opposition media. The situation of the media in Serbia in 1992 was nothing like that of Germany in 1942. So why this indifference on the domestic level, in a world where, at the end of the twentieth century, international communication is said to be transparent? Various theories have been put forward.

The first of these relates to the skill with which the regime pretended that Serbia was not even at war. This political culture of 'keeping up appearances' had its origins partly in the communist experience, and lulled the Serbian population along in a kind of 'bubble' of reassurance, completely removed from reality. The mainstay for this protective device was the official media, which provided a viewpoint completely divorced from the reality of the situation. A poll carried out in June 1992 shows, for example, that two-thirds of the population of Serbia did not know who had surrounded and was bombarding Sarajevo.[101] A few kilometres away from the besieged town, Serbian villages seemed to live on peacefully as though nothing was happening. Generally the population thought that both camps were responsible for atrocities, but since the Serbs had been attacked first, they were therefore the victims. Over and above the manipulation of the media, this culture of victimisation explains better the particular attitude of indifference that was manifested. If the Serbs were visibly insensitive to the suffering they caused, it was because they could only see their own woes, as a martyred people who had themselves been victims of 'genocide' during the Second World War. 'This obsession with no longer being victims transformed us into bullies,' admitted the former Bosnian Serb President, Biljana Plavsic, during his trial.[102]

It was precisely because they didn't want to experience the same fate again that they set out to defend themselves. Not for one moment, then, did the Serbian population seem troubled by the war being waged in Bosnia and Croatia. Of course, the unitary reflex played its part in adversity; but, as Slavenka Drakulic notes, the autism they demonstrate is utterly horrible, even incomprehensible.[103] An autism that goes hand in hand with the outright denial of reality referred to by the French journalist Jean-Arnault Dérens, when describing how a Serbian friend of his from the town of Bijeljina, the town where many Muslims were massacred in April 1992 in north-eastern Bosnia, while several thousand others were confined in the town centre. 'A kind of ghetto was thus created in this town, from the spring of 1992 to January 1994. But his friend, who claimed not to be political, passed by the barricaded streets without asking any questions. And no one seemed worried about the situation any more than he was.'[104]

It is also important to take into account the influence brought to bear by an authoritarian culture seeking to legitimise the regime in power. This was an authoritarian culture rooted in the deeply rural, paternalistic and conservative section of Yugoslav society, an environment in which communism had prospered. It was largely rural Serbia, along with the retired population in the suburbs of Belgrade, that backed Milosevic. Likewise, in Croatia the traditionalist Tudjman bastion was to be found above all in Slavonia. So from the standpoint of their social base the nationalist regimes of Milosevic and Tudjman bore some resemblance to each other. But it should not be forgotten that they both also acquired electoral legitimacy just before and during the war, because their respective parties won the 1990 and 1992 elections. How, then, could they come up against a powerful movement hostile to their political stance? To the national cohesion so conducive to war was added the international embargo declared against Serbia in 1992. Not only were nourishing foodstuffs increasingly rare and expensive, but nearly 60 per cent of the active Serb population found themselves technically unemployed. People were resigned and disillusioned, and had started to worry far more about the difficulties of everyday life than massacres being committed who knows where. In 1992–3 inflation was borne as an evil necessary to the defence of the Serbian people. For despite the difficulties, the patriotic reflex remained steadfast in a context where the media maintained that an international plot was being hatched against Belgrade.

There was also, however, a Serbia that rejected the nationalist politics that had led the country into war. It found expression notably through the tens of thousands of young people fleeing their enrolment in the army. But these recalcitrant Serbs could in no way manage to influence events politically because organisations working for peace remained weak in Serbia as in Croatia. So in July 1991 in Belgrade the Centre for Anti-War Action was created, and by actively developing multiple contacts abroad, organised two types of activity: assistance to deserters and refugees, and public demonstrations for peaceful conflict resolution. Another association called the Belgrade Circle, founded on 25 January 1992, brought together some 400 intellectuals from all over Yugoslavia. These writers, artists and journalists aimed to create a civic space that went beyond the framework of party politics to show that there were Serbs who disapproved of the politics being conducted by the country's leaders. But these organisations remained relatively unknown to the Serbian general public, especially in the provinces. They did not manage to stifle the deep-rooted political movements that the nationalist forces had succeeded in mobilising, in the name of defending the national territory.

Territorial defence. The dominant political climate consisted in fact of 'pulling together' for defence as a group, rather than conducting peaceful mediations over and beyond national differences. And the parties in opposition, themselves often divided, never managed to create a coherent alternative front to Milosevic's politics. And yet the Yugoslav people had been prepared for this defence of the territory since Tito's reign. Indeed one of the originalities of the Tito system was to have set up a military innovation referred to as TO—*Territorijalna Odbrana*—literally territorial defence, based on the idea of a 'people in arms'. Set up in the 1970s, it consisted of preparing society to mobilise to defend the nation against a potential enemy, as much from the outside as from within. This pre-militarization of society was supposed to have a dissuasive effect on an aggressor that might come from the West, but in fact would more probably come from the East (the Soviet Union). It was the invasion of Czechoslovakia in August 1968, and Moscow's decision to put an end to the Prague Spring, that had convinced Tito to create this territorial defence.

Conceived in this way as a self-defence mechanism for civilian society, it incorporated factories, administrations, and schools, with a potential mobilisation of nearly three million people. In practice, this territorial defence was placed under the responsibility of each of the republics, which led the former Minister of Defence, General Kadijevic to think that this military preparation of society was an important factor in the weakening of the *bona fide* federal army.[105] Events would prove him right. According to Marina Glamocak, 'it was precisely this territorial defence that made possible the process of arming which led to war and the advent of ethnic cleansing.... It 'served as constitutive core to the national forces.'[106] The role of territorial defence was precisely to defend what was perceived as legitimate territory.

At the end of the 1980s, with the replacement of the federal structure by the national structure, the foundations of this legitimacy were increasingly subject to upheaval. Realignment of political allegiances led in real terms to a desire to redesign the territories and, as a consequence, restructure the territorial defence units. Each town and village was thus redefined on the basis of an ethno-nationalist criterion: each territory must be defended by armed force. Did this mean that from now on it was necessary to hunt down those within this space no longer recognised as members of the group? Exclusion was not yet automatic. In Bosnia people could still be heard saying: 'We know these Muslims who live next door very well. To be sure, they are not Serbs or Croats, but they are good neighbours. They are nothing like those dirty Bosnian allies of the Turks, pillagers, rapists', etc. Good neighbourly relations still won over the plague of ideological discourse and protected people from exclusion. But for how much longer?

For a definitive rupture to occur, it would take the social tie coming under attack from some external element. It was the threat—then the reality of the violent act—that crystallised violence and provoked the massacre. As soon as the risk became imminent, the dialogue abruptly changed: 'Neighbour, you are well-liked. We have always got along fine. But you understand: you are Muslim, and I am Serb. I am telling you to get out. Because if you don't, tomorrow it will be too late.' And when tomorrow did come, the thunderbolt did, sure enough, fall on the village. Or at least, on a certain part of the village. The political-criminal militias did indeed go in, arriving from Serbia or Croatia, backed by the army. We are left to imagine what followed. Evil was done. Women were raped. Houses were burnt and corpses left scattered about. The mosque was destroyed.

Many observers have emphasised that the great majority of ethnic cleansing operations were apparently carried out by militias. There are not descriptions, as there are for Rwanda, of the population at large participating in the killings. 'Ethnic cleansing was more commonly militias and military against civilians than neighbour against neighbour', insists Antony Oberschall.[107] For example, of seventeen assaults against villages during the Prijedor ethnic cleansing in Bosnia in May–June 1992, Oberschall reported that the aggressors wore army or paramilitary uniforms in fourteen assaults out of seventeen, with survivors not recognising any of their aggressors, who didn't even make any attempt to hide their faces. 'We stumbled upon a gathering of some eighty opprobrious Chetniks camped down at Prijedor police station.'[108] Of course, when the militias arrived on the scene, some neighbours would inform on who should be hunted down or killed, and participate in the operation in this way. Others were forced to join in under the attentive eye of the paramilitaries. But active participation by civilians seems to have been consistently limited, an observation made also in various other instances of civil war.[109]

Such operations provoked massive movements of refugees trying to flee the combat zone. And the arrival of these refugees in another still unaffected region could become a source of considerable tension, and so of heightened violence. The proceedings of the International Criminal Tribunal for the Former Yugoslavia have sometimes brought this aspect of the conflict to light, as for example, in a judgement of a case in central Bosnia connected with the Croatian-Muslim conflict of 1992–3.[110] In April 1992 the Bosnian Muslims and Croats at first resisted the attack launched by the Serbs in eastern and western Bosnia-Herzegovina side by side. These ethnic cleansing operations caused a large number of Croatian and Muslim refugees to flee towards the centre of Bosnia, where their arrival provoked in turn overcrowding and tensions between the two nationalities. In the areas around Ahmici (central Bosnia) this huge flow of refugees contributed to mounting fear, and created in this way a propitious climate for the outbreak of violence. Ethnic cleansing operations then followed, this time orchestrated by Croats against Muslims, killed or forced to leave. It was as though violence and massacre had helped to 'clean' this region that had been overtaken by disorder and instability due to the arrival of these refugees. Through provoking separation, the aim of massacre is recreate order and tranquillity.

Bit by bit, violence will tend to propagate in a country where the former central power is no longer able to guarantee peace between the various communities. The political collapse of power has another consequence, and that is to favour the emancipation of local actors who assume they have the right to practise violence for their own ends. Because the state is no longer capable of ensuring law and order, they will profit from this to make their own law regime, settling scores hanging over from the past with neighbours. From the spring of 1992 onwards, the situation in Bosnia provides numerous examples. The Dutch anthropologist Marc Bax conducted a remarkable study in the Medjugorje region in the South West of Bosnia-Herzegovina.[111] This area presents an interesting 'condensation' between spiritual and warring forces typical of Croatian Catholic nationalism (very close to Muslim and Orthodox areas). Medjugorje had become a point of international pilgrimage since the Virgin was said to have appeared to six children there in 1981.[112] In this village also resided the main warlord of the region, Zdravko Primorac, a former Croatian soldier, who among other things ran a munitions factory there. The pilgrimage centre was operated by Franciscan monks who supported the activities of the man whom locals called 'Captain Zdravko'. From June 1992 to March 1994, the latter mobilised his own 'army' of mercenaries, and with the support of the nationalist Catholics, carried out several ethnic cleansing operations, of which the Muslims were the principal victims.

However, the Bax study shows that, over and above the ethnic cleansing question, quite a number of other issues were at the centre of these actions. These included the desire for revenge against Muslim families, jealous of the success of Medjugorje (where thousands of pilgrims had thronged), as well as the elimination of a village whose position hindered free access to the route by which Zdravko's men could gain access to their supply of fuel. Another factor was the massacre of a Muslim family that had acquired a monopoly on the region's wine, a situation that over time had created profound resentment among Croatian wine-growers.

Another local dimension of the war in Bosnia resides in the town-country antagonism, to the point that Bogdan Bogdanovic, the former mayor of Belgrade, coined the word 'urbicide' to describe the particular phenomenon of this violence directed against towns.[113] The driving force for the conflict was no longer 'ethnic' in this instance, but stemmed principally from a rural world feeling itself overtaken by the march of modernity: this it set out to reject, placing the blame on what it saw as its embodiment: city life, a place of mixing, culture, wealth etc. 'The war is (to be sure) firstly a rural war, rurals against rurals, and in the early days in the villages along the Sava in Slavonia,' Jean Hatzfeld observed, 'then rurals against city-dwellers, when the first shells fell on the towns. The sieges of Vukovar, Osijek, Dubrovnik, Bijelina, Mostar and Sarajevo will never cease to confirm this spirit of revenge of the country-folk, 'yokels', villagers, mountain-folk, the majority of them Serbs in Bosnia, who tried to launch their assault against (mostly Muslim and Croatian) towns, industries, shops, blocks of flats, museums. Confrontations between ethnic groups have obscured this other more ferocious, desperate, and all-out conflict, between the rural world on the wane like everywhere else in Europe, and the victorious city-dwellers.'[114] In other words, as in Rwanda, we can see that the ethnic dynamics of the conflict are in fact interwoven with other issues grafted on to it, seeming sometimes even to overwhelm it.

Elements from outside a region that kindle violence, an influx of refugees that causes tension to start mounting, local actors who profit from the situation for their own ends: we can see to what extent the factors determining how a massacre develops vary, and also how they interact. These are complex events, constructed just as much by central as by local actors, both adapting their destructive behaviour according to the adherence or intervention of nearby or distant third parties. To sum up, massacre is the product of a co-construction between a will and a context, the evolution of the latter being capable of modifying the former. The destruction process may go through phases of respite, just as it may also experience sudden accelerations, going as far as to sweep away in its tide people who were not meant to be victims. In Vichy France Pierre Laval took the step of arresting children of Jewish parents who were earmarked for deportation, following the Vel d'Hiv roundup in 1942, something the Nazis had not requested. This anticipatory action can provoke, in other circumstances, a phenomenon of massacre 'contagion', as for example the ethnic cleansing done in the Bosnian war, which ultimately affected all communities—Serbs, Croats and Muslims. All this validates an approach to massacre as a dynamic process—organised, certainly—but also subject to some relatively random modulations.

Ordinary rescuers. It should be remembered, however, that even when violence and death have the upper hand, other local actors are trying all the while to save lives. In these extreme situations a threshold can just as well be crossed into acts of 'rescue' as it can into acts of destruction. As well as engendering narratives of horror, war also gives rise to stories of mutual protection and services rendered, however limited. There are ordinary rescuers just as there are ordinary killers. In Nazi-occupied Europe, it is known that individuals—and also sometimes groups—came to the aid of those being persecuted, first of all the Jews, implementing in the process a veritable civilian resistance of rescuers.[115] In France the story of the village of Chambon-sur-Lignon (Haute Loire) that took in and protected Jews (many of them children) right from the start of the war[116] is well known: Chambon has become an international symbol of the actions of the 'Righteous'.[117] It would in other respects be useful to write a comparative account of the 'village rescuers', since there have been others, like those in Dieulefit, in France again (the Drôme region) and Nieuwlande (Netherlands). In the case of Bosnia, Svetlana Broz, the grand-daughter of Marshal Tito, wrote a book called *Good People in an Evil Time*,[118] recounting various positive stories, ranging from examples of individuals helping each other, to examples of a more collective kind of resistance, as in the mountain village of Baljvine, (south of Banja Luka) where Serbs and Muslims continued living together, and where the mosque remained intact. 'The Serbs of Baljvine have indeed always opposed the passage of the paramilitaries: they repaid, in a way, a debt that was fifty years old, because the Muslims from this village had themselves protected the Serbs during the Second World War'.[119]

In Rwanda the town of Giti (Byumba Prefecture) is also known for having saved 'its' Tutsis thanks to the determination of its burgomaster Sebushumba. In Kigali itself some places of asylum held good, such as the Grand Hotel des Milles Collines. This was probably because there were still 'a few foreign journalists' in the capital, as the journalist Philip Gourevitch reasoned.[120] It is interesting also to record the kind of tactics used by those who managed to restrain the killers. Paul Rusesabagina, the temporary manager of the Grand Hotel des Milles Collines, gave beer and money to the soldiers and militiamen who came in search of those they were protecting. Bishop Joseph Sibomana, from the diocese of Kivungo, did the same, giving all his money to the *Interahamwe* militiamen who arrived to kill the Tutsi hiding in his church.[121]

On the hills too there were ordinary rescuers who deserve the researcher's attention: a Hutu family sometimes took enormous risks to protect a Tutsi family. An even more remarkable fact: within the nation's tiny Muslim community (1.2 per cent) the feeling of mutual recognition, as a minority social and religious group, was stronger than the ethnic criterion. As a consequence, many Tutsis were protected by these Muslims, even though some Rwandan Muslims did also participate in the killing.[122] Some Hutus even cooperated with the Tutsis to ward off attacks by the militias, or fled with them to places of refuge. Often Hutus who took such decisions were driven to do so not because of political opinion but because of friendship or family ties with the Tutsis. At the scene of the killings expressions of disapproval were not as rare as one Hutu woman, who had been present at the massacre in the church at Nyamata, suggested: 'Many spectators appeared glad to see Tutsis die, shouting "The Tutsis are finished! Let's get rid of the cockroaches!" I can confirm too that a large number of people were extremely indignant to see them so cruelly killed and burned. But it was very dangerous to utter more than a murmur of protest, since the *Interahamwe* killed, without hesitation, any Hutu showing good relations with the Tutsis around them.'[123]

Resistance: the energy of despair. It should not be imagined, either, that victims falling prey to the persecutors always remained passively waiting quietly for their end to come. The cliché holding that Jews had accepted to go like lambs to the slaughter ignores the whole paralysing tragedy experienced by defenceless individuals, under threat of death. The interest of a comparative study is to show that victims react in roughly the same way in a situation of intense stress. Whether they were Jewish, Rwandan or Bosnian Muslims, the more they were socially marginalised, the less they were able to react collectively. It was as though, the closer death came, the more they were paralysed by the situation. Some individuals, more conscious than others, showed themselves able to interpret the situation correctly and to do everything possible to survive. The American psychoanalyst Bruno Bettelheim wrote penetrating pages on this subject.[124] As for the rest, some historical examples bear witness to this capacity for resistance on the part of victims in a situation of extreme danger, at the two ends of the chain of the process of their destruction. To prevent deportation some Jewish associations were set up secretly, like the Organisation de Secours aux Enfants (the OSE) in France and the Committee for the Defence of Jews (the CDJ) in Belgium.

As for the armed insurrection of the Warsaw ghetto on 19 April 1943, and the revolts of detained Jews even within the Treblinka (2 August 1943) and Sobibor (14 October 1943) extermination camps, these events remain exceptional moments of resistance offered by human beings with the energy of despair, knowing themselves to be doomed to die. It is precisely because they are conscious of being condemned sooner or later that they find the inner strength to rise up against their captors and put up a last fight in which they can save their honour, even if they can't regain their liberty.

Such events can be compared with the desperate armed resistance put up by Tutsi refugees in Bisesero, a mountain ridge in the Kibuye region, against their Hutu assailants between 8 April and 1 July 1994. Hiding in the surrounding woods, and living increasingly like hunted game, the Tutsis held off their aggressors. Even though the latter killed more and more, coming back with yet more men and weapons to 'clean' this region that had already been a Tutsi stronghold of resistance in 1959, the survivors still found the strength to battle on. They used, in particular, a so-called tactic of 'immersion', whereby they would lie in wait till their assailants approached and then suddenly loom up to confront them. In other places also, for which we still have few records, small groups of Tutsis fought their adversaries one by one, sometimes in their own homes, or out in the fields or on the roads.

In Bosnia the Muslims also tried to defend themselves. They were, it is true, unprepared for war, being very ill-equipped in terms of military resources. Their leader, Izetbegovic, requested the lifting of the embargo on weapons imposed by the UN: 'Let us defend ourselves,' he argued to Western powers. In 1993 this small Bosnian army was to prove formidable against the Croats, notably during the Vittez siege. In May, when confronted with the Serbian army, he had too few heavy weapons (tanks and wide bore cannons) at his disposal. Units from this Bosnian army nevertheless excelled in fighting against the Serbs, for example in the battle to take Bihac. During these confrontations the Bosnian fighters could themselves commit atrocities, as they did in Bratunac in January 1993.

In parallel, Izetbegovic tried implementing an alternative strategy to armed force. Taking advantage of heightened media coverage of the conflict, he managed to present the Bosnians to the international community as being innocent victims in order to accelerate military intervention by the major powers. This victimisation strategy led to the Bosnian Muslims being accused of bombarding their own population to arouse international compassion, as in the bombing of the Markalé marketplace on 5 February 1994.[125]

However, these little islands of humanity and attempts at resistance generally remained very rare and limited in scope. As the murdering dynamic amplified, it tended to acquire an unstoppable force of its own. Having started in Poland and then spread to the Soviet Union, the operations to exterminate Jews spread through all of Europe during the course of 1942. In Bosnia history seemed to repeat itself: regions where massacres were most terrible were those that had been the scene, during the Second World War, of previous massacres (of Serbs by Croats): Eastern Bosnia on the one hand, and the Kozara and Prijedor regions to the west on the other. In Rwanda, having been concentrated in Kigali and the centre of the country, the massacres spread to the east and the south, which had till then resisted the pressures of the extremists. It was as though a veritable cyclone had sprung up and swept along ravaging in its path an entire nation, or even a whole continent; but it was nevertheless a discerning cyclone, selecting its victims only to erase them from the earth; a cyclone against which shelter seemed to be almost always derisory, and its power of devastation to have no limits.

Morphologies of extreme violence

Violence unleashed in this way is irrepressible. It becomes extreme because it *tends to the extreme*. One might consider the use of such a word as containing a normative judgement: 'extreme' in relation to what? Here I give it an almost mathematical meaning: that of a violence tending to the extreme, as one says of a value or an equation that it tends towards infinity.

From a quantitative point of view this 'tendency' causes thousands, dozens of thousands, hundreds of thousands of deaths. From a qualitative standpoint, it tends to produce acts of cruelty and atrocities to the body, before and after death, that exceed the limits of our understanding. The characteristics of this extreme violence make one think moreover of what Clausewitz wrote about the war, when he remarked on exactly this point—that one of war's characteristics is its tendency to escalate to extremes. But for Clausewitz it is politics that must hold the reins of this runaway horse that is war. Politics makes an instrument of war by assigning to it objectives and conditions. There is 'something', as well, that restrains war: a taboo, a moral prohibition, a political limit—in short, a barrier. But in the instances examined here, there is no longer any barrier or any restraint that would seem capable of reining in violence as it unfurls. I shall then try to define with greater clarity the variables of this terrifying equation that seems to propel violence towards the unbounded.

In the light of the cases examined in these chapters, I would uphold that this equation depends on a particular combination of power, war and ideology. Political power first, because contrary to Clausewitz's view we are dealing with a political power that no longer assumes the role of containment of violence. Quite the opposite, in fact: politics 'heaps it on', whipping the galloping horse and urging it on faster to wreak ever greater ravages on everything its path. For all that, the animal is not totally out of control. Its destructive energy is directed towards very specific victims that are to be crushed in its passage. Politics seems indeed to be pursuing a plan to transform through destruction. The more this power is endowed with the means of exerting power, the more the violence that results from it will be devastating in terms of human lives. If power kills, Rudolf Rummel tells us, 'absolute power kills absolutely'. The formula seems to make sense: the less freedom a population has, the more it is subjected to the violence of the power that oppresses it. Without the opposition powers of a democratic system, power goes wild. Rummel was referring mainly to the twentieth-century communist states, which, he maintains, have been even more murderous of their own people than fascist states.

But what he is saying is more general in nature: if political science consists in studying systems of power and government, then it must explore much more the political motivations of those governments that transform the states of which they are in charge into immense mass graves. Nevertheless, Rummel's approach remains simplistic because he does not investigate when and under what circumstances these powers come to destroy their own people or the people they conquer. Because they do not spend all their time killing their own populations. They also experience phases of respite and apparent calm. How can this be explained?

I will use a somewhat paradoxical reasoning to address this question. In effect, a truly powerful power, precisely because it feels strong, has no need to perpetrate mass murder: it can just exhibit this power without going to such lengths. Didn't Machiavelli consider that the essence of power resides in the illusion of power? In which case the reasoning can be inverted: the practice of massacre would in reality be the sign not of a strong power but rather of a power that feels itself to be vulnerable and which aspires, via massacre, to cease to be so. If this power happens to be contested, it can then decide to express its power through massacre, to recover its authority. Massacre, then, would be the outward expression of a crisis of the state, from which the latter is seeking to extricate itself... through mass killings.

When the threatened state becomes the threatening state. In this regard we can distinguish between three situations of crisis. In the first a power under construction imposes itself on everyone else by resorting to the practice of massacre. Thus for the historian Jean-Clément

Martin the massacres that took place during the French Revolution (starting with those in the Vendée) cannot be understood without realising that they were the paradoxical expression of the state's weakness. One could say the same of massacres Tito's armies carried out at the end of the war, so that he could impose himself as the new military chief of communist Yugoslavia. In the same way the extreme violence of the Khmer Rouge in Cambodia would be explained by the fact that they were, and knew themselves to be, in an extreme minority. These revolutionary powers feel themselves pressed for time: to gain the upper hand as quickly as possible they freely engage in the most brutal forms of violence. In waging a kind of war against civilians, massacre aims to overcome a position of weakness and ensure their ascendancy over the population. If the state makes war as much as war makes the state, as Charles Tilly put it, we could say the same of massacre.

The next scenario is one of an already functioning state whose legitimacy is keenly contested, with individuals who refuse to accept—or no longer accept—their allegiance to this power and tending to reappropriate the right to violence. Under this heading comes the situation in former Yugoslavia, where various nationalist separatist movements undermined federal unity, eventually leading to the formation of new nation-states in the Balkans. Such, according to the Canadian political scientist Kalevi Holsti, is the principal source of contemporary wars; a government's lack of legitimacy is both the cause and the consequence of its collapse.[126] From this results a mixture of anarchy and tyranny that presides over the disputed constitution of new units. Thus war, including war waged in the form of massacre, leads to the formation of new powers that are often a fertile breeding ground for politically-oriented organised crime networks.

The third situation is that of states caught up in war that find themselves in a state of uncertainty, even vulnerability, over the conflict's outcome. Fighting an enemy from without at the same time as from within, these powers tend to invest all the more energy in destroying the enemy within as they fail on the external military front. One could almost say that the more these powers experience bitter defeat in war, the more they set upon the enemy in their midst, this foe being within easy reach and perceived to be complicit with the enemy on the outside. Such was the situation in Rwanda at the beginning of the 1980s: the RPF threatened effectively to seize power at Kigali, since the government's armed forces offered only token resistance. It is moreover plausible that if France had not come to President Habyarimana's aid at the time, this regime would have collapsed well before 1994. And because Hutu extremists perceived a close link between an evolving Tutsi threat on the outside and the Tutsi threat on the inside, they reached the conclusion that to win the war they had to destroy the threat posed on the inside.

Quite a similar kind of reasoning can also be applied to the Armenian massacres carried out following the crushing defeat of the Turks by the Russians in 1915. This took place against a backdrop of war in which the Ottoman Empire's Armenian minority was seen by the Young Turk government as being an accomplice and ally of Russia. In the case of Nazi Germany, we have seen how historians such as Philippe Burrin and Christian Gerlach established a relationship between the increasingly alarming turn of events the war was taking, from Berlin's standpoint, and the decision to go for a 'final solution'. This comparative approach lends weight to their argument that the decision to kill all Jews in Europe cannot be dissociated from the Germans' realisation, from the autumn of 1941 onwards, that they would not be able to win the war they had embarked on against the Soviet Union. It may well be, therefore, that it was awareness of imminent failure that prompted Hitler to take the decision to succeed at least in his other fundamental objective: the extermination of the Jews.

However, it is not the custom for all powers in positions of vulnerability to react by massacring segments of their own population. In the nineteenth century the Austro-Hungarian Empire was worn down on every side by nationalist movements, but did not react in this way. In the same way, when the Germans marched on Paris in 1870, it never occurred to French leaders that their best defence was to make an appeal to the people to slaughter all compatriots who sympathised with the invader. If the extent to which Nazi and Rwandan states set about destroying their 'enemies' from within partly reflected the difficulties they ran into on the military front, it was because they were predisposed to this by their very makeup. What these nations have in common is a definition of their identity in terms of an opposition to an ostracised and demonised 'other':

this is how they show the world who and what they are as a nation: as it were their trademark. Also, when a serious crisis threatens a state's existence in the short or medium term (as when there is a risk of losing a war) the strongest inclination is to survive—no longer simply by marginalising this 'other' at whose expense they constructed their own identity—but in going as far as to destroy it. It is in this case a paroxysmal reaction, induced by the identity profile of these governments. And only ideology, which spawned them and which therefore profoundly influences how their objectives are defined, can account finally for their destructive tendencies.

This ideological framework dictates their behaviour to the point where their actions seem 'demented'. But from what point of view? For the outside observer the behaviour of these powers seems completely irrational. So in 1944, even though the Reich had almost lost the war, how can we understand the efforts of Adolf Eichmann, who persisted in deporting the Jews from Hungary and in organising the hunt for Jews in Greece, as far as the islands of Corfu and Rhodes? Would not the means that he mobilised in these operations have been better deployed at the front line? Jean-Pierre Chrétien made the same remark with regard to Rwanda: 'When the 'war' everyone is talking about takes the form of massacring families of neighbours, women, children and the elderly included, even as the RPF continued to advance, how can we fail to remember the mobilisation in terms of equipment and men that had been assigned in Nazi Germany to 'supplying' Auschwitz when it would have been more usefully deployed at the various fronts of the world conflict?'[127] Nevertheless, this surprising behaviour is not without a degree of coherence from the viewpoint of the organisers. Their ideological convictions lead them to think that destroying enemy populations is in fact a legitimate wartime objective, just as soldiers fight other soldiers. The external front can not be dissociated from the domestic front, to the extent that the enemy is 'total' whether in uniform or civilian dress.

This special interweaving of power, war and ideology thus creates the conditions for an explosive cocktail capable of triggering an escalation of violence to extreme levels. The destructive potential of this combination of elements does not arise by chance. Each of them draws on the depths of the imaginary as described in Chapter 1:

power draws on identity, war on security, ideology on purity. And if this process of destruction is accepted collectively, it is precisely because it is '*grafted*' on to, and feeds on, this imaginary base that every individual aspires to. It can therefore assume the dimensions of a full-blown social incandescence—that of a purifying wave of destruction.

From partial to total destruction. Even when destructive processes have reached this stage, they should still be differentiated from one another. Some halt mid-way and only result in a partial destruction of the enemy. Others seem to rekindle endlessly, making their targets ever more widely inclusive, and going as far as total annihilation. The objectives assigned to mass murder alter over time as the conflict evolves or the war progresses. The same can be said of methods of destruction, which can change radically according to local and international constraints, and take different forms depending on the culture and geography of the countries in which they are deployed. I will complete this chapter by thus tracing different 'morphologies' of extreme violence, from the standpoint of their changing technologies and objectives.

Comparing various examples of mass murder enables us to measure the inventiveness of which man is capable in this domain. One can speak literally of know-how in the field of mass murder which, depending on the case, may resort to natural elements (cold, fire) or to man-made objects or machines (tools, weapons) to cause slow or immediate death. The various methods of putting people to death obviously bear a close relationship to the specific objectives being pursued. In the case of the Jews, the aim of reducing them to slavery in the East prevailed in the first instance over the aim of exterminating them. This is why till 1942 the process of their destruction remained utilitarian. To be sure, the Jews were bound to die, but working all the while! Thus the concentration camp was a place both of work and of death, because the tasks were exhausting, the climate was extreme, malnutrition was rampant, and so on. In the same way the ghetto that imprisoned the Jewish people reduced their access to food and health care, while forcing them to partake in certain activities. These two different methods of enclosure that in reality reduced all occupants to slavery necessarily provoked their slow death. In Nazi language the expression 'work in the East' in the end only meant one thing for the Jews: certain death.

In Rwanda the 'intermediary' phase of forced labour did not exist, except to use women sexually before killing them. The Hutu extremists did not envisage exploiting Tutsi labour; they simply wanted them to disappear. Hence the killings in 1994 attained to extremes immediately. In barely a few days the situation moved from a state of latent violence to a succession of episodes of slaughter designed to be 'definitive'. This paroxysm of violence went hand in hand with a furious exterminating discourse: this time, 'we will not let them go'; sub-text: 'we will kill them all'. From this arose techniques for systematically hunting down Tutsis that hinged on organising bush-beating operations as though hunting down wild animals, with the participation of the population at large. Ethnic cleansing operations in former Yugoslavia never attained this kind of intensity. The action of killing was associated with chasing people out. The slaughter was not an end in itself, but a means of sowing terror in order to precipitate the flight of any survivors. In this sense columns of refugees are not a consequence of massacres, but their prime objective.

Over and above such general differences, these mass murders had several points in common. They often began in the same way, under the pretext of eliminating elites of the enemy group: elites that were political, intellectual, economic etc. The aim was to reduce the adversary's defence capacities to nothing by going for its head. This involved preparing the attack with reference to pre-established lists. Using the Yugoslav example as a test case, James Gow has suggested calling this type of action an 'elitocide', a judicious term that could be applied to a number of other examples.[128] At the same time instigators of a massacre justify it as an act of war: even if the enemy was unarmed, it represented no less of a threat to be destroyed. It thus constituted a 'military target' as such.

This representation, according to which civilians are perceived as masked combatants, leads perpetrators first to arrest adolescents and men of the target group, and then to murder them. So long as this war-like representation of massacre dominates, the women, children and elderly are not threatened with the same fate as male individuals of combatant age. Nevertheless, those who were spared experienced the full force of various other forms of violence: loss of fathers, sons, brothers or husbands, the destruction of their homes, uprooting through flight and exile, not forgetting diverse sexual violence to which women, mainly, are subjected (with the exception of Jewish women under the Third Reich, with whom any sexual contact was prohibited).

A considerable qualitative leap is taken when the target widens to include women, children and elderly people. In the course of certain civil wars, we can thus observe that sometimes not only political and military leaders on the enemy side are killed, but also their families. In Kosovo, when armed resistance began in the Drenica region, such was the case, for example, of the Jashari family, in which not only the fighting men were executed by the Serbs, in February 1998, but every family member, of both sexes, from the latest born to the patriarch. 'Still more widely, it was soon whole villages that were taken as targets and pounded with heavy artillery fire, under the pretext that they must be harbouring 'terrorists".[129] In Kosovo extension of the target in this way to the close family circle was nonetheless a limited and occasional occurrence. In the case of Nazi Germany and Rwanda, such an enlargement became general, the criteria of sex and age no longer being respected. Thus, having started by killing all men of fighting age from June 1941 onwards, the *Einsaztgruppen*, advancing behind Wehrmacht lines, set about slaughtering women and children in August and September.

By the same token, in Rwanda, about one month after the start of the April 1994 massacres, more and more women and children were killed, on the pretext that Tutsi women could only give birth to Tutsi children (an argument that was nonetheless contrary to Rwandan tradition whereby the ethnic identity of a child came from its father). Whenever children are killed almost systematically, there is no doubt that a genocidal process is afoot. The way the slaughters evolved in Rwanda itself favoured this dynamic. In this instance fugitives trying to escape massacre tended to group together in places where they thought themselves safe, as in churches. The local authorities themselves advised them to do so, like for example the Prefect of Kibuye, Clement Kayishema, who asked the Tutsis to gather in the nearby stadium of Gatwaro (ostensibly earmarked as a safe area) or Bishop Augustin Misago (Bishop of Gikongoro) who asked the Tutsis to leave his church and proceed to a site where a school was being built in Murambi. In fact, these were traps enabling the militias, police and armed forces to kill the thousands or even tens of thousands of men, women and children gathered there more easily.

Another decisive criterion was the geographic widening of the target. In former Yugoslavia, only certain territories of the collapsed federation were affected by ethnic cleansing. In this case the spatial limits set for the massacres were related to their leaders' *political project*: to construct a 'Greater Serbia' here, a 'Greater Croatia' there. In Rwanda we have seen how Hutu extremists sought to spark massacres in those prefectures that attempted to resist the fury of violence. If they had had the political and military means, these would have probably tried to destroy the 'Tutsi threat' elsewhere in central Africa, starting in neighbouring Burundi,[130] but they were hardly able to do so because of the RPF's victory.

This was not the case for the Nazis when they became 'masters' of Europe. Their fundamentally racial vision of the world led them in effect to want to destroy the Jews wherever they were found. This meant their destructive ambitions were not restricted to German territory. They waged a war against the Jews across the entire continent, if not throughout the world. This nearly global extension of the racial enemy to be destroyed is in close relation not only to the nature of their ideology, but also to the context of the war, and a war that had become a world war. It was, moreover in the middle of a world war, and some weeks after the United States had engaged militarily in the conflict that the notorious Wannsee Conference took place on 20 January 1942. It is also known that Hitler was planning to seize Jewish refugees in Japan, or living in the Middle East. This mind-boggling 'purificatory' ambition on a worldwide scale justifies Hannah Arendt's assessment that the Nazis were the very first organisation ever to have desired the total disappearance of a people from the face of the earth.

Looking for a moment at procedures, mass murder often gives rise to the pillaging of the victims' property. Such practices cannot be considered in any way the true motive for the killings, but they undoubtedly contribute to stimulating perpetration of the acts. Either the killers are authorised to appropriate victims' belongings, or their leaders avail themselves of the right, unless the state has itself already laid claim to this privilege. But in any event it is always the case that those killed are pillaged. We should not, however, consider that mass theft leads necessarily to mass murder, even if the history of the spoliation of the Jews in France might lead us to believe so. From July 1940 onwards the Vichy government promulgated on its own initiative various laws that dispossessed the Jews of their property, by making a Jew legally 'unfit'. In the eyes of French law, the Jew was from then on considered to be a minor. From one day to the next, all those that had been defined by the law as Jews found themselves thus ruined, with their wealth and property all transferred to the state. Vichy intended in this way to show Nazi Germany with all possible speed that France could itself contribute to destroying Jewish influence by proclaiming them to be excluded henceforth from society. At no time can the Vichy authorities be said to have wanted the *physical* death of the Jews, but it is still evident that this state-instituted dispossession of their goods provoked their immediate social downfall, and that the application of French law had therefore been a way of 'killing' them socially. And this was just the first step that paved the way for other inhuman ways of treating Jews.

Mass murder technologies. To analyse killing methods, we must first manage to overcome the horror and repulsion which their description arouses. I come back to this fundamental point in Chapter V, when we look at the question of our 'understanding' of these atrocities. I will limit myself here to insisting on the fact that methods of killing should be viewed as a human activity: certainly not one that is really like any other...but one that is *also* like others. These methods always reflect to some extent a country's economic and technical development, its modes of cultural expression, etc. If the economy is predominantly rural, it is no surprise that farming and field tools (machete, knife, hatchet) are used to kill, and are wittingly invoked as the tools to use by extremist propaganda. Similarly, the perfection of the process of murder by gassing developed in Germany proclaims the particular level of scientific and technological development attained by that country.

Some killing methods can be common to several countries, like for example, execution by machine gun or firing squad. Used for the first time during the American Civil War, and then for repressing the

Communards of the Paris Commune, the machine-gun proved formidably efficient when it came to 'mowing down' the adversary and terrorising survivors. It also gave Westerners crushing superiority in their conquest of Africa at the end of the nineteenth century.[131] The use of this portable and powerful weapon thus became widespread: it crops up again and again in the majority of twentieth-century mass murders, from the Armenians to Rwanda and including the massacres of Jews by the *Einsaztgruppen*.

Once again it should be pointed out that like any other form of collective action, methods of destruction sometimes borrow from tradition, and in other respects constitute an innovation. So in Bosnia ethnic cleansing operations in the 1990s made partial use of procedures resorted to during the Balkan Wars at the start of the twentieth century, such as the burning of houses (to drive out inhabitants declared to be undesirable).[132] Analysing these forms of violence obliges us to distinguish between those that stem from tradition and those that derive from modernity or a re-invented tradition. When on 2 May 1991 Seselj's men set about massacring Croatian policemen at Borovo Selo, going so far as to pluck out their eyes and cut off their ears, they rekindled in a single stroke the painful past that some fifty years earlier had seen the Chetnicks and Ustashis massacring Croatians and Serbs respectively. And once again they were not alone, because Germans, Italian fascists and Tito Partisans alike had done the same. Against a background of nationalist revivals in the early 1990s, this event could not fail to arouse immediate and impassioned invective on Serbian and Croatian television screens, contributing just a little more to tipping the conflict over into war.

On the other hand there is no doubt that the development of the gas chambers, principally installed in Poland, is an unprecedented event in the history of mass murders. The first gas lorries (carbon monoxide) came into operation in Chelmno in November 1941, and then during 1942 several Zyklon B gas chambers were put into service at Belzec, Sobibor, Treblinka, Auschwitz-Birkenau and Majdanek[133]—constituting an incredible and terrifying 'advance' in the domain of techniques for putting large numbers of people to death. Even Joseph Goebbels seemed terrified by this 'invention'. In his diary entry for 27 March 1942, he noted for the first time: 'The procedure is a pretty barbaric one and not to be described here more definitely. Not much will remain of the Jews.... The prophesy which the Führer made about them for having brought on a new world war is beginning to come true in a most terrible way. One must not be sentimental in these matters. If we did not fight the Jews, they would destroy us. It's a life-and-death struggle between the Aryan race and the Jewish bacillus.'[134] These words are surprising, coming from an old fighting companion of Hitler's, who for years had been the author of so many public speeches preaching hatred for the Jews at every level and with violence and vulgarity. But in this month of March 1942, the most famous of the Nazi propagandists seemed himself to be 'de-stabilised', apparently not having learnt before that date that the Jews were being more and more systematically killed by gas. One cannot fail to notice how he immediately succeeded in integrating this information in the ideological framework with which he was familiar: that of the Aryans' fight to the death with the Jews. This is a telling example of the terrifying way mass murder can be rationalised.

The European Jews, nevertheless, were not the only people to have perished in the gas chambers. The first such experiments were practised, as we have seen, on German mental patients. Experimentation was extended, in Poland in the autumn of 1941, to Soviet prisoners of war. Other sectors of the population were also to die in this way, like the gypsies, themselves victims of the extravagant Nazi project to purify the race.[135] But it is without doubt the Jews who disappeared *en masse* in the gas chambers between 1941 and 1945, first in Poland, and then throughout Europe. What is literally stupefying is how massacre from this point on took on the character of an industrial activity of 'waste' disposal.

Indeed the 'killing centres', to borrow an expression of Raoul Hilberg's, operated like factories of destruction and recuperation, where the 'noxious' bodies were sent to be destroyed and burnt, care having been taken to remove anything that might have a market value such as jewellery, gold teeth etc. Who could have imagined that human beings would one day become capable of such innovation in murdering their own kind, except in interpretation of Hitler's terrible phrase in *Mein Kampf* with reference to the First World War: 'At the beginning of the War, or even during the War, if twelve or fifteen thousand of these Jews who were corrupting the nation had been forced to submit to poison-gas, just as hundreds of thousands of our best German workers from every social stratum and from every trade and calling had to face it in the field, then the millions of sacrifices made at the front would not have been in vain.'[136] What had possibly been no more than a fantasy of destruction in 1924 had become a terrifying reality in 1942.

Nevertheless, for the Nazis killing by gas was only an additional method of destroying the Jews: shootings had not ceased any more than the slower extermination techniques implemented in the camps. And when these camps had to be evacuated (when the Russians arrived) the Nazis organised 'death marches' in which tens of thousands of prisoners died. All too often we tend to boil down the history of the mass murder process to a single killing method. It is absurd, for instance, to state that the killings in Rwanda in 1994 were all done with machetes, as some Western observers have intimated.[137] Numerous reports claimed that the Tutsis were also killed with other instruments (cudgels, hoes, hammers), grenades and other firearms, not to mention when victims were burnt in churches where they had hoped to find refuge. Faced with the prospect of an appalling death, these people sometimes implored their murderers to kill them as quickly as possible, and would even pay them to do so. The historian José Kagabo reported that people referred to a luxurious death, when the victim handed over money in order to be shot rather than hacked to death with a machete.[138] In Bosnia knives were also used, along with grenades and machine guns as in Srebrenica. It was convenient also to make use of the steep terrain in this region, for example to dispose easily of bodies by throwing them into ravines or deep river gorges. In general mass murder combines several methods of killing—often complementary—that evolve depending on the circumstances, the killers' experience and the means at their disposal at the time.

A last point: the extermination of European Jews using gas fundamentally overturned the relationship between massacre and war. Clearly, as numerous authors have insisted, the destruction of European Jews is difficult to conceive of outside the context of total war. To paraphrase Pierre Hassner's comment with reference to Carl Schmitt, the formation of the total state (Bolshevik and then Nazi) in the lead-time before war led to a total war against a total enemy that had to be totally destroyed.[139] But looking at the situation from a purely empirical standpoint, it seems clear enough that with the machinery set up by the Nazis from 1942 on, slaughter had effectively become completely detached from the actual battlefield of the war. In effect the process that consisted of arresting and deporting Jews in trains from Western countries to the death camps in Poland no longer bore any relation to the methods used to execute Jews in 1940 and 1941 in the East.

In the assault on the Soviet Union the killing operations 'adhered' to the logic of war, with massacres being perpetrated to the rear of the advancing front, either by the *Einsatzgruppen* or by regular army battalions. As if it were an ordinary military operation, commandos of killers would close in on the 'enemy' and then destroy it. In Bosnia and in Rwanda paramilitary groups and other militias operated in the same way, but the system of arrest-deportation-extermination invented by the Nazis was completely different. Such an initiative was distinctive in that it was completely detached from the battlefield. The turnaround is spectacular: instead of death coming to strike the victims where they happened to be, it was the victims themselves who went towards death, shuttled to the places where they would be annihilated. To sum up, the process of destruction came to function autonomously as far as the military front was concerned. I identify this *autonomisation* of mass murder as being emblematic of a more general scheme of things that leads from massacre to the genocidal process, which will be the subject of the last chapter in this book. First, however, let us take a close look at the behaviour of individuals in charge on the ground, and how they perform the massacre. Can we really hope to 'understand' them?

V

THE VERTIGO OF IMPUNITY

We have now entered a world in which anything is possible. The level of violence has been steadily increasing one notch at a time. 'Now all bounds have been overstepped, there are no longer any limits'. This process is truly dizzying because man finds himself before a gaping hole, an anguish that no wall can contain and which risks drawing him towards the nothingness of death. In order to fashion himself, man needs limits, he needs the Law as a reference point. This is how he learns to moderate his drives. 'To make a man is to set him limits,' French philosopher Pierre Legendre has written. And 'to set limits is to bring into play the idea of the Father.'[1] The Father symbolises the Law, barring the way between desire and its object with taboos. In this way the man–child gains access to the symbolic and to speech, and learns to differentiate between his imaginary universe and the real world, between his fantasies and reality. Thus, 'in the course of our bloody history, when speech becomes unbearable to human beings, massacres appear once again.'[2]

But does this automatically mean that such a universe, in which all limits have been abolished, allowing all boundaries to be overstepped, thereby making the descent into violence possible, is without norms or codes? Absolutely not. It originates in both chaos and order. It is both organised and anomic. It is a universe in which unrestrained passions and destructive impulses are authorised. In actual fact, this universe of destruction comes into being out of an inversion of norms. Instead of the paternal figure safeguarding the murder taboo, he encourages or lets it happen. Either the state openly instigates massacre, or, in the event of collapse, it is no longer capable of preventing it. In either case the extreme violence that ensues ends up making impunity the rule.

238

But is it enough to say that individuals agree to kill because they believe they won't be punished? This is far too simplistic an explanation. It shouldn't for a moment be supposed that such action is the result of a well-thought-out decision, calmly weighed in terms of pros and cons beforehand. No, taking action of this kind is generally the product of a situation of social turmoil, and a collective dynamic in which people get swept along on the tide. Before the earthquake, doesn't the earth's crust become molten? I'd say the same of the society before mass murder: It develops into a 'socially molten' state that tends to lead individuals to support, if not actually participate in, massacre.

Taking this 'socially molten' state as its starting point, this chapter aims to explore the 'hard core' of the act of crossing the threshold into violence; or at least to get as close to it as possible. To this end I will start by rejecting psychiatric theories that try to explain such action as resulting from some kind of individual madness. Not all individuals who participate in the violence of massacre are psychopathic monsters. No doubt the context of impunity allows some people's sadistic or perverse traits to come to the fore, but this cannot be assumed for the majority. Individuals are not monstrous as such but only in as far as they are involved in the monstrous dynamic of mass murder. It is therefore social forces that carry them away and I agree with Zygmunt Bauman that cruelty is social in origin. But does this mean that individuals are more 'acted upon' than acting for themselves, that they are paradoxically 'subjected to' their own actions and that consequently they cannot be held responsible for them? Analysis of the facts refutes this position to the extent that individuals effectively subscribe to what is happening. While their degree of freedom may sometimes be greatly reduced, it is never nonexistent. They can always say 'no', or at least steer away from the path that would lead them to become executioners.

To understand this tipping process, I'd like to put forward two types of interpretation. The first leads on directly from the line of argument in Chapter I: that massacre always follows from one or more *frameworks of meaning* that prefashion it. In order to live, men need to make sense of their existence. They have to do the same in order to kill. This mental springboard leading towards mass murder depends on the constant interplay between the imaginary and the

real that abolishes all limits. Depending on the historical situation
and the actors on stage, these frameworks of meaning are tremen-
dously varied: individuals either effectively subscribe to the reasons
for killing put forward by the powers that be, or they find their own
reasons to kill, both these types of motives being compatible. Shifting into acts of violence follows on from a plurality of meanings that
factor in both impulse and calculation.

In parallel with these frameworks of meaning, which as we'll see
develop as much before as during a massacre, the taking of violent
action also supposes a *tipping mechanism* towards murder. Whatever
one can say, it is not easy for a man to resolve to kill a fellow human.
Even if he gives himself good reason for doing so, an individual can
experience, the first time, a moment of hesitation before the fatal act,
as if he was about to throw himself into the void. For this individual
to kill, not just once but dozens or even hundreds of times, he must
be part of a *tipping mechanism* towards murder. In this respect it is
somewhat paradoxical to talk about the individual as such as though
he were a molecular unit of society. But this individual only really
becomes a mass murderer once connected to a group within which
he is nothing but a link in the chain. I will explore the two main axes
of this tipping process towards murder: the one vertical, which most
often fits him into a hierarchical relationship, the other horizontal,
which immerses him in peer group dynamics.

Acts of mass killing, let us not for a moment forget, are a descent
into horror. They mean brutal and atrocious violence to the human
body. Approaching this kind of 'thing' too clinically is a mistake.
History is conventionally documented through tales of battles from
the epic or strategic angle without reconstructing their real core:
violence and its atrocities. Yet in order to fully understand extreme
violence, it is imperative to concentrate on the precise *moment* at
which the violent act occurs and on the way it destroys bodies
before, during and even after death. This dimension of violent action
is even more enigmatic than the ones explored previously. I will
therefore try to interpret the most relevant aspects of it.

Crossing the threshold into violence

Here we are, then, on the 'battlefield' at the fateful moment of killing. One thing is immediately obvious: the killers are in a *group*.

Whether they advance in disguise or openly, whether they're in uniform or civilian dress, they are together. The collective practice of massacre depends more often than not on the prior grouping of these bands of killers, whether hierarchically governed (military or police), more or less informally disciplined (militias) or sporadic (groups of citizens from several neighbourhoods). Killings are thus carried out by battalions, gangs, crowds. Each group has a different story, and operates under different circumstances. But one thing is certain: It is the group that acts as the collective operator of mass murder. It is the group that gives rise to individuals transformed into killers.

How does such a metamorphosis take place? It has first to be nurtured by the reigning power's ideology that rallies individuals to a burst of collective action by 'us' against a dangerous and harmful 'them'. By crystallising this identitarian polarisation, ideology distils the psychotic, then war-mongering climate described throughout these pages. By means of symbols, myths and slogans, ideology—qualified as ethnic, racist or nationalist—helps to aggravate fears (when people are already in a high state of anxiety due to an objectively difficult economic or political situation). Whether one subscribes to it or not, the now dominant ideology constitutes the *semantic matrix* out of which emerge the 'us against them' modes of physical aggression.

The observations of the ethno-psychiatrist George Devereux are interesting in this respect in that they take as their starting point the idea that all individuals possess a number of identities (family, community, political, professional, etc.).[3] In a crisis situation the collective identity tends to take precedence over the others, imposing itself as a common response and refuge in the face of the crisis. The other aspects of the individual's personality become subjugated by the group identity. They lose their individual character to the benefit of this hyper-collective investment. It is ideology that makes possible this very first political coagulation of 'us'. From this point on, groups formed to defend 'us' against 'them' seem naturally to come into being. Interviews conducted by the German historian Natalija Basic with twenty-five former combatants from the wars in Croatia and Bosnia confirm such observations.[4] At the beginning of the 1990s 'the idea of autonomous arming (*Selbstbewaffnung*) was an immediate success. For a while a spirit of camaraderie and enthusiasm dominated. It had never been so easy to get weapons.' Every ethnic community prepared to defend its territory. 'Not since the 1940s had there been so many men ready to fight to preserve their homes and protect their children, wives and elderly women. To refuse was a matter of public scandal. ... Military service for a young man, especially in Bosnia, was expected. Boots were worn every day. Some really seemed to love the 'work' they were called on to carry out. They named this period simply the 'time of killing'.'

However, we should not conclude from this that ideology explains everything. It is a necessary vector in the rising impetus leading to the act of massacre, but it is not enough to cause actual perpetration of the act. For this to happen, a group dynamic must be 'grafted' on to the ideology in such a way as to plunge individuals into killing. It can be assumed in effect that ideology possesses a very real murderous capacity. For violent action to occur, ideology must be combined with something else for the idea to crystallise into the act of massacre. Authors attempting to explain this tipping process put forward three main types of interpretation.

Massacre, pillage, business. The first type of interpretation views the ideological factor as combined with that of self-interest and greed. Men profit from the fact that a country's social and political climate designates this or that category of individuals as 'enemies' in order to relieve them of their wealth, even if it means killing. This is conducive to the formation of gangs with this purpose. Under the guise of fighting the enemy, as identified by ubiquitous propaganda, these groups operate for their own profit. The war in Bosnia offered numerous examples of mixing nationalism and 'business'. Either leaders of opposing camps made arrangements with each other to ensure that their affairs flourished, or everyone naturally took their victims' possessions as spoils. In the Bosnian region of Visegrad, only a few weeks after hostilities broke out in April 1992, a gang of young Serbs, whose leader Milan Lukic was a self-described Chetnik,[5] began attacking and pillaging the wealthiest Muslim families. The gang was known under various names such as the 'White Eagles' or the 'Drina Wolves'. They were a law unto themselves in the area and plundered, killed and/or evicted the local Muslim population.

'Milan Lukic's primary motive was not heroism or patriotism or family honour. It was profit.' But the result of the intrigues of his gang of fifteen or so men was to chase some 14,000 Muslims from Visegrad and the surrounding area.

'Muslims, Muslims, you yellow ants, black days have come.'

'For days thereafter, Milan and his gang cruised Visegrad's streets in the maroon Volkswagen. Chetnik songs blared from the car stereo. He called out with a megaphone for Visegrad's Muslims to leave: *'Muslims, Muslims, you yellow ants, black days have come.'*

Men in black wool balaklavas burst into Muslim homes. They demanded money and jewelry. They carried off whatever they could carry. Gold watches and rings and chains. Cash. Washing machines. Television sets. Candy. There was no resistance. They led Muslims, men and women, on to Mehmet Pasha's bridge and killed them with guns and knives, dumped them in the river, and shot at their bodies as they bobbed away on the current. The gang occupied the hotel next to the stone bridge. Young Muslim women were locked inside and raped. Older women were led on to the bridge to wash down the blood.

(…) On 27 June 1992, just after the evening curfew began, Milan's gang members rapped on the Turjacanin's door saying: 'Get out. You are to be deported to Bajina Basta.'

The gunmen led Zehra and her family into a nearby Muslim house. Zehra says she noticed that the doors and the windows were closed and blocked. She says she saw Milan standing near the balcony door. She knew Milan. Her brother had gone to school with him. After the balcony door was shut, the soldiers outside threw rocks through the windows. The people fell to the floor, she says. Gun bursts followed. Then three hand grenades blew up inside the room. Children screamed. A piece of shrapnel tore into Zehra's leg. The air filled with dust. The people coughed and gagged. Then the room went up in burst of flames. Zehra says she struggled to escape. She pulled her nine-year-old niece with her. She lunged time and again against the balcony door. It didn't open. The mass of burning women and children and men around them were wrestling, pushing, screaming. Zehra says she spotted a small window. She fought her way to it, and lifted herself out. She reached back, trying to grab her niece. But the flames tore into her face and hands and she turned away.

Music blasting from a car stereo drowned out the screams of the burning people. Milan and his men did not notice Zehra limp from the house. She stumbled into a nearby creek bed and hid there through the night. A Serb doctor bandaged her and gave her an injection the next day. He told her never to return. She went into the woods again and met up with a patrol of Muslim soldiers who were leading Muslim civilians away from Milan's gang. Ten members of Zehra's family were among the seventy-one people who died in that house.'

Extract from the article by Chuck Sudetic, 'Le criminel de guerre' in *Après-guerre(s), Autrement*, no. 199/200, January 2001, pp. 236–53.

On the basis of examples such as these, the political scientist John Mueller finds that ethnic warfare fails to fit the Hobbesian model of war of all against all, and considers it to be rather a matter of small bands of gangsters and hooligans sowing terror in an area and taking advantage of it to enrich themselves.[6] He has also highlighted the fact that to make up for the lack of numbers in the Serbian army, the Milosevic government freed common criminals to do the 'dirty work' in exchange for the opportunity to rob their victims. But Mueller neglects the role of the official military units, which were almost always there to prepare and support the actions of these groups.

Several pogrom case studies also highlight this profiteering dimension, for example the monograph by the historian Jan Gross on the massacre of Jedwabne in Poland on 10 July 1941. In this village in eastern Poland, occupied by the USSR between 1939 and 1941, resentment against Jews escalated, with them being accused of having been of the allies communists. The Wehrmacht had only recently departed in its push further East in the hope of conquering Russia. In this war context, several pogroms were carried out against

Jews with German approval if not actual support. So on 10 July 1941, with the help of local hooligans and peasants, the inhabitants of Jedwabne were to kill some 1,600 of the area's Jews (women and children included). Some were stoned to death, others drowned in a lake or beaten; most were burned to death in a barn.

According to Jan Gross, only a combination of factors can explain this incredible event. It took place at a time of political transition, after Soviet forces had left and while the German authorities were establishing themselves. The particularly virulent anti-Semitism of the local Polish Catholic peasants must also be taken into account: at least 50 per cent of the men in the town allegedly participated in the massacre. Nor was their action spontaneous, but rather it was a well-organised operation directed by the mayor, Marian Karolak, and several of his municipal advisers.[7] However, for Jan Gross 'the desire and unexpected opportunity to rob the Jews once and for all—rather than, or alongside with, atavistic anti-Semitism—was the real motivating force that drove Karolak and his cohort to organize the killing.'[8] But does this 'economic' interpretation, propounded as a decisive argument, really take into account the barbarous nature of what took place in the small Polish village?

Socialising into violence. A second model for explaining the descent into violence grafts the ideological factor on to the process of socialisation and conditioning of individuals for violence. Thus certain authors insist on the importance of preliminary training to prepare military, police and other special commandos for the killing of their peers. In fact all government authorities need to train those who serve their interests and kill on their behalf. Of necessity such training must be physically and morally tough—almost traumatising—if these men are to become agents of execution, totally insensitive to the violence they will inflict on others. Such is the theory of the criminologist Lonnie Athens, to whom the American writer Richard Rhodes refers in his account of the behaviour of the *Einsatzgruppen* in Russia.[9] In this instance the process can be described almost as the 'manufacturing' of executioners.

This type of explanation certainly contains a kernel of truth to the extent that all the world's police forces and armies develop pretty tough training programmes for new recruits. But according to the

French historian Christian Ingrao, who has a special interest in the history of the *Einsatzgruppen*, the importance of this prior training for men who become killers is greatly exaggerated. In the case of the *Einsatzgruppen*, for example, training lasted no more than two weeks before they were sent out into the field.[10] And what about the peasant-killers interviewed in Rwanda by Jean Hatzfeld? They had had no preliminary training or gruelling military discipline. They were simply asked, during a crisis, to use a familiar farm tool, the machete, not to work in the fields but to go and chop up the Tutsi enemy.

Becoming a killer on the battlefield. It is rather *in situ*, then, in and through action, that groups become killers, whether trained for the event beforehand or not. Here we are tackling the third interpretive framework for the process of spilling into violence: experience gained in the field is ultimately considered to be the most important causal factor in the descent into mass murder. Anyone who has worked with or led groups knows very well that group spirit is developed in the field, whether the leader's aim is to coach youths in an athletic activity, rally team spirit in a corporate setting, or lead soldiers into war. There is no reason why the training of a group of killers should obey any other rules. It is war that makes warriors, and it is through the act of killing that men become mass killers. The famous study by historian Christopher Browning on German Police Battalion 101 provides a striking example of this way of becoming a killer. Here were 500 men with nothing in their history to suggest they might be destined to become murderers. For the author these were 'ordinary men': fathers and family heads too old to be sent to the Russian front, recruited into the ranks of the Hamburg police. Once posted abroad in Poland, they were nevertheless to murder some 38,000 Jews and send another 45,000 to the gas chambers in Treblinka. They managed all this in sixteen months without having been in any way prepared for the task.

     Such a trajectory is mind-boggling. Browning's great achievement lies in the subtlety of his reflections on how best to shed light on such mysteries, a subject I shall come back to. However, Michael Mann criticised Browning for minimising the anti-Semitic leanings of some battalion members (and some commanders in particular), which in fact showed that the group was not entirely made up of quite such ordinary men. This criticism seems to be partly well founded.[11] These men probably exerted some influence over the others, although perhaps less so on the ideological front. But such an influence should not be overestimated. The only way of 'understanding' what happened to this battalion, as indeed the author invites us to do, is to put its action in context,—that of the all-out war triggered by German aggression against the Soviet Union (and reinforced by the United States' entry into the war). Such contextualisation is certainly difficult for anyone who hasn't experienced the overwhelming atmosphere of war, but it is nevertheless this context that gave rise to the primary framework of meaning that would influence these men's actions. Because it is through war that ideology breaks through into reality by being interwoven with an imaginary fear of the hideous and dangerous enemy, who is indeed there, on the battlefield. Even unarmed, he is still the enemy, and must be destroyed.

This last reading brings us much closer to the crux of things than the previous two, although they are without doubt of interest and do not necessarily pertain to the same perpetrators. Although very different, both are based on the same rational concept of action—that is, that people kill either for profit or because they have been trained to do so. In both cases a purposeful or instrumental notion of committing violent acts is put forward, in other words an explanation based on a certain kind of rationality. But I believe I have already shown, in the first chapter of this book, how important it is to take into account the role of imagined fear, the need for vengeance and omnipotence as drivers for killing.

Critics of Browning's book have perhaps not taken sufficiently into consideration the speech Major Trapp gave his men several hours before going into action: 'If it would make their task any easier, the men should remember that in Germany the bombs were falling on women and children.'[12] In other words, what 'they' have done to our children, we can and should do to theirs. It matters little that Trapp is talking about Anglo-American bombings. What counts is the link he establishes between this 'external enemy' that attacks innocent Germans and the 'Jewish' enemy that his police battalion must destroy. Here we find ourselves in the incredible intertwining between the reality of a physical aggression and an imagined threat supposedly coming from unarmed civilians. The onset of killing almost always seems to involve this astounding sleight of hand that assimilates the destruction of civilians with a perfectly legitimate act of war. From that moment on, massacre becomes an act of self-defence. Once again we are in the security dilemma typical of war logic: it is 'us' or 'them'. In Bosnia Natalija Basic tells us ethnic cleansing was experienced as an act of war, while in Rwanda, the killing of Tutsis was seen as a contribution to the defence of the homeland.

But are we indeed purely in the realm of the imaginary? No, because the sleight of hand seems real, and the threat does indeed seem to be partly well-founded. After all, some Jews could be communists and helping the Red Army, while Tutsis could be helping the RPF in its fight to gain power. The argument appears rational. But where does one draw the line on the likelihood of such a threat? Who is really accomplice to the enemy and who is not? It seems impossible to say. So the whole group becomes suspect, and becomes the enemy. This is why the boundaries between real and imaginary become so blurred. Shifting into violent action then makes the destruction of the whole group an obligation.

What do killers think about during the massacre? How do we know that those taking violent action really believe in this 'threat'? To a certain extent we do because they themselves provide the evidence by becoming killers. But such collective behaviour does not constitute absolute proof of individual conviction. Killers rarely provide us with their testimony at the moment they go into action. Christopher Browning's study is based on statements by police officers during their trial some twenty years after the event. Similarly, Jean Hatzfeld interviewed his peasant-killers in prison about ten years after they had been tried. In both cases the murderers had time to rationalise their past actions.[13] The vagaries of memory inevitably played their part in the subsequent reconstruction of the facts. To know what killers are thinking at the very moment when they act would mean having access to confidences made at the very moment killings took place. Not remarks they might make to friends to disguise their lack of composure but inner confidences that one might suppose would have a greater degree of authenticity, such as personal diaries or private family correspondence.[14] But such documents are extremely rare.

The war diary of SS Hauptscharführer Felix Landau falls into this category.[15] His diary begins at the time of the invasion into Russia, when he joined a 'Special Kommando'.[16] He was then in love with a young typist called Gertrude (although he had been married since 1938) to whom he writes regularly and whose letters he awaits with impatience. He seems very preoccupied with this relationship. At the same time he is obedient and hardworking, and has a very strong sense of duty toward his mission. He seems to have accepted once and for all that Jews and Poles were sub-human, and effectively slaves. Nonetheless he expresses regret at having to kill them, not out of any sort of human compassion but because he would have preferred a more noble task, that of fighting the 'real' war. 'I have little inclination to shoot defenceless people—even if they are only Jews. I would far prefer good honest open combat.' (5 July 1941). However, Felix Landau uses a wartime metaphor to justify his action: 'in addition I was officially assigned as "Judengeneral" (General to the Jews)' (10 July 1941).

He finds his mission somewhat tiring: 'Once again I've got to play General to the Jews' (5 July). But it was war nonetheless and as such seems to have deeply marked him. His unit follows the Wehrmacht's progress and the smell of death accompanies him every step of the way: 'We've seen things one rarely sees.' In this world of destruction his intimate thoughts are of his 'darling Trude': 'Like a small child I couldn't wait to get my post' (12 July 1941). He is often tormented by whether or not she'll be faithful to him. On the other hand he doesn't seem particularly troubled when he kills or orders the killing of Jews. This is how he relates participating in an execution: 'It's strange, you love battle and then have to shoot defenceless people. Twenty-three had to be shot, among them ... women. They are unbelievable.... The death candidates assembled with shovels to dig their own graves. Two of them were weeping. The others certainly have incredible courage. What on earth is running through their minds? ... Strange, *I am completely unmoved. No pity, nothing.* That's the way it is and then it's all over. My heart beats just a little faster when involuntarily I recall the feelings and thoughts I had when I was in a similar situation' (12 July 1941).

Despite being a member of the SS, his notes express displeasure at having to 'play executioner and then gravedigger' when he would have liked to be at the front fighting. He says that the executions are exhausting: 'the shots were fired and the brains whizzed through the air. … I came back dog tired but the work went on.'

In other passages of his diary we find that Felix Landau is someone who is interested in other cultures. For instance, he talks about an excellent evening spent with a Ukrainian family learning about their customs. But at night thoughts of his beloved return. He seems to be so in love with her that he wants her by his side and intends to take steps with his superiors to achieve this. Does he need her physical presence in order to withstand the difficulties of his 'work' better? Reading this diary leaves one with a deep sense of unease, even terror. Because this individual who learns how to kill Jews on a virtually industrial scale by 'playing General', as he puts it, is so very human: he loves, he suffers from the absence of his beloved and yet his being in love goes hand in hand with an extreme brutality towards Jews, about whom he has fully internalised the idea that their lives are worth nothing more than the condition of slaves.

Another staggering document is a letter by Walter Mattner, a Viennese police clerk recruited into the *Einsatzkommando* and on operations in Belarus. On 5 October 1941 he writes the following incredible lines to his wife: 'So I also took part in the day before yesterday's huge mass killing (*Massensterben*). When the first truckload [of victims] arrived my hand was slightly trembling when shooting, but one gets used to this. When the tenth load arrived I was already aiming more calmly and shot securely at the many women, children and infants. Considering that I too have two infants at home, with whom these hordes would do the same, if not ten times worse. The death we gave to them was a nice, quick death compared to the hellish torture of thousands upon thousands in the dungeons of the GPU. Infants were flying in a wide circle through the air and we shot them still in flight, before they fell into the pit and into the water. Let's get rid of this scum that tossed all of Europe into the war…'[17]

Such remarks tend to prove that perpetrators internalise rather easily the ideological frameworks concocted by those in power to justify such killings. Like Felix Landau, Walter Mattner appears at first to feel a certain uneasiness about shooting defenceless people.

But his scruples fade fairly quickly. He mentions that he 'gets used to' the killing (a point I shall return to). However, this father feels the need to explain to his wife how he comes to be killing babies when he has young children himself. He could doubtless have spared her such details, but he has to justify his behaviour to himself. And he has no choice other than to take the arguments used by the regime's propaganda and apply them to his personal situation and his own family. So he, a father of toddlers, accepts the killing of babies while thinking of his own children. By thinking of these babies as belonging to a 'horde', savages by definition, that has plunged Europe into war[18] and threatened the German people, he rids himself of the guilt of murdering young children. Note how this man also shows himself in a favourable light, boasting of his almost humane violence since he and his comrades inflict a 'nice, quick death' compared to the tortures inflicted by the Bolshevik enemy. Even as he is in the process of committing his barbaric actions, the bully will seek to inflate his own ego by claiming to be human.

These very rare writings by perpetrators at the time of killing tend to prove that they believe in what they're doing. One might wonder whether before taking such action they belonged to a minority of fanatics or rather to the majority of ordinary individuals in Browning's sense of the term. I believe that such a question is secondary as soon as these people become caught up in the dynamics of massacre. In fact, from the moment they agree to take part in mass killings they have to make 'sense' of what they're doing, otherwise it is impossible to see how they could continue to kill. Whether they were convinced ideologues beforehand or not, their behaviour in a way forces them to come up with justifications that in their own eyes explain their participation in the killings. Theorising massacre does not boil down to identifying a 'before' and 'after' the actual shift into action, as if the 'before' were ideological justification and the 'after' the physical act of killing.

Such a scenario is far too linear and does not sufficiently take into account the effects of the act of killing on the perpetrators themselves. The killers' representations continually evolve in line with what they do in the field. It is not just the framework of meaning that precipitates the act itself; it is the very act of massacring that recreates the contextual meaning of such an action. As the anthropologist

Alexander Hinton suggests, we can consider the perpetrators as 'meaning-makers'. He uses the metaphor of *bricolage* to qualify their acts: 'By regarding perpetrators as bricoleurs and not passive ideological automatons, we can gain a better understanding of their motivations for committing genocidal atrocities. Even if perpetrators are highly constrained in some circumstances, they remain active subjects who construct meaning and assert their self-identity through their violent practices.'[19]

Cognitive dissonance and rationalisations. Another way of apprehending the different metamorphoses of the descent into killing can be identified here: the group may enable the individual to turn into a killer, but the repeated act of massacring leads the perpetrator to reconstruct images of his victims in such a way as to justify his acts. Indeed, military rhetoric (as described above) is apparently not always enough to legitimise the destruction of defenceless individuals. The killers' own words bring into play other types of justifications, very often concocted on the spot. Thus the practice of massacre produces of itself a new rhetoric, a new vocabulary that uses words borrowed from a wide range of activities (hunting, work, health, etc.) to disguise the reality of murdering human beings. These representations are not so much the cause as the consequence of the act itself (even if they draw upon elements already present in former statements).

It is as though the perpetrators, at the moment of killing, and using words taken from their own culture, devise the various frameworks of meaning that by their very nature 'rationalise' what they are doing. In fact they find themselves plunged into a situation of intense 'cognitive dissonance', to use the expression coined by the psychologist Leon Festinger.[20] They are experiencing in effect an acute conflict between on the one hand their murderous practices and, on the other, their own self-image. How can they 'stand themselves' when in the act of massacring? The theory of cognitive dissonance holds that killers must of necessity restructure their beliefs about themselves in such a way that they conform to their actions. There is nothing exceptional in this: it is only one illustration among many of our capacity to rationalise our beliefs in line with our behaviour. The development of such representations by killers should not therefore be seen as pure propaganda so much as the formation, in action and through the act of massacring, of a varied and necessary vocabulary of mass murder, enabling the act to be performed time and again.

One of the most recurrent lexicons, often common to different cultures, is that of animals and hunting. We have already noted that a regime's propaganda may have previously described its enemies as animals (rats, lice, cockroaches, vermin). This kind of talk was part of more general rhetoric aimed at ostracising a population. When the killing has begun, these animal descriptions of victims may reappear in other guises, for example as a hunter's prey. Charles Mironko noted that the former peasant-killers he interviewed frequently used the word '*igitero*', which in Kinyarwandan has two meanings: it refers both to hunting and the need to stick together in the face of danger.[21] From there, as perpetrators' own words while in action often tell us, it is only a short step to launching oneself and the group to hunt down this menacing prey and feast on it.

Thus one survivor relates: 'they were brandishing machetes or axes and spears and yelled: "Here we are, here we are, and here's how we prepare Tutsi meat".'[22] In Croatia groups of Serbs entering Vukovar shouted almost the same refrain: 'Slobodan, send us some salad to go with the meat from Croats whose throats we've cut.'[23] What more is there to say about this 'loss of moral sense on the part of the Polish peasants'? 'A psychosis took hold of them and they emulate the Germans in that they don't see a human being in Jews, only some pernicious animal, which has to be destroyed by all means, like a dog with rabies, or a rat.'[24] To make the Lublin district forever 'free of Jews' (*judenfrei*), as of October 1942 those found wandering the countryside were to be killed without any form of administrative procedure. 'In official jargon, the battalion made "forest patrols" for "suspects". As the surviving Jews were to be tracked down and shot like animals, however, the men of Reserve Battalion 101 unofficially dubbed this phase of the Final Solution the *Judenjagd* or "Jew hunt".'[25] The victims of these roundup operations could also be Partisans or escaped prisoners of war. In order to carry out their task, officers of Reserve Battalion 101 developed a network of Polish informers, woodsmen and other such moles specialised in searching out hiding places.

At the moment of killing, murderers can still resort to other rhetorics to make sense of what they are doing. The use of certain words or expressions is a ploy designed to obscure and play down the realities of the massacre. In Rwanda the killing was often presented as a special type of 'work', which made it appear normal or even ordinary, and in any case useful for the community, a form of hill 'clearing', akin to farm work. Massacre is still often portrayed as a 'cleaning' task, a word that is present in the expression 'ethnic cleansing' but also in military language: 'clean up the area'. Consequently, the reality of 'massacre' disappears behind the positive notion of cleanliness or even health.

Moreover, words taken out of context that conjure up the idea rather of technical operations or the free movement of people or goods are also used to describe slaughter. We know that the Nazis had invented a euphemistic vocabulary to refer to the assassination of Jews, employed in various administrative reports, including expressions such as 'special treatment', 're-installation' or the notorious 'final solution'.[26] The protocol of the Wannsee Conference refers in this way to 're-installing' or 'evacuating' Jews. To carry out the massacre of the men of Srebrenica, Bosnian Serb political and military leaders used a code to communicate among themselves, referring to the groups of men to be executed as 'parcels'. This term is not, however, loaded with the same dehumanising meaning as the expressions used by the Nazis. But at least it allowed the Bosnian Serb nationalists to cover up what they were doing. Thus on 14 July 1995 Colonel Ljubisa Beara informed his superior that there were '3,500 parcels left to deliver'.[27] It should be noted that these different ways of naming victims contain contradictions: how can one be both an animal to be hunted and a parcel to be delivered? But the lexical universe of perpetrators is not troubled by such inconsistencies. What does it matter, so long as they fulfil their missions?

The way vocabularies of massacre have developed thus seems to be directly related to the development of the practices themselves. These expressions allow the killers to construct a 'common culture' among themselves and so facilitate group dynamics. But how can one believe that words alone, simple linguistic formulae, can hide the horrors of carnage, even from the murderers themselves? Who could really believe that these individuals to be eliminated are not humans just like everybody else? In reality, to slaughter human beings requires a high degree of physical and above all mental exertion from those who perform such acts. In order to come to terms with what they are doing, the executioners must persuade themselves that they are serving a higher cause, whether it is that of their identity group, of their nation, or even of humanity as a whole.

In short, the horror of their acts forces them to project themselves into a kind of transcendental state. This state is presented as a superior 'law', a categorical imperative, dictated by an absolute sense of duty. Rather than thinking 'what horrible things I have done', the perpetrator has to be able to say: 'what horrible things I *had to do*'. At the same time, the killer 'disconnects' from himself, having acted in the line of duty. True, he has performed some 'dirty work' but in his own eyes and in the eyes of others, he is a better person for it; it had to be done and it was moreover necessary for the survival of his group, for the common good. He can be proud of what he has done. In any case, if he had refused, others would not have hesitated to do it. And so what is the point of being stubborn? What a staggering reversal of values this is! In fact, it is a reflection of the inversion of norms in a society that rewards individuals who kill instead of punishing them.

This inversion also operates among many killers as a defence mechanism. To rid themselves of the idea that they are doing something evil, they have no other choice but to believe that this wickedness is embodied in their victims. This projection mechanism, well documented in psychology, is devastatingly powerful. Anchoring mass murder on the side of morality gives it an extraordinarily destructive force, and over a long period of time. The 'other' who must be destroyed is evil or the Devil incarnate. The victim may well have a human face, but the Devil does too. These diabolical representations of the other to be destroyed seem much more powerful than animal representations. They permit the executioner to kill these evil beings without any qualms. And consequently the perpetrator claims his innocence. The 'clear conscience' which killers have is not so much a prerequisite to doing the deed as a consequence of it: a false moral stance to which they cling ever more desperately as they sink deeper and deeper into repeated acts of murder.

Divine legitimation. Some way down this slippery slope of supposed innocence, the executioner has an appointment with the sacred.

Because in playing life and death games with the men and women that are his victims, the perpetrator ends up almost believing that he is the instrument of the hand of God. The need to justify the massacre morally can lead some people to claim for it a religious justification. God is summoned to bless their murders, as was the case in Rwanda where the Virgin Mary was invited to support the war, in May 1994, during an 'apparition' broadcast on the radio.[28] In Croatia apparitions of the Virgin Mary in Medjugorje appeared to prove that she was also on the side of the Croatian nationalist combatants; 'the Virgin Mary has been recruited in a war of independence' and has been appointed 'healer of all Croatian sickness'.[29] On the Serbian side there is no doubt that for one of the police officials, Brana Crncevic, 'Serbian crimes are God's responsibility, the crimes of others are the Devil's.'[30]

In Nazi Germany it was Hitler himself who was presented as the new God. In Omer Bartov's analysis, 'the troops' view of reality was composed of two interrelated elements: a progressive dehumanisation of the enemy and a parallel deification of the Führer'.[31] Should we be surprised then by the words uttered by Friedrich-Wilhelm Krüger, commander-in-chief of the SS and the police in Galicia, who supervised the massacre of the Jews in Stanislau? On 12 October 1941, a day when it proved impossible to have the planned number of Jews murdered, he declared: 'Those who are still alive can go home, the Führer has spared your lives.'[32] If the deification process is taken to its logical conclusion, the executioner could end up thinking he is God. After all, is this not exactly what the poets of ancient Greece have been telling us since Homer? As a consequence of continual killings the hero may fall into the trap of believing in his own immortality. Is this the feeling of omnipotence that he experienced just after killing the men in Srebrenica? Is this proof of his megalomania, or perhaps a temporary bout of madness? Whatever the case may be, when he arrived face to face with the Muslims of Zepa whom he was also intent on having executed (after those of Srebrenica), General Mladic declared: 'Not Allah, not the United Nations, not anything can help you. I am your god'.[33]

Not all organisers and perpetrators of massacres experience such a progression. I have described a range of executioners' representations in this chapter starting from the most common (massacres

experienced as military operations) to the most extraordinary (deification of the executioner). Once they are engaged in killing, the
perpetrators necessarily undergo great psychological distress and the
frameworks of meaning that they construct are a constant compromise between the propaganda that assails them from the outside
and the images that they harbour deep inside them. This was the case
with the SS member Landau: even though he had fully accepted that
he could kill Jews at will, he considered this activity to be something
inglorious, and not altogether compatible with his self-image; he
aspired to engage in 'real' combat. The psychological cost borne by
those who carry out these killings could thus cause many executioners to be reluctant to participate in them.

But this scenario hardly ever occurs in reality, because the killers
are carried along by a collective dynamic that leaves them little room
to refuse. In parallel to the semantic adjustments justifying massacre,
sliding into acts of violence requires some kind of organisational and
technical mechanism to trigger it. This mechanism has no other
function than to relieve the psychological strain on the perpetrators
so that they can get into the rhythm of killing on a long-term basis.
This trigger mechanism comprises two additional 'springs', one
vertical, the other horizontal, the operational dynamics of which
I will now elucidate.

The tipping mechanism

Within the group the individual is subjected to pressure from two
directions that can push him over the edge to commit the act of
killing. The first is exerted by those who are invested with authority,
while the second comes from the peer group—those who, like him,
are in the situation of perpetrators of the massacre. The two dynamics intersect and complement each other: the first acts along the
vertical axis, that of obeying orders, the second along the horizontal
axis, that of group conformity. In this way the individual is continually caught up in the mechanics of a sequence of events that
throws him off-balance, since his behaviour is defined not so much
by himself but by his superiors, as well as by the pressure to conform
to the image held up by his companions in slaughter.

Does this mean that the individual is swept up against his will in a
diabolical spiral? Such an affirmation would place him rather too

hastily in a situation of total irresponsibility. Has he not given his consent from the beginning? Of course, he is caught in the wheels of a machine he cannot control and which in some cases will take him further than he ever imagined. The more involved he becomes, the more difficult it is for him to escape. The fact remains that he agreed to take part at the outset. I shall briefly examine the two axes of this tipping mechanism by means of which this primary group of killers is formed, irrespective of the past history of the individuals of which it is composed.

The crime of obedience. Describing the vertical axis of the tipping mechanism involves assessing the role of the command hierarchy in triggering the killings. Depending on the nature of the groups in question, the hierarchy is more or less rigidly structured. Thus within a military unit the discipline is generally much more highly developed than it would be in a group of militiamen.[34] But because massacres almost always require a central driving force, even in such groups, it is rare for there to be no leader whom the perpetrators obey in a more or less formal manner. It is precisely by arguing from their standpoint as subordinates that perpetrators attempt to exculpate themselves from what they have done. We often hear them say, when they are called upon to defend themselves in court: 'I was only obeying orders.' The subordinate allegedly found himself in a situation of absolute compulsion: either execute the orders or be executed; kill or be killed.

This line of defence seems to be unanswerable. Nevertheless it can be countered by one serious objection, as Christopher Browning observed in the case of Nazi Germany: 'Quite simply, in the past forty-five years no defense attorney or defendant in any of the hundreds of postwar trials has been able to document a single case in which refusal to obey an order to kill unarmed civilians resulted in the allegedly inevitable dire punishment.'[35] Even within the ranks of Battalion 101 some men refused to participate in the mission as soon as they were informed about it by their commander, and they were not punished. In Yugoslavia some young people refused to join Milosevic's army, and I know of no case in which someone who refused to take part in the massacres was killed as a result. In Rwanda refusing to join in the slaughter was apparently more risky. Hutus who wanted to protect the victims were immediately killed. But to my knowledge cases of Hutus being executed because they refused to kill have not been reported. There seem to have been ways of avoiding the task by claiming that an urgent family matter had arisen, or that something needed attention in the fields, etc. on the day the 'work' was to be done.

The question of obedience to orders concerns all of us. Having frequently discussed this issue with my students, I have come to realise just how often they spontaneously ask themselves what they would have done if they were in the position of the German police, the Serbian and Croatian soldiers or the Hutu farmers. With hindsight we can judge their behaviour in the abstract and conclude that they could always have refused, but we do this from the comfortable position of knowing how the story ends, and that some said 'no' and went unpunished. But if we were really thrown into a similar situation, under pressure from leaders and afraid of being punished, how would we react? We can understand why the perpetrators say that they were 'carried along', as in the case of a young Croatian police officer, Darko Mrdja, who claimed at his trial in The Hague that refusing to partake in the slaughter was not an option.[36] This impression has a sound basis, because there is something in the logic of action characteristic of a group of killers that resembles a spiral, if not the behaviour of addicts. I will come back to this point later.

Does this mean that all the perpetrators must be considered as having acted against their will, as they often claim when on trial? Certainly not. Obedience is not a purely passive attitude; it presupposes and requires an initial voluntary consent. There are a multitude of reasons for this consent, as we saw previously. Ideological reasons, to begin with: the individual agrees to kill because he really 'believes', because he thinks he is truly serving his country, convinced that it is urgent to be rid of its 'enemies'. There are economic reasons as well, when it is apparent that there are material benefits to be gained from the situation. These two reasons are of course perfectly compatible. The majority mode of agreement to obey is another story again: it is when most of the perpetrators are convinced they are serving a legitimate authority. Max Weber's reflections are enlightening when it comes to understanding how power stamped with the seal of legitimacy draws the allegiance of indi-

viduals and the adherence of those who serve it to inflict violence in
its name.

Social psychology experiments have shed light on the devastating
effects of this process of obedience. The best known of all are those
conducted by Stanley Milgram at Yale University in the 1960s.[37]
The original experiment involved an experimenter and a 'teacher'
who was asked to give electric shocks of increasing intensity to a
'learner' who was supposed to learn pairs of words. In reality the real
subject of the experiment was the participant upon whom the
experimenter exercised his authority. Milgram's experiment has
been criticised for being artificial and thus not reflecting the complexity of the historical situation. This is true, of course, as is always
the case: laboratory experiments, when they manage to throw light
on the salience of certain phenomena, are only a source of inspiration to enable us to understand the complexity of the reality of
social or historical events.

In practical terms Milgram's experiment, reproduced in several
countries, highlights the central aspects of the obedience process.
The first is that the 'teacher' only agrees to give electric shocks to the
'learner' if he sees the experimenter as an authentic representative of
scientific authority. For example, if the experimenter is not wearing
a white coat, the 'teacher' does not follow his instructions. From this
we can infer that the scientific legitimacy he personifies is the only
factor that can make the 'teacher' agree to follow his instructions.
As the experiment progresses, this initial agreement will bind the
'teacher' more and more closely to the experimenter. The 'teacher'
is convinced that he is acting within a certain framework of meaning, that of science, in a laboratory at a prestigious university. This
set of circumstances leads him to agree to participate in such an
experiment.

Secondly, the entire thrust of this experiment comes from the
experimenter who continues to give instructions to the teacher, the
gist of which will always make him increase the strength of the
electric shocks to 'punish' the learner for failing in his task. The
vertical tipping action is triggered by the influence of the experimenter. It is he, by means of the constant pressure he applies, who
continues to 'command' the teacher how he should behave. The
experimenter, invested with scientific authority, seems to hold a post

similar to the commander identified during massacres, the one who decides who should or should not be killed. In passing, the importance of the three-participant model should be noted: experimenter-teacher-learner. This seems also to define the basic structure for massacre: instigator-perpetrator-victim. It is unfortunate that Milgram did not think of creating a variant of the experiment with just the teacher and the learner: such a combination would probably have produced much lower degrees of conformity, or perhaps none at all.

The constant pressure from the experimenter on the teacher rapidly comes into conflict with the learner's obvious suffering. This takes us to the heart of what Milgram wanted to test: how will the teacher get himself out of this situation? How will he behave? The results of the experiment are still rich in lessons for those who study phenomena relating to mass violence. The dominant response of teachers (between 60 and 80 per cent of cases) is to continue the experiment, putting themselves completely under the responsibility of the scientific authority. From the outset the teacher had already accepted the principle, merely by agreeing to carry out the experiment. But having reached this moment of extreme tension, and faced with the learner's simulated suffering, he deepens his allegiance and decides that he can no longer be held responsible for what might happen. At this point the teacher enters what Milgram described as an 'agentic state', complying rigorously with the experimenter's instructions, and concentrating assiduously on the dials of the machine. In one way he obeys the experimenter's 'rule', which instructs him to continue increasing the electric shocks. In so doing he cuts himself off from the learner totally and appears not to notice his suffering. So we can see a double process at work: total identification with authority, and emotional detachment from the victim, as the teacher applies himself to doing his 'job' well.

However, the aim of this experiment was not so much to study obedience as disobedience. More precisely, what was under study was to what degree and at what point the subject, the 'teacher', would decide to stop following the experimenter's instructions. Although none of the subjects refused to participate in the experiment, 20 to 40 per cent of them did not agree to administer the most dangerous electric shocks. In the majority of cases these refusals do not take the form of open rebellion against the experimenter. The teachers stop mostly because they cannot bear to hear the screaming and pleading of the actor-learners. They show compassion for the learners' suffering, and cannot distance themselves emotionally from what the experimenter asks them to do.

A link can be established between this observation and the desertions recorded by Christopher Browning among the men in Battalion 101. Somewhere around 10 to 15 per cent of the men disobeyed orders, but had no intention of entering into head-on conflict with their leaders. They simply claimed to be 'not strong enough' to fulfil the mission they had been given. By admitting their 'sensitivity', i.e. their supposed 'weakness', they managed not to take part in the killings. This sensitivity to suffering, which prompted disobedience, can in fact be seen as a displaying a 'stronger' personality and in this instance a more autonomous one, in other words one less likely to submit to commands from authority.[38]

Group conformity. Group conformity constitutes the second fundamental axis of the mechanism for tipping into massacre. Sociological and historical observations also help in the understanding of this phenomenon, and it has been the subject of various studies in social psychology. Besides the pressure applied by leaders, groups themselves can be considered as sources of power over individuals. This pressure, as much psychological as physical, arises from the fear of being rejected by the group and, in a broader sense, of being ostracised by society. The tendency to conform originates first and foremost from overall social pressure, which develops in a country in crisis in which everyone has to take sides: to be with 'us' or with 'them'. In 1994 in Rwanda the polarisation based on political and identity characteristics reached boiling point. The social environment favoured killings and it was very difficult to escape from that collective state of mind. 'Being alone is too risky for us,' says Alphonse, a former Rwandan killer. 'So the person jumps up at the signal and takes part, even if the price is the bloody work you know.'[39]

The quest for conformity also results from a tendency noted in many mass murders: the desire to implicate as many individuals as possible in the slaughter so that the responsibility for the killings will be shared collectively. 'Christine, the daughter of a Tutsi father and a

Hutu mother, tries to explain it this way, 'I think someone who was forced to kill wanted his neighbors to have to kill, too, so they would all be considered the same …, but you had to show yourself worthy by reddening your hands that one time.'[40]

Within a group of killers, this collective pressure became particularly potent. Regarding Bosnia 'Militiamen were not necessarily fanatics filled with hatred,' remarks Anthony Obershall. 'Peer pressure, fear, not only of Muslims but of extremist Serbs who might finger him as a "traitor", were the major reasons for joining a militia. Some of these men were unemployed and expected a job in the coming Serb government as militia or police. Once the young man "took out a gun" he became encapsulated in a quasi-military unit subject to peer solidarity and ethnic loyalty. He was trained in weapons and indoctrinated with the beliefs and norms of the crisis frame about other ethnics.'[41] In Rwanda networks of affinities in the hills contributed to the formation of local groups of killers. To carry out the 'work' in the marshes; the men grouped themselves together with people they knew. These groups did not take kindly to the *Interahamwe* militiamen from outside the region who came to pillage the victims' belongings.

To strike up a real team spirit, groups sometimes organise initiation rites in which newcomers are called upon to prove their loyalty by killing for the first time while all the others look on. In the Musebeya region, which had not yet been affected, Alison Des Forges tells us that Hutus who had not yet killed any Tutsis were called 'accomplices' ('*ibyitso*'). They were threatened: 'Come with us and join us or we will kill you.' Then the group would capture someone and be told: 'Now kill her to show that you are really with us!'[42]

However, these initiation rites are not always necessary since the tendency to do as the others do is dominant and therefore prescribes the behaviour of each and every group member. The paramount consideration in all this is the desire not to lose face, in other words not to appear cowardly. It is very difficult to go it alone when the leader demands that his men 'surpass' themselves, as on 13 July 1942, when the commander of Battalion 101 stated what he expected of his men. 'Nonetheless, the act of stepping out that morning in Jozefow meant leaving one's comrades and admitting that one was 'too weak' or 'cowardly'.[43] At this precise moment the perpetrators are no longer in a position to say: 'Why do I have to kill these people who have done nothing to me?' but rather: 'Can I let my comrades down by leaving them to do this dirty work?' Their participation becomes much more a question of personal pride, if not of courage, in following the others; and this overshadows their possible feeling of guilt at killing defenceless individuals. When it comes to the crunch, members of the group feel obliged to move into action all together. To appear 'strong', and to comply with an ideal of so-called masculinity, which is at the same time synonymous with brutality, they will become killers. At that particular instant their ideological representations of their victims do not seem to determine their behaviour to a great extent. Everything revolves around the way these men see each other, and around their pride, which does not allow them to show pity for those they are about to kill. And it all hinges on the manner in which they show unity, an *esprit de corps* in this sinister, virile camaraderie of massacre.

However, in this group all the killers are not alike they may exhibit different behaviour once the action begins. On this point another social psychology experiment conducted by Philip Zimbardo helps to refine our understanding. He decided to simulate a prison environment and asked students from Stanford University to play the roles of prison guards and prisoners. This situation, though artificial, had spectacular effects on the individuals involved. The students identified with the roles and started behaving like real prison guards and prisoners. According to Zimbardo they underwent a process of deindividuation that led them to conform to the role of passive prisoner and brutal guard. This polarisation of roles tended to be accentuated over time: the guards started being violent to the prisoners, and the experiment eventually had to be curtailed. One of the most alarming results was that it showed that individuals who could in no way be described as sadistic before the experiment actually started to exhibit increasingly sadistic tendencies as time went on.

Zimbardo nevertheless identified three types of behaviour among the prison guards. Almost a third of them proved to be cruel and uncompromising. They demonstrated imagination in humiliating the prisoners and seemed to take pleasure in inventing such 'games'. Others (almost half) restricted themselves to enforcing the rules, acting in a strict but fair manner. They did not seem to want to take advantage of the situation to mistreat the prisoners. Finally, a few (less than 20 per cent) turned out to be 'good' prison guards, not seeking to use any brutality with the prisoners and even allowing them small privileges.

According to Christopher Browning, this experiment is even more relevant than Milgram's in helping to understand the behaviour of the perpetrators. The range of behaviour identified by Zimbardo has similarities to the attitudes of the German police in Battalion 101. First, there was a hard core of zealous perpetrators, killers whose enthusiasm gradually increased, and who volunteered to take part in the executions. Secondly, there were the 'follow-my-leader' types, more numerous than the first group, who shot when asked to, but did not seek opportunities to kill. These people sometimes refrained from killing if the leaders were not there to check on them. Finally, a handful of 'reluctant' or 'resistant' subjects (less than 20 per cent) refused to kill or attempted to shy away from killing.

Despite repulsion or even resistance on the part of certain individuals, the overall group tendency is therefore to agree to carry out the killings. Do they resemble the hunting packs that Elias Canetti refers to? Do they advance in close formation as if they were confronting an army? Seeing them pass by, they already cause fear. Generally they wear special suits or uniforms to show their membership of a group, a single police or military unit: the sinister 'death's head' worn by the SS; the more discreet slogans tattooed on the arms of Serbian nationalists; the banana leaves worn by certain Hutu attackers. Sometimes they donned balaclavas or blackened their faces to avoid being recognised. Suddenly, the carnage starts: bodies fall to the ground, blood spurts everywhere, heads crack open. The perpetrators are not necessarily accustomed to carrying out these deeds. This can be an entirely new experience for them, in which case it is definitely a mental ordeal, a kind of 'baptism of blood'. How can they protect themselves psychologically from the effects of the carnage? At the same time they must complete the task efficiently to get the mission over quickly. A dual learning process is involved in the perpetration of extreme violence: the task of psychological adaptation and at the same time mastery of various procedures for killing victims, some more effective than others.

The dual learning process of massacre

Besides constructing frameworks of meaning and setting up trigger mechanisms, what can really prepare the perpetrators for the shock of the forthcoming carnage? Very little indeed. The act of massacre implies both a psychological and technical learning process: the men must become 'accustomed' to their job of mass murderer. And to live with themselves in the performance of this macabre activity more easily, they tend to acquire more and more professional skills to turn their destructive behaviour into a routine activity. From a psychological standpoint participating in a massacre is far from a trivial experience. The collective practice of killing immediately transports the perpetrators into a sphere of omnipotence. They suddenly enter another world, created by the terror of their weapons alone. It is a world in which human beings entirely at their mercy have already ceased to exist, even as they reach the point where they become corpses.

As regards the world of Nazi concentration camps, David Rousset, a French survivor of Buchenwald, spoke of this world as one where 'Anything is possible', a phrase Hannah Arendt used to introduce the first chapter of her major work *The Origins of Totalitarianism*.[44] The frightening brevity of this statement also characterises, in minimalist fashion, the real dynamics of mass killing. Once a massacre begins, anything is indeed possible, everything becomes possible. How will the perpetrators react psychologically and how will they adapt to this world of impunity?

Some seem to adapt right away with pleasure. They experience a form of unconcealed glee. They throw themselves on their prey like savage beasts. Anyone would think they had long been waiting for this very moment. They race headlong into the violence, throwing themselves wholeheartedly into their task. The German sociologist Wolfgang Sofsky describes this type of perpetrator with indulgence. The killer 'wants to wallow in blood', he writes, 'to feel with his own hands, with his fingertips, what he is doing. The knife affords him a direct, tactile sensation. The violence that he perpetrates affects him, his muscles, his arm, his hand. By crushing, cutting, dismembering, he is in contact with his own violence. It is his body that conceives of the evil that he is doing, his hand that feels the force of destruction. The more the killer enters the skin of the other and cuts him into pieces, the more his triumph takes on a bodily consistency, a physical reality'.[45] But what Sofsky considers to be unquestionably the psychology of a perpetrator, is in fact just one of its facets. His approach is in my opinion far too systematic.

Other perpetrators, by contrast, can feel a profound unease as they gradually sink deeper and deeper into the massacre. They find this experience particularly disturbing or even traumatic. Browning provides us with a few testimonies of policemen from Battalion 101 who state that they found it hard to bear what they were forced to do. We should not misinterpret the meaning of such observations. It would be out of place to 'pity' the executioner while he is slaughtering defenceless individuals. It is precisely because such an act is morally scandalous and psychologically difficult that it will probably have a traumatising effect on the person who commits it. In reality the perpetrator is faced with this dilemma: How does he carry out this 'task', and carry it out efficiently, while protecting himself psychologically from the world of death that he himself is helping to create? To do so he must have recourse to methods or procedures that will allow him to remove himself from the situation—while at the same participating in it.

The murdering self. Two 'solutions' are available to perpetrators, which can be complementary. The first is 'artificial': it consists in taking drugs or alcohol, often with their superiors' permission, before taking part in, and even during, the operations. Those in command are well aware that their men require encouragement to give them enthusiasm for their work. Many accounts of massacres testify to the killers having operated under the effect of these stimulants. For good reason: they have the advantage of suppressing the individual's inhibitions and immersing him in an artificial state of well-being or even euphoria that helps him function in the blood and death-stained environment in which he is operating. It is as if, at the decisive moment, to facilitate shifting into action, an additional factor is required to 'push' the individuals into committing the irreparable. Consumption of these stimulants and other mood-altering drugs that produce a chemical reaction in the brain allows them to reach an altered state, in which they will be able to do what is asked of them. But not all perpetrators use these stimulants and in any event not necessarily on a systematic basis.

The second escape route available to them is purely psychical, and does not arise from a conscious decision but is based upon a reaction often observed in human beings in moments of intense stress. To protect himself from a world of death, the individual generates a kind of psychic numbness in response to the outside world: he is there but no longer there. He is actually performing certain actions, but it is only his body, while his mind is elsewhere. Soldiers on the battleground or prisoners in concentration camps can consequently dissociate themselves from the situation to escape from the destructive environment that is assailing them, from the vision and stench of corpses, etc. In short, to survive. This human capacity to 'separate from the self' can be just as useful to live with oneself while slaughtering others. According to the psychologist Robert Lifton, it would probably be impossible to kill another human being without 'numbing' the brain to the plight of one's victim. The more deeply the individual is involved in murder, the more he creates another 'self', that is detached from the first 'self' and which even takes control of it.

The governance of the 'self as killer' over the whole individual enables him to 'undo' his behaviour as a killer by freeing him theoretically from all feelings of guilt.[46] In effect a kind of personality dissociation occurs, and is the sole means of accepting oneself during the act of slaying. Robert Lifton considers that this personality splitting process in order to wreak destruction is founded upon a 'Faustian contract' between these two 'selves', and refers to the work of Goethe and Thomas Mann: 'Two souls, alas! reside within my breast,' says Faust, 'And each withdraws from and repels its brother.' And the devil replies: 'We lay upon you nothing new, but only ingeniously strengthen and exaggerate all that you already are.'[47]

Has the perpetrator therefore reached the point of no return? By becoming more and more deeply involved in the most abject violence, has he no way out? To say this would be to forget that some, who have already reached this stage, have, by arresting the collective dynamic, managed to escape from the process. These refusals, even when the individual has started killing, though rare, are among the possible reactions of perpetrators in the field. Although their margin of freedom is very slight, some individuals do manage to say no. A policeman from Battalion 101, George Kageler, decided to take such action when he realised that they were killing German Jews. This thirty-seven-year-old tailor, having taken part in one series of killings, recalls: 'After I had carried out the first shooting and at the unloading point was allotted a mother with daughter as victims for the next shooting, I began a conversation with them and learned that they were Germans from Kassel, and I took the decision not to participate further in the executions. The entire business was now so repugnant to me that I returned to my platoon leader and told him that I was still sick and asked for my release.'[48]

In Bosnia, on the first day of the Srebrenica massacre, Drazen Erdemovic, a Croat married to a Serb, decided to run away. 'They told us that a busload of civilians would come from Srebrenica,' he said during his trial in The Hague. 'I said immediately that I did not want to take part in that and I said 'Are you normal? Do you know what you are doing?' But nobody listened to me and they told me, 'If you do not wish to, if you—you can just go and stand in line together with them. You can give us your rifle.' He said that during that day he took part in the execution of around 100 prisoners. But when he was called to another location to kill more people— another 500 or so—he refused to carry on, and in this instance a faction within his unit supported him.[49]

For the remainder there are a thousand and one ways of coping with killing. After the initial shock perpetrators gradually manage to get used to it, developing various techniques. In short, they work through their own apprenticeship in collective murder, becoming professionals in committing violent acts against civilians. The historian Natalija Basic identified several phases of this progression based on interviews with ex-combatants in Bosnia: 'At first, there is a phase of cumulative radicalisation during which the perpetrator learns to kill. In the second phase, the violence carried out is reinterpreted as being a 'moral' action. Then comes the phase of habituation to homicide. Finally, the act of killing is defined as 'work', a profession in its own right; a job that has its own specific routines. At this stage the perpetration of violence becomes 'routine' and acts of cruelty are demystified'.[50]

In the case of Battalion 101 Christopher Browning points to more or less the same progression. He observes the increasingly brutal behaviour of the men and the setting up of increasingly routine killing procedures. They were not necessarily brutes before the action but once they had killed on a routine basis, they became brutal. 'As in combat, the horrors of the initial encounter eventually became routine, and the killing became progressively easier... brutalisation was not the cause but the effect of these men's behavior.'[51] But habituation of the perpetrators to slaughter does not mean that they have adapted to it. If the process of diminishing empathy for the victims is curtailed or suddenly interrupted, then the men can be subject to traumatic pathologies, the first symptoms of which are often recurrent nightmares and/or insomnia.

'The journey from Poniatowa'

Himmler could not expect to liquidate the Lublin work camps gradually or one by one without encountering further Jewish resistance born of desperation. The inmates of the Lublin labor camps would therefore have to be killed in a single massive operation that would catch them by surprise. Such was the genesis of the *Erntefest*....

On the evening of 2 November Sporrenberg met with the commanders of the various forces, which included the Waffen-SS from the districts of Krakow and Warsaw, Police Regiment 22 from Krakow, Police Regiment 25 (including Reserve Police Battalion 101) and the Lublin Security Police, as well as the commanders of the camps at Majdanek, Trawniki and Poniatowa, and Sporrenberg's SSPF staff. The meeting room was full. Sporrenberg gave instructions from the special folder he had brought back from Krakow. The massive killing operation began the next morning.

Members of Reserve Police Battalion 101 participated in virtually every phase of the *Erntefest* massacre in Lublin. They arrived in the district capital on November 2 (so Trapp presumably attended Sporrenberg's conference) and were lodged overnight. Early on the morning of November 3 they took up their stations. One group from the battalion helped to march Jews from various small work camps around Lublin to the Majdanek concentration camp several kilometres from the city center on the main road leading southwest. The largest contingent of Reserve Police Battalion 101 took up positions five meters apart on both sides of the angled street that led from the main highway past the Commandant's house to the entrance of the inner camp. Here they watched as an endless stream of Jews from various work sites around Lublin filed past.

Women guards on bicycles escorted 5,000 to 6,000 women prisoners from the 'old airport camp' where they had been employed in warehouses sorting the clothing collected at the death camps. Another 8,000 male Jews were also marched past in the course of the day. Together with the 3,500 to 4,000 Jews already in the camp, they swelled the victim pool to some 16,500 and 18,000. As the Jews passed between the chain of reserve policemen into the camp, music blared from two loud-speaker trucks. Despite the attempt to drown out other noise, the sound of steady gunfire could be heard from the camp.

The Jews were taken to the last row of barracks, where they undressed. Arms raised, hands clasped behind their necks, totally naked, they were led in groups from the barracks through a hole cut in the fence to the trenches that had been dug behind the camp. This route too was guarded by men from Reserve Police Battalion 101.

Stationed only ten meters from the graves, Heinrich Bocholt of the First Company witnessed the killing procedure: 'From my position, I could now observe how the Jews were driven naked from the barracks by other members of our battalion… the shooters of the execution commandos, who sat on the edge of the graves directly in front of me, were members of the SD… Some distance behind each shooter stood several other SD men who constantly kept the magazines of the submachine guns full and handed them to the shooter. A number of such shooters were assigned to each grave. Today I can no longer provide details about the number of graves. It is possible that there were many such graves where shooting took place simultaneously. I definitely remember that the naked Jews were driven directly into the graves and forced to lie down quite precisely on top of the pile of those who had been shot before them. The shooter then fired off a burst at these prone victims … How long the action lasted, I can no longer say with certainty. Presumably it lasted the entire day, because I remember I was relieved once from my post. I can give no details about the number of victims, but there were an awful lot of them.'

... In the memories of many men from the Reserve Police Battalion 101, the two massacres in the two camps merged into a single operation of two or three days at a single camp, either Majdanek or Poniatowa. But some witnesses—at least one from each of the companies—did in fact remember shooting operations at two camps. It seems clear, therefore, that early on the morning of November 4 the men of Reserve Police Battalion 101 traveled the fifty kilometres from Lublin to Poniatowa.

This time the battalion was not dispersed. The men were stationed either between the undressing barracks and the zig-zag graves of the site or at the shooting site itself. They formed a human cordon through which the 14,000 work Jews of Poniatowa, stark naked and with their hands behind their necks, marched to their deaths while the loudspeakers once again blared music in a vain attempt to cover up the noise of the shooting. The closest witness was Martin Detmold:

'I myself and my group had guard duty directly in front of the grave. The grave was a big zigzag-shaped series of slit trenches about three meters wide and three to four meters deep. From my post I could observe how the Jews...were forced to undress in the last barracks and surrender all their possessions and were then driven through our cordon and down sloped openings into the trenches. SD men standing at the edge of the trenches drove the Jews onward to the execution sites, where other SD men with submachine guns fired from the edge of the trench. Because I was the group leader and could move about more freely, I went once directly to the execution site and saw how the newly arriving Jews had to lie down on those already shot. They were then likewise shot with bursts from the submachine guns. The SD men took care that the Jews were shot in such a way that there were inclines in the piles of corpses enabling the newcomers to lie down on corpses piled as much as three meters high.

...The whole business was the most gruesome I had ever seen in my life, because I was frequently able to see that after a burst had been fired the Jews were only wounded and those still living were more or less buried alive beneath the corpses of those shot later, without the wounded being given so-called mercy shots. I remember that from out of the pile of corpses the SS [sic] men were cursed by the wounded.

Excerpt from Christopher R. Browning's book, *Ordinary Men: The 101st Reserve Battalion of the German Police and the Final Solution in Poland*, New York, HarperCollins, 1992, pp. 137–41.

In parallel with these attempts to adapt psychologically to the practice of massacre, the procedures themselves can undergo technical advances over time and with the benefit of experience acquired. This knowledge, gleaned through trial and error, can be used to devise methods meeting three objectives: to facilitate the perpetrators' slide into violence, to protect them from traumatising exposure and to increase efficiency. Executioners always prefer to shoot a person in the back, or blindfolded, so that their eyes do not meet. 'I just happened to start by killing several without seeing their faces.... The eyes of the killed, for the killer, are his calamity if he looks into them. They are the blame of the person he kills,' the farmer Pancrace Hakizamungili explained to Jean Hatzfeld.[52] And if they have to slit their victim's throat, the perpetrators know that it is better to make the person kneel down and then to cut his throat from behind, as if they were killing animals.

In Rwanda and Bosnia these killing methods were borrowed from farming. In Nazi Europe they were clearly taken more from experience gained in war, be it the 'massing' of individuals or recourse to digging anti-tank trenches, on the edges of which the victims were lined up before being killed. The simple fact of bringing together the future victims together as a mass helps to de-individualise them. Quantity depersonalises and consequently desensitises. Thus the manner in which the Jews were grouped together and deported was preparation for their destruction. And killing two people is in a sense harder than killing two thousand. During the remarkable interview that the Hungarian journalist Gitta Sereny conducted with Franz Stangl, the former commanding officer of the Sobibor and Treblinka extermination camps, he acknowledged that he perceived the Jews arriving as 'a load', and added: 'I rarely saw them as individuals. It was always a huge mass. ... They were naked, packed together, running, being driven with whips like...'[53]

The experience accumulated by the *Einsatzgruppen* leads to what Christian Ingrao called the 'constants' of extermination by shooting, observed in all commandos in mobile SS units. These constants are the 'dissociation between killers and guards responsible for the transporting, collective shooting, prior digging of communal graves, shooting of victims in the back to ensure they fall into the grave due to the impact of the bullet or killing of victims lying down and lined up in rows one on top of the other in the grave. They are a sort of ... empirical skill of the killing method developed by the killers themselves.'[54] In these procedures of mass slaughter, it is important for the whole group to be involved. Thus 'almost all unit commanders obliged their men, no matter what their post, to take part in an execution and to shoot somebody, obviously with the aim of spreading the psychological load over the entire army. Some officers militarised the procedure by forming groups that had to shoot when the order was given; others designated two gunmen per victim, regulated the shooting distance, automated the gun reloading movements to prevent the executioners from having to suffer the spectacle of the grave; still others used native militias to perform the executions of women and children.'[55]

Task specialisation and the professionalisation of slaughter. When massacres are carried out over a long period and a large area, a degree of task specialisation tends to occur, as it does for other human activities. Browning observes this in the way Battalion 101 developed over the sixteen months of operations in Poland. After first handling the execution of Jews itself, the battalion used Ukrainian, Latvian and Lithuanian groups of prisoners of war taken from prison camps and selected for their anti-communist and anti-Semitic sentiments, and forced them to perform the most revolting tasks. Consequently, the policemen from Battalion 101 became responsible only for arresting and transporting Jews to the execution site, a much easier task. They also took care of driving them to the local train station from which point the Jews were transported to a death camp.

In Bosnia massacres were often a coordinated effort among several types of actor: the army first bombed a town or village, then police units or paramilitary groups entered the fray, arresting, killing, burning, raping and expelling their victims. Local civilians sometimes joined in these operations as well.

In Rwanda the distinct roles of military staff, police, and militias need to be studied area by area, even if only to assess the exact involvement of the local population in the slaughter. But the organisers do not appear to have actively sought a division of labour. In this sense the extermination of Rwandan Tutsis and European Jews was based on two completely different dynamics. In Rwanda those who initiated the massacres encouraged the Hutu population to become involved on a massive scale. This tendency can be observed in many mass murders: the more the murders rely on group participation, the more the responsibility is shared. In Rwanda this phenomenon is particularly striking. The participation of all the Hutus in the killings was completely over-dramatised, and presented as a matter of group survival in the face of the advancing '*Inyenzi*' (cockroaches). As a result every Hutu was urgently called upon to kill Tutsis. In fact, instead of tending towards the division of labour, this 'model' of mass murder rests on the 'spontaneous' involvement of everyone in killing right where they live, because the '*Inyenzi*' are everywhere. And in this collective swing, the killing population retains its full identity. It is by drawing on its own practices and values that the people can knuckle down to the task of mass murder. Hence the Hutu killers went up into the hills to kill as if they were going to do their work for the community.

And as they marched off they sang traditional songs to give themselves heart. At the end of the day, the men could go back to their cabarets (the equivalent of pubs and bars), as is the tradition of the *Ibyivugo*. The cabarets were the place where each man could describe and declaim his accomplishments: 'I am the one who..., I did..., I achieved...'. During the massacres, and at such gatherings, the farmers would take turns to speak, as is customary in celebration ceremonies. As one *Ibyivugo* followed another, the claims regarding the violence committed spiralled: 'I am so and so and I killed so and so with this club...', 'I killed ten...', 'yes but I killed twenty...'. 'More than pride in their participation in genocide', remarks the French political scientist Pierre-Antoine Braud, 'these claims are part of the local context whereby the influence of all concerned is redefined, by calling up the mood of raids and a highly militarised monarchical society.'[56]

The Nazis, on the other hand, rarely called upon the local populations to destroy 'their' Jews. Under the influence of Himmler and Heydrich, a 'colder' and more 'rational' vision of slaughter was implemented, involving secrecy and an increasingly sophisticated division of labour. As we know, after having tested the efficacy of other killing techniques, they decided on gassing with Zyclon B, this procedure being particularly well suited to removing responsibility from the perpetrators (cf. chapter IV). It was the gas that acted, not the man who pulled the machine-gun trigger. Moreover, gas chambers concealed the victim's moment of death, whereas a gunman must necessarily focus on his target to kill the victim and thus witness his death. This is one of the reasons why gassing was also applied to the extermination of the Jews, in addition to, or in place of, shooting, because shooting affected the perpetrators psychologically to a much greater extent. In some ways the gassing process makes the executioner 'vanish', as his participation is limited to the technical act of putting the Zyclon B into the machine, without having to worry about anything else.

Therefore, the gassing technique appears as a 'clean', hygienic method that does not causing atrocities but is more 'humane' for the victim… but also for his executioner. If we subvert Norbert Elias' expression, here the very civilising process is fully given over to a destructive enterprise. For the Italian philosopher Enzo Traverso, this conception of mass killing should be seen as part of the long-term evolution of European history through the invention of the guillotine and the prison. He writes: 'The guillotine paradigm—mechanical execution, serialised death, indirect killing, ethical de-responsibilisation of the executioner, killing as a 'subjectless' process—has celebrated its triumphs in the technological massacres of the twentieth century.' To this can be added the 'prison paradigm—the fencing principle, dehumanisation of prisoners, withering and discipline of the body, submission to hierarchies, administrative rationality—(which) reached its apogee in the concentration camp system of totalitarian regimes.' The author concludes: 'the Nazi extermination camps merge these two paradigms by giving birth to something appallingly new and historically original … they create a system of killing on an industrial scale in which modern technology, division of labour and administrative rationality are mutually integrated as they are in a company. Its victims were not strictly speaking 'inmates' but 'raw material' formed of downgraded living beings of the human race, required for the mass production of corpses.'[57]

Another characteristic of the extermination system set up by the Nazis further demonstrates its perverse ingenuity. Not only did it aim to make the executioner 'vanish' but it goes as far as enlisting the participation of victims in their own destruction. This occurred at both ends of the line: from the control of the Jews (in countries that were under Nazi domination) up to their entry into the gas chambers. In fact, right from the outset, forced cooperation was ensured by the establishment of Jewish councils, in both eastern and western Europe. The creation of such bodies had immediate practical value, since the Nazis did not have adequate human resources to administer the Jewish communities. The role of these Jewish councils has generated intense controversy, mainly in response to Hannah Arendt's book *Eichmann in Jerusalem*, in which she suggested that the Jews cooperated with the Nazis, and that this cooperation, which was often voluntary, made the lot of the Jews worse instead of improving it.[58] It should be pointed out, however, that these organisations were useful in providing a structure for assisting and organising life in the communities, in increasingly disastrous living conditions.

But it is clear that in many cases the '*Judenräte*' were forced to carry out the work of the Nazi authorities, for example by policing the ghettos themselves and, even worse, by being ordered to hand over Jews who were then sent to their deaths. This untenable position drove some Jewish leaders to despair and even suicide. Adam Czerniakov, for instance, took his own life in Warsaw on 23 July 1942 when he realised that his organisation had become an instrument of the Nazi extermination policy.

And the worst was yet to come—at the end of the deportation process, at the very heart of the killing centres. There the Nazis created the *Sonderkommandos*, groups of prisoners who were made responsible for maintaining order before new arrivals entered the gas chamber, and then to remove the corpses, extract the gold teeth, cut off the women's hair, etc. The fate of these prisoner-guards was also sealed: they performed menial tasks in the gas chambers for a few weeks or months, then were replaced by newcomers who were eventually subjected to the same fate. Nobody was to be left to testify to what they had seen and done. A few German, Russian and Polish prisoners took part in these *Sonderkommandos* as well, but the majority were Jews. In other words, certain perpetrators of mass murderer were also victims! The creation of *Sonderkommandos* could well be the most monstrous version of mass murder, one in which the system's dynamics forces the victim to take part in his own destruction. Not only the executioner seems to have vanished, but he is replaced by the victim. 'One is stunned by this paroxysm of perfidy and hatred', writes Primo Levi. 'It must be the Jews who put the Jews into the ovens; it must be shown that the Jews, the subrace, the submen, bow to any and all humiliation, even to destroying themselves'.[59]

The killers' profiles: revisiting 'the banality of evil'

One often wonders whether those who become mass killers have a particular psychological profile that might explain why they slide into violence. Some authors have explored this avenue, such as the psychiatrist Henry V. Dicks whose book, now forgotten, explored the personal histories of various Nazis, including Rudolf Hoess, commandant of Auschwitz, in order to interpret their fanatical violent behaviour. Dicks thought he had identified common tendencies in the Nazi criminals' childhood that Hitler's regime enabled them to develop and satisfy.[60]

Better known is the research that the philosopher Theodor Adorno conducted on the authoritarian personality, allegedly at the root of all fascist and totalitarian power.[61] But such studies have shown their limitations. It is difficult to identify in infancy or in the upbringing of individuals or even in their personality traits, sufficiently convincing elements that could account for what might have pushed them at a later stage into mass violence. The main reason for such a failing is simple: mass murder is above all the product of a socio-political process, and the upshot of that is that any individual, whatever his personality type or social status, can potentially become involved in it. Of course, particularly troubled and perverted personalities can take centre stage in the system, with the complicity of the authorities who exploit them.

In Bosnia Goran Jelisic, a Serbian guard at the Luka camp, is probably an example of such a pathological case. When he first appeared in court at The Hague on 26 January 1998, he introduced himself to the judges as 'the Serbian Adolf'; which is what he always told his Muslim prisoners to let them know that they would soon be killed. According to one witness, Goran Jelisic declared that before he could drink his morning coffee, he had to execute twenty to thirty people.[62] The conditions of impunity in which these individuals are placed allow them to give free rein to their murderous fantasies. However, as Bruno Bettelheim already noted more than sixty years ago in his observations on the behaviour of the SS guards, when, as a young psychiatrist, he was interned in the camps of Dachau and then Buchenwald, these sadistic or perverted personalities are in a tiny minority in relation to all perpetrators, whether they are guards or killers.[63]

Ordinary executioners. Just who are they? The stereotype of 'family man-executioner', handed down from the Nazi period, does not really correspond to what is known about them. Apart from the wide diversity of their profiles, most of the killers have several common characteristics: they are young, even adolescent, single and male. Most of the potential killers are recruited from among the thirteen to twenty-five year-old age group. At this stage in life, human beings are both the most psychologically malleable and physically vigorous. They are often idealistic and in search of guidance that an authority figure who would take charge of them might be able to provide. They seek also to fit in with people in their own age group by acting the way they do.

In short, the main characteristics described above to account for what triggers the act of killing, whether this is from the standpoint of frameworks of meaning (good/evil) or from that of tipping mechanisms (obedience/conformity), are particularly salient at this stage of human development. It is thus hardly surprising that people in power the world over recruit their agents from this age group. Youth organisations make up the main breeding ground from which authorities select those who will become their devoted servants. There is no need to recall the role of the Hitler Youth organisations or the manipulation of sporting associations by the Nazi regime. In former Yugoslavia the anthropologist Ivan Colovic has explained how young paramilitaries were recruited among supporters of the Serbian and Croatian football clubs.[64]

In Rwanda the *Interahamwe* militias also found volunteers among Kigali football club supporters. An ex-killer who was seventeen years old in 1994 recounts: 'we had long enjoyed listening to Ferdinand Nahimana's commentaries of football games on the radio. When we saw that he wanted to save the country by supporting President Habyarimana, we all joined the *Interahamwe*. We had a great time and at the same time, we were protecting the Republic against the *Inyenzi*.'[65] These *Interahamwe* militias started recruiting from among the 'many young men who had hung out on the streets of Kigali or smaller commercial centers, with little prospect of obtaining either the land or the jobs needed to marry and raise families.'[66] Should we conclude that the killers are all young dropouts, and the poor belonging to a kind of lumpen proletariat? This would lend credence to another cliché in this field. In fact, other studies show that the recruits may also have a high educational level. They are qualified but jobless. In other economic and social circumstances, they would have done other things, if they had work opportunities. When war broke out in their country, the best they could find was to be recruited as militiamen, policemen or into the forces, turning them into killers.

However, it should not be believed that job qualifications and employment prevent individuals from straying on to the social and political pathways that lead people to commit mass murder. Teachers, lawyers and doctors are just as likely to 'get their hands dirty' by organising idle youths, offering them an exciting future. In Rwanda one survivor, a Tutsi teacher Jean-Baptiste Munyankore, speaks of some of his colleagues in these terms: 'these learned people were calm, and they rolled up their sleeves to get a firm grip on a machete. So for people like me who have taught Humanities their life long, criminals such as these are a terrible mystery.'[67] It must once again be noted that education does not in itself constitute a barrier against murder, no more than culture is a differentiating factor in the acting out process. The same profile of young men who become killers is found in Europe, Africa and Asia as well. They can find themselves involved in the perpetration of a massacre out of conviction, opportunism or chance, on a small or large scale.

The involvement of women and children. In certain circumstances the range of perpetrators can broaden. This was especially the case in Rwanda where the entire Hutu population was called on to participate in the killings. Thus women were sometimes implicated in the massacres. Their involvement, hardly studied to date, must still not be overstated. It probably ranged from widespread indirect support to occasional participation in murderous acts.[68] Indirect support could take the form of Hutu women standing by their men and encouraging them to go to 'work' in the hills. Once this 'work' was accomplished, they also trooped up to the hills to strip the victims of their belongings. Some women also joined in with groups of killers, either as passive onlookers, or cheering them on in their task. In other cases they fulfilled a 'supervisory' role with young militiamen, and even went as far as to encourage them to rape Tutsi girls. Such incitement by women to commit sexual violence against other women seems incomprehensible. Those who participated actively in the killings included civil servants, shopkeepers and teachers. There are reports of other equally baffling incidents, such as women accused of having killed their husbands or their children because they had Tutsi fathers. Equally stupefying is the fact that some nuns participated in the slaughter, such as the Mother Superior of a convent in Sovu (Butare), Gertrude Mukangango, who was tried in Belgium for having helped the *Interahamwe* militiamen to burn Tutsis who had taken refuge in one of the convent buildings.

Such examples, though rare, testify to the fact that the mass violence in Rwanda reached extremes that are rare in history, practically unheard-of even in 'totalitarian' regimes. This violence stemmed from a dual transgression: of the taboo against murder within the family, which can completely destroy the family unit, and of the basic tenet 'Thou shalt not kill', leading people of the cloth to cease protecting the lives of their fellow men but instead becoming accomplices in their destruction.

The participation of young adolescents in slaughter is also an indicator of such total social destructiveness. In Nazi Germany children were sometimes driven to denounce members of their families. In Rwanda children were also used to denounce 'enemies'. 'It is customary in this country to send children to neighbours' houses to ask for salt, water or matches,' reports the Rwandan Tutsi survivor

Annick Kayitesi. 'During the genocide, the adults used this form of solidarity to flush out Tutsis hidden by family members or by Hutu neighbours who were helping them.'[69] Children seem to have taken part in the massacres only very rarely, but as the schools—exceptionally—were closed, children spent most of their time following on the heels of the killers. Rows of corpses by the roadside became playgrounds that children were quick to occupy. As they did not have the physical strength required to kill adults, they sometimes hit the victims with machetes. 'A.B. confided in me: "We enjoyed ourselves more than at home or in the deserted hills. Here we had enemies to fight. Every day there were different enemies. They were bigger and stronger than us and we were very proud."'[70] In Rwanda children traditionally leave school at the age of fourteen or fifteen to work in the fields. This introduction into working life probably corresponds to the age at which these children-adolescents were allowed to join in the killings with the adults. However, their murderous behaviour probably differed according to their social class. Young people from middle-class families preferred to conceal their acts from most people, whereas few in rural areas were able to do the same. For the very poor young people, murder was often rewarded by a small payment in kind. A shirt, a pair of shoes, or perhaps even a watch were the most sought-after spoils. The chance of material gain fed their enthusiasm for the task.

The involvement of women and occasionally children in massacre is certainly the most significant and the most baffling social indicator of the extreme nature of the swing of a whole population towards mass murder. This does not imply that every one of its members is transformed into a killer. As in every community, some appear more motivated by the task, derive greater benefit from it, or have little choice in the matter, and so on. On the other hand, this means that the fundamental social norm of this population is no longer to forbid murder, but rather to allow it. And at this very special point when killing is performed with impunity, anyone can join in the macabre dance and try to find in it his own personal rewards.

The ambiguity of evil. In this sense understanding the reasons for individual acting out, in the context of massacre, implies always taking account of at least two distinct but intertwined levels.

The first is that of the official public arena: that of ideology, security, and the imaginary. There is no reason to doubt that certain perpetrators 'believe' in what they are doing: they are convinced that they are carrying out a civilising mission, defending their country at a critical time when 'the enemy' is everywhere, participating in an exalting collective task, and so forth. They carry out mass killings because they consider it necessary. These collective reasons for massacre are both the product of passion (exploited by the authorities) and of a context conducive to it (helping to give these reasons historical resonance).

The second level is that of a more unofficial arena, a private stage, made up of the thousand and one reasons for which and by which individuals will commit violent action. Here too passion and interest can be combined, first for reasons of greed and profit-seeking, as we have already seen. In other cases the incentive for committing murder is purely financial: the individual simply becomes a mercenary, accepting payment for killing, with no ideological motives whatsoever for his destructive behaviour. Career and social promotion motivations must also be taken into account, above all in organised corps such as the police and the army, where promotion is at stake; strict obedience to orders elicits approval from one's superiors. But this careerism, which came into play for instance in officer promotions during the war in Bosnia, is only one of the many factors at work. In other circumstances an emergency rationale will prevail, dictated by the security dilemma: kill or be killed. In the case of neighbourhood massacres, old resentments can also partly explain local outbreaks of violence. Whether they can be tied, in certain situations, to the material success of a particular person, property conflicts or perhaps lovers' quarrels, these unresolved conflicts from the past can lead neighbours to join in the killing out of jealousy or revenge. The multiple intrusions of private micro-conflicts, in the very midst of the public macro-war, occur frequently and are often observable in what we term 'civil wars'.

Although individuals are indubitably swept up by the dynamics of mass murder, they still know how to reap benefits from it. People can be extremely opportunistic and calculating in exploiting the effects for their personal gain. So on an individual level, the reasons for crossing the threshold into violence are manifold. What is true for one individual at a given time will not be true for another. But it is precisely this variety of converging private motives that lends massacre its massive dimension. Individuals join in the murderous dynamic not as automata droning on with the same stereotyped ideological discourse, but with different histories, and hence different expectations and personal motivations. Their shared involvement in killing results from a variety of ambiguous behaviour patterns.

In this behavioural mosaic, there is moreover room for some forms of protective action. We are sometimes at pains to understand why certain killers will save some people's lives even as they are killing others. But it is so difficult to see that they might harbour a secret need to give themselves precisely that positive image of rescuer? This double face is perfectly compatible with the phenomenon of the split personality, described by Robert Lifton. While the 'murdering self' goes about its daily activities in the open, a 'secret self', the saviour, acts behind the scenes. Perpetrators can continue to take part in slaughter while at the same time taking risks to save *one life*. The act of destruction is developed against another as a whole and dehumanised, while the act of protection is focused on a specific person, human and respectable. The motives for this protective behaviour also vary widely.

In Rwanda Jean Hatzfeld reports the story of a Tutsi woman, Marie-Louise, shopkeeper in Nyamata, whose husband and family were massacred by the *Interahamwe*; having made a narrow escape, she seeks refuge in the house of her neighbour, Florian, a Hutu who is the head of military intelligence in the region. Before the war the two families were on good terms. Florian, who took part in the massacres in town, does not want to kill his ex-friend's wife. He does everything he possibly can to save her, and manages to help her escape to Burundi. In another case a young Hutu militiaman showed great zeal in killing the '*Iyenzis*'... so that his Tutsi mother should be spared. And then there was a Hutu soldier who hid a young Tutsi girl as long as she agreed to have sexual intercourse with him. In this case the notion of 'rescue' is a highly relative concept since it rests upon a relationship of blackmail: 'Your life in exchange for sex'. In Rwanda there are hundreds of stories in this vein in which violence, love and self-interest are the ingredients. In Bosnia Serbian combatants are known to have helped members of the other communities, either Croatian or Muslim.

Similarly, Christopher Browning considers that among the German police from Battalion 101, pity and brutality could coexist in the same individual and at the same time.[71] This interweaving of sentiments, he remarks, is very difficult to accept. We find it extremely difficult not to see the executioner as being a single monstrous whole, the incarnation of evil. But we are mistaken: it is here in many cases that the biggest obstacle to understanding such evil resides. To reassure ourselves, we would like things to be conveniently cut and dried. This conviction is all the more powerful because it is taken directly from our childhood, when we believe the world was peopled with good and bad individuals. Human beings do not really behave like that. Even executioners can display unexpected and ambiguous behaviour, where just for an instant a spark of humanity will suddenly shine through. On the other hand, even those who seem to be on the side of good, those who have saved lives, might— at some time in their lives—have had blameworthy attitudes. The moral nature of an act never totally defines the moral identity of the author of that act. With regard to Kurt Gerstein, a German mining engineer who witnessed the gassing of Jews and communicated this information to the Allied forces, Saul Friedlander wrote of 'the ambiguity of good'. According to the author the resistance fighter may in certain circumstances seem to resemble the executioner.[72] Looking at this the other way round, it could also be argued that in some circumstances an executioner can exhibit the behaviour of the resistance fighter. It is appropriate in this case to talk of the ambiguity of evil, bearing in mind this residue of humanity which is still present in the psychological make-up of the executioner, and shows itself when the killer acts as protector, even if it is to save just one life.

The banality of evil revisited. On this subject Hannah Arendt's notion of the banality of evil arising from her analysis of Adolf Eichmann does not seem sufficiently all-embracing when it comes to grasping all the different faces the perpetrators of massacre can show. Looking at the behaviour of the *Einzatsgruppen* in Poland, the *Interahawme* militiamen in Rwanda or the paramilitary groups operating in Bosnia, we find no connection here with the 'white collar crimes' perpetrated by zealous and obedient civil servants far removed from the actual theatre of operations. This shortcoming arises from the

limited scope of her study (self-imposed, and therefore, in fact, irre-
proachable): Hannah Arendt does not tackle the case of the actual
killers involved in massacre, but of one man in the course of his trial,
a man who, at the nerve-centre of the Nazi administration had
been in charge of transporting Jews to the death camps. Moreover,
Hannah Arendt never denied that the perpetrators could have other
faces. However, she leaves herself open to criticism when making
generalisations about the question of evil on the basis of Eichmann's
case alone. Having adopted a larger but above all comparative field of
vision, I was led to 'revisit' the expression 'banality of evil'. Before
writing these pages, I took care to reread the passages of her book
where she offers a definition of this notion, only to realise that in fact
this definition was practically non-existent![73]

The expression is of course given a certain prominence due to the
fact that it is the book's subtitle, which certainly contributed to its
success. But one is at great pains to find a developed definition of the
concept. In the few lines where she makes reference to it, in the Post-
script, she considers that Eichmann is not an 'abnormal monster' but
an individual who is characterised above all by his 'thoughtlessness'.
'He was not stupid,' she writes. 'It was sheer thoughtlessness—something by no means identical with stupidity—that predisposed him to
become one of the greatest criminals of that period. And if this is
'banal' and even funny, if, with the best will in the world, one cannot
extract any diabolical or demonic profundity from Eichmann, that is
still far from calling it commonplace'.[74]

But Eichmann's crimes, as she wrote, were not ordinary crimes,
nor was he an ordinary criminal. In this sense what struck Arendt
during Eichmann's trial was the man's extraordinary sense of duty,
with no real thought given to the meaning of duty. Eichmann
proudly claimed to have always 'been a law-abiding citizen', and
executed orders 'to the best of his ability'.[75] This conduct goes
beyond the problem of whether orders were given or not. As Arendt
noted, Eichmann experienced the need to refer each of his acts to a
higher law: that embodied by Hitler himself. We can see that this is
not really a 'simple' case of deference to authority in Milgram's
sense: obeying or disobeying orders and instructions given by an
outside authority. Adolf Eichmann was rather an example of a civil
servant who had internalised the 'law of a system', an unwritten law

which is tantamount to identifying oneself with the will of him who is its incarnation: the Führer.

It was only several years after her essay was published that Hannah Arendt advanced a definition of her notion of the 'banality of evil' in the journal *Social Research*: 'I spoke of 'the banality of evil',' she says, 'and meant with this no theory or doctrine but something quite factual, the phenomenon of evil deeds, committed on a gigantic scale, which could not be traced to any particularity of wickedness, pathology, or ideological conviction of the doer, whose only personal distinction was perhaps extraordinary shallowness. However monstrous the deeds were, the doer was neither monstrous nor demonic, and the only specific characteristic one could detect in his past as well as in his behaviour during the trial and the preceding police examination was something entirely negative: it was not stupidity but a curious, quite authentic inability to think.'[76] These various passages show that the philosopher groups several things under the expression the 'banality of evil'. By 'banal' she means a 'normal' individual, neither a Satan figure nor a psychopathic monster. From this it follows that the executioner does indeed belong to our common humanity, and therefore can be held criminally responsible for his acts.

Nevertheless Arendt ably shows the gulf that exists between this ordinary perpetrator and the extraordinary nature of his crime. And she stresses his 'thoughtlessness', this trait being the focus for her definition of banality. Indeed, for her Eichmann does not think: he becomes the zealous instrument of an ideology, that is to say, a 'logic of the idea', of which Hitler is the veritable expression. As he said himself during his trial, 'Hilter's orders ... had possessed the force of law in the Third Reich.'[77] We get an inkling here of the influence of her work on totalitarianism and the role of 'the mind' in subjugating all totalitarian fetters. Thinking in effect serves to 'dismantle' all ideology that by definition is the mark of a lack of thought.

Therefore, a perpetrator such as Eichmann asks no questions: he works routinely and without pondering the possible consequences of his acts. The effects of this 'thoughtlessness' reside in the increasingly 'de-realised' relationship of the perpetrator with the world and in his lack of guilt for the acts he has committed. Such ideas are in keeping with those resulting from research on direct perpetrators. As a description it corresponds in part to Browning's 'ordinary men', who become more deeply involved through the routinisation of their actions. One is tempted to suggest that there are probably thousands of lesser Eichmann-type executioners, even among the ranks of the direct perpetrators of massacre. Why not apply this notion of the banality of evil to Rwanda as well? In one sense it seems to be even more pertinent, since unlike SS killers operating outside social normality, the Hutu killers carried out their 'work' in broad daylight, surrounded by villagers, and were encouraged and even celebrated. This was surely the ultimate trivialisation of the extraordinary.

But the philosopher's observations are debatable on several important points. First regarding the very viewpoint from which she studies Eichmann: that of the role of the civil servant within society at large. Of course the prototype of this thoughtless agent of the state, concentrating on following his leader's will, certainly appears to exist. We should bear in mind, however, that the administrations in which they worked were managed by individuals who did indeed have a specific plan for Germany and for Europe. We cannot maintain that these people assigned by Nazi authorities to key posts did not think, but rather that they 'had bad thoughts', or that their 'thoughts were evil'. For this reason German historians such as Christian Gerlach or Dieter Pohl, describing these ideological warriors, have called into question the interpretation put forward by Hannah Arendt, or at least have considered it inadequate.

Secondly, she takes the risk of generalising her ideas on evil, although her reasoning is actually based on a single individual. Consequently, she is a prisoner of her observation method, and this causes her to miss important factors that enable us to understand better why an 'ordinary' individual becomes a mass murderer, if only through the role of the group which causes such a metamorphosis to take place. Regarding the core idea in her thesis, i.e. that the banality of evil is a synonym for thoughtlessness, it is likely to perplex anyone who wishes to pursue this line of inquiry even further. Hannah Arendt is careful to point out that we are all inclined towards this thoughtlessness, so common in everyday life, where we hardly have the time and still less the desire to stop and think.[78] To trace the roots of Eichmann's mechanical behaviour in our own as 'normal people', carrying out the routine activities of daily life, follows on from a bold and frightening parallel, which is doubtless partly true. But thankfully, our own disposition for 'thoughtlessness' does not necessarily lead us to slaughter our fellow man. What is missing from Arendt's analysis is above all some reflection on the issue of sliding into the act of violence *in itself*, i.e. on the manner in which banality, at the end of a highly complex process, serves to facilitate a collective monstrosity. Finally, Hannah Arendt's thesis regarding evil does not tackle the most enigmatic and uncomfortable dimension of all: that of cruelty, often associated with the act of slaughter.

Sexual violence and other atrocities

The analysis of occurrences of atrocities, often associated with massacres, constitutes one of the most demanding challenges in social science, first of all for researchers themselves. They are human too, and like anyone else feel the full force of their accounts. Although I have collected many such stories over time, each more horrible than the last, I still surprise myself by being shocked when I hear some accounts, such as that of Reverien Rurangwe, a young Tutsi aged twelve in 1994, the sole survivor of a family group of forty-two people.[79] This instance left me with a feeling of total incredulity and revulsion. Yet there was no real reason to be frightened: it is 'only' an account. But one is nonetheless overcome by a sensation of terror provoking something akin to a suspension of the intellectual faculties, or even a kind of mental paralysis. However, the attempt to comprehend the process of crossing the threshold into violence would be incomplete if one balked at 'grasping' these phenomena of cruelty. This would belie a reluctance to follow through the inquiry to its logical conclusion, whereas such practices have considerable traumatic effects. It is neither masochism nor voyeurism on the part of the researcher, but just the intuition that, in this terrible act lies one of the keys, if not *the* key to the explosive power of massacre. It is the horror of an act of cruelty which will probably forever remain in the memory of the surviving victim, and which can nourish a furious desire for revenge.

Let me start by pointing out two very different possible positions, which practically amount to ways for the social sciences to elude this analysis. The first consists of simply masking its importance. Considering it 'unseemly' as a subject for research is to react as though atrocities did not exist or should be seen as secondary. Many international relations theorists, in their analyses of war, simply refuse to broach this question, including those who belong to the so-called 'realist' school. This tendency is true of some historians as well: accounts of battles tend to emphasise strategy or the epic dimension without really recreating the central theme: violence and its atrocities. On the other hand, the second position consists of allowing oneself to be overwhelmed by the symbolic power of the cruel act by placing it at centre stage, or even the forefront of the account of massacre. The result is an almost aesthetising narration of the atrocities, which feeds on attention to detail and dramatisation. Sofsky's writings, sometimes made up of short fictitious descriptions, adopts this quasi-literary style, which conveys a very ambiguous relish for violence. Neither of these two positions, the one rooted in a denial of the atrocities, the other in their exhibition, helps us at all in our analysis. Behaving as if they did not exist amounts to committing the error of not wishing to grasp a phenomenon that is central to many contemporary conflicts. However, to study it too closely would be to risk becoming paralysed by macabre contemplation.

For my part I would argue that an appropriate distance must be sought, this perspective being vital when embarking on an analysis of this hideous object. This pre-supposes the construction of intellectual frameworks that enable us to draw nearer, as near as possible, to an understanding of this monstrosity. In this perspective, John Horne and Alan Kramer's work is of valuable assistance precisely because it is aimed at uncovering the atrocities of war.[80] And such atrocities are not of course only the acts of 'Nazi hordes' or of 'savage Africans' but of representatives of the 'civilised' West, such as the American soldiers studied by John Dower who, during the war in the Pacific, had no qualms about taking trophies—an ear, a scalp, a penis—from the bodies of their Japanese enemies.[81] However, the study of the massacre of non-combatant populations, while it must be grounded in work on the subject of war, also raises specific questions that go beyond this 'frenzy of the battlefield'. In this respect it is not only history as a discipline that must be summoned but every one of the social sciences, to arrive at an understanding of such disconcerting phenomena.

A variety of indefinite interpretations. In general, two approaches are employed in the study of atrocities. The first raises questions about their *meaning.* Primo Levi poses this problem in a striking manner in one of his most eloquent texts. Although the aim is to destroy civilians *en masse,* he remarks, why, then, on top of it, make them suffer, humiliate them, mutilate them before killing them? Hence the pertinence of his question: 'Why this useless violence?'[82] Why does massacre provoke cruelty before, during and even after the act? Is there a distinction to be made between instrumental violence directed at achieving a specific goal, and apparently gratuitous violence—with no specific goal—frequently called cruelty, as suggested by the anthropologist Véronique Nahoum-Grappe in her work on Bosnia?[83] More generally we must ascertain whether or not these acts of cruelty have any meaning, and if so, what is it?

The second type of inquiry relates to *the intentionality* of such practices. Even though they are apparently aimless, we always tend to think that they are deliberate, controlled, if not orchestrated. For example, the discovery in 1992 of rape centres during the war in Bosnia led observers and activists to say that there was a deliberate policy of cruelty, implemented through planned programmes of mass rape. However, with hindsight such an affirmation seems exaggerated. In various places in Bosnia it is unquestionable that rape was encouraged, indeed organised, especially on the Serbian side and mainly against Muslim women.[84]

This role of management is always decisive in the field, whether it is to encourage rape or to prohibit it. The case of Rwanda offers a multitude of examples of incitement to rape, including those rapes encouraged by Hutu women.[85] On the other hand, in Nazi Europe Germans soldiers were strictly forbidden to rape Jewish women in accordance with the absolute prohibition of all contact between Aryans and the Jewish 'race of the damned'.

But should we for all that, in the case of Bosnia, conclude that Serbian leaders instigated a concerted policy of systematic rape, as various activists' statements claimed during the war? The judgement of the International Tribunal for former Yugoslavia, which on 22 February 2001 described rape for the first time as 'a crime against humanity' in the *Kunarac* case (known as the 'rape camps'), is very cautious in this respect. When the judgement was handed down,

Judge Mumba declared: 'It is to some extent misleading to say that systematic rape was employed as a weapon of war. This could be understood to mean a kind of concerted approach or an order given to the Bosnian Serb armed forces to rape Muslim women as part of their combat activities in the wider meaning. There is no sufficient evidence for such a finding before the Tribunal. What the evidence shows is that the rapes were used as an instrument of terror, an instrument they were given free rein to apply whenever and against whomsoever they wished.'[86]

How can we distinguish then between what clearly stems from a calculated policy and a free initiative taken in the field in a general climate of impunity? The free lance journalist Tim Judah argued that atrocities spiral out of control. He refers to statements made by Dr Milan Kovacevic, one of those responsible for the creation of the Serbian camp of Omarska, who claimed it was originally planned as a reception centre for displaced persons. But because of the escalation of the war, its function changed and the camp became a concentration camp. Such statements should probably be viewed with caution, in that their author was seeking to protect himself against legal proceedings. But they may contain a grain of truth since Milan Kovacevic admitted that he could not totally explain this loss of control. According to him, 'I don't even think the historians will find an explanation in the next fifty years.'[87]

On these scales of sense and nonsense, of the intentional or the unintentional, interpretations of atrocities are manifold and hesitant.[88] However, some authors remain categorical and often propose a unilateral interpretation. The monstrosity of the subject under study arouses unequivocal judgements on their part. This, in my opinion, is a mistake. When considering something unbelievably difficult to understand, one should on the contrary inspect it from all possible angles to multiply the analytical approaches taken. This is precisely what the social sciences may be able to bring to bear on the debate. There is no way to side in favour of a single intellectual posture considered the most relevant. The only certainty we can allow ourselves is therefore to refuse to imprison ourselves in *one* explanatory model. So now I will attempt to summarise several interpretative frameworks, specifying each time that it in no way excludes another type of approach.

Rational choice? The first type of interpretation argues that there is rational calculation on the part of political and military decision-makers who take specific measures designed to develop the ferocity of the men who serve them in the field. The perpetrators are thus pressed to adopt ever more brutal and cruel conduct when in action. The most important of these measures is naturally the guarantee that their superiors will not punish them for committing abuses. Assurance of impunity is a prerequisite for the performance of cruel acts. To this can be added the incisive and inciting role of propaganda disseminated to these servants of the cause. Ah, propaganda again! We have already seen it at work at the very outset of the conflict when, with simple but terrible words, it helped crystallise hateful representations of the enemy.

It crops up again, logically enough, on the battlefield, when the perpetrators are about to shift into action. Here it acts as a mental catalyst for cruelty. Be it in Africa, Europe or elsewhere, the method is always the same: the danger of the acts about to be committed are denounced: 'they're disembowelling our women and killing our children', 'we must show no mercy for these brutes! Let them suffer the same fate!' As explained earlier, the instrumentalisation of an *imaginaire* of fears, fed by both shocking and revolting images with a high emotional charge, literally enables the perpetrators to shift from fantasy into action: from the fear of being viciously destroyed to the concrete action of destroying viciously.

The soldiers of the Wehrmacht were flooded with this apocalyptic discourse that depicted what the Judeo-Bolshevik hordes from Asia would do to the Aryans if ever they fell into their clutches. And Roy Gutman, who at the beginning of the war in Bosnia came across a leaflet circulating among the soldiers of Milosevic's army, describing the horrors that the Serbs were supposedly undergoing, immediately guessed that these same Serbs were probably committing the very same acts that they were denouncing. Such mutual recriminations, which act as 'mirrors of destruction', to use Omer Bartov's phrase, whether they are true or false, certainly succeed in stirring up the ferocity of the killers. Already, in the earlier Balkan wars, a Greek officer claimed with brutal simplicity in reference to the Turks: 'When you have to deal with barbarians, you must behave like a barbarian yourself. It is the only thing they understand.'[89]

By studying specific cases of violence committed against individual victims, one is able to detect the strategic intentions contained in acts of cruelty. Analyses of rapes carried out during the war in Bosnia are based on just such an approach. Rape is not seen as a consequence of war but as a fighting tactic that targets—over and above women, who are the primary victims—the entire identity group. The Croatian sociologist Jadranka Cacic-Kumpes has often noted the extreme cruelty and perversity of rapists, whose acts sometimes go as far as to be carried out in the presence of the parents or children of the victim, who is penetrated by several assailants.[90] The question now is: how is the meaning of such acts to be deciphered? Some see rape in the war in Bosnia as a method of marking territory and humiliating the opposing community, so as to reinforce the separation and territorialisation of the communities. Others have seen it as the desire to destroy the identity and perpetuation of this community and have therefore described the rapes as an attack on parentage. However, this second position is criticised by those who point to the fact that in Bosnian society a child born of a rape is not considered a Serbian child (as this position claims) but as an illegitimate child.[91] In any event, the deliberate perpetration of atrocities is a reliable method of causing lasting trauma not only in the victims, but also in the witnesses and, beyond that, all the members of their entire community. In this sense atrocities are directed at the future since they are part of the deliberate strategy of separating the rival groups for ever. By rendering any prospect of reconciliation impossible for several generations at least, they serve the political goal of segregation and 'ethnic cleansing' perfectly.[92]

This instrumental approach to atrocities, however, falls far short of addressing their full complexity. A 'bottom up' study is also needed, even if it only entails analysis of the rumours that circulated in a region that was in the grip of violence. Indeed, what has just been said of the role of propaganda could have been formulated regarding gossip about the enemy. From this point of view, is the role of these rumours in times of war and/or massacre of civilians really so different? Fear quickly spreads through people's imaginations and reaches armies in the field just as much as the civilian population. When Germany invaded northern France in 1914, rumours started to circulate, such as the one that affirmed that 'the Boches were cutting off children's hands'. The French historian Marc Bloch studied such rumours after the war. German soldiers certainly committed atrocities against civilians, but that particular act was never documented. One of the most horrible rumours, if not the most horrible, stuck in peoples' memories, yet it was false. What then does it mean when such rumours spread?

It is as if the population, in an intense context of war and insecurity, 'invented' frameworks of interpretation, as plausible as they were outrageous, for what was happening to them or for what they deeply feared. Rumours are part of these modes of justification of the crisis: they usually convey a demonisation of the enemy in a very stark light. At the same time they may contain a grain of truth, but how do they arise? Who invents them? The 'origins' of rumours are always difficult to identify. It is nevertheless certain that rumours provide a fertile medium in which propaganda can put down the roots of 'shock arguments' and appear 'credible' to a disoriented and traumatised population.

For instance, the trial, of Milosevic enabled a better identification of the genesis of a rumour that circulated in Kosovo after the massacre perpetrated by the Serbs in Racak in February 1998. A survivor of this massacre had testified that the assailants had cut out the eyes of one of their victims, but in reality this interpretation was false: the court investigation revealed that the victim in question was actually killed by a bullet in the head, and that it was the impact of the projectile that had caused the eyeballs to 'pop out'. In other words, the surviving witness had propagated in good faith a false interpretation (that of an atrocious mutilation committed by the Serbs on an Albanian) on the basis of an accurate but extremely traumatising observation of the corpse.[93]

Towards orgiastic violence. Hence this first approach to atrocities, viewed as calculation, does not take into account the possible effects of another phenomenon: the dynamics of the conflict which are themselves induced by the perpetration of atrocities. Very often reprisals and counter-reprisals build up to a level whereby the conflict gets out of proportion. In other words, the initial rationality, detected in the act of massacre, tends to 'get out of hand' and to create irrationality. To terrorise the enemy camp further, it must be subject to even worse acts of cruelty. The question is: what frame-work of interpretation can be applied to decipher what is perceived as 'irrational'? I will come back to this. The specific characteristic of rumours is to mix inextricably elements of truth with what is defi-nitely false. Just like in the cliché of the 'children with their hands cut off', that of 'disembowelled pregnant women' was circulated in the Balkans too often to be true. But this does not mean that the con-flicting groups are not guilty of horrendous abuses on innocent people, including pregnant women. In the same way, when the RPF re-opened the hostilities in Rwanda, the wildest rumours circulated about atrocities for which the Tutsis were said to be responsible. True or false, they contributed to the terror experienced by the Hutus and also to creating a situation where they were likely to carry out acts of violence against their Tutsi neighbours, and to do to them what the Hutus thought that the Tutsis intended to do to the Hutus.

But are not the very conditions of neighbourhood massacre, which *de facto* implies the physical proximity of executioners to their victims, necessarily conducive to the committing of atrocities? Killing while meeting the eyes of the other, and while gazing into his eyes seems almost impossible. On the contrary the performance of massacre confirms an one of the strongest assertions made by the philosopher Emmanuel Levinas, namely that the recognition of our common humanity necessarily rests on meeting the other face to face. Even though the enemy is depicted by propaganda as having frightening, hideous features, he retains a dreadfully human face. This being the case, it could be why perpetrators of massacre feel a need to 'disfigure' this fellow human as quickly as possible to prevent any risk of identification. To be able to kill him involves dehuman-ising him, not 'just' in the imaginary constructs conveyed by pro-paganda, but now in one's acts: by cutting off his nose or ears, we ensure right away that he no longer has a human face. Cruelty is truly a mental operation on the body of the other, intended to de-stroy his humanity.

And why stop once one has started? Why not continue dismem-bering the body, cutting off a woman's breasts, a man's penis, break-ing their limbs? The vertigo of impunity hurls the executioner into a bottomless pit of cruelty. This spiral of bodily destruction can even continue after death. Although bereft of life, bodies can still resemble the living. And so they must be scalped, torn into pieces, crushed into unrecognisable objects; or, even worse, arranged in a variety of unimaginably grotesque positions, or carved up into pieces to turn them into waste material or even rubbish. In all these various acts of cutting or disembowelling it is the executioner who is protecting himself. Seen in this way, the perpetration of atrocities is the means by which perpetrators establish their own radical psychological distance from the victims, and convince themselves that these are in no way, and no longer, human beings.

In this connection the Nazi leaders developed a more sophisticated methodology of dehumanisation. In the preceding cases it is the executioner who is the direct artisan of this mutilation of the enemy. The perpetrator is in a way forced to produce the atrocious act that will detach him from his victim on his own. However, the Nazis managed to move away from such 'makeshift methods' by creating a system that automatically achieved dehumanisation. Its constituent elements are well known: the journey made in cattle cars, the tattooing, the shaving, etc. This psychological distancing is produced by an organisation operating upstream from the perpetration of the violent act. It is on this precise point that Primo Levi sees the sole utility of useless violence: to make the victims seem like animals so as to facilitate the work of the perpetrators. He bases his assertion on the words of Frantz Stangl, the commandant at Sobibor and Treblinka. In answer to the question 'If they were going to kill them anyway, what was the point of all the humiliation, why the cruelty?', Stangl replied: 'to condition those who actually had to carry out the policies. To make it possible for them to do what they did.'[94] In other words, atrocities have a clearly functional purpose: that of conditioning future perpetrators to carry out what is demanded of them.

But in seeking to discover 'rationality' in what seems to be the extremes of horror, are we not going down the wrong path? It is a desperate attempt to find 'meaning' where there is none, where it no longer exists, where there is only senselessness. After all, is not what has just been labelled 'irrational' not simply madness? Primo Levi cannot get away from this idea: 'I cannot avoid the impression of a general atmosphere of uncontrolled madness that seems to me to be unique in history,' he writes in *If This Is a Man*.[95] In Rwanda Jean Hatzfeld also sometimes uses the metaphor 'the wind of madness' that took over the country, as if its inhabitants had been caught up in a 'tumult'. This image of the 'wind' ('*umuyaga*') had already surfaced during the massacres of 1959. 'It became a madness that went on all by itself', said Joseph-Désiré, 'You raced ahead or got out of the way to escape being run over. ... The one who rushed off, machete in hand, he listened to nothing any more.... Our arms ruled our heads, in any case our heads no longer had their say'.[96] At this point anything could have happened, including atrocities. The individuals seemed to have gone into a trance.

In psychiatry, passing states of madness are referred to as a 'delirious episode' that can take hold of any normal individual at a particular time in his life. In general, when an affected person returns to his normal behaviour he remembers nothing at all about what happened in this period of 'madness'. Perpetrators of atrocities can be said to enter just such delirious episodes, and this metamorphosis can occur all the more easily when it is authorised by society, in as much as murder and all kinds of trangressions are encouraged. In this regard the approach of philosopher Eric Vogelin on the subject of Nazism has a much wider application. He describes it as a regime that exploits the basest instincts of human beings not only because they elevate the rabble to positions of power; 'it is the problem of the simple man, who is a decent man as long as society as a whole is in order but who then goes wild, without knowing what he is doing, when disorder arises somewhere and society is no longer holding together.'[97]

In this case social de-regulation facilitates the development of orgiastic violence: 'a time of folly' is also a time for celebration. Roger Caillois has explored these relations between war and celebration, this 'simultaneous convulsion' which occurs when the norms of society are turned on their head: 'Both appear as prolonged periods of widespread debauchery,' he writes, 'which naturally lead to a climate of outrageous acts and spiralling violence, and where the rules of civilisation are temporarily abolished: binge drinking and feasting, rape and orgies, boasting, making faces, obscenities and swearing, betting, challenges, brawls and atrocities are all on the agenda.'[98] In the same vein the French historian Alain Corbin gave a

THE VERTIGO OF IMPUNITY

remarkable account of a 'little massacre' committed by farmers on a market day in a village in Perigord in the nineteenth century.[99]

There are traces of this festive dimension of the violence in Rwanda: 'In case after case, killers quit at the day's end to go home and feast on food and drink they had pillaged or been given, ready to come back the next morning, rested and fit for "work".'[100] This description cannot help but remind us of the binge drinking recounted by Christopher Browning in relation to the policemen in Battalion 101 who met up in the evening to get drunk, united in a kind of virile fraternity. Was this their way of 'forgetting' the scenes of horror of the day and the brutal treatment they had personally meted out? Was it a way of giving themselves Dutch courage for the tasks that awaited them the following day? The fact remains that the perpetration of atrocities also arises from this collective unbridling, a synonym for drunkenness and loss of inhibitions. The notion of intoxication in this instance contains a much broader meaning than just alcohol or even drug consumption by killers before, during and after having performed the act. Intoxication is also the state produced by violence itself, by means of which perpetrators experience a feeling of omnipotence from being able to kill without restraint. Acting out the killing, once in place, and continually repeated, seems to lead to compulsive forms of behaviour, close to addiction. There is a real intoxication, both perverse and entrancing, in being able to play with the body, with life and death, to cause sufferings, to humiliate, torture, enjoy, cut, kill and kill again and again.

Delighting in cruelty. However, there is a tendency all too often to label something as 'mad' if it seems strange and incomprehensible. The supposed folly of the killers is perhaps not as irrational as all that. Atrocities do have a meaning if we analyse them from other angles, from the standpoint of certain historians or anthropologists of Antiquity. Have we forgotten for example the horrible way bodies are described as being treated in the *Iliad*? In his comments on Homer's epic, the French Hellenist historian Jean-Pierre Vernant distinguishes between the concepts that the Greeks had of a 'beautiful death' and of an 'insulted corpse'.[101] The 'beautiful death' is a reward for heroes and for valiant warriors in general. Hector knows he has to die but does not want to go without a struggle and without glory, knowing the memory of a hero and his exploits will be sung after he has gone; this goes hand in hand with the ritual of embellishing the body, before burning it, to preserve what characterised the deceased: his youth, his heroism and his beauty.

However, it is precisely this beautiful death of which his adversary wishes to deprive him. The first type of offence consists in dirtying the bloody corpse with dust and dirt, in tearing his skin so as to mar his distinguishing features, his colour and his radiance. When Achilles, the victor, undertakes to desecrate Hector, he attaches him to his chariot to tear off his skin and leave just his body, making sure that especially his head and hair would be dragged in the dust. By reducing the body to a shapeless mass indistinguishable from the ground on which he lies, remarks Jean-Pierre Vernant, not only are the distinctive features of the corpse erased, but what separates inanimate matter from living creatures is obscured as well. A second type of cruelty is to dismember the body, cutting it into pieces. The head, arms and legs are detached and then the body is carved up. Ajax in a fit of rage cuts off Imbrios' head and sends it rolling in the dust. In losing its unity of form the human body is reduced to the state of a thing and at the same time disfigured.

The dismembering of a corpse, the fragments of which are scattered, culminates in the practices alluded to in the first verse of the *Iliad*, and returned to all through the poem: that of throwing a body to the dogs, to the birds or to the fish. Instead of burning it so that it can be restored whole in the hereafter, it is devoured raw by wild animals. It is thus dissolved into confusion, delivered up to chaos, to total inhumanity. The last way of adding insult to injury is to deny a body burial, to allow it to decompose and rot unceremoniously, to be destroyed by worms and flies that will penetrate through its open wounds. The body left to decompose is the complete antithesis of a beautiful death. We cannot help but spare a thought for all those bodies that, in our contemporary massacres, are denied burial, left by the roadside or piled up in common graves, like piles of rubbish, deprived of their funeral rites. These various ways of mistreating corpses, observed in Greek culture, seem incredibly modern. The difference today is perhaps more quantitative than qualitative! What the Greeks did on a small scale twenty-five centuries ago, we have managed to do in a much more systematic way to hundreds of thousands and perhaps even millions of people.

Anthropologists put forward other analytical perspectives. If it is accepted that methods of cruelty are rooted in the executioners' psyche (as was postulated above), then these practices are characterised by specific cultural features. The ways in which bodies are taken over, twisted, cut into pieces, constitute wholly cultural acts, through which the perpetrator expresses something of his own identity. Such, for example, is the point of view of the anthropologist Arjun Appaduraï: 'It is clear that the violence inflicted on the human body in ethnic contexts is never entirely random,' he writes, 'or lacking in cultural form. Whenever the testimony is sufficiently graphic … even the worst acts of degradation—… beheading, impaling, gutting, sawing; raping, burning, hanging, and suffocating—have macabre forms of cultural design and violent predictability.'[102] This violence embodied in cruelty, while it is shattering to any witness, is apparently not random for all that. In a moment of intense crisis and uncertainty, paradoxically, these barbaric acts install certainty by stamping irreversible cultural markers on the victims' bodies.

In the case of Rwanda the anthropologist Christopher Taylor has proposed an anthropological interpretation of the 1994 massacres (part of which he witnessed).[103] According to him, the anatomy of the enemy is likened to an animal's anatomy. Thus a very common practice is the sectioning of the Achilles tendon, generally of an enemy's oxen, as a reprisal. Besides animalising the man, this process reflects a Rwandan symbol of the body. Rwandan cosmology of the body attributes a very precise characteristic to it: circulation. An obstructed body constitutes a danger to itself and society. Sectioning the Achilles tendon, and so immobilising the enemy, amounts to causing obstruction of a thoroughfare, and recognises *after the event* the obstructive character of the enemy ready for sacrifice. In the same way the Hutus threw Tutsi corpses into the rivers, and hence eliminated objects that obstructed the global Hutu body.

Rwandan ontology, according to which the body politic is in direct relation to the individual body, is clearly expressed here. The body politic is the country, which has a discharging organ, the river, by which it evacuates 'indigestible' objects. Taylor remarks that in the perpetration of massacres, a great number of acts conform to a cultural model, to a structured and structuring rationale, the violence appearing to be culturally or symbolically determined. 'The torturers not only killed their victims—they transformed their bodies into powerful signs which resonated with a Rwandan *habitus* even as they improvised upon it and enlarged the original semantic domain of associated meanings to depict an entire ethnic group as enemies of the state.'[104] This interpretation of events in Rwanda in 1994 is nevertheless met with scepticism by other authors more used to reasoning with the categories of analysis of history or political science. It remains true nevertheless that the anthropological approach to massacre offers new perspectives, as is maintained by Alexander Hinton.[105]

Should not inquiring into atrocities open finally on to a broader and rather more disturbing approach, the matter of the pleasure that cruelty affords to the executioner? It is known and accepted that the reason why violent practices are so widespread that they seem to be inherent in the human condition is partly because they give some pleasure, even if this seems unsavoury and ambiguous. Humiliating others and, worse still, making them suffer, can provide a form of enjoyment: either by sexually possessing their bodies, or by torturing their bodies in various ways before annihilating them. As I have already pointed out, the situation of impunity creates the conditions for becoming drunk on violence. This is the way the perpetrator can feel genuine pleasure, not only at making others suffer but by enjoying the all-powerful state over the victim who is completely at his mercy.

Those who have survived such ordeals testify sometimes to this particular transformation undergone by an executioner. In his superb writings on torture, the ex-resistance member and deportee Jean Améry writes eloquently on this subject, explaining that psychology cannot offer a profound comprehension of what he himself underwent (having been tortured by the Nazis): 'But probably they *were* sadists if we leave the sexual pathology aside and attempt to judge the torturers according to the categories of, well, the *philosophy* of the Marquis de Sade.'[106] Such a reference may be surprising and even shocking. But historical, sociological or political research sometimes amounts to shedding light on questions that literature, and more generally art, has already explored. Is it not the case for the accursed writings of Sade? Jean Améry's remarks encourage

us to delve deeper into this issue. For example, in *Justine* he describes just how this very intoxication of violence gives pleasure to those inflicting it on others: hence the need to enjoy their humiliation and their screams once more before killing them. And then once again on other bodies, other prey.

To consider this book as a treatise on eroticism or pornography would be to interpret it too narrowly and, ultimately, erroneously. There is certainly in Sade's work a great indulgence for recounting sex scenes, through which he effectively depicts the corruption of certain social circles. In this sense the book is a particularly acid panorama of the morals in which he claims eminent representatives of elites indulge, be they of the courts, the police or the Church. But what exactly is he describing? Secret trading in young girls, several cases of paedophilia or incest, group sex, homosexual or otherwise. Sade in fact revealed more or less marginal behaviour that is today more widely acknowledged and openly discussed.

However, beyond his delight in recounting stories of vice and transgressing taboos, his work is in fact very well argued discourse on violence, and death. In reality, *Justine* is certainly a novel that advocates not moral liberty but rather an apology for the destruction of the other. It is a book on violence in its pure state—one might say a total violence meted out upon a man or woman who has sided with virtue, incarnated by the character of Justine, emblematic victim figure, always humiliated and on the losing side. As all Sade's hero-executioners say, one must give oneself up to crime, it is the law of nature and there's no point in fighting it. And Sade cites La Fontaine: 'Might makes right'! Yet, by indulging oneself in this natural inclination toward destruction, man goes in search of pleasure: an extremely intense pleasure since it is the ultimate expression of crime to delight in the suffering of one's victims, of others humiliated.

I must acknowledge that the power of Sade's writings strikes home as regards the subject of this book. Throughout these pages, and especially in this chapter, I have been searching for what the executioner experiences, what he thinks when he carries out the act. Sade devotes long, even somewhat repetitive passages to exposing their arguments and describing their emotions at the fateful moment. In his own way of course: every scene of torture, rape, and killing is preceded or accompanied by long speeches given by the execu-

tioner to his victim before inflicting brutality upon him. What is
even more remarkable in the portraits of his characters, is that none
of them seems to be mad. Certainly, Sade tells us sometimes that they
are monsters, but never that they are abnormal. They are above all
driven by egoism and cupidity. It is therefore apparent that most of
the themes explored herein are discussed: the feeling of impunity,
the exhilaration of violence, the marking of the bodies, the desire to
break taboos, to eliminate all sexual and generational barriers. In this
sense Sade appears as an explorer of total transgression, of the situations of extreme violence in which he portrays his characters.

When he goes as far as to describe a so-called medical experiment
which a doctor carries out on the body of his own eighteen-year-
old daughter, the passage seems to be almost premonitory of what,
two centuries later, the Nazi doctors like Josef Mengele in Auschwitz would do, although he performed his 'experiments' not on his
own children but on the children of others. Beyond the description
of specific situations, Sade tells us that what counts above all, is the
executioner's fantasy, his faculty of imagination, his whims designed
to take full advantage of his omnipotence over his victim. Sade draws
here on the story of Gilles de Rais, *Maréchal* of France and former
comrade-in-arms of Joan of Arc, who, after retiring from the court,
kidnapped and sequestered in his castle more than a hundred young
boys and sexually abused them before killing them. What we would
now describe as paedophilia and serial killing also fascinated Georges
Bataille[107] and Wolfgang Sofsky. These authors joined together to
affirm that absolute power has no other goal beyond itself, simply
the pleasure of violence for violence's sake. Absolute power facilitates absolute action on its victims. And so as to make this pleasure
last longer, it is important to delay the victim's death. To make the
suffering linger, to see the victim bleed profusely, to hear him scream
as long as possible, begging for mercy from his executioner, is to
ensure that the latter experiences the sensation of absolute pleasure:
the ecstasy of total power.

The abyss of the 'grey zone'. Captivating though this approach is, is it
not based on pure fantasy? The realities of the descent into violence
are surely much more complex than these authors would have us
believe. What we have learned about the perpetrators' psychology

does not support the Sadian, exclusive vision, the pleasure of destroying others. It is undoubtedly one of the dimensions contributing to going through with the act of killing, and for some individuals can even be the predominant factor. But in no way can it be considered as the only basis for interpretation. What Sade, Bataille or Sofsky do not mention—I dare say—is the suffering of the perpetrator himself. It is obviously of a very different nature to that of the victim. And the perpetrator is not about to lose his life. It is nevertheless probable that the transgressive nature of the acts perpetrated by the executioner produces a form of profound and durable trauma. For one who has raped women or men, split open stomachs or skulls, carved up bodies, nothing will ever be the same again. Becoming a mass murderer, whether as leader or perpetrator, is to undergo a process of intense psychological degradation comparable to a form of dehumanisation. Perpetrators are also victims of a system of coercion they nevertheless agree to serve.

In this regard the notion of a 'grey zone' that Primo Levi writes about in his famous analysis of the relationships between guards and prisoners inside Auschwitz has much wider relevance.[108] In view of the fact that both executioners and victims are crushed by the same system that annihilates their common humanity, Primo Levi invites the reader to shatter any frozen and Manichean images that he may have. Such a perspective seriously destabilises all the certainties that attempt to set in stone ideas about the roles of the 'good victim' and the 'bad' executioner. No, the realities of relationships of violence are, once again, more complicated and fluctuating, and oblige one continually to re-examine these two very disturbing questions: in what way do victims sometimes identify with their executioners? And also: in what respect do the executioners become closer to their victims? For example, at the very moment when they carry out the act or afterwards, perpetrators sometimes express clear signs of intolerance towards the massacring of defenceless individuals, like the members of the *Einzatsgruppen*, who had fits of vomiting or uncontrollable weeping, or were overtaken by a depressive state which made it impossible for them to fulfil their duties.

Others committed suicide or drifted into madness. Such was the case of a Hutu killer who had buried his Tutsi neighbour alive in a hole behind his house: 'Eight months later, he heard his victim call to him in a dream. He went into the garden, he removed the earth, he pulled up the corpse, he was arrested. In prison ever since then, he walks day and night, carrying this fellow's skull in a plastic bag. He cannot let go of the bag even to eat. He is haunted in the extreme.'[109]

Many killers do not react in this way and manage to remain sane after the event. This may well be the case, but often they remain silent. They do not want to talk about what they have done, trying to bury what they once agreed to do deep inside themselves, whether they did it of their own accord or against their will. Their silence is accompanied by extremely diverse forms of rationalisation, as soon as they are questioned to find out more about their past: 'It was war', 'our enemies did the same to us', 'they got what they deserved', etc. But do not expect them to talk to you personally: you will be met with utter silence.

This silence is very often the mark of a profound *denial*, that is to say a total inability after the fact to accept the realities of the previous behaviour, at the moment the threshold was crossed. Where the outrageousness of their crimes is concerned, perpetrators no longer 'see': they are literally incapable of recognising the facts. If they become conscious of the significance of their transgression, they can simply break down psychologically and be totally shattered. For this reason perpetrators behave as if their crimes did not exist or had never existed. The honourable image that they give of themselves is in total contradiction with their bloody past. This is how contradictory and parallel memories arise between executioners and victims, which make their reconciliation very improbable. It is also in this way that completely revisionist accounts are constructed, and through which the massacres of the past are denied in a political context.

Whether we perceive meaning or senselessness in the perpetration of atrocities, whether we consider that executioners experience pleasure or are psychologically damaged, there cannot be an unequivocal understanding of manifestations of extreme violence. The reader who was hoping for a definitive, systematic explanation of human barbarity, will probably be disappointed. Scholars must however show modesty. The social sciences can certainly help understanding of *how* killers carry out certain acts. They can also throw light on the reasons *why*. But large grey areas will remain, impervious to all analytical approaches. Are such limits to knowledge specific to the study of massacre and of its atrocities? Probably not. I devoted several years of research to the study of the Resistance, which after all, constitutes another form of shifting into action.[110]

However, in studying this 'resistant subject', we are beset by the same perplexity. Why should one individual and not another be moved to take part in the resistance? Very often, one cannot say for sure. In the same way, why does one individual, and not another, become an executioner? We lose ourselves in hypotheses. As Raymond Aron pointed out, there will always be mystery surrounding a person's decision.[111] These doubts, these hesitations clearly show that the goal of building a system to explain the shift into action necessarily relies upon an open form of questioning, which is renewed over and over. It is certainly better that way. Because it is evidence that man, despite the constraints that weigh upon him, retains a certain degree of freedom, which means that his conduct remains unpredictable. It is the greatness of his condition that allows him the possibility, at every instant, of showing courage—or of throwing himself into the abyss.

VI

THE POLITICAL USES OF MASSACRE AND GENOCIDE

Even while Auschwitz was still operating and Germany was far from having lost the war, on the other side of the Atlantic an American legal scholar of Polish stock, Raphael Lemkin, then professor at Yale University, invented the word 'genocide'. While he had very little reliable information about what was going on at the core of Nazi Europe, Lemkin had an intuition that something totally unheard-of was happening, which in his eyes justified the coining of a new term. He therefore devoted an entire chapter to it in a book published in 1944.[1] Scarcely four years later, the United Nations adopted the new notion in the context of the International Convention on the Prevention and Repression of the Crime of Genocide, passed in Paris on 9 December 1948, just before this same assembly approved the Universal Declaration of Human Rights. What an achievement for an academic to see a word he had coined himself recognised so quickly on an international scale! The international Nuremberg and Tokyo tribunals set up by the victors of the Second World War had nevertheless resorted to a new notion in November 1945 and January 1946—the 'crime against humanity'—in prosecuting the Germans and Japanese responsible for such acts. But realisation at the end of the war of the true nature of the crimes the Nazis committed against European Jewry probably explains why the notion of 'genocide' was so readily adopted within the newly-emerging 'international community'.

And so the word *genocide* gradually came into use in ordinary language to denote absolute evil, the crime of all crimes perpetrated against innocent populations. The term has been applied, aptly or not, to all sorts of violent situations. Journalists, activists, scholars and the commoner alike have in turn used it in relation to nearly all the conflicts in the second half of the twentieth century that claimed large numbers of civilian victims: from Cambodia to Chechnya, including Burundi, Rwanda, Guatemala, Colombia, Iraq, Bosnia, and Sudan. The notion has also been used retrospectively to qualify the massacres by the Greeks of the inhabitants of Melos (5th century BC), the *Vendéens* in 1793 during the French Revolution, the native Americans of North America, the Armenians in 1915, and not forgetting the famine in Ukraine, the various deportations in the former USSR under Stalin as well as, of course, the extermination of European Jews and gypsies, but also the Americans dropping the atom bomb on Hiroshima and Nagasaki. This list is, of course, not exhaustive...

Applying the notion of 'genocide' to these very different historical cases has raised a number of objections, and continues to fuel the most heated of debates. The problem the term poses is an apparently inextricable one of taxonomy, stemming from the various and sundry meanings invested in this term. These multiple uses reflect a need to resort to a broad-sweeping term describing a massive phenomenon in the twentieth century: the destruction of civilian populations. Other terms appeared subsequently such as 'politicide', coined by Ted Gurr and Barbara Harff in 1988.[2] However, the word 'genocide' continues to dominate the field, to the extent that several universities throughout the world have created departments or centres for 'genocide studies'.

The current notion that the twentieth century will have been the 'century of genocides' is nevertheless worth examining. That it has been the age of extremes, to use historian Eric Hobsbawm's excellent expression,[3] and consequently, of mass murders, would seem to be corroborated by numerous historical observations. But to argue that the twentieth century is a genocide 'era' is an assertion that requires further substantiation, if it is indeed admitted that genocide is only one of many possible forms of mass murder. In fact, the term's very success poses a number of problems for the social scientist.

Any group today that wants to construct itself as a victim in the eyes of the entire world claims to have been a victim...of genocide. The word is thus exploited to all sorts of identitarian and militant ends that must first be deciphered. Scholars, being themselves affected by these same moral and political issues, have barely managed to agree on a definition of what genocide means. In fact, since Lemkin's groundbreaking work, genocide studies have mainly developed at the nexus between law and the social sciences. This elemental overlapping between the normativity of international law and socio-historical analysis engenders considerable conceptual difficulties that give rise to numerous controversies. Is it possible to disentangle them and, if so, how?

I believe it is crucial for genocide research to disengage itself from the legal approach in order to come into its own in the field of the social sciences. To do so I recommend the use of a non-normative vocabulary, and the notion of 'massacre' can serve here as a basic lexical unit of reference. Extricating genocide studies from the field of law further means seeking to understand the political uses of massacres according to their dynamics of destruction. Such is precisely the aim of this chapter in suggesting an interpretation of twentieth century (and earlier) mass killings on the basis of three ideal-type configurations: *subjugation, eradication* and *insurrection*. We will then see how, drawing on the comparative analysis developed in the preceding chapters, it becomes possible to redefine the notion of 'genocide' and, more broadly, the *genocidal process* from the standpoint of the social sciences.

Instrumentalisations of a word that is impossible to define?

The first problem posed by the word 'genocide' has to do with the many ways in which it is instrumentalised. Today the word 'genocide' is endemic to all kinds of identitarian, humanitarian and political rhetorics. This in itself could constitute an entirely separate field of research, so extensive are the issues tied in with its use. *Remembrance issues* are in the forefront, and involve obtaining acknowledgement by all of the particular genocide of which any group claims to have been a victim.

The most emblematic battle in this area is that of the Armenian community. But others can be mentioned: the Greeks, who believe they were victims of a genocide perpetrated by the Turks between 1915 and 1923, the Ukrainians, seeking to have the famine of

1932–1933 recognised as genocide, or yet again the descendants of the Aborigines in Australia who are seeking reparations and an apology from the Australian government for massacres perpetrated by the first colonists and the forced assimilation of their children.[4] In France a one-article law passed on 18 January 2001 officially recognises the Armenian genocide of 1915. It is very rare that a country's elected officials are called upon in this way to make such a statement regarding *the nature* of a historical event, and the more noteworthy in this case since the event contributed only very obliquely to French national history. This way of officially stating how an event should be named and interpreted—via legislation—has provoked sharp criticism among historians;[5] not that they refuse to acknowledge the genocidal nature of the event but more because they find it intolerable that the law should thus qualify history, proclaiming its view as definitive historical truth. This situation leaves the road wide open for an official history, a dogmatic history, poles apart from the professional calling of the historian.[6]

The use of the word 'genocide' raises other issues related to immediate action when a population seems to be, or is indeed, in danger of extinction. In such dramatic circumstances recourse to the word 'genocide' constitutes a kind of final distress signal broadcast in order to prevent a tragedy. In 2004 the Darfur crisis in Sudan was a new illustration of this issue. Several NGOs had already claimed that genocide was underway there, an affirmation picked up by the US Holocaust Museum in Washington, DC, then by Colin Powell (US Secretary of State at the time),[7] and then by the Swedish government and the European Parliament. During the same period, this position was not, however, shared by the United Nations High Commissioner for Human Rights, Louise Arbour,[8] nor even by NGOs such as Human Rights Watch (which instead rather denounced in the Sudan the perpetration of a 'crime against humanity') or Médecins Sans Frontières. This does not mean that these organisations intended to remain inactive with respect to the tragedy.[9] In January 2005 the United Nations investigative commission, led by the legal scholar Antonio Cassese, also came to the conclusion that the violence being committed in Darfur came under the heading of 'war crime' and 'crime against humanity', pressing the international community to intervene and put a stop to it; an appeal reiterated by Kofi Annan who spoke of Darfur as 'a little short of hell on earth'.[10]

Whether use of the word 'genocide' is justified or not, the term aims to strike our imagination, awaken our moral conscience and mobilise public opinion on behalf of the victims. The objective is not just to alert public opinion by creating a wave of sympathy toward them, but above all to legitimise ahead of time a possible international intervention by invoking the 1948 UN Convention. Under these circumstances, anyone daring to suggest that what is going on is not 'really' genocide is immediately accused of weakness or sympathising with the aggressors. Morality always seems to side with those who denounce genocide in progress. And it is true that the 'genocide or not' debate seems callous at a time precisely when human beings are threatened with death or are indeed dying. As a result, the word 'genocide' is literally over-used in a general 'hyping up' of situations in such a way as to mask what it really signifies. The historian Henry Huttenbach had already noted this in 1988: 'Too often has the accusation of genocide been made simply for the emo-tional effect or to make a political point, with the result that more and more events have been claimed to be genocide to the point that the term has lost its original meaning.'[11]

In parallel to these battles for remembrance or the emergency protection of populations, the notion of genocide as a crime has a strictly legal use, especially since the 1990s, in prosecuting political or military leaders before international tribunals. Are such indict-ments, for which the political stakes are obvious, always justified? This, too, is debatable. The fact remains that the former Chilean dictator Augusto Pinochet was accused of genocide by the Spanish magistrate Baltazar Garzon. Such charges have also been made against Slobodan Milosevic and the former Iraqi dictator Saddam Hussein. Many NGOs, Amnesty International being one, base their hopes on this combat in their work to overturn the impunity of those personally responsible for ordering and organising massacres. And these NGOs set out, naturally, to draw support for this mission from the International Criminal Court (which they in fact helped to create, to the great dismay of certain governments). This new court, which came into being on 1 July 2002, can make use not only of the Convention of 1948 but also the various legal provisions relating to the notions of war crime and crime against humanity (see inset).

Finally, but by no means less significantly, the term genocide can be used as a propaganda tool by becoming the hinge for a venomous rhetoric against a sworn enemy. Given the powerful emotional charge the word genocide generates, it can be used and re-used in all sorts of hate talk to heap international opprobrium on whoever is accused of genocidal intent. Thus, as we know, in the 1980s the Serbs in Kosovo declared themselves victims of a genocide perpetrated by the Albanians. Likewise, during the Durban conference in South Africa in September 2001, Arab delegates accused Israel of committing genocide against the Palestinians. The obvious conclusion: the word is used as much as a symbolic shield to claim victim status for one's people, as a sword raised against one's deadly enemy.

'Genocide': a legacy of international law. Can social science researchers provide any conceptual clarification? As mentioned earlier, work in this field is permeated by moral issues and struggles related to identity. At one end of the spectrum, the psychologist Israel Charny considers that any massacre amounts to genocide, including an industrial accident such as the Chernobyl nuclear disaster. He adopts this very broad definition to avoid exclusion from the definition of genocide[12] any human group that is made a victim. At the other end, the historian Stephen Katz considers that there has been only one incidence of genocide in history: that of the Jews. But he gives a preliminary definition that is so restrictive and hewn to the case of the Holocaust that his reasoning leads him necessarily to the conclusion that throughout history only the Jews have been victims of genocide.[13] Between these two extremes, the range of definitions offered by researchers is particularly wide and diverse. Admittedly, there is no consensus among them as to what does or does not constitute genocide. How can this state of affairs be explained?

To understand why, we need to retrace the development of the notion and what it was intended to mean since the foundational writings of Raphael Lemkin were published, and even further back. Lemkin was not actually the first to pose the question of the extermination of a group as such. Montesquieu had already raised the issue of genocide as a possible 'treatment' of a people, without seeing the need to coin a word for it. In *The Spirit of the Laws*, he notes that 'one state that has conquered another treats it in one of these four ways: the state continues to govern its conquest according to its own laws and takes for itself only the exercise of the political and civil government; or it gives its conquest a new political and civil government; or it destroys the society and scatters it into others; or, finally, it exterminates all the citizens. The first way conforms to the right of nations we follow at present; the fourth is more in conformity with the right of nations among the Romans.'[14] In the context of the French Revolution, the journalist and polemicist Gracchus Babeuf spoke of a 'system of depopulation' (and of '*populicide*') to describe the massacre of the *Vendéens*.

Lemkin's contribution thus has more to do with the creation of the word 'genocide' itself, and allocating a specific name to this process of annihilation of a people, and this in the context of the Second World War. In that regard he shrewdly makes the connection between the plan to destroy the Jews and the Nazi project itself, basing his intuition on an analysis of Hitler's thought as expressed in *Mein Kampf.* Lemkin argues that the notion of genocide first has a biological basis, even a genetic one, rooted in the Führer's vision of race; this explains the presence of the radical *genos* in the word genocide. With respect to the supposed 'superiority of the Aryan race', the Nazi plan for society aimed to thwart the reproductive capacity of the other races. In this sense mass execution is just one method among many linked to the term genocide, which also implies, for example, measures to restrict births and unequal treatment of other peoples regarding food and health care. To support his demonstration Lemkin reproduced a chart ranking the 'required basic nutrients' the Nazis granted to the population as a function of their hierarchical conception of races. He concludes from this that implementing genocide presupposes a pre-determined plan to organise such arrangements (in matters of sexuality, health, etc.) and that these measures are not applied to isolated individuals but on the basis of their real or supposed membership of a particular group.

However, Lemkin's thinking suffers from considerable ambiguities. The first has to do with his particularly broad conception of genocide. He conceived it as a general way of treating population groups that could be applied not only to the Jews (doomed to disappear),[15] but also to the Poles, the Czechs, the Slovenes, and others. Moreover, he believed that the populations of Luxembourg, the Eupen and Malmedy areas of Belgium, and the Alsace-Lorraine region were victims of genocide. This judgement, which is surprising to say the least, remains consistent with the author's theory in that Lemkin extends the notion of genocide to the attempt at cultural destruction of a groups' identity. For him these regions annexed by the Reich were subjected to a forced policy of deculturation of their identity and Germanic reculturation. Such measures, which thus aimed to interrupt the 'cultural reproduction' of peoples (like the above-mentioned measures) and which halt biological reproduction, are an integral part of a genocidal plan. Some would call this policy of destroying groups by annihilating their culture 'ethnocide'. But Lemkin does not really distinguish between genocide and ethnocide, as he states in a footnote at the outset.

This broad and relatively heterogeneous meaning given to the notion of genocide has had the effect of fuelling the determination of those who want to set the extermination of European Jews *apart*. In itself this evolution is rather paradoxical, for as pointed out above, the UN's adoption of the 1948 Convention can only be understood in the postwar context with the discovery of the Nazi death camps. But the term genocide, 'as a hodgepodge concept' according to the Belgian historian Maxime Steinberg's brutal phrase, has had the effect of 'allowing the object of history to escape from the story told about it'.[16] It is thus not surprising that those who have insisted on the 'singularity' of the Jewish 'catastrophe' have sought to impose other words: 'Holocaust' in the United States and 'Shoah' in France.[17] Irving Horowitz's book published in 1976 (and succeeded by several new editions) is based on just such a distinction, not hesitating, in all good faith, to classify in the miscellaneous category of 'genocides' the policy of apartheid in South Africa or the collective suicide of Jim Jones and the 910 disciples of his sect in Guyana in 1978.[18] However, the term 'Holocaust' is also becoming more and more inflationary, as though to prevent the Jews from monopolizing the word, and thereby preventing them from singling themselves out by dint of the unique character of their destruction.[19] Here again, through the usage of words a political battle for remembrance is being waged in what the Belgian sociologist Jean-Michel Chaumont has called a 'competition of victims'.[20]

Lemkin's work raises another problem at the very foundation of the word 'genocide', constituting in a sense his original hallmark. In fact, the Yale law professor clearly did not content himself with merely noting that mass violence against civilians in Nazi Europe required the coining of a new term. He also set out to suggest concrete legal measures to combat this new crime in the future, and so took the trouble to compile a list of legal recommendations to this end. In other words, from the very start the word 'genocide' was constructed as straddling the social sciences and international law. It thus carries a strongly normative character, which makes its use particularly problematic for scholars. I shall return to this later. Most genocide research is indeed heir to this juridical approach: the field of international law spawned genocide studies.

This can be verified simply by analysing works published by the first authors following Lemkin who attempted to develop a comparative perspective on genocide. Nearly all of them use the 1948 Convention as their point of departure and main point of reference. To a certain extent, the UN text has provided them with a framework of analysis through which to examine history. What exactly does this Convention say? It first emphasises the fact that genocide arises from an *intentional plan* to destroy a group as such and spells out the criteria for identifying these groups. Two items in the text should be pointed out: first, genocide does not occur without prior *selection* of the victim population, which boils down to saying that genocide presupposes a *sorting process*; second, this Convention only legally protects 'national, racial, ethnic or religious' groups, which amounts to saying that it does not protect other groups, for instance those defined according to political, economic or cultural criteria. Thus the UN Convention gives genocide an ambiguous definition, which is obviously the outcome of a compromise among all the signatory states. Some, like the Soviet Union, were staunchly opposed to including the political criterion for fear of being accused of the crime of genocide for its past actions.[21]

Pioneer studies in the social sciences. Despite such limits, the UN Convention prompted the first socio-historical studies on genocide, such as the work of Leo Kuper. On the basis of the UN definition, he suggested a classification by 'genocidal process' and 'motives of the crime'.[22] While regretting the exclusion of political criteria, he disregards 'political murders', simply because the UN Convention does not take them into account. As for Israel Charny, he rightly believes

*Convention on the Prevention and Punishment
of the Crime of Genocide*

UN Resolution 230 approved on 9 December 1948

Article 2

'In the present Convention, genocide means any of the following acts committed with intent to destroy, in whole or in part, a national, ethnical, racial or religious group, as such:

(*a*) Killing members of the group;
(*b*) Causing serious bodily or mental harm to members of the group;
(*c*) Deliberately inflicting on the group conditions of life calculated to bring about its physical destruction in whole or in part;
(*d*) Imposing measures intended to prevent births within the group;
(*e*) Forcibly transferring children of the group to another group.

Article 3

The following acts shall be punishable:

(*a*) Genocide;
(*b*) Conspiracy to commit genocide;
(*c*) Direct and public incitement to commit genocide;
(*d*) Attempt to commit genocide;
(*e*) Complicity in genocide'.

that the criterion of intent is in no way adequate when it comes to qualifying genocide in mass societies in which the levels of responsibility are diluted.[23] Frank Chalk and Kurt Jonassohn criticise the UN definition of being too narrow (because it excludes political criteria) and at the same time far too broad, because one paragraph in article 2 stipulates that genocide also applies in the case of 'serious bodily or mental harm to members of the group'.[24] They thus recommend integrating this political criterion in the definition of

Definition of Crime against Humanity, article 7

International Criminal Court 17 July 1998 (Rome)

For the purpose of this Statute, 'crime against humanity' means any of the following acts when committed as part of a widespread or systematic attack directed against any civilian population, with knowledge of the attack:

(*a*) Murder;

(*b*) Extermination;

(*c*) Enslavement;

(*d*) Deportation or forcible transfer of population;

(*e*) Imprisonment or other severe deprivation of physical liberty in violation of fundamental rules of international law;

(*f*) Torture;

(*g*) Rape, sexual slavery, enforced prostitution, forced pregnancy, enforced sterilisation, or any other form of sexual violence of comparable gravity;

(*h*) Persecution against any identifiable group or collectivity on political, racial, national, ethnic, cultural, religious, gender as defined in paragraph 3, or other grounds that are universally recognised as impermissible under international law, in connection with any act referred to in this paragraph or any crime within the jurisdiction of the Court;

(*i*) Enforced disappearance of persons;

(*j*) The crime of apartheid;

(*k*) Other inhumane acts of a similar character intentionally causing great suffering, or serious injury to body or to mental or physical health.

genocide (breaking away, in this, from Kuper and his reservations on this point) and excluding the notion of 'mental harm'. For them, genocide is first of all the physical destruction of defenceless human beings outside the conduct of war: what they call 'one-sided killings'.

The sociologist Helen Fein has opted to adhere to the UN definition while attempting to translate it into sociological terms. She thus winds up defining genocide as 'A sustained purposeful action by a perpetrator to physically destroy a collectivity directly or indirectly, through interdiction of the biological and social reproduction of group members, sustained regardless of the surrender or lack of threat offered by the victims.'[25]

The historian Yves Ternon, a pioneer of genocide studies in France, also drew from this initial legal approach in his seminal work *L'Etat criminel*.[26] To summarise all the various approaches that have been taken in this area would seem nearly impossible. In 2001 Scott Straus for instance attempted to compare the various definitions formulated by all these authors on the basis of the following key points: the question of 'intent', the modes of annihilation of the target group, the way the victims and perpetrators of their destruction alike are defined. Result: divergences are far from incidental and relate to the core variables of the destruction process.[27]

Other researchers have attempted to break free from the UN Convention to explore new avenues. Since the Convention left out political mass murders, they have simply suggested naming them as such. The word 'genocide' being a neologism, they have felt justified in coining other terms to refer to different phenomena. Thus Barbara Harff and Ted Gurr forged the notion of 'politicide' to designate mass murders of a political nature. In truth their approach remains modelled on that of the UN, their notion of 'politicide' being in all appearance a lexical solution to compensate for the lack of a political criterion. Thus they consider that genocide refers to the case of mass murders that target groups of a 'communitarian' nature defined by ethnic or religious criteria, whereas politicide targets groups whose victims are considered according to their opposition to the dominant power. These authors thus see an analytical advantage in differentiating the two notions which they believe elsewhere to be complementary, whence their tendency to speak of 'geno-politicide'.[28]

Rudolph Rummel casts aside the notion of 'genocide' in favour of a term of his own invention: 'democide'. He defines democide as being any mass murder perpetrated by a government leaving at least one million dead, whether it is genocide, politicide or any other mass murder.[29] However, an attentive reading reveals that he suggests this term more for moral than scholarly reasons, primarily to cover all the victims of state-perpetrated violence. In this he is closer to

Charny's approach, except that unlike the latter he refuses to define genocide in broad terms. Furthermore, his definition poses a problem in that, although it strives to cover all cases of massacre, it does not take into account those perpetrated by non-state actors.

Other new notions have appeared that have no more legal substance than the others. We could mention 'Judeocide'[30] (to refer to any massacre of Jews), 'ecocide' to describe the destruction of an ecosystem,[31] 'feminicide' referring to the specific destruction of women,[32] 'libricide' for the destruction of libraries,[33] 'urbicide' for that of cities and 'elitocide' for that of elites, and 'linguicide' and 'culturicide'[34], not to forget 'fratricide', 'classicide' and 'ethnocide'.[35] This proliferation of terms, most of which have appeared since the Second World War, attests to a new tendency in the social sciences that strives to explore phenomena of destruction as such. At first it was as if researchers' attempts had focused on how to *name* them in order to be able to *think about* them. There are in fact no research traditions in this area from which to draw. Such terminological abundance can thus be interpreted as an indicator of the wealth of a field of studies under construction. But such diversity also attests to another fact: the huge difficulty of grasping the object studied, of delimiting it, of framing it properly through definitions. The result is reflected in the countless misunderstandings and disagreements between researchers themselves who are nevertheless often studying the same historical cases.

Distancing genocide studies from the frame of law

I will now dare to ask a rather provocative question: do we still need the word genocide in the social sciences? Since using the term always seems to create misunderstanding, does it not pose scholars with more problems than it helps to resolve? I am inclined to believe so. Dropping it would mean leaving the term 'genocide' to its identitarian, activist and legal uses described above. In the social sciences the general notions of 'mass violence' or 'extreme violence' might then seem adequate, provided that one differentiates between their specific dynamics (depending on their political objectives) and their actual morphologies. The German historian Christian Gerlach advocates such a solution, having decided to banish from his work the very use of the notions of 'crime' and 'genocide'.[36] But some will continue to object that even if the word 'genocide' has become highly problematic, it is difficult to do without. This is why I will nevertheless attempt here to defend its continued use in the social sciences, by clarifying the key problems that determine the future of this academic field.

Genocide studies today are at the intersection of two very different paths. The first takes the UN definition of 1948 as the main category for analysing genocide. Most genocide scholars identify with this approach, among whom Helen Fein's work remains the most influential. Their position is fairly coherent: noting that scholars are unable to agree on a common definition of genocide, they feel justified in sticking to its legal definition. Such is for instance the viewpoint defended eloquently by the historians Robert Gellately and Ben Kiernan.[37] Their approach also rests on a conception of the academic's commitment to bringing perpetrators of genocide to trial. For them scholars should not hesitate to commit themselves and place themselves in the service of magistrates to help prosecute such criminals. The political scientist Eric Markusen adds that the 1948 Convention can all the more serve as a basis for reference having demonstrated its flexibility in proving both general and precise enough to be used in such dissimilar international tribunals as the ones for Yugoslavia and Rwanda. This approach is also upheld by Eric Weitz in his important study: he embarks on his research on the twentieth century using the UN definition as the starting point, while acknowledging that the notion of 'intent', at the crux of the 1948 definition, is not easy to verify in history.[38]

But this research current, which I will call 'the UN school', runs up against a serious question: to what extent is it legitimate to adopt an international legal norm resulting from a political compromise between states as a basis for historical, sociological or anthropological inquiry? It in fact implies using a norm that is political by definition, because the wording of this Convention is obviously the result of an international compromise made between governments in 1948, in the postwar context. This is a truly problematic state of affairs. It brings to mind Durkheim's arguments on suicide published in the early twentieth century relating to the normative use of the notion of 'crime' in sociology. In the twenty-first century we must also develop a criticism of the normative use of the notion of 'genocide' in the social sciences. It is by extricating it from the frame of law, and thus politics, that genocide research will someday manage to attain maturity. This is not necessarily in fashion at a time when everything is tending to become a legal issue and when, conversely, law is used in politics, legislation itself being political.

This criticism does not, of course, seek to cast any doubt on international law as such. I should probably clarify this point to avoid any risk whatsoever of so serious a misunderstanding. There is no doubt that adoption of the 1948 Convention bore witness to a considerable step forward in twentieth-century international law as regards recognition of the crime of genocide. And today, excellent published work on the contribution made by international law and on its philosophical foundations is available for all to read.[39] Nor is there any doubt that court hearings of organisers and perpetrators of massacres provide an essential source of documentation for scholars, even if this information is not always easy to exploit from a research standpoint: a trial is designed to prosecute a criminal, and not to aid understanding of a historical event. It is precisely here that the difference in roles emerges most strikingly: as historians, sociologists or anthropologists, scholars simply do not exercise the same profession as magistrates.

'Massacre' as unit of reference. The first authors, I believe, who tried to distance themselves from the UN definition were the historian Frank Chalk and the sociologist Kurt Jonassohn.[40] Although they acknowledge the importance of this definition, they nevertheless seek to redefine the notion of 'genocide' in the social sciences by suggesting it be separated from that of 'ethnocide', an ambiguity that was already present in Lemkin's early writings and that reappeared in the 1948 essay. The French historian Bernard Bruneteau follows in their wake.[41] The historians Marc Levene and Martin Shaw work in a similar direction, although both seem to liken genocide to a large-scale massacre.[42] Norman Naimark and Michael Mann also both emancipated themselves from the legal definition of genocide (or even disregarded it) in their works on ethnic cleansing and mass violence.[43] The political scientist Benjamin Valentino does the same, preferring to use the general term of 'mass murder'.[44] By the same token, Manus Mildlarsky, Daniel Chirot and Clark McCauley have based their comparative research on a framework that does not rely on the 1948 UN Convention alone.[45] I obviously feel an

affinity with this research current, which I would like to problematise further.[46]

Indeed, the first step in moving away from the legal approach
involves bringing into play a non-normative, non-legal vocabulary
to construct massacres as an object of research. The notion of 'mass
crime', which I used for a while, does not meet this requirement.[47]
True, it presents the advantage of serving as a bridge notion between
law and the social sciences. The word 'mass' announces the exceptional proportions of the crime under consideration, in the sense
that it targets a group or a mass of individual victims. The expression
can also suggest that the spectacular crime under study is not committed by a single individual but instead by a group that very probably enjoys the support of the mass. However, the word 'crime'
bears the stamp of its normative and thus possibly legal and penal
nature.

Hence I have ended up recommending the use of the word
'*massacre*' as lexical unit of reference in this field of study. It is much
less general than 'violence'. I first give it a sociological, empirical
definition: a generally collective form of action, involving the destruction of non-combatants, men, women, children or disarmed
soldiers.[48] I might point out that this word also has, since the European Middle Ages, referred in French to killing animals. The connection between the massacre of animals and that of human beings,
on both a historical and a semantic level, is not insignificant. It certainly does not solve the question of defining genocide from a social
science standpoint. But before doing so, research must first concentrate on massacres; not all massacres can be considered as genocide, and genocide necessarily involves one or several massacres. It is
therefore simple good methodological sense that leads me to privilege 'massacre' as an object of study, the question being particularly
one of identifying at what point and in what circumstances a massacre becomes genocide.

We can distinguish between various morphologies of massacre by
their scope, the possible distance between killers and victims, and the
structure of the conflicts that these forms of extreme violence engender. A massacre implies the death of several people, although it is
impossible to specify a minimum figure. There is nevertheless a difference in magnitude between the series of 'small-scale massacres'
such as those that took place in Algeria or Colombia, and a very

large-scale massacre, such as the one perpetrated in Indonesia in 1965 in the space of a few weeks (nearly 500,000 dead) or Rwanda in 1994 (nearly 800,000 dead). In the second case it seems justifiable to speak of mass murder or mass killing just as we distinguish intuitively between a 'demonstration' and a mass demonstration.[49] Similarly, it is important to differentiate between massacres close at hand (describing face-to-face contact between murderers and victims), and massacre from a distance (such as aerial bombing performed by a pilot who does not even see the people his bomb will hit). The meaning of the massacre is again very different when dealing with a situation of bilateral massacres between adversaries in conflict (i.e. a civil war) or a unilateral massacre perpetrated for instance by a state against its own people. It is also essential to know whether the massacre is committed by a state or a militant organisation and if the authors of the act are prepared to die with their victims, as in the case of the 11 September 2001 suicide attacks in the United States (see below, pp. 000–00). Each of these different cases requires a specific study.

Analysing destruction processes. The study of massacres must necessarily fit within the broader framework of a *destruction process*, of which it is the most spectacular expression. As a form of extreme violence, a massacre needs to be understood in the context of the dynamic of violence that precedes and accompanies it. The rise in violence in Kosovo in the 1990s is a particularly significant example in this regard. A controversy arose about the number of dead in this former Yugoslav province, following the 'ethnic cleansing' operations undertaken by the Serbian army and various militias. When NATO intervened in 1999 with the official mission to end the killings, the various parties involved put forward very different figures for the number of those killed: 3,000? 10,000? 50,000? However macabre it may be, such reckoning is certainly necessary, if only from a legal point of view. But it is far too simplistic to account for the destruction caused in Kosovo since 1998 (if not since 1990) in terms of people who have disappeared, displaced families, women raped, homes burned, etc. Wherefore the importance of theorising massacres as being 'simply' the most spectacular and tragic form of an *overall destruction process*. A massacre can either 'accompany' this process or be the outcome of it.

In this respect the socio-psychologist Ervin Staub suggested the interesting expression 'continuum of destruction'.[50] The term 'continuum' seems inadequate, however, since it might suggest an inescapable progression that would necessarily go from event *a* to event *b*, for example from increased persecution of a minority to its slaughter. Such a view was undoubtedly inspired by the history of the Holocaust. Nevertheless, it is now admitted that this is a misinterpretation reconstructed with hindsight (because the end of the historical event is known): the persecution of German Jews at the very beginning of Hitler's regime did not in any way imply that the Auschwitz scenario was already written. For that reason the concept of a 'process' is preferable to that of a 'continuum' since the former implies the idea of a dynamics of destruction that is liable to change, slow down or speed up, in short not a scenario foretold, but one shaped according to the will of the perpetrators and to the circumstances. Such is the approach that has been adopted in this book.

To be even more precise, I could instead refer to *an organised process of destruction of civilians directed at persons and their property: Organised* because this is not 'natural' destruction (such as an earthquake) or accidental destruction (such as the Chernobyl nuclear disaster). Far from being anarchic, this process of violence is channeled, directed and even structured against a particular group. It takes the concrete form of collective action, most often fostered by the state (and its agents), with the will to organise such violence. That does not rule out possible improvisation or even spontaneity on the part of the perpetrators in ways of inflicting suffering or of killing. *Process* because the collective action of a massacre can be regarded as the outcome of a complex situation created primarily by the combination of a particular long-term political history, cultural environment and international context.

Destruction: the term is broader than 'murder' and encompasses the possible demolition or burning of houses or religious or cultural buildings in order to wipe out the presence of the 'other', i.e. the enemy, which could also include dehumanising the victims before their elimination. Forced marches and other deportation techniques, which often carry a high mortality rate, also form part of these processes of population destruction. The word 'destruction' does not

326 PURIFY AND DESTROY

predetermine the method of killing, be it by fire, water, gas, starvation, cold or any other slow or quick means of causing death.

Civilians because it has to be acknowledged that, while such violence might at first be directed against military (or paramilitary) targets, it tends to move away from such targets and focus primarily or even exclusively on noncombatants, and hence civilians. The phrase 'destruction of civilian populations' is a familiar term found in strategic vocabulary. However, it conveys too strongly the idea of aerial bombing and hence the wiping-out of an entire community (for example, the inhabitants of a town). We need to envisage a more differentiated destruction process targeting civilians scattered throughout the same society. The expression 'destruction of civilians' is therefore preferable since it encompasses both these dimensions, which range from the elimination of scattered individuals to that of established groups and even entire populations.

These collective acts of destruction in all cases entail a totally asymmetrical relationship between aggressor and victim, referred to as one-sided destruction, where victim individuals and groups are not in a position to defend themselves. Note, however, that this does not in any way dictate the former or future status of the victims, who may have been, or could become, murderers in their turn.

Disengaging genocide studies from a legal approach also means adopting a different analytical perspective: not so much examining the effects of the violent act on the victims[51] as seeking to detect among perpetrators of massacres the reasons for their descent into violence. Such a change in perspective is decisive: one stops looking at massacres through the lenses of the legal expert to don those of the political scientist. Again, such is the fundamental approach adopted in this book: to examine the various political uses of massacres, even of genocides. This approach may seem shocking, since it suggests that massacres have 'meaning' or, more precisely, that they mean something to those who perpetrate them. But taking the viewpoint of the perpetrators by no means implies espousing their cause. As Max Weber has taught us, 'One doesn't have to be Caesar to understand Caesar.'[52] Thus there is rationality behind the practices of extreme violence, even if this rationality seems delusional to us. The diversity of historical situations leads to distinguish between three fundamental political dynamics of mass killings, i.e. the will to destroy a targeted group partly and even totally, depending on whether the aim is

— subjugation;
— eradication;
— insurrection.

I will attempt a brief historical overview of these murderous dynamics that will provide a better understanding of possible genocide definitions from the social science standpoint.

Destroying to subjugate

The goal here is to annihilate a group partly in order to force the rest into total submission. The destruction process is, by definition, *partial* but it is intended to have an *overall* impact, since those responsible for the deed rely on the effect of terror in order to impose their political domination on the survivors. That is why the act of massacre is particularly suited to such a strategy. The slaughter need not be wholesale; it only has to become known to the public so that its terrorizing effect will spread among the population. Pillage and rape increase the impact of terror. In some cases these practices can take on incredible proportions, one of the best-known examples being the mass rape of Chinese women by Japanese soldiers in Nanjing that went on for more than six weeks, from December 1937 to January 1938.

As I have already pointed out (Chapter III), warfare often leads to massacre. The civilian subjugation dynamic can in fact be fully incorporated within a military operation to precipitate an adversary's surrender and hasten the conquest of its territory and the subjugation of its people. This is what Michael Walzer calls 'war against civilians', which according to him includes various forms of siege and blockades aiming at the fall of a city or at a country's collapse. Such methods of warfare are universal and shared by all types of political and military powers. Authoritarian or totalitarian states are far from having a monopoly on them. Democracies may also use them, as during the Second World War with the Allied bombing of German cities, the most notorious being that of Dresden on 13 and 14 February 1945. The atomic bombing of Hiroshima and Nagasaki by the United States on 6 and 9 August 1945 was also motivated by the intention to terrorise an entire country and thereby force its leaders to capitulate, a type of military operation against civilians that philosopher John Rawls has deemed immoral.[53]

On a lesser scale, destruction/subjugation methods can also be found in contemporary civil warfare, where a distinction is no longer made between combatants and non-combatants. Even if women and children in a given village are unarmed, they may be suspected of helping the enemy guerrilla by supplying food and ammunition. Women and children thereby become potential targets for the opposite camp, who believe they should be destroyed. When a village does fall into the hands of these enemy forces, they are always tempted to 'set an example' by killing the inhabitants, using this form of 'punishment' to send a message to the entire area. Massacres are thus used to win the allegiance of all those living in the surrounding area. Sometimes a few people are spared so they can share the horror of what they have witnessed with all around them. Everyone will thus be forewarned of the fate awaiting anyone trying to resist the conqueror. But if the population indeed complies with the enemy, it is then in danger of being taken as a target by the defeated camp that sets out to take revenge. And so civilian populations are always caught in the crossfire between armed groups in conflict, causing the number of civilian deaths to surpass by far those of armed combatants *per se*. Such practices can be identified in countless wars past and present, from Vietnam, Lebanon to Guatemala, including Algeria, Mozambique, Colombia, Sierra Leone and Chechnya.

From warfare to ruling over the population. The destruction/subjugation practices forged through warfare can also be extended to ruling over a people. For instance, wars of conquest have been conducted through massacre, followed by economic exploitation of the conquered population, with further recourse, where necessary, to the killing of some of its members. This, for example, was the basic attitude of the Conquistadors towards the Indians, whom they perceived as worthless beings, existing only to do their masters' bidding. The accounts written between 1527 and 1561 by the Dominican monk Bartholomew de Las Casas, bear a particularly poignant testimony to this.[54] Many other examples could be cited of stories of colonial conquest, be it in South America, Africa or Asia. The revolution in firearms in the late nineteenth century with the appearance and then improvement of machine-guns, gave European expeditionary forces a crushing superiority in their conquest of the Sudan, Angola and Rwanda.

History offers other, more 'political' variants of this destruction/subjugation dynamic that anticipates the shift from warfare to domination. In this instance, Clausewitz's formula could be reversed. Instead of war being the continuation of politics by other means, politics becomes the means of pursuing war... against civilians. The winning side of a civil war is also very logically drawn into this power-building dynamic, as illustrated to some extent by the example of revolutionary France, which sent 'fiery columns' to put down the Vendée rebellion in 1793. Here we find again the figure of the suspect described in Chapter I, made officially dangerous by the law of 17 September 1793, thus enabling the government to imprison 500,000 people.[55] It was in this period, known as the Terror, that the expression 'terrorism' emerged, conceived as a state policy.

In Lenin's revolutionary Russia, the Bolsheviks similarly continued the war against their enemies of all sorts, former royalists or socialists, or members of classes deemed 'reactionary', such as the peasants. The Bolsheviks wanted to remain in power longer than the seventy-two days of the Paris Commune and thus enacted measures of terror previously unknown in Tsarist Russia. In November 1917 they officialised the notion of 'enemy of the people', later extending it to all sorts of 'counter-revolutionary' categories. And they always justified their use of violence on a 'class' basis, in the perspective of the dawning of a new world. The figure of this many-faced traitor seems closely associated with the political dynamic of destruction/subjugation, reaching in communist regimes the scale of mass violence.

It is true that whether or not civil war was involved, the process dates back a long time. Torture and killing to 'set an example' constitute one of the standard techniques for any tyrant seeking to quash an internal rebellion. Authoritarian or colonial powers, even democratic ones, have often used such lethal methods. One such example is the Amritsar massacre in India perpetrated by the English Brigadier-General Reginald Dyer against a crowd of non-violent demonstrators on 13 April 1919 (379 dead, 1,200 wounded). In South Africa the racist regime was no less abashed about firing on a peaceful crowd in Sharpeville on 21 March 1960 (69 dead, 180 wounded).

In Algeria, on 8 May 1945 (the very day of Germany's surrender in Europe), the French police and gendarmerie opened fire on a parade of demonstrators waving the Algerian flag in Sétif, which sparked a revolt. That same evening, another massacre was perpetrated in Guelma, with the participation of armed colonists.[56] Subsequently, during the war of independence, the French military, with the support of Guy Mollet's government, developed the practice of wide-scale torture against the population (including women), suspected of backing the Algerian resistance. This systematic use of torture, justified in the name of intelligence gathering and also for security reasons, actually appears as the preferred instrument of a political system of terror that aims not to make people talk but to keep them quiet.[57]

For its part, the National Liberation Front (FLN) committed abuses not only against French settlers but also against the Algerian population suspected of collaborating with the colonisers, murdering and kidnapping in the process several tens of thousands of people.[58] And Latin American dictatorships in the 1970s, led by Argentina and Chile (these governments benefiting from advice offered by the French and, even more so, North American military officers), organised systematic 'disappearances' of all those they deemed suspicious. The technique involved arresting real or assumed political and union enemies of the regime, without ever informing their families. Were they dead or alive? Generally they were tortured, and then killed. But their loved ones did not and could not know. The uncertainty surrounding the fate of the 'disappeared' was aimed specifically at creating a psychological climate of terror and paralysis in the entire population.

Communist regimes: Reshaping the social body. Dynamics of destruction/subjugation were also developed systematically by twentieth-century communist regimes, but against a very different domestic political background. The destruction of the very foundations of the former society (and consequently the men and women who embodied it) reveals the determination of the ruling elites to build a new one at all costs. The ideological conviction of leaders promoting such a political scheme is thus decisive. Nevertheless, it would be far too simplistic an interpretation to assume that the sole purpose of inflicting these various forms of violence on civilians could only aim at instilling a climate of terror in this 'new society'. In fact, they are part of a broader whole, i.e the spectrum of *social engineering* techniques implemented in order to transform a society completely. There can be no doubt that it is this utopia of a classless society which drives that kind of revolutionary project. The plan for political and social reshaping will thus logically claim victims in all strata of the society. And through this process, communist systems emerging in the twentieth century ended up destroying their own populations, not because they planned to annihilate them as such, but because they aimed to restructure the 'social body' from top to bottom, even if that meant purging it and recarving it to suit their new Promethean political *imaginaire*.

In the case of the Soviet Union, one of the great projects of this social reshaping was the enforced collectivisation of agriculture, which involved ruthless and systematic measures of 'dekulakisation', namely the deportation of supposedly well-off peasants who could only oppose such a plan. The deportation operations (mainly to Siberia) should thus be understood as part of a vast, coherent policy brutally to transform the economy and society. By so doing the budding Soviet state went to war against a multitude of small farmers who did their best to resist. In 1930, notes the French historian Nicolas Werth, 'nearly 2.5 million peasants took part in approximately 14,000 revolts, riots, and mass demonstrations against the regime. The regions most affected were the Black Earth region, the Northern Caucasus, and Ukraine, particularly the western parts, where whole districts, and notably the areas that bordered on Poland and Romania, temporarily slipped out of the control of the Soviet regime.'[59] By way of reprisal, Stalin provoked extensive famine in 1932–3, claiming some 6 million victims. His intent was to subjugate the most rebellious regions, starting with Ukraine, once and for all. Afterwards, this mass violence implemented against the peasants was applied to other social groups.

The purges of Stalin's great terror in the years 1937 and 1938 went on in the same vein, inspired by these same dekulakisation methods. Those purges, which targeted all kinds of 'enemies', affected not only the elites but society as a whole. The aim was to rid the country of all its 'anti-Soviet' and 'anti-social' elements. No one could feel sheltered from this because everyone became a suspect. The Party set quotas of 'enemies' to be arrested according to category and region, the same way that it set production quotas for mining iron and coal.

Another basic element of Soviet-style social engineering was the vast network of labour camps that the Russian writer Alexander Solzhenitsyn named the 'Gulag Archipelago'. The basic idea of the camp was punishment/re-education, the prisoners being subjected to forced labour in prison camps in conditions that jeopardised their health, if not their lives. But unlike the Nazi camps, the aim of the Soviet camp system was not to kill the prisoners; Hanna Arendt intuited this difference when she pictured the Soviet camp as being 'to Purgatory what the Nazi camp was to Hell'. The most recent historiography confirms this idea that, although a Soviet citizen could die in the Gulag, he could also get out after several years of imprisonment. Thus the Gulag could be a place of passage and not only death.[60]

Communist China under Mao Zedong is another variant of total social engineering. The father of the Chinese Revolution himself gave a very broad definition of his enemies when in 1949 he declared: 'Once the armed enemies are annihilated, there are still unarmed enemies; those who will fight us to the death. We must never underestimate them. If we do not face and understand the problem in this way right now, we will make serious mistakes.'[61] And in 1951 he undertook a virulent terror campaign directed at 'counter-revolutionaries', restarted in 1955 against 'hidden enemies of the revolution', etc.

It is impossible here to reproduce all the serial murderous mobilisations launched regularly against intellectuals, or more broadly against city-dwellers, former Party leaders, Buddhists, etc. These Party-orchestrated operations had also set quotas of enemies to be arrested. From the beginning of its struggle in the 1920s up through the massacres in the 1960s, and including the period of 'Cultural Revolution', the Chinese Communist Party used violence not only as an instrument to terrorise the population but also as a weapon by which to establish and 'regenerate' its regime, which was supposed to breathe new life into the grandiose revolutionary project of Marxism-Leninism.[62] Like the Soviet Union, Communist China

also produced a concentration camp system, which the French political scientist Jean-Luc Domenach has named 'the forgotten archipelago'.[63] It was made up of some 1,000 huge labour camps and a
multitude of detention centres. Tens of millions of individuals—50
million in all till the mid-1980s—perished in what were known as
laogai (meaning 'reform through labour').[64]

The risk of losing one's life seems to have been higher than in the
Soviet camps. Most of the prisoners were incarcerated under the
pretence of 'reform through labour'—or, to borrow Harry Wu's
expression, of 're-education through labour'. Some have compared
this enslavement of individuals in Chinese camps to the trade and
enslavement of Negroes by the European powers. But there is a huge
difference between these systems. In the case of Chinese communism, men are subjugated in the name of their 're-education':
they are detained not really as punishment but to give them an
opportunity to reform, to hone closer to the ideal of the 'new man'
that the Party wanted to reproduce by the millions. The entire system thus aimed at encouraging everyone to absolute submission, as
attests this terrifying statement: 'Please give me the authorization to
show repentance for my sins by working in the camps.'[65]

The paradigm of 'Democratic Kampuchea'. In Cambodia Pol Pot's
'Khmer Rouge' wanted to make even deeper, and above all faster,
inroads than their Chinese and Soviet counterparts. Between 1975
and 1979, Democratic Kampuchea (the new name given to communist Cambodia) constituted something of a paradigm of destructive social engineering on a nationwide scale. Over and above their
staunch determination to bring down the hated regimes of General
Lon Nol, backed by the United States, their aim was to build an
entirely new society, the 'ancient Khmer people' (mainly uned-
ucated peasants) serving as its base and most authentic expression.

So the Khmer Rouge set out to destroy all signs of modern civilisation left by the 'new people' who resided mainly in urban areas,
and more generally everything that embodied bureaucracy and
western technology. They also made the radical decision literally to
empty the country's major cities, beginning with the capital Phnom
Penh, as soon as it fell under their control (17 April 1975). This
mind-boggling feat, which in the space of a few hours saw millions

of people on the road (including the sick and elderly), enabled them to wipe out the urban fabric within which their political enemies might move. But more 'constructively', so to speak, it was based on the idea of building a new society and a new economy by putting all the Cambodians to work in the rice paddies and fields. The country was soon entirely cut off from the outside world, and became a huge labour camp where the causes of mortality were numerous: summary executions, of course, but also the harsh physical labour, forced marches, hunger and disease.

Ben Kiernan believes that a racist vision on the part of the Khmer Rouge was also a decisive factor, leading it to want to eliminate religious or ethnic groups, such as the Muslim minority (the Cham).[66] But from there to claim that such racism was the very essence of Pol Pot's regime requires taking a step that Steve Heder, another specialist on Cambodia, is reluctant to take. In his view the founding principle of the Pol Pot regime truly remains the Marxist-Leninist model inspired by its Chinese 'big brother': a specific plan for rapid modernisation aiming to bring about the glorious dawn of the communist system in Cambodia. It was in the context of this radical political program that those perceived as possible opponents were stigmatised in terms of race. Moreover, Heder points out, from the Soviet Union to China, progress toward achieving communism was made to the detriment of many national minorities. The extraordinary regime of terror that reigned in Democratic Kampuchea was thus not purely the fact of mere racism, it resulted from the attempt to implement Marxist-Leninist policy.[67] As in China, the 'individual re-education' aspect is essential, since mandatory re-education sessions were scheduled in the workplace. It mattered little if the individuals were on the verge of exhaustion and often starving. The salvation of the 'new people' depended on the notion of converting individuals to the communist doctrine, which, according to François Bizot, was grafted on to the religious structure inherited from Khmer Buddhism.[68]

Destroying to eradicate

The destruction/eradication dynamic, the second dynamic I have identified, is altogether different. It aims not so much to subjugate individuals to a given political power as to *eliminate a community* from a more or less extensive territory controlled or coveted by a state. This process involves 'cleansing' or 'purifying' the area of another's presence, deemed undesirable and/or dangerous. For this reason the concept of *eradication* seems particularly relevant since its etymology conveys the idea of 'severing roots' or 'extracting from the earth', in short 'uprooting', as would be said of a harmful plant or contagious disease.

This identity-based destruction/eradication process can also be associated with wars of conquest. Such is the meaning behind the popular expression 'move over and make room for me'. Mass killing, combined with rape and pillage, is the means by which one makes one's intentions clear and consequently hastens the departure of the 'other', who is deemed undesirable. The partial destruction of the group and the effect of the resulting terror are thus able to bring about and accelerate such departure. This was, for example, the tactic employed by the European settlers in North America against the Native American peoples, who were driven farther and farther west, beyond the Mississippi. The words of one of the United States' founding fathers, President Thomas Jefferson, are unambiguous in this respect: 'If ever we are constrained to lift the hatchet against any tribe, we will never lay it down till that tribe is exterminated, or driven beyond the Mississippi. ... In war they will kill some of us; we shall destroy all of them.'[69]

In the Balkans such forced movement of populations out of a territory has been termed 'ethnic cleansing', in particular to describe the operations conducted mainly by Serbia and Croatia in the early 1990s. But the methods used (slaughtering people, burning villages, destroying religious buildings, etc.) can be linked to earlier practices in that region, dating at least back to the nineteenth century, in the context of the rise of nationalism and the decline of the Ottoman Empire. All nationalist movements in the Balkans resorted to ethnic cleansing, be it in Greece, Serbia and Montenegro and later in Bulgaria. The Balkan wars in the early twentieth century fit into this continuum, observers at the time already using the expression 'extermination of civilian populations'.[70] In some cases the purifying reputation of an army was such that the inhabitants deserted their villages even before the army arrived.[71]

After their inception in the United States and Western Europe, similar practices of massacre associated with the formation of a nation-state spread throughout the world, progressing from West to East in the nineteenth and twentieth centuries, then from West to South in the twentieth century (decolonisation in Asia, South America and Africa). This general trend seems to be far from over, given the vigour still manifest in national aspirations of some peoples across the planet. It is as if the modern state, viewing itself as a homogenous self, an 'us' imagined on a political, ethnic and/or religious basis, necessarily had to build itself against an other to be expelled, if not destroyed. The figure of the enemy becomes in this case that 'other in excess', deemed both very different from oneself—the collective self—and far too numerous on the coveted territory.

The formation of the state of Israel at the end of the 1940s did not escape this foundational political dynamic. Israel's history is clearly rather singular given the age-old persecution of the Jews, and Nazi Germany's attempt to eradicate them totally in the twentieth century. In this regard, the creation of Israel, which was meant to provide Jews with security once and for all, constitutes a before and after in their timeless history. But as is so often the case, constructing this state was possible only at the expense of an 'other' perceived as undesirable. A new school of Israeli historians has revealed the truth about the expulsion and massacre of Palestinians perpetrated in 1948 by Israeli military units, the best known being those of 9 April 1948 in Deir Yassin and 11 July 1948 in Lod and Ramle.[72]

In his *Nouvelle Histoire d'Israel*, the Israeli political scientist Ilan Greilsammer shrewdly shows how these facts demolish historical Zionist myths such as the one claiming that the Arabs left of their own accord following a radio appeal issued by their leaders.[73] Similarly, the myth constructed around the memory of Joseph Trumpeldor, a pioneer of Russian origin who died in battle against the Arabs as he was defending the early Jewish settlements north of Galilee, stands up no better to historic method. Before he died in the battle of Tel-Hai, he supposedly declared: 'It doesn't matter. It is good to die for our country.' Although it is true he was killed in combat on 1 March 1920, he never actually spoke those words. But 'if the myth has worked so well, it is because the hero corresponded perfectly to what was expected of him.'[74] These words of the 'valiant pioneer' in effect broadcast a message of bravery and sacrifice, enjoining others to fight to conquer the right to live in Palestine. Didn't Ben Gurion say that Trumpeldor's comrades had blessed the country with their blood? Such claims to land rights, rooted in the memory of blood spilled by the Jewish pioneers, thus in return justified violence they deemed legitimate in remaining faithful to their memory. It is as if the powerful mechanism of sacrificial violence was inaugurated right at the start, within the foundations of the state of Israel, and naturally at the expense of those living on that land, the Arabs of Palestine. This foundational violence subsequently went through apparent moments of respite. But every time that feelings of insecurity resurface among Israelis, violence against the Palestinians immediately resurges, seemingly all the more justified since the latter are also engaged in armed combat against those they perceive as an occupying force. Thus on both sides the most radical elements believe that there is an 'other in excess' on a territory they want to be theirs alone; this other is far too close, and so they make it their mortal enemy. As a result, the most extreme discourses on both sides are based on this logic of total exclusion, typical of the security dilemma: 'it's us or them.'

These processes used in warfare to build a nation can be re-used later in the internal 'governance' of the population. This is so in the full range of ethnic conflicts studied by Andrew Bell-Fialkoff, Norman Naimark, Béla Vardy and Hunt Tooley.[75] Generally, new elites in power instrumentalise the ethnic criterion for the purpose of one group's political domination over an entire community. In some cases, the other in excess is tolerated as long as he submits to the law of the dominant ethnic group, or if he is deemed quantitatively to present little danger. In the aftermath of a war, forced population displacements are thus sometimes organised. For instance, after the fall of the Third Reich in 1945 nearly 16 million Germans were forced to leave Central and East European countries to rejoin Germany, now split in two. This happened to 3.5 million Sudeten Germans, most of whom had lived in the Sudetenland for centuries. Nearly 200,000 Hungarians were subjected to the same fate in 1945–6, though to a lesser extent, when Edward Benes recreated Czechoslovakia and forced them to cross the Danube into Hungary. However, in some cases, recourse to more radical violence, in other words a massacre *per se*, can hasten a departure movement. Such operations are naturally presented as being taken in self-defence, in order to solve once and for all a problem regarded as insoluble.

Although such practices are mainly impelled by the governing elites, the people sometimes participate directly, as in the reciprocal slaughters of Hindus and Muslims during the Partition of India, which in 1946–7 caused approximately one million deaths and displaced over 100,000 people. The sociologist Donald Horowitz has done an interesting study on the communal, ethnic or religious violence that has broken out in Malaysia, Kyrgyzstan, Nigeria and Lebanon. Even if such incidents sometimes seem to be set off by an unpredictable 'spark', they nevertheless often remain manipulated and organised and sometimes refer to traditions that hark back to the nineteenth century, if not earlier.[76]

Surgical practices in politics. Ultimately the incapacity of the modern sovereign state to tolerate significant minorities within its borders leads either to forced assimilation programs or operations of ethnic cleansing. It all depends on the political circumstances and the historical context. But this homogenising ardour runs all through the twentieth century. It thus seems clear that the development of an all-powerful state must be viewed in the longer historical perspective, as Michel Foucault's work invites us to do. I have in mind here in particular his analyses on the birth of a 'bio-power', embodied in this state that disciplines, controls, interferes in family life, identifies and banishes dangerous groups, etc.[77] And the examples provided by the twentieth century confirm that much more is going on than simply the establishment of social control over bodies. The state is no longer content merely to 'discipline and punish'.

With the multiplication of ethnic cleansing practices, the state crossed a new threshold in the twentieth century: that of *purifying and banishing* populations deemed undesirable or dangerous. For the state henceforth takes the liberty of carving up the social body: it planes off the rough edges, and removes contagious and impure elements when it doesn't simply crush them without qualms. In short, it shapes the social body in its own way, *to its own design*. It can perform the work of a gardener, or rather a political surgeon,[78] all the better now since it has new instruments to identify and quantify, for

example statistics to inform about population, allowing governments to take action as required to fulfil a particular policy. Never
before have authorities had at their disposal such powerful tools for
governing the masses (administration), speaking to them (radio) and
displacing them (trains). To accomplish this great political reshaping,
we see *a new form of social engineering* emerge, that consists not only of
subjugating a rebellious people (as we saw earlier) but of carving
it up, removing the undesirable elements by deporting them and
allowing them to die *en route* if need be.

Here again Europe was the grand worksite for the mass uproot-
ings that took place especially during the Second World War. It is
hard to imagine today how, inside the Soviet Union, entire populations were deported by Stalin's regime toward settlement areas in
Siberia and Kazakhstan. The historian Robert Conquest devoted a
pioneer book to what long remained a 'blank spot' in the history of
this period.[79] The first to be subjected to such fate, in 1940 and 1941,
were the Poles, the Germans in the Volga region, the peoples of the
Baltic states and later, in 1943 and 1944, the Talmuks, the Ingush, the
Tatars, the Chechens and so on. These 'damned' peoples were perceived by Moscow as potentially dangerous, even accused of collaborating with the Nazi enemy. The deportation operations were a
particularly terrible blow to these people's integrity, even if they
were not actually slaughtered. Deportation for them amounted to a
brutal de facto uprooting, their transfer resulting in a mortality rate
between 20 and 25 per cent. In this regard, such operations really do
arise out of an intention to eradicate.[80]

The process can take on an even more radical form when individuals are killed without even having the chance to flee, or when
they are slaughtered once they have been deported. The notion of a
'territory to be purified' in this case becomes secondary in relation
to the aim of totally exterminating a group. The objective becomes
to destroy all its members, including children. Some colonial massacres were probably perpetrated with this in mind, like that of the
Herero population of Namibia in 1904 by the German settlers.[81] Are
there other examples? This is subject for debate, and more research
needs to be done, particularly on the nineteenth century.[82] There is
no doubt, however, that it was the leaders of Nazi Germany who
went furthest in this process of total eradication. The extermination

of European Jews between 1941 and 1945, which followed the partial elimination of mentally ill Germans, is the paradigmatic example of this eradication process.

The essentialised figure of this 'Jewish' enemy constitutes the prototype of the 'other in excess' that was slated to disappear in the grandiose, entirely 'purified' (*judenrein*) Aryan Third Reich. More generally the elimination of the Jews was part of the huge plan to reshape all of Europe that also included, for reasons of racial hygiene, the mass murder of gypsies and homosexuals and the partial destruction of those 'subhuman' Slavs. In these actions experts of all sorts—economists, demographers, statisticians and so on—played a major role alongside the politicians. In very different historical contexts, a destruction/eradication process was also undertaken in 1915–16 by the Young Turkish government against the Armenian minority under the Ottoman Empire, as well as by the Hutu extremists in Rwanda 1994 at the expense of that country's Tutsi minority. The aim here was not to disperse a people across other territories. It was, in Hannah Arendt's words, to cause a people to disappear not just from *their* own land but from *the* land.

The Holocaust paradigm. At this final stage of total eradication, the notion of 'genocide' can be reintroduced, this time as a concept in the social sciences. The public at large sees genocide as a form of large-scale massacre; whenever the death toll reaches several hundred thousand, and even more so when it reaches the millions, it seems reasonable to speak of genocide. But this intuitive approach, which takes the large number of victims as its yardstick, is not specific to a genocidal undertaking. Moreover, no expert today could say from *how many* deaths genocide begins. What offers a more reliable definition of genocide is a *qualitative* criterion *combined* with this quantitative criterion, i.e. the intention to achieve the total annihilation of a group. This is why I will define genocide as that particular process of civilian destruction that is directed at the total eradication of a group, the criteria by which it is identified being determined by the perpetrator.

Naturally, like any definition, this one implies a choice and is thus debatable. I would therefore justify it in the light of the broad categories of destruction/subjugation and destruction/eradication just outlined. One can certainly decide that the notion of genocide holds for both categories, and some authors readily adopt this approach. Why should they not? Because if the concept covers both categories, it cannot be expected to have any discriminatory value. It cannot then in any way serve as an analytical tool in the social sciences. Its function is more of a moral nature, operating as a 'catch-all' notion to qualify all the mass murders on earth.

Another defining option involves reserving the notion of 'genocide' for all massacres targeting the eradication of groups rather than their subjugation. Many have argued in favour of such a choice, and rightly so, reasoning on the basis of the example of the American atomic bombings of the two Japanese cities, Hiroshima and Nagasaki. Those actions indeed cannot be considered as genocidal operations, since the United States had the intention not of destroying all the Japanese but of forcing the government to surrender. However, extending this same reasoning to the mass murders perpetrated by the communist regimes is problematic. If we so easily admit that a war operation is not genocide (when conducted by a western democratic state), why wouldn't the same hold true for 'civil war' operations undertaken by a communist state against its own population? In both cases we are nevertheless in the rationale of destruction/subjugation. But the ideological nature of communist violence, defined as totalitarian, lends another 'quality' to this destruction process, which would then tip it over into the category of genocide. In fact, any totalitarian power would then necessarily be genocidal in nature.

The consequence of such reasoning is considerable because genocide would then be as much the product of Nazism as of communism. It poses a sort of lethal equivalence between the two systems: the communists set out to destroy class enemies, the Nazi regime racial enemies. This position is partly coherent, which is why its advocates define as genocide, for instance, the case of Cambodia under Pol Pot or the famine in Ukraine. The French historian Stéphane Courtois has advocated this in his introduction to *The Black Book of Communism*, more generally using the arguments of the German historian Ernst Nolte that 'relativise' the Nazi crimes with respect to those of communism. However, other historians dispute such an approach.[83] François Furet himself marked his distance from this position in his correspondence with Ernst Nolte, when he wrote that 'genocide stands apart from other figures of evil because it targets men, women and children for the very fact that they are born as they are, regardless of any intelligible consideration stemming from struggles for power. The anti–Semitic terror lost all relationship to the political sphere from which it stemmed.'[84] In other words, François Furet clearly states here that the Nazi violence against the Jews does not fall into the same category as the communists' political violence against the 'enemies of the revolution'.

Without going into an excessively technical historiographical debate, let us point out that this approach, which boils down to equating totalitarianism with genocide, gives hardly any attention to showing the considerable differences in the dynamics of violence at work inside of each system. We have seen how the figures of the enemy corresponding to the destruction/subjugation process and the destruction/eradication process are in no way the same. In the case of subjugation, the figure of the suspect engenders a dynamic of violence that 'scans' the entire social body: each individual becomes a potential suspect. If he is arrested, then this suspect is by definition guilty. That is because the criteria defining an 'enemy of the people' are so vague that it is the actual arrest that serves as proof of his guilt.

On the other hand, in the case of eradication the destruction process focuses on the identity of individuals defined as belonging to that 'other in excess'. It is thus their very identity that betrays them in advance: they are guilty because they were born Jewish, Tutsi or Muslim. Before even being arrested, they are condemned. Their situation is thus the exact opposite of the previous one. The type of violence resulting from it is also not at all the same. Far from being random, as in the first case, the violence concentrates on those precise targets that must be 'extracted' from the social body that they contaminate by their very presence. These two dynamics are thus opposites: one radiates through the entire society, the other focuses on a specific group, which is to be destroyed. It is in the second case that the notion of genocide takes on its full meaning, if in any event it is to remain coherent with the very first definition outlined by Lemkin, who viewed genocide as the destruction of a group as such.

Those who remain hostile to this type of analysis can still retort: 'You may be right: the dynamics of violence are probably different. But so what? We are thus simply facing two distinct forms of genocide: the first 'political', the second 'identity-based'. This is in fact a major drawback of the 1948 Convention, which recognises the existence of the second but not the first. To this objection I would reply that, in the guise of being a supposedly 'scientific debate', it actually conceals major issues related to remembrance and immediate action (reviewed earlier in this chapter). The insistence on keeping the word 'genocide' then proceeds either from the intention not to release communist violence from the incrimination of genocide, or from the moral desire, no less commendable, of maintaining a broad definition of the term to provide protection today for potential victims of political or social repression in the future. But if one sticks to a more rigorous approach—and rigour should, after all, prevail in the social sciences—we must admit that the use of one and the same notion to refer to two different phenomena is likely to result in unfortunate and lasting confusions. This seems all the more necessary since the two logics are so often intertwined in one and the same historical situation.

The dynamics of subjugation and eradication tend in fact to coexist, one being dominant, the other relegated to the background. In actual fact they complement each other by targeting different groups. This is precisely what emerges in comparing Nazi Germany and the USSR under Stalin: the Nazi genocidal power began by subjugating and/or destroying its political opponents, whereas the USSR, having undertaken all kinds of battles with the 'enemies of the people', undertook huge deportation operations displacing entire peoples, that were genocidal by nature. In Rwanda the genocide of the Tutsis, undertaken by Hutu extremists, started with the murder of their political opponents who themselves were Hutus. On the other hand, in Cambodia the Khmer Rouge, as soon as it came to power, began massacring all its political opponents and also undertook to eradicate groups that resisted them, starting with the Cham Muslim minority. The work of the scholar is precisely to identify these different dynamics of violence. This is often a complex task because they may not only be intertwined, but may also shift with time, for example from subjugation to eradication.

Politicidal regimes? If the term 'genocide' is not adequate to describe the crimes of communism, what other expression should be used?

'Classicide', in counterpoint to genocide, has a certain appeal, but it doesn't convey the fact that communist regimes, beyond their intention of destroying 'classes'—a difficult notion to grasp in itself (what exactly is a 'kulak'?)—end up making political suspicion a rule of government: every individual can potentially be accused of ideological deviance, even within the Party (and perhaps even mainly within the Party). The notion of 'fratricide' is probably more appropriate in this regard. That of 'politicide', which Ted Gurr and Barbara Harff suggest, remains the most intelligent, although it implies by contrast that 'genocide' is not 'political', which is debatable. These authors in effect explain that the aim of politicide is to impose total political domination over a group or a government. Its victims are defined by their position in the social hierarchy or their political opposition to the regime or this dominant group.[85] Such an approach applies well to the political violence of communist powers and more particularly to Pol Pot's Democratic Kampuchea. The French historian Henri Locard in fact emphasises this, identifying with Gurr and Harff's approach in his work on Cambodia.[86]

However, the term 'politicide' has little currency among some researchers because it has no legal validity in international law. That is one reason why Jean-Louis Margolin tends to recognise what happened in Cambodia as 'genocide' because, as he points out, to speak of 'politicide' amounts to considering Pol Pot's crimes as less grave than those of Hitler.[87] Again, the weight of justice interferes in the debate about concepts that, once again, argue strongly in favour of using the word genocide. But those so concerned about the issue of legal sanctions should also take into account another legal concept that is just as powerful, and better established: that of the crime against humanity. In fact, legal scholars such as Antoine Garapon and David Boyle believe that the violence perpetrated by the Khmer Rouge is much more appropriately categorised under the heading of crime against humanity, even if genocidal tendencies can be identified, particularly against the Muslim minority.[88] This accusation is just as serious as that of genocide (the latter moreover being sometimes considered as a subcategory of the former) and should thus be subject to equally severe sentences. I quite agree with these legal scholars, believing that the notion of 'crime against humanity' is generally better suited to the violence perpetrated by communist regimes, a viewpoint also shared by Michael Mann.[89]

From 'ethnic cleansing' to 'genocide'. Applying the notion of 'genocide' to all destruction/eradication processes raises still other difficult issues. It would mean no longer discerning the difference in destructive intensity and extremity between what has been called here 'ethnic cleansing' on the one hand and 'genocide' on the other. Now, the comparative analysis developed throughout this book concludes in favour of such distinction. We have seen that the ethnic violence in Bosnia had certain limits, whereas it apparently had none in Nazi Europe or Rwanda (cf. chapter IV). That is why I believe, along with authors such as Norman Naimark and Michael Mann, that the distinction between 'ethnic cleansing' and 'genocide' is a relevant one. Michael Mann moreover devised a six-point scale for this destruction process, the ultimate stage of which is the physical extermination of the group targeted:

(1) coerced assimilation;
(2) biological assimilation (laws restricting marriages, enforced sterilisation);
(3) coerced emigration;
(4) deportation;
(5) murderous cleansing and organised murders;
(6) genocide (rare according to him before the twentieth century).[90]

But the 1948 Convention pays no heed to these socio-historic observations, which is another source of confusion. It tends to blur this distinction because in article 2, it considers that there is genocide when there is intent to destroy a group in whole or in part. Any 'ethnic cleansing' operation can thereby be legally defined as a crime of genocide. The justices on the International Criminal Tribunal for the Former Yugoslavia referred to this very article in the judgement rendered on 2 August 2001 against Major-General Radislav Krstic, for his involvement in organising the massacre of Muslims in Srebrenica between 10 and 19 July 1995. This judgement, confirmed on appeal on 19 April 2004, broke new ground in the legal recognition of certain mass killings as genocides. The justices in The Hague decided that the massacre of Srebrenica attested that 'the alleged perpetrator intended to destroy at least a substantial part of the protected group', in other words all the Bosnian Muslims. Their reasoning is coherent enough, but is also debatable, in that the criteria used to determine that a 'substantial' part of the group was destroyed are relative.[91] In any event the ICTY judgement marks a major evolution in international law.

There is now in fact a considerable discrepancy between recognition of the crime of genocide for all the massacres of Tutsis in Rwanda, which claimed some 800,000 victims in the space of three months throughout an entire country, and recognition of the same indictment for massacre of 8,000 men in the space of a few days in one city. The ICTY judgement thus considerably expands the potential indictment for genocide in contemporary conflicts, for a mass murder such as that in Rwanda fortunately does not happen every day. On the other hand, massacres such as the one in Srebrenica are more common. So if the ICTY judgement creates a precedent, other massacres of this sort will thus be qualified as genocide. This evolution will consequently vindicate scholars such as the political scientist Robert Melson who, referring precisely to the UN Convention, has suggested a distinction between 'partial genocides' and 'total genocides'.[92] But other scholars and legal experts do not share this position: they point out that what Melson calls 'partial genocide' often actually involves encompassing under the generic term 'genocide', specific destruction processes they prefer to label differently for instance as 'ethnic cleansing', as do Antonio Cassese and the members of the United Nations International Commission of Inquiry on Darfur previously mentioned.

Comparative analysis prevents these two concepts from being confused. True, 'ethnic cleansing' and 'genocide' are indeed on the same continuum of destruction with the purpose of eradication. We could even say that in the dynamics of ethnic cleansing, in some places a more intense impulse to eradicate can appear, as in Srebrenica (Bosnia). But genocide is clearly different from ethnic cleansing where the ultimate fate of the victims is concerned. In the case of ethnic cleansing, even if some of the individuals are killed, others are allowed to flee, while in the case of genocide all exits are blocked, as Helen Fein has remarked.[93] That is why the phrase that still best characterises the genocidal paradigm is not only 'purify and banish'. A qualitative threshold is crossed: the aim is to *purify and destroy.*

However restrictive, this definition of genocide is based on Raphael Lemkin's initial approach, or at least on the 'essence of his definition', as Eric Markusen would say, that is, the destruction of a group as such.[94] Nevertheless, our approach makes two breaks with former research. First of all, the law is obviously no longer the starting-point. The opposite approach prevails, i.e. studying the nature of processes of extreme violence at work in a given historical situation in order to determine whether, ultimately, the destruction process aims to eradicate a group entirely. In other words, application of the term 'genocide' can only be the result of a researcher's analysis, an approach he can then discuss with the legal scholar.

Another distinction has to do with the very way the notion of genocide is understood. To speak of a 'process' or an 'evolution' means to consider genocide as a *specific dynamic of violence*. This constitutes a break with descriptive, virtually statistical approaches that dominate the field of genocide studies today. These in fact qualify as 'genocide' an act or an event using a battery of items: *a, b, c, d*, and so on. Such approaches are precisely the legacy of law, and explicitly that of the UN Convention. Thus it is always better to speak of a *genocidal process*, in order to emphasise this particular dynamic of destruction/eradication.[95]

Destroying to revolt

We should demarcate finally a third possible use of massacre, perpetrated mainly by non-state actors (or purportedly so). In this case the aim is to strike the target group in a single blow to provoke an intense traumatic shock likely to influence its leaders' policies. Since those who perpetrate the massacre know they are a minority in the society in which they are operating, recourse to this spectacular method allows them instantly to assert themselves in the public arena to promote their cause. Whether they claim responsibility or remain anonymous, they believe that the political effects of this destructive action will weigh on policymakers, for instance by causing an institutional crisis or by blockading a turn in policy of which they disapprove.

The practice of massacre thus clearly fits within a strategy of opposition or resistance to state policy. Obviously the procedure described here is at the very basis of so-called 'terrorist' acts, which rest mainly, according to the Israeli historian Ariel Merari, on the common denominator of a strategy of insurgency or revolt.[96] The word 'revolt' has a dual advantage: first, it refers to provoking a violent insurrection *against* a despised system, and second, it also refers to self-revolt in that it is hoped that the massacre will trigger an emancipating dynamic of the 'masses'. For the action is supposed to have a driving effect, not only leading to a political blockage but it should also 'deblock' a situation by attracting new militants and, more broadly, by fostering the population's 'detachment' from its leaders.

The rhetoric of terrorism. Is the word 'terrorism' the most apt to denote this form of collective action that has an aim of destruction/ insurrection? The enormous emotional charge associated with it makes analysis particularly tricky. In fact, grasping the notion of 'terrorism' poses the same type of problem as does 'genocide'. Both being contemporary incarnations of evil in politics, they both partake of the propaganda rhetoric used by the actors in conflict. This is why it is so difficult to break free of the political instrument- alisation of the term 'terrorist' that authorities so often use to stig- matise their adversaries, accusing them of killing innocent victims. In 1942 one might remember that the Germans as occupiers label- led the anti-Nazi resistance fighters as 'terrorists'. And in Chile un- der General Pinochet all opponents to his dictatorship were also called 'terrorists'.

Such political manipulations seem wholly to disqualify the use of this notion. For the French political scientist Didier Bigo, 'terrorism does not exist: or more precisely, it is not a concept that can be used in the social sciences and strategy studies.'[97] Amnesty International has in fact banned the use of the term from its annual reports on human rights abuses throughout the world. Nevertheless, can a non- partisan analyst dispense entirely with making reference to it, if only to explore the meaning of the word, to find out whether or not it can refer to a particular use of massacre in politics (whatever the cause defended)? Striving to break free from any moral judgement, Tony Oberschall has attempted to interpret what we call 'terrorism' in the light of collective action theory.[98] And the sociologist Michel Wieviorka defines terrorism as 'an extreme, degenerate, and highly particularized variety of social antimovement' in which the actors stray from the actual experience of those in whose name they are acting.[99] A distinction must be made between terrorism and guerrilla warfare, given that the actors in the latter case are theoretically at one with the population in whose midst they are fighting.

Here Walter Laqueur's often cited definition of terrorism—'the use of covert violence by a group for political ends'—is insufficient.[100] It can lead to considerable confusion between terrorism and any other form of political violence that could end up falling into the same category (be it guerrilla attacks or even banned demonstrations). For then any and all illegal violence would constitute a terrorist act, and governments could without scruple criminalise any sort of opposition to their power, as the Russian President Vladimir Putin does when he labels all Chechen combatants 'terrorists'. But is not the main issue at stake in wars that pit state actors against non-state actors precisely to determine who is legal and who is not?

History offers numerous examples of combatants who, after having been considered terrorists, have become heads of state. One such was Menahem Begin. In 1943, when Palestine was under British mandate, he became the leader of Irgun,[101] an ultra-nationalist underground organisation that was responsible for the attack on the King David Hotel (British administration headquarters) in July 1946, that caused over ninety deaths. When the state of Israel was founded, this organisation was incorporated into the Israeli army, Tsahal. He thus pursued his military career before becoming Prime Minister of his country. It leaves one to wonder if the word 'terrorist' does not simply refer to all those who fail to conquer power, all of history's losers. In any event, the reference to the legal status of actors is thus not relevant in settling the question pertaining to the nature of violent acts committed.

The 'legal/illegal' distinction tends to become even more blurred in cases where internationally recognised states provide logistical and financial support for terrorist groups operating within other countries. Shielded by its international legitimacy, a state can perfectly well orchestrate and remotely control illegal and violent actions. Such was the case in Iran under Ayatollah Khomeini, who provided support for the Hezbollah operations that organised several attacks in France in 1986 (most likely with the aim of forcing Paris to take a more favourable position towards Teheran in the Iran-Iraq war). Likewise, in the 1990s Afghanistan served as a base camp for the Saudi Osama Bin Laden, who was accused in particular of having ordered the operations conducted in 1998 against the American embassies in Kenya and Tanzania.

Finally, as we have seen, terrorism first designated a state policy historically in the context of the French Revolution. Previously it was used to describe lawless combatants, as is the case today, the original meaning of the word was thus to describe a government practice, *state* terrorism, based on a policy of terror, whether it was embodied in a manner of ruling or of making war. In fact all the practices of destruction/subjugation described earlier come under this terrorist rationale. Merari, for example, resorts to the use of the word terrorism in his writings about strategic bombings of cities during the Second World War: 'The dropping of atomic bombs on Hiroshima and Nagasaki which ended World War II can also be viewed as a case which fits the definitions of terrorism, albeit on a huge scale.'

From there it is only a short step to linking the methods of destruction carried out by states and those undertaken by non-state groups and networks, a step taken by the French political scientist Isabelle Sommier. She does indeed believe that terrorism (which she prefers to call 'total violence') is actually an imitation and a reinvention of methods used to destroy civilian populations that states initiated on a much larger scale. This is why I believe a reflection on terrorism ultimately has its place in a book dealing with genocide and other forms of mass murder. Certainly, the small-scale massacres perpetrated by terrorists cannot really be compared to the large-scale massacres qualifiable as genocide. The fact nevertheless remains that there are historical and political ties between them. What we call 'terrorism' today could finally be, on a small scale, the 'hideous double' of the policy of terrorist states, a typical product of our modernity.[102]

To define terrorism by the very nature of the acts perpetrated, I could start with the word's etymology, as Christian Mellon suggests: 'Any act of violence whose primary aim is to instil intense fear in order to reap the political benefits of this fear, is terrorist. In this regard, the most standard form of terrorism is what is called the "indiscriminate" attack, one that randomly strikes a population without targeting anyone in particular. For if violence strikes at random, then everyone feels threatened. The expression "blind terrorism" is basically pleonastic.'[103] For this reason I know no better definition of terrorism than this: a terrorist act is one that aims to kill anyone, anywhere, at any time. This definition incidentally helps to distinguish terrorism from tyrannicide, which by definition has a precise political target. In this regard it is wrong to consider the *Sect of Assassins* as being part of the first terrorists in History, because it attacked representatives of authority and not what we call today civilian populations. In effect that group never indulged in blind massacres and never targeted foreigners. Their attacks had specific targets: politicians, soldiers, and high-ranking religious figures in the Sunni hierarchy.

In fact a terrorist act fits into the category of so-called 'indirect' strategies, whereas a 'direct' strategy takes on opposing combatant forces. 'Terrorist violence is "indirect" in that it does not seek to achieve its objectives by eliminating a given category of persons, but by influencing the adversary's political will: the terrorist combatant supposes—often wrongly, but that is another question—that the population, terrorised by its attacks, will put political pressure on its leaders to make them yield to its demands in exchange for a halt to the terror.'[104] To give this dynamic of indirect confrontation optimum political power, the terrorist act relies on a strategy of public communication in order to maximise its impact. It is indeed hard to imagine a terrorist act without spectators. It is thus legitimate to speak of a 'terrorist relationship' induced by the necessity of having a third party to terrorise.[105] This prompted Brian Jenkins, in the 1970s, to speak of terrorism as a form of theatre in the emotional relationship that is created between the terrorist and his 'audiences': 'Terrorists want a lot of people watching, not a lot of people dead.'[106]

Thus the media's role as a sounding board is essential to the effectiveness of terrorist action, the very aim of which is to provoke, through a 'little massacre' and by surprise, a huge wave of public emotion that brings the political process under way to a screeching halt. In 1994 Hamas launched suicide attacks as a last resort to sabotage the painstaking Israeli-Palestinian peace process. The enormous media impact these attacks had in Israel immediately lent credit to all those who believed that it was impossible to trust the Palestinians. Thus by organising their action in such a way as to have maximum emotional effect, the terrorists exploited the media in advance, first of all those that could provide live coverage: the television stations. For television, in its quest for larger audiences, is eager for exceptional events with which the public can identify and commune in a shared emotion, be it compassion or fear.

The spectacle of suffering and death is one of the situations particularly suited to televised media. And so for entirely different reasons terrorism and the media stretch a hand out to one another, thereby entertaining an extremely ambiguous relationship. What could be more extraordinary than the theatricalisation of one's cause by the spectacle of death via a live broadcast? A spectacle that, moreover, can have *suspense*, and thus keep the public on tenterhooks, for instance when hostages' lives are at stake. The media, while condemning a terrorist attack that has just occurred, is visibly fascinated by it. And the constant repetition of scenes played in a loop on a screen in one's living room is the best way to increase the audience's emotion.

The 11 September 2001 paradigm. The prototypical example of this quasi co-dependent relation between a terrorist attack and the televised media is that of the 11 September 2001 suicide attacks in the United States. The destruction of the Twin Towers of the World Trade Center in Manhattan, hit successively by two airplanes, is indeed a textbook example without parallel, bringing together in a very short sequence the violence of the impact, the virtually cinematic aesthetic effect of the collapse of the towers, the whole scene signifying absolute tragedy because the television viewer knows that thousands of people are trapped inside the towers. This case embodies the very quintessence of a terrorist strategy from the standpoint of its media impact: that unique moment when the occurrence of mass murder *merges* with the instantaneity of an international broadcast. This particular terrorist act is an extraordinary product of the globalisation of communication.

It has perhaps not been remarked on sufficiently that the media 'originality' of this event has to do most of all with the impact of the second plane. In effect televised images of the first plane's impact remain in the spirit of 'media coverage after the event'. We are at this point still in a familiar scenario where a terrorist bomb has just exploded in a public place, and a few moments later a television crew arrives on the scene to film the damage. But with the impact of the second plane, the media novelty is total because television viewers saw and heard it hit its target in real time. In other words they attended a live performance of a massacre. Never to my knowledge has a mass murder been thus 'captured' on camera in this way and the footage immediately broadcast throughout the world. Some have written of Rwanda that it was the first media-covered genocide. Nothing, however, supports this statement. Although some rare footage of the killing was shown, it was after the genocide. As for the video images of the bombs dropped by American pilots on Iraq in 1991 during the first Gulf war, they showed nothing of their final impact, in other words of the destruction wrought on the ground. Their trails of light across the screen had more of an aesthetic than an agonising effect.

Did those who organised 11 September then consciously plan that the arrival of the second plane would be filmed, the television crews being already on the scene because of the first impact? Or was this just a matter of chance, a mere combination of circumstances? We will probably never know. In any event the effect was totally staggering and the constant replaying of the same footage helped intensify the traumatic power of these images.

The immaterial broadcast of these images in fact produced a veritable *emotional earthquake* throughout the western world,[107] whose epicentre was obviously at the place of impact: in the United States. It is moreover revealing that the Americans have called the place where the disaster occurred 'Ground Zero', the name that the physicist J. Robert Oppenheimer gave to the place where the first atom bomb was tested in a New Mexico desert three weeks before the United States dropped it on Hiroshima. In other words, in the American subconscious this expression refers to total catastrophe, the apocalyptic destruction of innocent victims. The use of 'Ground Zero' could also signify a return of repressed memory, something like a guilty conscience: America has become the victim of the same thing that it did to others (the Japanese). Establishing such a parallel certainly makes no sense from a strategic standpoint: 9 August 1945 and 11 September 2001 cannot be compared. But from the standpoint of collective representations, the expression 'Ground Zero', attached to the very place where the Twin Towers collapsed, says a lot about the depth of the trauma felt throughout the entire American nation.

No press release came in from the perpetrators of the suicide attacks claiming responsibility for them, so what exactly did they want? Some observers have emphasised the turnaround in meaning that these attacks represent, since they were perpetrated outside of any national and social context. They certainly have nothing to do with the political demands of Basque or Irish terrorism, or revolutionary terrorism of the sort formerly practised by the Red Army Faction in West Germany and the Red Brigades in Italy. This was a case of transnational, seemingly decontextualised terrorism with vague political demands. Other analysts however pointed out that the 11 September attacks did indeed have political significance that was closely related to the spread of religious terrorism in the Middle East that had developed since the Islamic revolution in 1979 in Iran. I am hardly qualified to settle such a debate, but my research into massacres leads me to accord considerable importance to the public discourse of those identifying with such actions, or even claiming responsibility for them. In this connection the statements made by the Saudi Osama Bin Laden provide a 'framework of meaning' for these suicide operations that must be deciphered at all costs, all the more so since he had already openly called for attacks to be committed against Americans (and Westerners in general) and had even claimed responsibility for some of them in the recent past.[108] Consequently, the content of his videotaped message broadcast on 7 October by the Qatari television station Al-Jazeera is particularly interesting since it was his first 'public appearance' since the attacks on New York and Washington.

'Prophet' Bin Laden's televised address (7 October 2001)

Appearing on screen in combat fatigues, Bin Laden, with his very first sentence, associates God and death: '*Here is America struck by God Almighty.*' Why was America attacked by the hand of God in this way? Let us first make note of the fact that some of his arguments are pertinent to a degree, for example when he points to the West's responsibility in a number of situations of violence. He observes, for instance, that the West pays little heed to suffering and death in the countries of the southern hemisphere, twice using Iraqi children as an example (which of course is no accident). He also recalls that the United States itself has used war tactics without making a distinction between combatants and non-combatants, citing the example of the nuclear bombing of Hiroshima (which is not an innocent choice either). Bin Laden tries here to appeal to America's guilty conscience with respect to the United States' historical responsibility in the atom bomb attack on the Japanese cities. More generally, he seeks the sympathy of those who might think, even in the western world, that the Americans only got what they deserved, that they asked for it, etc. As if there was cause for rejoicing in seeing the strongest country in the world a victim, for a change, of such a massacre. Bin Laden declared in this vein: '*What America is tasting now is only a copy of what we have tasted.*' Here we recognise the standard discourse of a murderer who draws on real or imagined atrocities committed by the other camp to justify his own.

Bin Laden's speech then goes off on a truly delirious tangent, borrowing from the repertoire of religious terrorism. Over twenty years earlier, Ayatollah Khomeini had already amply exploited the theme of 'diabolical America' to mobilise the masses in support of his cause during the Iranian revolution. Bin Laden's speech aims to be international, if not global, in scope. So the primary source of evil, he asserts, is '*the modern world's symbol of paganism*', America and its allies.

This target of 'America' is presented as a polymorphous monster. It has many faces, each in turn denounced as the primary enemy: the great infidel Bush, the United States military, America the country or more generally the Americans, to such an extent that it is hard to tell if Bin Laden is targeting the military and political leadership, the American territory *per se* or even its entire population; probably all of these at once. Such a speech against a global and indistinct target is extremely alarming: carrying a total threat against those it designates, one can be sure it announces or accompanies a massacre.

Opposite the figure of Evil America is that of God-Muhammad. This is the thread of his speech from the very first sentence. The mention of the hand of God returns as a leitmotiv in nearly every sentence. In a televised address that hardly lasted 4 minutes, he pronounced the word 'God' (or 'Muhammad') 12 times and the word 'America' or 'Americans' 9 times, as if the two were engaged in a merciless battle: '*Since America is Evil, since America desecrated the holy lands of Islam, God has punished it. And the Muslims that died in that event on 11 September were the instruments of divine will.*'

Then comes the supreme condemnation: the Americans are accused of desecrating Islamic holy lands by their presence in Saudi Arabia. The consequence is all too clear: the '*infidels*' must be run out to restore its purity. This imperious necessity to fight the apostates is thus transmuted, given its religious essence, into an act of redemptive purification.

Videotaped message broadcast by the Qatar television station *Al-Jazeera*, translated in the *New York Times*, Monday, 8 October 2001, p. B7.

During this period in which the United States was already beginning to prepare its 'retaliation' (military intervention in Afghanistan), Bin Laden was seeking both to scare the West (primarily the Americans) as well as to galvanise the Arab Muslim masses. He remains consistent with his earlier statements in which he had called for a holy war (*jihad*), an appeal he reiterated two weeks after the attacks.[109] His statements in February 1998 on establishing the World Islamic Front for Jihad against the Jews and Crusaders particularly reveal his intent and that of his new organisation: 'The ruling to kill the Americans and their allies—civilians and military—is an individual duty for every Muslim who can do it in any country in which it is possible to do it, in order to liberate the al-Aqsa Mosque and the holy mosque (in Mecca) from their grip. ... We—with Allah's help—call on every Muslim who believes in Allah and wishes to be rewarded to comply with Allah's order to kill the Americans and plunder their money wherever and whenever they find it. We also call on Muslim ulema, leaders, youths, and soldiers to launch the raid on Satan's U.S. troops and the devil's supporters allying with them.'[110]

In his 7 October 2001 message he again dons the face of the 'Prophet', but in battle fatigues. He claims that the 11 September attacks are proof of God's vengeance against 'the Great Satan, America'. He more generally describes the stakes in the fight to the death in Allah's name, against all the infidels who have desecrated the sacred land of Islam. It is thus not difficult to identify in his statements the theme of destructive purification: once again, purify and destroy go hand and hand. There is nothing peculiar to Islam in this: We have seen enough throughout this book of the extent to which the *imaginaire* of purity could serve as a springboard for massacre, in a variety of cultural and religious contexts. But the 'malady of Islam', according to Abdelwahab Meddeb, is precisely to wish for 'a return to the purity of the letter'.[111] What makes Bin Laden's apocalyptic discourse 'modern' is the use of the rhetoric of eradication to terrorist ends, a rhetoric that governments have freely used in the past.

Moreover, this intimate association between God and death surely warrants closer examination. It is certainly part and parcel of the rhetoric of religious terrorism, which is not really anything new.[112] But should we not also investigate its purely nihilistic signification? For there was also a desire for purification in the Russian nihilism at the end of the nineteenth century in reaction against the 'rotten west'. And Nietzsche's warning inescapably comes to mind: 'What I relate is the history of the next two centuries. I describe what is coming, what can no longer come differently: the advent of nihilism.'[113]

Let us recall that madman who, in his *Merry Knowledge*, calls to the passers-by, a lantern in hand, shouting: 'I'm looking for God!' and who, offended by the jeering of his audience, hurled the following accusation at them: 'We are all assassins of God.' He was a nihilist hero.[114] He proclaimed the 'death of God', meaning that the belief in the Christian God had become discredited. A few decades later Nietzsche already appeared to have been proved right. With the rise to power of Nazism, the revolution of nihilism was under way, Herman Rauschning wrote. It was a nihilism whose trilogy was based on the death of liberty, the domination of violence and the enslavement of the mind.[115] With religious terrorism, which some qualify as a new totalitarianism, does not Nietzsche's prophecy continue to be indicated? In this decadent West that no longer has faith in any divine transcendence, there are those who willingly affirm, in the name of Islam, that God has almighty power over their lives, to such an extent that they are prepared to die for Him. They proclaim loud and clear a God-unto-the-death that orders them to annihilate all the infidels who have betrayed and even destroyed him. What have those 'unbelievers' made holy in his place? Money, business and sex. There too the World Trade Centre was not a random target. And so that abhorrent form of insurrection of the sacred through death has come about to destroy one of the arrogant symbols of the rottenness of the infidels, to avenge God and restore His purity. One may as well admit that from a western viewpoint, the chances for communication and 'dialogue' with those who advocate this new holy war are virtually nil. According to Brian Jenkins, all that matters to jihadists is to claim as many victims as possible among 'unbelievers' in their actions. After 11 September, he revised his initial approach to terrorism 30 years previously, now offering an apocalyptic vision: 'Terrorists want a lot of people watching *and* a lot of people dead.'[116]

'Ordinary' candidates for sacrifice? Meanwhile, the West is afraid, or lives in denial of this fear. For in the year of this writing, 2006, the United States is still living in a sort of morbid fear of an attack, and this fear is exploited to some extent by its own leaders. As for Europe, it seems to be yielding to a certain lethargy, giving the impression of not having taken seriously the attack on the Atocha train station in Madrid on 11 March 2004—the 'mini 11 September'. If only Raymond Aron could still be right when in 1962 he wrote that an action is called terrorist when its psychological repercussions are disproportionate to its purely physical results.[117] Playing the media chord, terrorism has in fact always been fairly economical in terms of human lives. It has been estimated, for instance, that terrorism claimed 3,000 lives between 1968 and 1984, or an average of fewer than 200 deaths per year.[118]

But suddenly with the 11 September attacks (which also included the attack on the Pentagon in Washington), there was a drastic change in scale, for the number of victims was 3,000 dead or disappeared.[119] This figure is still far from those reached with the carnage of the great mass killings in southern hemisphere countries, with several thousand dead in a few months (such as Indonesia in 1965–6 and in Rwanda in 1994). But Westerners tend to remain indifferent to these large massacres that do not affect them directly. On 11 September 2001, on the other hand, the very heart of the western world was hit and the feeling of horror was all the more intense.

The shock of 11 September thus crystallised the fear of a terrorism of mass destruction, the development of which many experts had dreaded for years. According to the French military expert Gérard Chaliand, this inventive and daring operation nevertheless remains an example of 'classic terrorism', the worst aspect being that its authors had no arms other than pocket knives.[120] However, the scenarios of apocalyptic terrorism were described in the press on the basis of the assumption that atomic, bacteriological and chemical weapons of mass destruction had fallen into the hands of private groups. These technologies of destruction are theoretically under the absolute control of a handful of states, but for how much longer? The most pessimistic predictions seem all the more credible when one remembers the precedent set by the Japanese sect Aum Shinrikyô when it attacked the Tokyo subway system with sarin gas on 20 March 1995.[121]

Even before such possible technological advances are made, the most worrisome fact must be the psychological evolution represented by the development of what François Geré calls the 'volunteers for death', referring to those who agree to die along with their targets. In the history of massacres their voluntary sacrifice is a novelty.[122] The Nazis certainly did not plan to die along with the Jews any more than the Hutus did with the Tutsis. Their aim was indeed to build a safe and pure world that they would control. To sacrifice one's life by killing oneself at the same time as one's mortal enemy is assuredly an absolute defiance of any power. For if an authority does not receive voluntary consent to obey it, it can only exercise power through fear and, finally, through the threat of death it wields over everyone. Consequently one who is not afraid to sacrifice his life cancels out by definition the powerful effect of this authority.

The French sociologist of Iranian origin, Farhad Khosrokhavar, has demonstrated in a remarkable way how such martyr profiles appeared on the one hand in the context of the Israel-Palestinian conflict and on the other within western societies themselves. These two ways of dying voluntarily in suicide attacks in the name of God actually have little inter-relationship. The first way of killing oneself by fighting for a group cause is that practised by the Palestinians: it is clearly directed against the enemy Israel, which is perceived as an occupying force. 'In Palestine martyrdom is achieved through the sanctification of despair that is overcome by acting in the name of a religious ideal entirely reconstructed around a sense of apocalypse.' The second way of killing oneself voluntarily for a cause characterised the 11 September hijackers, representing an infinitesimal minority of Muslims who, though well integrated into western countries, ended up harbouring a savage hatred of the West, starting with the United States, which they accused of dominating and violating the land and values of Islam. For them the West, demonised, seductive and corrupting all at once, destroys the very bases of Islam, each western individual contributing to this undermining endeavour. This is why the total and absolute war against westerners, without distinction in terms of individual guilt or innocence, becomes a 'religious duty'. Consequently, terrorist networks can recruit their operatives in the very midst of hypermodern societies.[123]

The American psychiatrist and political scientist Marc Sageman has devoted an interesting study to such networks, which in many ways echoes what has been said here about the perpetrators of massacres (even if their profiles differ). On the basis of a sample of 172 militants who had joined the *Salafist jihad*, he shows that their individual biographies alone are not able to explain why they turn to terrorist action. Neither psychopaths nor sociopaths, they are 'ordinary' individuals who are often university graduates from a middle-class background. They have virtually no history of violence: it is thus impossible to deduce from their biographies that they will become terrorist combatants.

However, cut off from their home country, they experience in western society a sort of desocialisation on the basis of which a resocialisation develops along the lines of religious rhetoric, which leads them to identify with the *jihad*. But, as Marc Sageman points out, this ideological convergence is still not what makes them turn to violence. He concurs with the observation also emphasised in these pages: It is the *formation of a group* that turns out to be the preliminary operator to a slide into terrorist action. It is revealing to examine the history of those who prepared the 11 September attacks. Originally they were people who moved in the same circle of friends living in Hamburg, Germany, who, once their group was constituted, intended to work for the cause of the *jihad* and one day allowed themselves to be recruited to this end. It is this phenomenon of aggregation of isolated individuals that prevails. In time this group of friends will gradually become an operational cell and work its way into militant fundamentalist networks.[124] To what extent can this distressing pattern reproduce itself today?

Finally, the great victory of 11 September is fear; a fear that has spread throughout the West, a vague fear that crystallises henceforth around the frightening figure of the 'terrorist', an enemy both internal and external, whose presence is difficult to detect in our own societies. The 'terrorist' indeed embodies the modern representation of the 'suspect' in our midst who is working towards our downfall. Do we not refer now to a 'dormant enemy', one who is by definition unassailable? The murder of the Brazilian youth Jean Charles Menezes by the London police on 22 July 2005, although he had nothing to do with the 7 July bombings that left at least 55 dead and over 700 wounded, could well be the symptom of a disturbing evolution: that of a democratic state which, declaring itself above the law in the name of the fight against terrorism, grants itself the right to kill whomever it wishes to triumph over "Evil".

As the time to conclude our study approaches, we again find these inextricable relationships between real and imaginary that were central to the first chapter in this book. Let us then have the clarity of mind to apply this analysis to ourselves in the historical moment at which we are living. Certainly there are objective reasons to be worried about the possibility of new terrorist attacks. And yet are we westerners not in the process of becoming excessively paranoid? For it is very difficult to distinguish between the real risk of further terrorist acts and what remains pure fantasy, associated with the morbid fear of a terrorism of mass destruction that many anti-terrorist security agents amplify to their advantage. Heads of government themselves have an interest in playing on the risk of terrorism to present themselves as the guarantors of everyone's security. To defy this daunting future, the historian's eye is probably what helps us the most to take a step back from the convulsions that currently besiege us. I have particularly in mind the great work by the French historian Jean Delumeau, published in 1978, of which the title was precisely *La peur en Occident*... Except that his study was on the evolution of Europe between the fourteenth and eighteenth centuries. And the French subtitle of the book was 'a society under siege'.[125] And what do we find in the table of contents? The fear of Jews of course, the fear of women naturally, but also 'the Muslim threat'! Therein, we can be sure, lies food for thought on the 'novelty' of our own fears in this nascent twenty-first century.

CONCLUSION

THE 'NEVER AGAIN' REFRAIN

I wrote this book to try and understand the genocidal process. However, the reader would be well justified in asking the use of this research in preventing such hideous events from recurring. This concern is without doubt fully justified morally when we consider the violence on a massive scale to which ordinary civilians are subjected. After the Second World War everybody said 'Never again!' From then on we were all going to 'draw lessons from catastrophe', 'combat racism in all its forms', 'teach tolerance', etc. What remains today of these pious intentions? A scene of desolation in every corner of the world—Cambodia, Indonesia, Chechnya, Biafra, Guatemala, Iraq, Rwanda, Darfur to mention only a few. Here and now at the beginning of the twenty-first century the cry of 'Never again!' has become almost unbearable to hear. Rather than merely talking about it, surely it would be better to face up to the realities of the situation, however outrageous, and seek to understand the reasons for this tragic reiteration that is repeated mass murder.

If we dare to admit it, the truth is that those researching the genocidal phenomenon often experience a kind of psychological dissociation vis-à-vis their object. On the one hand they share the moral indignation of all those denouncing the hypocrisy of the so-called 'international community' that, even in the wake of Rwanda, allows yet more massacres to take place, whether in Darfur, the Congo or Chechnya. But on the other hand the knowledge they have acquired gives them a better grasp of the reasons for this passivity, encountered often enough to leave them ultimately feeling sceptical about how feasible it would be to implement an effective policy for the prevention of mass murder worldwide. Clearly this is an uncomfortable position, to say the least: to find oneself constantly torn between the demands of a universal morality and the realities of international relations. But are there not other positions, short of succumbing to the most foolish form of naivety, or the darkest cynicism? To accept living with this contradiction, we have to develop a kind of para-doxical thinking; one that reasons from the vantage point of antago-nistic propositions. A statement made by F. Scott Fitzgerald seems to me especially well suited to our purpose: 'the test of a first-rate intel-ligence is the ability to hold two opposed ideas in mind at the same time, and still retain the ability to function. One should, for example, be able to see that things are hopeless and yet be determined to make them otherwise.'[1]

Crisis prevention: arguments and illusions

So let us turn to hope, and hence to those channelling their endeavours toward prevention. Here we can observe some very encouraging developments. Of the sum total of the dramas this planet has known, there are indeed one or two that have produced a kind of electric shock crystallising an emergent global conscience. Despite the prevailing apathy, and a more or less contemplative 'remote suffering',[2] individuals can in fact be transformed into ver-itable social actors, and become collective entrepreneurs of a common task aiming to limit, stifle and subdue the causes or effects of mass violence. It is useful to recall that it was the butchery at the battle of Solferino in 1859 that convinced the Swiss-born Henri Dunant to set up an organisation specially devoted to war victims, today called the Red Cross.

Similarly, in the wake of the 1967–70 Biafra war, new non-gov-ernmental organisations such as *Médecins Sans Frontières* were formed, setting out to aid victims while also putting pressure on the Interna-tional Community via the media: Bernard Kouchner referred to this as the 'law of hype'.[3] Some thirty years later, after Bosnia and Rwanda, new organisations were still appearing such as the Interna-tional Crisis Group, this time with a very different objective: to provide analyses of conflicts taking place with the aim of raising consciousness among decision-makers well-placed to have a bearing on the way they develop. The role of this new NGO clearly illus-trates the realisation at the end of the 1990s that the aim should be not to intervene only *after* the crisis, but rather *before* it happens, to prevent it from degenerating into a catastrophe. In this regard, some scholars and activists believe that educating people against the repetition of genocide is possible, and have attempted to undertake such action for Darfur.[4]

The question of *prevention* has thus become a major topic for discussion in international relations. An appropriate, if somewhat muddled vocabulary has developed: 'early warning signals' are discussed, as well as 'structural prevention' and 'preventive diplomacy',[5] and so on. But what are we really talking about? Conflict prevention or crisis prevention? If it is a question of conflicts, then we are really going down the road of formulating a superbly pious wish: because conflict is obviously inherent in the history of man, and so any intention to prevent it is doomed to fail from the start—and to inspire many a spell-binding discourse. The expression 'crisis prevention' seems more judicious if by this we mean that the aim is to control the evolution of a conflict that may potentially lead to a serious regional or international crisis. But how can we differentiate between that which pertains to crisis prevention and what which falls within the auspices of international conflict management? Some countries, such as Canada and Sweden, have tried to make headway in the thinking on these issues.

In 2001 a report submitted by the UN Secretary General made some contribution to this advance.[6] Then in addition, having first admitted the serious failures of the United Nations in the Rwandan crisis, Kofi Annan announced in 2004 the creation of a new post of special reporter for the prevention of genocide, directly attached to the Security Council. A report published in 2004 by the 'high-level panel' asked that, in the framework of a major overhaul of the UN, the permanent members of the Security Council would pledge themselves, 'in their individual capacities, … to refrain from the use of the veto in cases of genocide and large-scale human rights abuses'.[7]

The concern with preventing genocide was already a driving force behind a campaign led by Raphael Lemkin, and the 1948 Convention inspired in part by him sets out to work to this end as the title of the Convention describes.[8] And most researchers working in the field of comparative studies on genocide are also working with a view to its prevention. They look to the social sciences to shed light on any identifiable common causes of massacre in the hope that acting on these causes might prevent them from being repeated. Doesn't this book show, moreover, that hardly anything is ever left to chance in the matter? But in the end these processes of extreme violence nevertheless remain, and fortunately so, uncertain. This is fortunate because they will always be subject to the will of actors set on a course of engaging in action, but they will also depend on circumstances favourable to precipitating their development. It must therefore be possible to halt their monstrous evolution, or at least to restrain it. Research has been carried out in this area to try and identify 'early warning signals' that could sound an alarm when the situation in a particular country approaches the danger point. We have looked at some of the most important among them in the preceding pages: increasing incidence of inflammatory discourse emanating from intellectuals, rise of the 'hate media', increased marginalisation of a particular group, public denunciation of a double-sided enemy: *the enemy without and the enemy within*, etc. The sociologists Ted Gurr and Barbara Harff have attempted to provide structural models of conflicts likely to lead to increasingly wide-scale forms of violence aimed at minority groups,[9] an approach shared by sociologist Helen Fein.[10]

In real terms, measures of prevention envisaged will consist of, for example, supporting 'antidote intellectuals' who have the courage to take a stand against those pouring oil on to the fire, to favour the development of media channels oriented towards cooperation rather than confrontation between groups,[11] or striving to inform victims of the fate awaiting them if they remain passive.[12] More generally, one can qualify as being 'preventive' any political, social or cultural action aiming to establish or reinforce links with individuals of a group that is marginalised or at risk of being marginalised.[13] Inventorying ways to mitigate conflicts between communities, Daniel Chirot and Clark McCauley have proposed one of the most interesting studies on prevention of mass murders. Researching conflict resolution processes within pre-state societies as well as in modern nation-states, they argue that if human beings know perfectly well how to kill each other, they have also invented different means to prevent mass violence. Consequenly, Chirot and McCauley suggest a 'package of policy oriented solutions' to promote telerance, from large-scale institutional reforms to local programs, including the development of civil society institutions, particularly ones that bring members of different ethnic and religious groups together.[14] One such preventive measure involves alerting the outside world to the risk of possible tragedy, putting pressure on international community policymakers to intervene. Indeed, if warning signals are generally well known (due to the circulation of reliable information issued by NGOs, journalists or researchers on the ground indicating a serious worsening of the situation of a particular group) what is nearly always lacking is the political will to intervene to bring this situation to a halt.

To stimulate this political will, partisans of preventive intervention set forth at least four types of argument. First, an urgent reaction is legitimised in the name of international law itself: the judicialisation and therefore the criminalisation of acts observed in a given country construct a legal framework by means of which preventive measures (or even measures of intervention) are judged to be legitimate in the eyes of international law.[15] Whence the specific role of NGOs such as Amnesty International or Human Rights Watch in encoding information collected in the legal vocabulary of the violation of human rights.

Another argument presented by advocates of prevention is pragmatism. They maintain that it is wiser to intervene immediately in a crisis, even if this is only to avoid movements of vast numbers of refugees likely to threaten stability in neighbouring areas and so effectively spread the conflict. Moreover, such action would cost less than having to manage tens or hundreds of thousands of refugees (housing, food, epidemic control etc).[16] With figures to support their claims, a report produced by the Carnegie Commission similarly asserts that prevention is far less costly than belated intervention. According to this report, the international community spent US $200 billion during the 1990s on managing conflicts in the framework of seven major interventions (Bosnia-Herzegovina, Somalia, Rwanda, Haiti, the Persian Gulf, Cambodia and El Salvador), but could have saved $130 billion if it had opted for a more effective, preventive approach.[17]

Other authors claim an early intervention can be effective in so far as massacres are generally perpetrated by a minority of individuals, and so technically it should be more than possible to prevent aggressive action from taking place.[18] Examples of preventive missions that are apparently encouraging are cited, like the measures taken by the European Union and NATO to bring the civil war unfolding in Macedonia in 2001–2 to a halt. Similarly, during the summer of 2003 the European Union, at the instigation of France, deployed a military force in Ituri in the North East of the democratic Republic of the Congo (RDC) in order, it claims, to prevent a possible genocide.

But have the expected results been obtained? Such actions are also perceived by some to be, like post-colonialist programmes conducted notably in Africa, initiatives that only solve the problems in a very superficial manner, or even contribute to making them worse. These commentators point out that such interventions are rarely inspired by humanitarian concerns, and more often than not stem from calculated self-interest, even on the part of those who actually participate. Rather than resorting too hastily to 'technical fixes', to use Marc Levene's expression, which range, according to him, from the search for early warning signals to military intervention, and include the creation of the International Criminal Court as well as mediation, he advocates adopting a more solidly based approach to prevention that is structural by nature.[19] No longer should the international community play a kind of fire brigade role, putting out fires that have already been started (i.e. military intervention), but we should be working more towards strategic design of our 'houses' so that they have built-in firewalls. In any case, today's international system does not even permit the fire brigade to intervene in countries allied to the West (like Turkey) or in permanent member states of the UN Security Council (like Russia or China). Only a policy of prevention, then, tackling structural causes of conflicts at their roots can have some chance of success in putting the brakes on genocide. Marc Levene writes: 'To paraphrase [Auguste] Comte': if one cannot understand causation, one cannot anticipate; if one cannot anticipate, one cannot prevent.'[20]

But how in practice can we implement this vision of structural prevention? Marc Levene offers no solution except that of striving for a more equitable world, a world that is fairer in economic terms, based on sustainable development, etc. Such general objectives can only elicit the support of the majority—all those living in poverty and insecurity, to begin with—but these aims draw on a vision of political and structural change that is so global and radical that one could justifiably remain sceptical as to the feasibility of achieving them. The author even betrays his own underlying doubt when he predicts that in the absence of such transformations, entire zones of the globe are at risk of being subjected imminently to ecological devastation, famine, illness, genocide and other forms of extreme mass violence.

Let us now look at the problem from the point of view of those critical of prevention. The desire to act on causes of conflict with a view to curbing their murderous dynamic seems to engender scepticism, whatever approach is suggested. While partisans of prevention clearly feel themselves to be on the moral high ground, they run into criticism from some who question the very basis for their initiative. Michael Freeman sharply criticises the dominant positivist approach in this field of study. This research, he explains, makes an assumption: that knowing the causes of genocide would necessarily lead to our being able to anticipate them, and so to being able to implement appropriate measures to halt their progress. Consciously or not, researchers believing in prevention effectively put themselves in the school of Comte. One could even go on to say that the approach they adopt is a medical one: perceiving genocide as a hideous illness, like a cancer eating away at the social body, they advocate as the only effective therapy preventing its progress as soon as the first symptoms appear. Thus David A. Hamburg and Alexander George suggest a public health model of prevention that considers major risk factors for the entire population and ways to absorb their impetus before serious damage is done.[21]

However, such an analogy is simply erroneous; the social sciences do not share the same experimental validation models as medical science. Identifying the 'causes' of a historical event still remains problematic in history, and subject to lively controversy. As Hannah Arendt suggested: 'The event illuminates its own past, but can never be deduced from it.'[22] The social sciences can therefore have only a weak predictive capacity: how can we hope to apply 'lessons' of history to new crises that come about at a necessarily different moment in time, and the progression of which remains unpredictable? The non-reproducibility of historical events casts doubt on any attempt to apply known remedies, because the diagnostic cannot be identical. To go further, it would be to give in to the 'experimental illusion' in sociology, against which the French sociologist Jean-Claude Passeron has put us on our guard.[23]

It is, of course, vitally important that researchers work to identify early indicators of possible genocide. This research, says Michael Freeman, represents a kind of debt we owe to survivors of all mass murders. But he warns us not to be misled over the results this research might possibly yield: 'Probability not necessity is the category which should guide our attempts to understand genocide.'[24] This critique is taken up by Thomas Cushman, who denounces the ideology of 'preventionism'. He claims that all those working on genocide fall prey to this illusion to some degree, in that the essential aim of their work is to try and prevent it from happening.[25] Cushman knows of no researchers whatever working on this object having as their sole objective the progress of scientific knowledge.

The consequence of this unpredictability? We may suspect that prescribed initiatives, whether modest or ambitious, may not bring about the effects anticipated. Intellectuals seeking to exert an antidotal influence on a discourse of hatred may of course be acting in good faith, but it can also happen, against their wishes, or through clumsiness, that their words ultimately add fuel to the fire rather than appeasing high levels of tension. In the same way the effectiveness of economic sanctions against regimes accused of serious violations of human rights is also hotly debated, because of the harmful effects these can have on the local populations in the countries concerned—the sanctions against Iraq under Saddam Hussein are an often cited example. Still more concretely, NGOs or other countries intervening in crises with the laudable intention of restraining or halting massacres cannot control the effects of their interventions: because they are not the party best placed to intervene, or because their knowledge of the realities of the country is limited, their actions may not have the desired impact, or could even provoke the opposite effect to the one intended. The case of the American intervention in Somalia in 1992 is a well-known example of this, as is the US-led intervention in Iraq to bring down the regime of Saddam Hussein.

An ethics of responsibility

But should airing these criticisms prevent us from trying to do something, with actors crippling themselves by the very thought of the negative effects, contrary to the original objectives, that could potentially result? True, situations of mass violence are often of paralysing complexity, and it is vital to exercise caution and clear-sightedness. But it is too easy for scholars to criticise, in the very name of the complexity that it is their job to decipher, those who try to 'do something'. From the point of view of all who have died in massacres, and of those who still risk the same fate, this position is not morally tenable. Moreover, it would disqualify the very basis for any political or social action, whatever the objective in view, to argue that because we can never be sure of the outcome it is futile to intervene. Any political action in the name of change would, by definition, be in vain. We would effectively be advocating a contemplative immobilism regarding world misfortunes. To surmount these contradictions, I will conclude this book by proposing two platforms for action that are sufficiently pertinent and future-oriented, one in the domain of international action and the other in that of the social sciences *per se*.

As for international crisis management in situations where massacre is a potential risk, the report written by Gareth Evans and Mohamed Sahnoun aiming to establish a new consensus among international experts seems to me a good starting point in this first decade of the twenty-first century.[26] The authors insist that the principal motivation guiding their research was to do something practical to prevent another Rwanda from happening. Rather than emphasising the 'right to intervene' (that risks ruffling the feathers of nations sensitive about defending their sovereignty), Gareth Evans and Mohamed Sahnoun prefer to speak of the *responsibility to protect* which is incumbent on these states. But, they insist, if states are incapable of protecting their citizens from catastrophe (such as murders on a grand scale, rape, famine, etc.), or unwilling to do so, then such a responsibility must be assumed by the 'community of states' (principally in the framework of the UN or regional organisations). And claiming such a responsibility involves three specific obligations:

(1) the responsibility to prevent: eliminate both the underlying and direct causes of internal conflicts and other crises that are man-made, and which put populations in danger;
(2) the responsibility to react: to react in the face of situations where protection of human beings is an imperious necessity by resort-

ing to appropriate measures, including coercive ones (sanctions, international criminal proceedings and, in extreme cases, military intervention);

(3) the responsibility to rebuild: to provide, above all following military intervention, assistance at every level to facilitate the resumption of activity—reconstruction and reconciliation by addressing the causes of the abuses intervention was called upon to halt, or that it had tried to prevent.

For each of these themes, the authors put forward often worthwhile, constructive solutions. As for prevention, they distinguish clearly between measures that must be applied to underlying causes (involving programmes of economic and financial aid) and those that relate to immediate causes (calling for rapid reaction on the part of international organisations, including military intervention).[27]

It is true their work is not totally immune from criticism. To the responsibility to prevent, the authors are right to add those to react and rebuild. This forms a perfectly coherent whole. But to achieve this remains extraordinarily difficult in view of the instability and poverty of some regions. On numerous points one wonders how what they recommend could be achieved in realistic terms. For example: sustainable prevention can only come about where a region, in the wake of conflict, can experience appreciable economic development. But, when more than 60 per cent of the population are unemployed—as they were in Kosovo, five years after NATO's intervention—how can we not fear that serious tensions will break out again because of absence of hope for the future? To sum up, the Evans-Sahnoun report articulates general principles that are certainly useful for formulating an international doctrine on the subject, but it does not dwell sufficiently on the problem of how they should be implemented in practice, a difficulty that is nonetheless always highlighted in research surveys conducted on the ground.[28]

Moreover, the authors do not emphasise sufficiently the importance of the work on remembrance and memory issues without which a nation may be at risk of plunging once more into repeated episodes of mass killings. Throughout this book we have seen just how much the past can be instrumentalised by political actors, traumatic events being hyped up and invested with new value by some, who present a one-sided reading, while others simply seek to hide them. School textbooks are often repositories of these biased readings of the past, to such an extent that books destined to be read by a nation's youth will often reinstil the ideological seeds of tomorrow's conflicts. Therefore the prevention of mass-scale violence must include work on memories of the past, memories that could just as well serve to stir up passions as to contain them in working for reconciliation.[29]

As regards prevention of extreme crises, there exists no single recipe; this has to happen on a case-by-case basis. In the domain of the social sciences, what can researchers do in real terms? They can advise political decision-makers, compiling notes and recommendations for them to consult and act on as appropriate. They can also engage in militant activity, metamorphosing into men of action defending the cause of a particular martyrised people. But as researchers working on massacre and its prevention, how, and at what objective, can they direct their efforts more particularly?

While the researcher cannot exercise any protective responsibility, he can at least take on the *responsibility to know and to make known*. Is this not, moreover, his primary mission, that of constructing knowledge and teaching it? This book aims to make a contribution in precisely this sense. But other tools for disseminating knowledge can be imagined that are useful as much for research as for informing the general public. For example, despite the scale on which massacres occur during conflicts, there is no reliable database bringing together our knowledge on the subject. This is why, while writing this book, the idea came to my mind to create *The Online Encyclopedia of Mass Violence*, www.massviolence.org, that can be consulted free of charge. This project could make a key contribution to the history of Humanity (or more precisely to the history of the destruction of humanity). Over and above what it brings to our knowledge of the past, such a tool would also be precious for researchers everywhere (decision-makers, journalists, NGO officials, legal experts, etc.) in the field of international relations, to analyse in-depth contemporary crises and—who knows?—prevent them from happening. This is an ambitious, global project that depends not only on my own personal dedication, but also on the committed involvement of top scholars in the field.

As regards research programmes, the study of the pertinence of 'early warning indicators' mentioned above is another priority. For more than ten years at the time of writing some university teams and NGOs have been working on projects aiming to define these types of parameters, the most interesting of these having been in the framework of the *Minorities at Risk* programme at the University of Maryland.[30] The central idea is excellent: it consists essentially of gathering reliable information about a conflict and the possible ways it could deteriorate so political decision-makers can take practical steps to halt the degeneration before it is too late. The decision-makers in question must, of course, have a will to do something, and whether they have this will, as I have insisted in these pages, may be quite another matter. But when this political will is indeed present, it is crucial that policymakers have access to the most pertinent indicators. But can these early warning criteria really prove to be reliable in an actual crisis situation? Nobody really knows, especially since academic research in this area is generally liable frequented by experts in international relations. Besides, there is always a minimum time-lag between evaluating a situation and any decision-taking: an early warning is one that has been given *in time*, that is, three weeks to twelve months in advance of the anticipated event. With any less warning than this, it is considered impossible to exert any influence on the way events will unfold. So research needs to be carried out to fathom the nature of the various warning indicators, and how they interrelate: their temporality in relation to crisis chronology, for example, and ultimately whether or not they are acted upon by decision-makers.[31]

'The revenge of passions'

Whether geared towards action or towards knowledge, however, these proposals cannot ignore the new climate of international relations model in the wake of the 11 September 2001 terrorist assault on the United States. As we all know, the attack on the Twin Towers turned the analyses of experts on their heads. From one day to the next, the prevailing discourse was no longer focussed on the responsibility to protect populations in danger (was it, in fact, ever focussed on this?) but on a will to *protect oneself* against international terrorism. The death of 3,000 people in the West, in the United States, was much more important in the end than that of 800,000 people in the South, in Rwanda.

A new paradigm had imposed itself on the international scene. Pierre Hassner commented that we had entered another epoch, that of the 'the revenge of passions', characterised by a forceful return of terror and power.[32] In response to an intangible adversary, the United States did not hesitate, in the very name of their demand for security, to give themselves the right to ignore the law. Humanitarian intervention schemes of the 1990s were immediately replaced by *security interventions* (or what were assumed to be) in Afghanistan first, and then in Iraq. However, various experts pointed out that going to war was not necessarily the best way to prevent further terrorist attacks, and that the only thing that would really prove to be efficacious would be to continue gathering intelligence about those groups and networks likely to commit new attacks. Nothing worked: the US did not listen. To avenge itself for the public humiliation suffered, the great America wanted publicly to demonstrate its power, that is, its singular capacity to respond militarily anywhere in the world. Although the operation against Kabul was meaningful in relation to 11 September,[33] all the arguments put forward to justify war against Saddam Hussein's regime have proved unfounded.

In so doing, and in the very name of their conception of good, American leaders therefore rearranged the notion of 'prevention', transforming it into 'pre-emption'. This notion, in their eyes, justified in advance recourse to armed force against any state presenting a potential threat to their country. As it happened, this commitment to the world crusade against terrorism proved useful to many other heads of state. What indeed could be more tempting for a political leader than to wave the red flag of the terrorist threat so as to present one's own nation as the only guarantor of security for all? In the aftermath of the 9/11 attack, Stanley Hoffmann quickly pointed out that the main political beneficiaries of terrorism were going to be *states*:[34] on the pretext of attempting to eradicate it, they would be able to wield a powerful emotional rhetoric to legitimate ferocious repressive policies against their opponents, whether in Russia, China or elsewhere.

Will Europeans be capable of asserting another vision of the world, and further, of implementing this vision, at the same time as responding appropriately to the terrorist threat? Will the United States agree to follow a less unilateral political programme? Will the

UN succeed in bringing about internal reforms? Will the Israelis and the Palestinians manage to establish peaceful relations? Etc., etc... This book can only come to a close by posing these questions, that is by looking ahead to a future that has still to be written. A future that is certainly open, but one that remains dark. Because this era in which passions run high is heavy with new wars. And it goes without saying, that these will again be justified in the name of civilisation and security, of God and purity to be found again, and so on. Once more it will be civilians who pay the price for these devastating assaults on humanity.

In January 2004 delegates from fifty-five states at the Conference on Genocide Prevention, organised by Sweden, showed themselves to be well aware of these dangers, even though the results of their work have gone almost unnoticed. According to their research, there was a risk of genocide in thirteen countries: Sudan, Myanmar/Burma, Burundi, Rwanda, DR Congo, Somalia, Uganda, Algeria, China, Iraq, Afghanistan, Pakistan and Ethiopia.[35] Let us hope that they were wrong, at least in part! Early warning signals or not, the role of the media and NGOs remains primordial, even if just to prevent a tragedy unfolding from being simply erased from international public attention. But public opinion is becoming weary of the dramas with which the media assail them. And yet another catastrophe will always follow in the wake of the last on our television screens. As for the United States, being generally guided by selfish interests, like other states, including France, it is rarely to be seen rushing to the aid of foreign populations, and this is why the 'never again' refrain inexorably comes round again. A huge amount of political determination is needed if we are to put the spectres of massacre and mass violence behind us.

APPENDIX A

INVESTIGATING A MASSACRE

Conducting empirical case studies on a particular massacre constitutes a preliminary and indispensable line of inquiry, to free the research from ideological and normative approaches. The facts need to be reconstructed almost as they would in a police investigation. Nevertheless this task is a difficult one because massacre is often carried out in secret. Also, the basic questions are always the same: who did the killing and gave the orders to kill? Who is dead? Who can act as witness to what happened? This triptych of aggressor, victim and witness comprises the 'basic triangle' for any study of massacre, an inquiry that must clearly avail itself of the socio-historical background to oral accounts of events in addition to rounding up the written material available.

Researching a massacre often causes discomfort to the person seeking to know and understand. To assist such a person in this endeavour, I have drawn up a questionnaire that could prove useful for undertaking this preliminary investigation. It needs to be regarded as an initial work tool and a starting point for collecting data. Then, as one 'gets into' the scenario under scrutiny, new questions arise of their own volition. In this way the case begins to 'speak' and the questionnaire becomes less necessary. Moving on subsequently from the stage of analysing the individual scenario to a comparative analysis constitutes a new and especially critical stage (see also Appendix B).

(1) Who has done the killing?
— Can we establish the killer profile in greater detail (age, sex, social origin)?
— Motives: are they acting with a view to territorial conquest, political domination or 'purification'?
— To what extent will the massacre procure political benefits for some of the perpetrators?
— What economic stakes might be involved in the massacre?

376

(2) Targeted Victims

— Are civilians killed at random or in a discriminatory fashion (for example, from lists of names, professional categories, according to political, religious or ethnic criteria)?
— Are men separated from women before being killed?
— Are the women systematically killed? Similarly, are children and the elderly systematically killed?
— How can we assess the number of victims, by age, gender or occupation?
— What problems arise from the quantification of victims and their identification?
— Is it possible to produce a cartographic description of the massacre?

(3) Constructing the figure of the enemy

— What are the representations of the 'enemy' slated for destruction?
— What universe—ideological and of the *imaginaire*—do the killers inhabit?
— How would one set about analysing the themes of the propaganda that preceded and accompanied the massacre?
— What importance should be attributed to fear and the collective feeling of insecurity in relation to a worsening economic situation?

(4) Modus operandi

— Can we break down the criminal procedure into clear-cut stages (preparation, decision and implementation)?
— Description of 'methodology' (massacres occurring directly on-site, deportation-abandonment, death camps?)
— What can we learn from the nature of the weapons used?
— Are the victims killed coldly and rationally or with savagery?
— Are sexual rituals associated with the act of massacre? Is a systematic policy of rape associated with it?

(5) Time frame of the massacre

— Premonitory signs: what indicators, if any, are there of a break in the social tie between future victims and their immediate environment?
— Is there a 'time' or 'opportunity' for the massacre in relation to the political situation in the country, or in relation to the international situation?
— Is there a context of war or collapse of an empire?

— Postures taken in the local community and further afield: is there tacit consent or are there gestures of protest, or even actions taken to protect victims?

(6) Political and media effects

— Was there a desire to hide the massacre or to make it public? Under the same heading, were attempts made to cover up the existence of bodies or to display them publicly?

— Does the event exert a political influence on the conflict in progress, and in what way?

— Does the massacre procure new legitimacy for some of the actors?

— How does news of the massacre spread?

— Will the massacre remain undiscovered for a certain length of time, or will it be revealed straight away?

— Was the massacre committed in order to frighten potential victims? Or to make them flee a coveted territory? Or to foment political instability?

(7) Aftermath narratives

— On the part of witnesses: who knows 'what really happened'? Structural analysis of journalists' accounts, and of the accounts of non-governmental organisation members.

— On the part of any survivors: Who can speak? Who can recount the horror? How best to separate reality from distortion, or sheer fabrication?

— On the part of the perpetrators of the massacre: negation and denial or justification for the crime? A guilt that is impossible to bear?

APPENDIX B

COMPARING MASSACRES

Comparative approaches are one of the most fertile avenues along which to advance our knowledge in the social sciences. And so there are the disciplines of comparative history, comparative sociology and of course comparative political science, which have been justified by many authors, starting with Max Weber.[1] This is not the place to rehash the legitimacy, the conditions and the limits of the exercise of comparison, a question that has prompted a considerable body of literature. The task of comparison nevertheless remains as difficult and risky as ever. Difficult because the comparative scholar sets himself the ambition of acquiring an in-depth knowledge of a number of historical events (or political regimes) that have taken place in a number of countries, which requires a tremendous work of erudition. Risky because the comparative scholar then opens himself to possible objections from a colleague who is a renowned specialist on a single country, of which he would have even more erudite knowledge. This is why comparison implies de facto a collective approach through discussion and cooperation among researchers. However, it requires them to agree not only on a common line of inquiry but also on the nature of the cases to be compared as well the method of comparison used. Now these methodological problems often turn into memory and remembrance issues, if not ideological and identitarian battles, as we have seen in the controversy surrounding the Communist crimes or the uniqueness of the Holocaust.

The problem here is that the comparison has to do with a highly sensitive subject. We are not dealing, for instance, with the comparison of different molecular structures or the geological masses over several different geographical areas. No, we are dealing with the comparison of various processes by which populations are slaughtered, in other words processes of mass death. Correlatively, we are dealing with authorities who have killed, of corpses that still scream their innocence, of survivors whose flesh still bears the consequences of these tragedies and who are demanding justice, revenge or reparation. The emotional charge connected with massacre as

379

an object can thus make one doubt that it is even possible to perform scholarly analysis of it.

In this regard there is no doubt that comparing massacres first poses the question of the neutrality of the person who decides to compare them. For the researcher can be more or less directly involved with one of these tragedies, over which he will feel greater sympathy due to the history of his own community or his political convictions. It is understandable for him to feel greater compassion for a particular group of victims, neglecting or even refusing to see the suffering of a group other than his own. In short his reasoning can be diverted toward the sole aim of accusing one power or another. That is understandable, but unacceptable from the standpoint of the scholar's mission: how can he then trust his affiliations and his emotions? Before outlining a methodology for comparison, I will start by identifying the main pitfalls or impasses that comparison can encounter.

The pitfalls of comparison: equivalence and uniqueness

One of the most frequent errors involves thinking that mass murder is always the same, particularly with regard to counting the dead. There is a tendency to equate very different historical examples as long as they involve hundreds of thousands or even millions of victims. Once that point on the scale of mass of human destruction has been reached, what is the point of maintaining that there are 'differences' between the dead? The exercise seems futile, if not indecent, in showing insufficient respect for their memory. Indeed, by what criteria can one declare that the victims in a particular case are 'more important' than those in another? Is not the pain and suffering of all of them beyond computation? To undertake a comparison on such a basis is doomed to fail and in addition will inevitably arouse heated controversy.

The publication of the *Black Book of Communism* amplified such debates, which were often highly emotional. Some argued that, where the number of dead ascribable to the communist authorities was concerned, the crimes perpetrated by these regimes were 'equal to', if not worse than, those of Nazism. This idea is explicitly formulated in the book's introduction, in which Stéphane Courtois writes: 'The deliberate starvation of a child of a Ukrainian kulak as a result of the famine caused by Stalin's regime "is equal to" the starvation of a Jewish child in the Warsaw ghetto as a result of the famine caused by the Nazi regime.'[2] What scale of measurement does the author use to speak thus of dead who 'are equal'? At that rate could he not also have affirmed that beyond the process used to kill, the death of a Jewish or a Ukrainian child is 'equal to' the death of a German or Japanese child crushed by the allied bombs that fell on Dresden or Hiroshima? In fact, such affirmation, in its apparent symmetricality (famine in both cases) and emotional equivalence (the death of a child) is a way not by any means of introducing comparison but of placing it out of bounds by making one believe that the two events are similar from a human standpoint. This reasoning then comes down to instrumentalising the moral argument (the death of children who are by definition innocent) to neutralise a comparative investigation aiming to point out the differences in nature between the powers that were behind these tragedies. There are collective volumes aiming to compare the Nazi and Stalinite systems, edited respectively by historians Ian Kershaw and Moshe Lewin, and Henry Rousso, that have shown the extent to which these two totalitarian systems differed.[3]

Conversely, defending at all costs the uniqueness or exceptionality of a historic event, as some Holocaust specialists have done, is to close the door to any comparative attempt: since the Holocaust is unique, it is not susceptible to comparison. This attitude is probably in part a reaction to the first, which, in the name of some sort of 'sameness', aims to downplay or nuance the destruction of European Jews. But this position of uniqueness is not tenable from an academic point of view because all historic events are in principle unique. The American Revolution was a unique event. The French Revolution was also a unique event. But that did not prevent de Tocqueville from giving us a remarkable piece of work based precisely on the comparison of these two events and political systems that sprang from them. To state the obvious, a fact or an event can be singular, or differ from another by one or more salient features, without being different on every point.

Thus, from a social science standpoint, no event can be extracted from history or placed in a position of perceiving an event to transcend history. This approach, in fact, has been criticised by certain Jewish historians of the Holocaust, such as Yehuda Bauer, who has challenged the religious or metaphysical a-historic position defended for instance by the writer Elie Wiesel.[4] Of course the literary quality and the great value as testimony of the author of *The Night Trilogy* are not being questioned here. By the same token Annette Wieviorka[5] and Omer Bartov both recognise the existence of other genocides and are open to the exercise of comparison.[6] Advocates of uniqueness sometimes become trapped by their own discourse: if the aim is to show that the Holocaust is an unprecedented event, then one must agree to the principle of comparing it with other mass murders in order to get from postulate to proof. And this is simply a question of intellectual coherence. Actually there is no fundamental contradiction in affirming that the massacre-event is *both* unique *and* can be compared: it is to admit that its features are both a singular and universal.

Methodologies for comparison

But how can progress be made in designing a methodology in this area? Developing comparative studies already implies disengaging oneself from the pathos of the ideological confrontation between Nazism and Communism, even from the question of totalitarianism, by opening the analysis to cases that do not fall under these categories. This is one of the reasons that led me to study the history of Rwanda up to the genocide in 1994. But grouping together very different case studies is not satisfactory either. Too many of the books published in this field are actually mere juxtapositions of a hodgepodge of historical examples. The contribution of such works to a comparative outlook is very limited. The difficulty lies in moving from an assemblage of case studies to a coherent comparative analysis of them.

In this perspective one of the first stages involves deciding on a common notion that can be used to classify the events that will be compared. In this sense early research adopted 'genocide' as a minimal concept on the basis of the definition adopted by the United Nations in 1948. I have already discussed the thorny issues posed by the adoption of this legal notion by the social sciences. This is why I prefer to take as a unit of reference the notion of 'massacre', without making assumptions about what is or is not genocide. Given that the notion of massacre still refers to a multitude of heterogeneous cases, the research has limited itself to examining a single class of events: those arising from a dynamic of *eradication*.[7] The trickiest and most perilous task remains, that of constructing the actual procedure for comparing them.

One of the most common avenues involves identifying the similarities and differences between the cases studied. The political scientist Robert Melson has conducted pioneer research in this area in his in-depth and subtle comparison between the Armenian and Jewish genocides.[8] I should point out that such a way of comparing in no way evens out the differences but rather throws them into relief, without for as much masking what the events might have in common.

The task of comparison can however be carried further if *common problematics* can be constructed between the events analysed which can account for their *specificities*. By 'problematics' I mean questions that intersect all the cases and that can to a certain degree be theorised—the answers to which can be ordered differently depending on the historical situation examined. In this book, for instance, these problematics focus on the role of the *imaginaire* and ideology, the crisis of the state and sacrificial violence, the international context and war, etc. In this way comparative conceptualisation enables the analyst to consider each case singly. The French historian Paul Veyne has in fact advocated using this approach in the field of history:

'conceptualise to individualise'. A similar perspective has been adopted herein: *problematise to differentiate.* To this end the study questionnaire (appendix A) is an indispensable research tool.

The comparative research conducted both by Norman Naimark and Eric Weitz partly fall within this perspective.[9] Both works are based on a limited number of cases the authors have submitted to comparative inquiry. However, the present work is based on an even more ambitious approach. Naimark and Weitz's works are composed mainly of historical monographs, which they then subject to comparative scrutiny. I believed it was possible to skip this step to offer the reader a constructed problematic right off. The table of contents reflects its basic structure. From that point on, writing the book involved a constant to-ing and fro-ing between the singular and the general, the universal and the particular, all the while maintaining an interdisciplinary perspective. Naturally I could never have undertaken such an exercise without first allowing my thinking and investigations several years to mature. Given the complexity of such a method of analysis, discussion and criticism seem to me more than ever necessary in order to advance the research, provided that it is done on meticulous intellectual bases.

SELECT BIBLIOGRAPHY

This bibliography presents the most representative works that study the processes of extreme violence, massacres and genocide from a comparative standpoint. It therefore does not include works on war as such, or even those dealing with a specific case of genocide or massacre. Works by single authors and edited volumes are listed separately.

As a supplement to these references, a list is given of other titles dealing with connected themes: international law, 'truth and reconciliation' committees, and genocide prevention. Specialised journals and websites are listed at the end.

EXTREME VIOLENCE AND GENOCIDE

Individual works

ALVAREZ, Alex, *Governments, Citizens and Genocide: A Comparative and Interdisciplinary Approach*, Bloomington, Indiana University Press, 2001.

ARENDT, Hannah, *Eichmann in Jerusalem: A Report on the Banality of Evil*, New York, Penguin, 1994.

BAUER, Yehuda, *Rethinking the Holocaust*, New Haven, Yale University Press, 2001.

BAUMAN, Zygmunt, *Modernity and the Holocaust*, Cambridge, Polity Press, 1989.

BELL-FIALKOFF, Andrew, *Ethnic Cleansing*, New York, St Martin's Press, 1996.

BRAUD, Philippe, *Violences politiques*, Paris, Le Seuil, 2004.

BRUNETEAU, Bernard, *Le siècle des génocides. Violences, massacres et processus génocidaires de l'Arménie au Rwanda*, Paris, Armand Colin, 2004.

CHAUMONT, Jean-Michel, *La concurrence des victimes*, Paris, La Découverte, 1997.

FEIN, Helen, *Genocide: A Sociological Perspective*, London, Sage Publications, 1990.

HASSNER, Pierre, *La violence et la paix*, Paris, Seuil, 2000.

————, *La terreur et l'Empire*, Paris, Seuil, 2003.

HOLSTI, Kalevi J., *The State War and the State of War*, Cambridge University Press, 1996.

HOROWITZ, Donald, *Deadly Ethnic Riots*, Berkeley, University of California Press, 2000.

JAULIN, Robert, *La paix blanche. Introduction à l'ethnocide*, Paris, Seuil, 1970.

KALYVAS, Stathis N., *The Logic of Violence in Civil War*, New York, Cambridge University Press, 2006.

KNUTH, Rebecca, *Libricide: The Regime-Sponsored Destruction of Books and Librairies in the Twentieth Century*, Westport, CT, Praeger, 2003.

KOTEK, Joël and Pierre, RIGOULOT, *Le siècle des camps. Détention, concentration, extermination. Cent ans de mal radical*, Paris, Jean-Claude Lattès, 2000.

KUPER, Leo, *Genocide: Its Political Use in the Twentieth Century*, London, Penguin Books, 1981.

MANN, Michael, *The Dark Side of Democracy: Explaining Ethnic Cleansing*, Cambridge University Press, 2005.

MARKUSEN, Eric, and David KOPF, *The Holocaust and Strategic Bombing: Genocide and Total War in the Twentieth Century*, Boulder, CO, Westview, 1993.

MAZOWER, Mark, *Dark Continent: Europe's Twentieth Century*, London, Allen Lane, Penguin Press, 1998.

MELSON, Robert, *Revolution and Genocide: on the Origins of the Armenian Genocide and the Holocaust*, University of Chicago Press, 1992.

MIDLARSKY, Manus, *The Killing Trap; Genocide in the Twentieth Century*, Cambridge University Press, 2005.

NAIMARK, Norman, *Fires of Hatered: Ethnic Cleansing in the Twentieth-Century Europe*, Cambridge, MA Harvard University Press, 2001.

POWER, Samantha, *A Problem from Hell: America and the Age of Genocide*, New Republic Book, Basic Books, 2002.

REVAULT D'ALLONES, Myriam, *Ce que l'homme fait à l'homme. Essai sur le mal politique*, Paris, Le Seuil 1995.

RUMMEL, Rudolf J., *Death by Government*, New Brunswick, NJ, Transaction Publishers, 1994.

SIRONI, Françoise, *Bourreaux et victimes. Psychologie de la torture*, Paris, Odile Jacob, 1999.

SEMELIN, Jacques, 'Analyser le massacre. Réflexions comparatives', coll. *Questions de Recherche/Research in Question*, CERI, 2002, www.ceri-sciencespo.com/cerifr/publica/question/menu.htm

SHAW, Martin, *War and Genocide: Organized Killing in Modern Society*, Cambridge, Polity Press, 2003.

SOFSKY, Wolfgang, *Traité de la violence* (transld.), Paris, Gallimard, 1998.

STAUB, Ervin, *The Roots of Evil: The Origins of Genocide and Other Group Violence*, Cambridge University, Press, 1989.

TATZ, Colin M., *With Intent to Destroy: Reflecting on Genocide*, London, New York, Verso, 2003.

TERNON, Yves, *L'état criminel. Les génocides au 20ème siècle*, Paris, Le Seuil, 1995.

TILLY, Charles, *The Politics of Collective Violence*, Cambridge University Press, 2003.

TODOROV, Tzvetan, *Face à l'extrême*, Paris, Seuil, 1990.

UEKERT, Brenda K., *Rivers of Blood. A Comparative Study of Government Massacre*, Westport, CT, Praeger, 1995.

VALENTINO Benjamin A., *Final Solutions: Mass Killing and Genocide in the Twentieth Century*, Ithaca, NY, Cornell University Press, 2004.

WALLER, James, *Becoming Evil: How Ordinary People Commit Genocide and Mass Killing*, Oxford, Oxford University Press, 2002.

WEITZ Eric D., *A Century of Genocide: Utopias of Race and Nation*, Princeton University Press, 2003.

WIEVIORKA, Michel, *La violence*, Paris, Balland, 2004.

Edited volumes

ANDREOPOULOS, George J. (ed.), *Genocide: Conceptual and Historical Dimensions*, University Park, University of Pensylvania Press, 1994.

AUDOUIN-ROUZEAU, S., A. BECKER, C. INGRAO, H. ROUSSO, *La violence de guerre, 1914–1945*, Brussels, Complexe, 2002.

BARTOV, Omer, Phyllis MACK, *In God's Name: Genocide and Religion in the Twentieth Century, Oxford, New York, Berghahn, 2001*.

BARTOV, Omer, Atina GROSSMAN, Mary NOLAN, *The Crimes of War: Guilt and Denial in the Twentieth Century, New York, The New Press, 2002*.

BELA VARDY Steven, T. HUNT TOOLEY, *Ethnic Cleansing in Twentieth Century Europe*, New York, Columbia University Press, 2003.

CHALK, Frank and Kurt JONASSOHN, *The History and Sociology of Genocide*, New Haven, Yale University Press, 1990.

CHARNY, Israël W. (ed.), *Toward the Understanding and Prevention of Genocide: Proceedings of the International Conference on the Holocaust and Genocide*, Boulder, CO, Westview Press, 1984.

———, William S., PARSONS and Samuel TOTTEN, *Century of Genocide: Eyewitness Accounts and Critical Views*, New York, Garland, 1997.

CHARNY, Israel (ed.), *Le livre noir de l'humanité. Encyclopédie mondiale des génocides*, Toulouse, Privat, 2001.

CHIROT, Daniel and Martin E.P. SELIGMAN (eds), *Ethnopolitical Warfare: Causes, Consequences and Possible Solutions*, Washington DC, American Psychological Association, 2001.

CHOBARDJIAN, Levon and Georges CHIRINIAN, *Studies in Comparative Genocide*, New York, St Martin's Press, 1999.

COQUIO, Catherine (ed.), *Parler des camps, penser les génocides*, Paris, Albin Michel, 1999.

COURTOIS, Stéphane (ed.), *Le livre noir du communisme. Crimes, terreur, répression*, Paris, Robert Laffont, 1997.

FRIEDRICH, David O. (ed.), *State Crime*, Aldershot (UK), Ashgate, 1998.

EL KENZ, David (ed.), *Le Massacre, objet d'histoire*, Paris, Gallimard, 2005.

JANSEN, Steven L.B (ed.), *Genocide: Cases, Comparisons and Contemporary Debates*, Copenhagen, Danish Center for Holocaust and Genocide Studies, 2003.

JONASSOHN, Kurt, Karin Solveig BJORNSON, *Genocide and Gross Human Rights Violations in Comparative Perspective*, New Brunswick, NJ, Transaction, 1998.

JONES, Adam (ed.), *Gendercide and Genocide*, Nashville, Vanderbilt University Press, 2004.

HANNOYER, Jean, (ed.) *Guerres civiles, dimensions de la violence, économies de la civilité*, Paris, Karthala, 1999.

HERITIER, Françoise (ed.), *De la violence*, Paris, Odile Jacob, 1996–9.

HINTON, Alexander L. (ed.), *Genocide, An Anthropological reader*, Oxford, Blackwell, 2002.

—— (ed.), *Anihilating Difference: the Antrhopology of Genocide*, Berkeley, California University Press, 2002.

KIERNAN, Ben, and Robert GELLATELY, *Spectre of Genocide: Mass Murders in Historical Perspective*, Cambridge University Press, 2003.

LEVENE, Marc, and Penny ROBERTS (eds), *The Massacre in History*, New York, Bargain Books, 1999.

RADFORD, Jill, and Diana RUSSELL, (eds), *Femicide: The politics of woman Killing*, Buckingham, Open University Press, 1992.

REVUE D'HISTOIRE DE LA SHOAH, *Génocides. Lieux (et non-lieux) de mémoire*, no. 181, 2, 2004.

REVUE INTERNATIONALE DE POLITIQUE COMPARÉE, *Les usages politiques des massacres*, vol. 7, 1, spring 2001.

REVUE INTERNATIONALE DE SCIENCES SOCIALES, *Violences extrêmes*, no. 174, Dec. 2004.

SHELTON, Dinah L. (ed.), *Encyclopedia of Genocide and Crimes Against Humanity*, 3 vols, Thomson Gale, 2005.

SMITH, Robert W. (ed.), *Genocide: Essays Toward Understanding, Early Warning and Prevention*, Association of Genocide Scholars, 1999.

ZARTMANN, William (ed.), *Collapsed States: The Disintegration and Restoration of Legitimate Authority*, Boulder, CO, Lynne Rienner, 1995.

INTERNATIONAL LAW

BALL, Howard, *Prosecuting War Crimes and Genocide: The Twentieth-Century Experience*, Lawrence, University Press of Kansas, 1999.

BASS, Gary Jonathan, *Stay the Hand of Vengeance: The Politics of War Crimes Tribunals*, Princeton University Press, 2000.

BEST, Goeffrey, *Nuremberg and After: The Continuing History of War Crimes against Humanity*, University of Reading, 1984.

BETTATI, Mario, *Le droit d'ingérence. Mutation de l'ordre international*, Paris, Odile Jacob, 1996.

BLOXHAM, Donald, *Genocide on Trial: War Crimes Trials and the Formation of Holocaust History and Memory*, Oxford University Press, 2003.

BOUCHET-SAULNIER, Françoise, *Dictionnaire pratique du droit humanitaire*, Paris, La Découverte/Syros, 2000.

BOUSTANY, Kathia, DORMOY Daniel (eds), *Génocide*, Réseau Victoria, 'Droit international', Brussels, Bruylant/Editions de l'Université de Brussels, 1999.

DELMAS-MARTY, Mireille (ed.), *La justice pénale internationale entre passé et avenir*, Paris, Dalloz, 2004.

————, *Vers un droit commun de l'humanité*, Paris, Textuel, 2005.

DELSOL, Chantale, *La grande méprise. Justice internationale, gouvernement mondial, guerre juste*, Paris, Editions de la Table Ronde, 2004.

GARAPON, Antoine, *Des crimes qu'on ne peut ni juger ni pardonner. Pour une justice internationale*, Paris, Odile Jacob, 2002.

GOLDSTONE, Richard J., *For Humanity: Reflections of a War Crimes Invetsigator*, New Haven, Yale University Press, 2000.

GUTMAN, Roy and David RIEFF (eds), *Crimes of war: What the Public should know*, Singapore, Norton, 1999.

LEMKIN, Raphael, *Axis Rule in Occupied Europe*, Washington DC, Carnegie, 1944.

METTRAUX, Guenaël, *International Crimes and the Ad-hoc Tribunals*, Oxford University Press, 2005.

OSIEL, Mark, *Mass Atrocity, Collective Memory and the Law*, New Brunswick, NJ, Transaction, 1997.

OSIEL, Mark, *Obeying Orders: Atrocity, Military Disciplines and the Law of War*, New Brunswick, NJ, Transaction, 1999.

SCHABAS, William, *Genocide in International Law*, Cambridge University Press, 2000. juridique.

PEACEBUILDING, JUSTICE AND RECONCILIATION

BARKAN, Elazar, *The Guilt of Nations: Restitution and Negotiating Historical Injustices*, Baltimore, Johns Hopkins University Press, 2001.

CHESTERMAN, Simon, *Just War or Just Peace? Humanitarian Intervention and International Law*, Oxford University Press, 2001.

COUSENS, Elisabeth, KUMAR Chetan (eds), *Peacebuilding as Politics: Cultivating Peace in Fragile Societies*, Boulder, CO, Lynne Rienner, 2001.

DESTEXHE, Alain, *L'Humanitaire impossible ou deux siècles d'ambiguïté*, Paris, Armand Colin, 1993.

FATIC, Aleksander, *Reconciliation via the War Crimes Tribunal?*, Aldershot, Ashgate, 2000.

HAYNER, Priscilla B., *Unspeakable Truths: Facing the Challenge of Truth Commissions*, New York, Routledge, 2000.

LEDERACH, John Paul, *Building Peace: Sustainable Reconciliation in Divided Societies*, Washington DC, United Institute of Peace Press, 1997.

LEFRANC, Sandrine, *Politiques du pardon*, Paris, Presses Universitaires de France, 2002.

MINEAR, Larry, Thomas WEISS, *Mercy under Fire: War and the Global Humanitarian Community*, Boulder, CO, Westview Press, 1995.

MINOW, Martha, *Between Vengeance and Forgiveness: Facing History after Genocide and Mass Violence*, Boston, Beacon Press, 1998.

NEWMAN, Edward, Albrecht SCHNABEL (eds), *Recovering from Civil Conflict: Reconciliation, Peace and Development*, London, Frank Cass, 2002.

OFF, Carol, *The Lion, the Fox and the Eagle: A Story of Generals and Justice in Rwanda and Yugoslavia*, Toronto, Random House Canada, 2000.

POULIGNY, Béatrice, *Peace Operations seen from Below: UN Missions and Local People*, London, Hurst (transl.), 2005.

ROTBERG, Robert, Dennis THOMPSON (eds), *Truth versus Justice: The Morality of Truth Commissions*, Princeton University Press, 2000.

STOVER, Eric and Harvey WEINSTEIN (eds), *My Neighbor, My Enemy: Justice and Community in the Aftermath of Mass Atrocity*, Cambridge University Press, 2004.

TEITEL, Ruti G., *Transitional Justice*, Oxford University Press, 2000.

TERNON, Yves, *Du négationnisme. Mémoire et tabou*, Paris, Ed. Desclée de Brouwer, 1999.

PREVENTION

CHIROT, Daniel, Clark McCAULEY, *Why Not Kill them All: The Logic of Prevention of Mass Political Murder*, Princeton University Press, 2006.

CROKER, Chester A., Fen Osler HAMPSON, Pamela AALL (eds), *Herding cats: Multiparty Mediation in a complex world*, Washington, DC, United States Institute of Peace Press, 1999.

BUSSIÈRE, René, *L'Europe de la prévention des crises et des conflits*, Paris, L'Harmattan, 2000.

EVANS, G. and M. SAHNOUN '*The Responsability to Protect*', Report of the International Commission on Intervention and State Sovereignty (ICISS), appointed by the Government of Canada, published in *Foreign Affairs*, vol. 81, no. 6, November 2002. One can also consult the whole report on www.crisisweb.org.

FEIN, Helen, and Joyce APSEL FREEDMAN, *Teaching about Genocide: A Guidebook for College and University Teachers*, Human Rights Internet, Institute for the Study of Genocide, Ottawa, New York, 1992.

GURR, Ted. R, *Minorities at Risk: A Global View of Ethnopolitical Conflicts*, Washington DC, USIP Press, 1993.

HELTON, Arthur C., *The Price of Indifference: Refugees and Humanitarian Action in the New Century*, Oxford University Press, 2002.

HAMBURG, David A., *No More Killing Fields: Preventing Deadly Conflict*, New York, Rowman and Littlefield, 2002.

HEIDENRICH, John G., *How to Prevent Genocide: A Guide for Policymakers, Scholars and the Concerned Citizen*, Wesport, CT, Praeger, 2001.

GURR, Ted R. and John L. DAVIES, *Preventive Measures: Building Risk Assessment and Crisis Early Warning Systems*, Lanham, MD, Rowman and Littlefield, 1998.

RIEMER, Neal (ed.), *Protection Against Genocide: Mission Impossible?*, Wesport, CT, Praeger, 2000.

ROCARD, Michel, *L'art de la paix*, Biarritz, Atlantica, 1997.

RUBIN, Barnett R. (ed.), *Cases and Strategies for Preventive Action*, New York, The Century Foundation Press, 1998.

JOURNALS

Journal of Genocide Research
Journal of Holocaust and Genocide Studies
Journal of International Criminal Justice
Revue d'Histoire de la Shoah

WEBSITES

http://www.genocidewatch.org
http://www.crimesofwar.org
http://www.crisisweb.org
http://www.hrw.org
http://www.amnesty.asso.fr
http://www.cidcm.umd.edu
http://www.usip.org

http://www.un.org/icty/index-f.html
http://www.ictr.org/FRENCH/index.htm
http://www.ushmm.org
http://www.iwm.org.uk
http://migs.concordia.ca
http://www.chgs.umn.edu/index.html
http://www.yale.edu/gsp
http://www.iearn.org/hgp
http://www.dchf.dk/index.html
http://polisci.la.psu.edu/faculty/BERNHARD/extremeregimes.htm
http://www.holocaust-education.dk/Default.asp
http://www.holocaustef.org
http://www.fondationshoah.org

NOTES

Introduction

1. 'In the silence of abjection, when no sound can be heard save that of the chains of the slave and the voice of the informer, when everything trembles before the tyrant, and it is just as dangerous to incur his favour as to merit his disgrace, the historian appears, entrusted with the vengeance of peoples; Nero prospers in vain, the empire has already seen the birth of Tacitus.' François-René de Chateaubriand, *Mémoires d'outre tombe*, Paris, Gallimard, 1990.

2. Claude Lanzmann, 'Les non lieux de la mémoire' in the *Nouvelle Revue de Psychanalyse*, no. 33, 1986, p. 20.

3. Christopher R. Browning, *Ordinary Men: Reserve Police Battalion 101 and the Final Solution in Poland*, New York, HarperCollins, 1992, p. xx.

4. Marc Bloch, *Apologie pour l'histoire ou métier d'historien*, Paris, Armand Colin, 1974, cited by Christopher Browning, *Ordinary Men, op. cit.*, p. xx.

5. Primo Levi, *Si c'est un homme*, Paris, Julliard, 1958, 1988, p. 29. Transl. into English as *If This is a Man*, Abacus, 1991.

6. Zygmunt Bauman, *Modernity and The Holocaust*, Cambridge, Polity Press, 1989.

7. And I still do not claim to have the erudition of colleagues specialised in the history of each of these cases. In fact I have benefited hugely from their advice and comments, as acknowledged in the opening pages of this volume. There is, however, a notable gap in historiographic knowledge between the case of Nazi Germany on the one hand and the cases of Rwanda and Bosnia on the other. Research on the persecution and extermination of the Jews has spawned thousands of books and articles, while ten years after the event work on the massacres in Bosnia and Rwanda have not really reached maturity. This discrepancy results in often emotional debates among researchers from which I have tried to keep my distance. This has not prevented me from asserting my own analyses in the light of the knowledge I have gained and the comparisons I have made.

8. For these problems of definition and comparison, see Chapter VI as well as appendix I.

9. Michel Foucault, *Discipline and Punish; The Birth of the Prison*, transl. Alan Sheridan, New York, Vintage, 1977.

Chapter 1 *The Imaginary Constructs of Social Destructiveness*

1. Gaston Bouthoul, *L'infanticide différé*, Paris, Hachette, 1970.

2. Estimates of the number of Jews living in Germany at the end of the 1920s vary between different authors. I take my information here from the estimate Renée

Neher-Bernheim provides in *Histoire juive de la Révolution à l'Etat d'Israël*, Paris, Editions du Seuil, 2002.

3. Claude Lévi-Strauss, *Race et histoire*, Paris, Ed. Folio Essais, 1952, 1987, p. 22.
4. Jean-François Bayart, *The Illusion of Cultural Identity*, London, Hurst, 2005 (trans. *L'illusion identitaire*, Paris, Ed. Fayard, 1996).
5. Robert Kaplan, *Balkan Ghosts*, New York, St Martin's Press, 1993.
6. Marc Levene, Introduction to *The Massacre in History*, edited by Marc Levene and Penny Roberts, New York, Oxford Books, 1999, p. 19.
7. Donald Horowitz, *The Deadly Ethnic Riot*, Berkeley, University of California Press, 2001.
8. It is estimated that this purge by massacre, perpetrated between 15 May and 15 June 1945, claimed at least 30,000 lives. On this subject see Milovan Djilas, *Wartime*, New York, Harcourt Brace Jovanovich, 1980.
9. Harold Lydall, *Yugoslavia in Crisis*, Oxford, Clarendon Press, 1989, p. 9.
10. In 1991 (date of the last census), the total population was 7.5 million. Rwanda had the highest density on the continent, with 271 inhabitants per km.^{2}, actually over 300 if the uninhabitable areas (parks and reserves) are subtracted. And the urbanisation rate is only 7 per cent.
11. Danielle de Lame, 'Le Genocide rwandais et le vaste monde. Les liens du sang', *Annuaire de l'Afrique des grands lacs*, 1996, pp. 156–77.
12. Norman Cohn, *Warrant for Genocide: The Myth of the Jewish World-Conspiracy and the Protocols of the Elders of Zion*. New York, Harper Row, 1967, pp. 268 ff.
13. Albert Einstein and Sigmund Freud, *Why War?*, International Institute of Intellectual Cooperation, League of Nations, 1933.
14. Melanie Klein, *Contributions to Psycho-Analysis*, London, Hogarth Press, 1948.
15. Which Freud had already lain to waste by speaking of the child as a 'polymorphic pervert'.
16. Infants have no notion of time. They cannot understand why the mother's breast doesn't come when they cry. They experience it as the action of a 'bad object' against which they develop destructive fantasies. On the other hand, the oral gratification of suckling, on which their entire life as an infant depends, causes them to have feelings of contentment and omnipotence and perceive the breast as a 'good object'. The mother is thus experienced at a very primitive level as a good object to keep and a bad object to be destroyed.
17. Franco Fornari, *Psychanalyse de la situation atomique*, Paris, Gallimard, 1969, p. 36.
18. Franco Fornari, *ibid.*, p. 35.
19. Franco Fornari, *Psychanalyse de la situation atomique, op.cit.*, p. 65.
20. On this topic see the introduction to Ch. II in which reference is made to Norbert Elias's theory.
21. Frank Chalk, Kurt Jonassohn, *The History and Sociology of Genocide*, New Haven, Yale University Press, 1990.
22. Bruno Bettelheim, *The Uses of Enchantment: The Meaning and Importance of Fairy Tales*, Alfred A. Knopf, 1976.
23. Paul Valéry, *Regards sur le monde actuel et autres essais*, Paris, Gallimard, 1945, p. 43. 'L'histoire est le produit le plus dangereux que la chimie de l'intellect ait

élaboré ... Il fait rêver, il enivre les peuples, leur engendre de faux souvenirs, exagère leurs réflexes, entretient leurs vieilles plaies, les tourmente dans leur repos, les conduit au délire de grandeur ou à celui de la persécution, et rend les nations amères, superbes, insupportables et vaines.'

24. George L. Mosse, *Fallen Soldiers: Reshaping the Memory of the World Wars*, New York, Oxford University Press, 1990.

25. Philippe Burrin, *Nazi Anti-Semitism: From Prejudice to the Holocaust*, trans. Janet Lloyd, London, The New Press, Oct. 2005, pp. 77–8. The author notes that the notion of 'existential power' is borrowed from the philosopher Eric Voegelin. For a philosophical approach to this notion, see in particular Paul Zawadzki 'Le ressentiment et l'égalité. Contribution à une anthropologie philosophique de la démocratie' in Pierre Ansart (ed.), *Le ressentiment*, Bruxelles, Bruylant, 2002, pp. 31–56.

26. See Joseph Krulic, *Histoire de la Yougoslavie*, Brussels, Ed. Complexe, 1993.

27. John B. Allcock, *Explaining Yugoslavia*, London, Hurst, 2000.

28. *Ibid.*, p. 418.

29. Jean-Pierre Chrétien, *L'Afrique des grands lacs. Deux mille ans d'histoire*, Paris, Ed. Aubier, 2000 and Mahmood Mamdani, *When Victims become Killers. Colonialism, Nativism and the Genocide in Rwanda*, Princeton University Press, 2002. We should also cite the important work of French sociologist Claudine Vidal who, after living for several years in Rwanda, completed an in-depth study on these 'ethnic' representations in *Sociologie des passions*, Paris, Karthala, 1991.

30. Even if some Hutus were farmers and vice versa.

31. According to statistics that remain approximate, Hutus represent 84 per cent of the population, Tutsis about 15 per cent and Twa 1 per cent. The physique of the Twa is very different from the Hutus and Tutsis; they are small, and they make a living by farming and cottage industries.

32. We will return at the beginning of Ch. II to his historical role as an important intellectual, and later political figure in the construction of the Rwandan republic's identity on an 'ethnic' basis.

33. Thus the first chapter of his book is entitled 'Rwandese Society and the Colonial Impact: The Making of a Cultural Mythology (1894–1959)'. See Gérard Prunier, *The Rwanda Crisis. History of a Genocide*, London, Hurst, 1995.

34. Denis-Constant Martin, *Cartes d'identité: comment dit-on 'nous' en politique?*, Paris, Presses de la FNSP, 1994, pp. 31–2.

35. Benedict Anderson, *Imagined Communities: Reflections on the Origin and Spread of Nationalism*, revised edition, London and New York, Verso, 1991.

36. Ernest Gellner, *Nations and Nationalism*, Oxford, Basil Blackwell, 1983, p. 55. See also Anne-Marie Thiesse, *La création des identités nationales. Europe XVIII–XXè siècle*, Paris, Le Seuil, 1999.

37. The *Ustashis* (the word means 'insurgents') under Ante Pavelic made an alliance with Hitler to create a fascist Croatian state whereas the *Chetniks* led by Draza Mihajlovic fought against the German occupation and so also against the Croatian nationalists. The word '*Chetniks*' comes from 'Cheta' meaning 'military company', traditionally referring to nationalist fighters against the Turks.

38. Michel Wieviorka (ed.), *La différence*, Paris, Baland, 2002.
39. Michel Hastings, 'Imaginaires des conflits et conflits d'imaginaires', in Elise Feron and Michel Hastings, *L'imaginaire des conflits communautaires*, Paris, L'Harmattan, 2002, pp. 45.
40. Sigmund Freud, *Group Psychology and the Analysis of the Ego*, trans. New York, Norton Library paperback, 1959, p. 42.
41. Michael Ignatieff, *The Warrior's Honor: Ethnic War and the Modern Conscience*, London, Chatto Windus, 1998, p. 53.
42. Victor Klemperer, *I Will Bear Witness*, 2 vols, trans. Martin Chalmers, New York, The Modern Library, 1999.
43. See for instance Alain Blum, *Naître, vivre et mourir en URSS (1917–1991)*, Paris, Plon, 1994.
44. Marie Kahle, *Tous les Allemands n'ont pas un cœur de pierre*, Paris, Liana Lévi, 2001, p. 27.
45. Hannah Arendt, *The Origins of Totalitarianism*, San Diego, Harcourt Brace Jovanovich, 1979.
46. Claude Lefort, *L'invention démocratique. Les limites de la domination totalitaire*, Paris, Fayard, 1994.
47. Mary Douglas, *Purity and Danger: An Analysis of Concepts of Pollution and Taboo*, London, Routledge and Kegan Paul, 1966.
48. See André Pichot, *La société pure de Darwin à Hitler*, Paris, Flammarion, 2000.
49. This law considered that 'citizenship' pertained only to individuals 'with German blood', the only ones 'to enjoy full political rights'.
50. Philippe Burrin, *Nazi Anti-Semitism, op. cit.*, p. 55.
51. Ivan Colovic, 'The Renewal of the Past: Time and Space in Contemporary Political Mythology' in *Other Voices*, vol. 2, no. 1, 2000, http://www.othervoices.org/2.1/colovic/past.html#N19. See also *The Politics of Symbol in Serbia: Essays on Political Anthropology*, London, Hurst, 2002.
52. Quoted by Ivan Colovic, *ibid.*, p. 65.
53. Michael Mann, *The Dark Side of Democracy: Explaining Ethnic Cleansing*, Cambridge University Press, 2005, p. 3.
54. See his Ch. IV, 'Genocidal Democracy in the New World', pp. 70–110, which is one of the most convincing in his book as regards the founding relations between democracy and ethnic cleansing.
55. See in particular Stéphane Courtois (ed.), 'The Crimes of Communism', *The Black Book of Communism*. Cambridge, MA, Harvard University Press, 1999.
56. Michael Mann, *The Dark Side of Democracy, op. cit.*, p. 17.
57. Alison Des Forges explains that this term was already used to refer to the Tutsis who invaded Rwanda in 1963. It was brought back into use in the 1990s to refer to the RPF. See Alison Des Forges (ed.), *Leave None to Tell the Story: Genocide in Rwanda*, New York, Human Rights Watch, 1999, p. 55.
58. Dominique Colas, *Le léninisme*, Paris, PUF, coll. Quadrige, 1982, 1998, quotes from ch. VIII 'Epuration', in the section entitled 'Nettoyer la terre russe', pp. 196–201.
59. Quoted in Stéphane Courtois (ed.), *The Black Book of Communism, op. cit.*, p. 577.

60. These quotations are all taken from Ch. 8, 'L'épuration, pratique centrale du léninisme', of Dominique Colas, *Le léninisme, op. cit.*, pp. 195 ff.

61. David Chandler, *Voices from S21: Terror and History in Pol Pot's Secret Prison,* Berkeley: University of California Press, 1999, p. 44.

62. Nicolas Werth, 'A State against Its People: Violence, Repression, and Terror in the Soviet Union', in S. Courtois (ed.), *The Black Book of Communism, op. cit.*, pp. 33–268.

63. Jean-Clément Martin, 'La Révolution Française: généalogie de l'ennemi' in *Raisons politiques,* Feb.–April 2002. See also Chs 4 and 5 of his book *Contre-révolution, révolution et nation en France, 1789–1799,* Paris, Le Seuil, 'Points', 1998.

64. Quoted by David Chandler, *Voices from S21: Terror and History in Pol Pot's Secret Prison, op. cit.*, p. 44.

65. Georges Bernanos, *Les grands cimetières sous la lune,* Paris, Plon, 1938, pp. 83–4.

66. Véronique Nahoum-Grappe, *Du rêve de vengeance à la haine politique,* Paris, Buchet-Chastel, 2003, p. 106.

67. Ian Kershaw, *Hitler,* Longman, 'Profiles in Power' series, London New York, 1991, p. 26.

68. 33 editions were published before Hitler's rise to power and countless others followed. See Norman Cohn, *The Pursuit of the Millennium; Revolutionary Millenarians and Mystical Anarchists of the Middle Ages,* Oxford University Press, 1957 and Pierre-André Taguieff, *Les Protocoles des Sages de Sion,* 2 vols., Paris, Berg International, 1992.

69. Saul Friedlander, *Nazi Germany and the Jews,* Volume I: *The Years of Persecution, 1933–1939,* New York, HarperCollins, 1997, p. 95.

70. Michel Hanus, *Psychiatrie intégrée de l'étudiant,* Paris, Maloine, 1975.

71. Here I particularly have in mind Erich Fromm, *The Anatomy of Human Destructiveness,* New York, Holt, Reinhart and Winston, 1973, that includes two psychoanalytical studies on Hitler and Stalin (an otherwise interesting book).

72. Saul Friedlander, *Nazi Germany and the Jews,* Volume I: *The Years of Persecution, 1933–1939, op. cit.*, p. 99.

73. Jacques Semelin, 'From Massacre to the Genocidal Process', *International Social Sciences Journal,* no. 174, Nov. 2002, pp. 483–491.

74. Raymond Aron, 'Existe-t-il un mystère nazi?' in *Commentaires,* automne 1979, vol. 2, no. 7, pp. 349.

75. Barry R. Posen, 'The Security Dilemma and Ethnic Conflict' in *Survival,* spring 1993, vol. 35, no. 1, pp. 27–47.

76. The French political scientist of Lebanese origin Joseph Maïla has offered an interesting interpretation of ethnic or religious conflicts in the context of 'globalisation': 'Identité et violence politique' in *Etudes,* Oct. 94, pp. 293–312. The Francophone Lebanese author Amin Maalouf also penned a fine essay on the theme: *Les identités meurtrières,* Paris, Grasset, 1998.

77. Carl Schmitt, *The Concept of the Political,* University of Chicago Press, 1996, p. 26.

78. Simone Weil, 'The *Iliad* or the Poem of Force' in *Simone Weil: An Anthology,* New York, Grove Press, 1986, p. 163.

79. Georges Lefebvre, *La Grande peur de 1789 suivi des foules révolutionnaires*, Paris, 1932, Ed. Armand Colin, 1988, p. 232.

80. Merton drew inspiration on this point from the definition of 'situation' as suggested by a pioneer of American sociology, W.I. Thomas (see ch. 4, in particular p. 475, in Robert K. Merton, *Social Theory and Social Structure*, New York, The Free Press, 1949 and 1957).

81. Jean-François Bayart, *The Illusion of Cultural Identity, op. cit.*, p. 177.

Chapter 2   *From Inflammatory Discourse to Sacrificial Violence*

1. Norbert Elias, *The Civilising Process: Sociogenetic and Psychogenetic Investigations*, Oxford, Blackwell, 1994.

2. Jonathan Fletcher, 'The Theory of Decivilizing Processes and the case of Nazi Mass Murder', *Amsterdams Sociologisch Tijdschrift*, 1994. See also (in French), S. Mennell, 'L'envers de la médaille: les processus de décivilisation', in A. Garrigou and B. Lacroix (eds), *Norbert Elias, La politique et l'histoire*, Paris, La Découverte, 1997, pp. 213–35.

3. Zygmunt Bauman, *Modernity and The Holocaust, op.cit.*,

4. Abram de Swaan, 'La décivilisation, l'extermination et l'Etat', in Yves Bonny, Jean-Manuel De Quieroz and Erik Neveu (eds), *Norbert Elias et la théorie de la civilisation*, Presses Universitaires de Rennes, 2003, pp. 63–73.

5. Even though the meaning assigned here to this word is close to that attributed to it by Jacques Julliard and Michel Winock through the notion of commitment: 'intellectuals are not merely those who sign petitions. They are people who, via this action, mean to offer society at large an analysis, a direction, a moral framework that their earlier works qualify them to undertake. ... By convention it is assumed that those who engage in intellectual activities (the arts, science, literature, philosophy), justified or not, are inclined to be familiar with the general ideals concerning society or how it is managed'. See Jacques Julliard and Michel Winock, *Dictionnaire des intellectuels français*, Paris, Le Seuil, 1996, p. 12.

6. Ian Kershaw, *Hitler, op.cit.*, p. 23.

7. Works in English include. *A Time of Death*, trans. New York, Harcourt Brace Jovanovich, 1983.

8. Quoted by Paul Garde, *Vie et mort de la Yougoslavie*, Paris, Fayard, 1992, p. 54.

9. Mirko Grmek (ed.), *Le nettoyage ethnique. Documents historiques sur une idéologie serbe*, Paris, Fayard, 1993, p. 251.

10. Quoted by Gérard Prunier, *The Rwanda Crisis: History of a Genocide*, London, Hurst, 1995, pp. 45–6. In Kinyarwanda, *Muhutu* and *Mututsi* are the generic terms used for Hutu and Tutsi. *Bahutu* is the plural of Hutu and *Batutsi* the plural of Tutsi.

11. See Julie Mertus' study, *Kosovo: How Myths and Truths Started a War*, Berkeley, University Califronia Press, 1999.

12. René Lemarchand, 'Comparing the Killing Fields: Rwanda, Cambodia and Bosnia' in Steven L.B. Jansen (ed.), *Genocide: Cases, comparisons and Contemporary Debates*, Copenhagen, Danish Center for Holocaust and Genocide Studies, 2003, pp. 141–73.

13. Author of a work on anatomy named after himself, he became Dean, then Rector, of the faculty of Medicine in Vienna following Hitler's accession to power.

14. The first, head of the neuro-psychiatric hospital in Sibenik (on the Dalmatian coast) started his dazzling career in 1988 with prolific writing and speeches in which religious, nationalist and psychoanalytic references were all thrown in together; the second was to take over leadership of the nationalist party (the PDS) and ultimately become the most popular Bosno-Serb political leader.

15. Robert Ian Moore, *The Formation of a Persecuting Society: Power and Deviance in Western Europe, 950–1250*, Oxford, Blackwell, 1987.

16. Quoted by Jean Hatzfeld in *Into the Quick of Life. The Rwandan Genocide: The Survivors Speak*. Trans. Gerry Feehily, London, Serpent's Tail, 2005, p. 78.

17. Arlette Farge, 'Le parcours d'une historienne. Entretien avec Laurent Vidal', dans *Genèses*, no. 48, Sept. 2002, pp. 115–35.

18. Interview with Ian Kershaw, 'L'Allemagne rêvait d'un grand homme', in *L'Histoire*, Jan.–March 2003, pp. 60–3.

19. Vesna Pesic, 'La guerre pour les Etats nationaux', in N. Popov (ed.), *Radiographie d'un nationalisme. Les racines serbes du conflit yougoslave*, Paris, Ed. de l'Atelier/ Ed. Ouvrières, 1998, pp. 45–6.

20. John Allcock, *Explaining Yugoslavia, op. cit.*, pp. 430–1.

21. Jean-R Hubert, *La Toussaint rwandaise et sa répression*, Brussels, Académie Royale des Sciences d'Outre-Mer, 1965.

22. Claudine Vidal 'Le génocide des rwandais Tutsi: cruauté délibérée et logique de haine' in Françoise Héritier, *De la violence*, vol. I, Paris, Editions Odile Jacob, 1996, p. 339.

23. In 1961, Rwanda had 2,800,000 inhabitants. The Tutsi, representing 15 per cent of the population, numbered around 420,000, some 120,000 of whom had already chosen exile by the end of 1963.

24. Aaron Segal, *Massacre in Rwanda*, London, The Fabian Society, 1964 and Luc Deusch, 'Massacres collectifs au Rwanda?' Brussels, *Synthèses*, 1964, pp. 418–26.

25. André Guichaoua (ed.), *Les crises politiques au Burundi et au Rwanda (1993–1994)*, Paris, Karthala, 1995, p. 22.

26. André Guichaoua, *Destins paysans et politiques agraires en Afrique centrale*, Vol. 1, *L'ordre paysan des hautes terres du Burundi et du Rwanda*, Paris, L'Harmattan, 1989.

27. Peter Uvin, *Aiding Violence. The Development Enterprise in Rwanda*. West Hartford, Kumarian Press, 1998. Uvin uses the term of "structural violence" suggested by Johan Galtung in "Violence, Peace and Peace Research", *Journal of Peace Research*, 6, 1, 1969.

28. The historian appeals here to the notion of 'charisma' as developed by the German sociologist Max Weber. See Ian Kershaw, *Hitler, op.cit.*

29. Milosevic's father, a priest in the Orthodox church (excommunicated after 1945 for having denounced his colleagues to the new authorities), ended his days by committing suicide. A few years later, his mother (a teacher, and an extremely authoritative woman) also committed suicide. See Adam Le Bor, *Milosevic, A biography*, Bloomsbury, London, 2002, pp. 26–7 (father's suicide) and pp. 36–7 (mother's suicide).

30. Hearing at the International Criminal Tribunal for the Former Yugoslavia, 31 Aug. 2004, the Hague.

31. This appeal was made by the President Kayibanda to Rwandan émigrés and refugees abroad, in Kigali on 11 March 1964 (document communicated by Marcel Kabanda).

32. Radé Veljanovski, 'Le revirement des médias audio-visuals' in N. Popov (ed.), *Radiographie d'un nationaisme, op. cit.*, pp. 299 ff.

33. See Jean-François Dupaquier in Jean-Pierre Chrétien (ed.), Rwanda: *Les médias du génocide*, Paris, Ed. Karthala, 1995, pp. 29 (republished in 2003).

34. Joseph Krulic, 'Réflexions sur la singularité serbe', *Le Débat*, no. 107, Nov.–Dec. 1999, pp. 97–117, and Jordane Bertrand, *Rwanda. L'opposition démocratique avant le génocide (1990–1994) le piège de l'Histoire*, Paris, Karthala, 2000.

35. Quoted in L. Gayer and A. Jaunait, 'Discours de guerre contre dialogues de paix. Les cas de l'ex-Yougoslavie et du Rwanda', *Cultures et Conflits*, 40 (I). See also Philippe Braud, *Violences politiques*, Paris, Le Seuil, 2004.

36. Galatians 6:10.

37. Dietrich Bonhoeffer, 'Die Kirche vor der Judenfrage' in *Berlin 1932–1933*, Christian Kaiser Verlag, Munich, 1997, pp. 349–58, pp. 350–4. Partial English translation 'The Church and the Jewish Question' in *A Testament to Freedom: The Essential Writings of Dietrich Bonhoeffer*, Geffrey B. Kelly and F. Burton Nelson (eds), New York, HarperCollins, 1990, 1995, pp. 130–1. I would like to register here my gratitude to Andrea Tam, who introduced me to this unpublished work, translated by her into French.

38. The Law for Restoration of a Professional Civil Service, promulgated 7 April 1933, was also applicable to civil servants employed by the Church. The result was that the Church had to refuse from that point on to employ or hire Jewish-Christian priests; this is what Bonhoeffer referred to as the 'Aryan paragraph'.

39. Karl Barth adds: 'For a very long time I have felt personally guilty for not also having defended it during the Kirchenkampf as being a decisive question, at least not publicly (for instance in the two theological declarations of Barmen I wrote in 1934)'. Quoted by Andrea Tam, 'Dietrich Bonhoeffer et la question juive', *Les engagements catholique et protestant contre le nazisme en France et en Allemagne, Journée d'Etudes du CIERA*, Paris, 21 May 2003.

40. Saul Friedlander, *Nazi Germany and the Jews*, vol. I, *op. cit.*, p. 41.

41. On this point see the qualified, but uncompromising, work by Michael Phayer, *The Catholic Church and the Holocaust, 1930–1965*, Bloomington, Indiana University Press, 2000.

42. Radmila Radic, 'L'Eglise et la question serbe' in N. Popov (ed.), *Radiographie d'un nationalisme, op. cit.*, p. 137.

43. Ibid., p. 147. Branimir Anzulovic's book also shows how cultural myths or religious beliefs have been reinterpreted in this way by champions of the revival of nationalism so as to vindicate their politics in the eyes of the greatest number: see Branimir Anzulovic, *Heavenly Serbia: From Myth to Genocide*, London, Hurst, 1999.

44. Ibid., p. 162.

45. Quoted by Jean-Pierre Chrétien, *L'Afrique des grands lacs. Deux mille ans d'histoire, op. cit.*, p. 264.

46. Véronique Avril, *L'Eglise, le Rwanda et la décolonisation. Influences et alliances*, Mémoire de DEA de l'Institut d'Etudes Politiques de Grenoble, 1996–1997, 175 pp.

47. Alison Des Forges (ed.), *Leave None to Tell the Story, op. cit.*, p. 44.

48. Guy Theunis, 'Le rôle de l'Eglise dans les événements récents' in André Guichaoua (ed.), *Les crises politiques au Burundi et au Rwanda (1993–1994), op. cit.*, p. 295.

49. René Girard, *Violence and the Sacred*, Patrick Gregory transl. Baltimore, Johns Hopkins University Press, 1979, p. 31. (*La violence et le sacré*, Paris, Grasset, 1972).

50. Custom that consisted in ritually loading all Israel's sins on to a goat and then hunting it down in the desert.

51. Paul Veyne, *Les Grecs ont-ils cru à leurs mythes?*, Paris, Le Seuil, 1983.

52. See for example Martin Broszat, Eike Frohlich *et al.*, *Bayern in Der NZ-Zeit*, 6 vols, Munich, Oldenbourg, 1977–1983. Tone Bringa, *Being Muslim the Bosnian Way: Identity and Community in a Central Bosnian village*, Princeton University Press, 1995. Danielle de Lame, *Une colline entre mille où le calme avant la tempête. Transformations et blocages du Rwanda rural*, Tervuren, Musée Royal de l'Afrique Central, 1996.

53. Etienne de La Boétie, *The Politics of Obedience: The Discourse of Voluntary Servitude*, introd. by Murray N. Rothbard; translated by Harry Kurz, Montreal and New York, Black Rose Books, 1997.

54. Pierre Aycoberry, *La Société allemande sous le IIIe Reich*, Paris, Le Seuil, 1998.

55. Alexis de Tocquevile *The Old Regime and the Revolution*, trans. Alan S. Kahan, University of Chicago Press, 1998, p. 207.

56. Elisabeth Noelle-Neumann, 'The Spiral of Silence: A Theory of Public Opinion', *Journal of Communication*, Spring 1974, p. 44.

57. *Ibid.*

58. Omer Bartov, *Hitler's Army: Soldiers, Nazis, and War in the Third Reich*, Oxford University Press, 1991, p. 112.

59. Helen Fein, *Accounting for Genocide: Victims and survivors of the Holocaust. National Responses and Jewish Victimization during the Holocaust*, New York, The Free Press, 1979, p. 4.

60. Jean Améry, *At the Mind's Limits: Contemplations by a Survivor on Auschwitz and Its Realities*, Bloomington, Indiana University Press, 1980, pp. 94–5.

61. See Jean-François Gossiaux, *Pouvoirs ethniques dans les Balkans*, Paris, PUF, 2002.

62. In these three domains it obeys strict rules of respect and reciprocity, symbolised by the sharing of a sugary cup of coffee between neighbours.

63. Anthony Oberschall, 'The Manipulation of Ethnicity: From Ethnic Cooperation to Violence and War in Yugoslavia', *Ethnic and Racial Studies*, vol. 23, no. 6, Nov. 2000, pp. 982–1001.

64. Danielle de Lame, *Une colline entre mille ou le calme avant la tempête, op. cit.*

65. Xavier Bougarel, *Bosnie: anatomie d'un conflit*, Paris, La Découverte 1996, p. 84.

66. *Ibid.*

67. Léon Poliakov, *Harvest of Hate: The Nazi Program for the Destruction of the Jews of Europe*, Foreword by Reinhold Niebuhr, Westport, CT: Greenwood Press [1971, 1954].

68. David Bankier, *The Germans and the Final Solution: Public Opinion under Nazism*, Oxford, Blackwell, 1992.

Chapter 3 *International Context, War and the Media*

1. Pierre Hassner and Roland Marchal (eds), *Guerres et sociétés. Etat et violence après la Guerre froide*, Paris, Editions Karthala, coll. CERI, 2003.

2. Leo Kuper, *Genocide: Its Political Use in the Twentieth Century*, New Haven, Yale University Press, 1981, p. 161.

3. Rudolf J. Rummel, *Death by Government*, New Brunswick, NJ, Transaction Publishers, 1994. While the means Rummel used to reach these figures produce sometimes questionable results, the scale is probably accurate.

4. Rummel created the word 'democide' made up of 'demos' (in Greek, the people) and 'cide' (kill). The term designates in its spirit the mass murder by a government of a population of at least one million individuals.

5. Mario Bettati, *Le droit d'ingérence. Mutation de l'ordre international*, Paris, Odile Jacob, 1996.

6. See on this point the suggestions made by the high-level panel (including Robert Badinter) in the report *A More Secure World: Our Shared Responsibility*, High-Level Panel on Threats, Challenges and Change, New York, United Nations, 2004, which can be viewed at http://www.un.org/secureworld/

7. Who in fact, at the Fifth Conference for the Unification of Penal Law held in Madrid in 1934, recommended making punishable what he called 'acts of barbarity', defined as 'an act of oppression and destruction against individual members of a social, religious or racial collectivity', as well as 'acts of vandalism' defined as the 'systematic and organized destruction of the art and cultural heritage in which the unique genius and achievement of a collectivity are revealed in fields of science, arts and literature'.

8. For example, Robert Hayden during round table discussions on the theme of Michael Mann's book on the occasion of the 10th World Convention of the *Association for the Study of Nationalities* at Columbia University, New York (16 April 2005).

9. Marc Levene, 'Why is the 20th Century the Century of Genocide?', *Journal of World History*, vol. 11, no. 2, 2000, pp. 305–36.

10. Norman M. Naimark, *Fires of Hatred: Ethnic Cleansing in Twentieth-Century Europe*, Cambridge, Harvard University Press, 2001.

11. Carnegie Endowment for International Peace, *Reports of the International Commission to Inquire into the Causes and Conduct of the Balkan Wars*, Washington, DC, 1914, p. 73.

12. Arnold J., Toynbee, *Armenian Atrocities: The Murder of a Nation*, first published by Hodder Stoughton, 1916, republished by Fawcett Publishing 1999, 124 pp.

13. Eric Hobsbawm, *Nations and Nationalism since 1780: Programme, Myth, Reality*, Cambridge University Press, 1990, p. 133.

14. Cf. Rogers Brubaker, 'Aftermaths of Empire and the Unmixing of Peoples: Historical and Comparative Perspectives', *Ethnic and Racial Studies*, 18 (2), April 1995, pp. 189–218.

15. Eric Hobsbawm, *Nations and Nationalism since 1780, op. cit.*, p. 133.

16. Analysed by Mirko Grmek, Marc Gjidara and Neven Simac in *Le Nettoyage ethnique. Documents historiques sur une idéologie serbe, op.cit.*, p. 150.

17. Jean-Pierre Chrétien, 'ethnicité et politique. Les crises du Rwanda et du Burundi depuis l'indépendance' in *Guerres mondiales et Conflits contemporains*, no. 181, spring 1996, p. 116. See also Claudine Vidal's article, 'Situations ethniques au Rwanda' in J.L Amselle and E. M'Bokolo, *Au cœur de l'ethnie*, Paris, La Découverte, 1985, pp. 167–84.

18. René Lemarchand, *Burundi: Ethnic Conflict and Genocide*, Cambridge University Press, 1997.

19. To learn more about the complex story of Rwandan refugees, see in particular José Kagabo and Théo Karabayinga, 'Les réfugiés, de l'exil au retour armé', *Les Temps modernes*, 1995, pp. 63–90.

20. Led by Omer Bartov, the interdisciplinary and international research programme '*Borderlands: Ethnicity, Identity, and Violence in the Shatter-Zone of Empires Since 1848*' explores the origin and manifestations of ethnic, religious and social violence in frontier zones of Central, Eastern, and South-Eastern Europe, and of the emergence of nationalism from the 19th century up till the present time, including the Holocaust. The programme is coordinated by the Watson Institute for International Studies at Brown University in the United States and can be consulted at http://www.watsoninstitute.org/borderlands/region.cfm.

21. Paul Garde, *Les Balkans*, 2nd edition, Paris, Flammarion, Coll. Dominos, 1996, p. 57.

22. Ivo Andric, *The Bridge on the Drina*, University of Chicago Press, 1977.

23. The growth of this Hutu political opposition and its subsequent failure is explored in the book by Jordane Bertrand previously referred to, *Rwanda. Le piège de l'histoire, op. cit.*

24. Created in May 1990, *Kangura* published in its December issue a portrait of Mitterrand entitled: 'Un véritable ami du Rwanda. Et c'est dans le malheur que les véritables amis se découvrent'. It was in this same issue that the ten bahutu 'commandments' were also printed. Cited in Jean-Pierre Chrétien (ed.), *Les médias du génocide, op. cit.*, p. 141.

25. For an analysis of the parliamentary commission's enquiry report on France's role in Rwanda (a commission created in 1998 and chaired by Paul Quilès) see Marc Le Pape, 'Le Rwanda au Parlement: enquête sur la tragédie rwandaise', *Esprit*, May 1999, pp. 81–92. The journalist Patrick de Saint-Exupéry's more incisive point of view (he was convinced that France had gone as far as to provide assistance to those responsible for the genocide of April–June 1994) can also be consulted in *L'inavouable. La France au Rwanda*, Paris, Editions des Arènes, 2004. More recently, the *Survie* association published the works of the 'Commission d'Enquête Citoyenne' on France's involvement in the Rwanda genocide: Coret Laure, Vershave François-Xavier, *L'horreur qui nous prend au*

visage. L'Etat français et le génocide au Rwanda. Rapport de la commission d'enquête citoyenne, Paris, Karthala, 2005.

26. Alison Des Forges (ed.), *Leave None to Tell the Story, op. cit.*, p. 65.

27. International Criminal Tribunal for the Former Yugoslavia, Milosevic court case, hearing on 23 Oct. 2003.

28. Ernst Nolte, *Der europäische Burgerkrieg, 1917–1945. Nationalsozialismus und Bolschewismus*, Berlin, Propyläen Verlag, 1987.

29. Ch. IV, *Ibid.* which includes a section about the 'image of the self and the image of the other in literature and propaganda'.

30. Somewhat as Milosevic and Tudjman later tried to reach agreement about dividing up Bosnia-Herzegovina.

31. Ian Kershaw, *Hitler*, Profiles in Power series, *op. cit.*, p. 144.

32. See on this subject the memoirs of the last American ambassador in Yugoslavia, Warren Zimmermann, *Origins of a Catastrophe: Yugoslavia and its Destroyers, America's Last Ambassador Tells What Happened and Why*, New York, Times Books, 1996.

33. Quoted by Alison Des Forges, *Leave None to Tell the Story, op. cit.*, p. 148.

34. Jean-Pierre Chrétien, 'Le noeud du génocide rwandais', *Esprit*, no. 7, June 1999.

35. Stephen Smith, 'France-Rwanda. L'évirat colonial et abandon dans la région des grands lacs' in André Guichaoua (ed.), *Les crises politiques au Burundi et au Rwanda (1993–1994), op. cit.*, p. 452.

36. Ian Kershaw, *Hitler, op. cit.*, p. 124.

37. Quoted by Dominique Vidal, *Les historiens allemands relisent la Shoah*, Brussels, Editions Complexe, 2002, pp. 43–5.

38. Rita Thalmann and Emmanuel Feinermann, *Crystal Night*, trans. Gilles Cremonesi, London, Thames and Hudson, Holocaust Library, New York, 1974, p. 141.

39. *Ibid.*, p. 158.

40. *La Suisse, le national-socialisme et la Seconde Guerre Mondiale*, final report of the Bergier Commission, April 2002, p. 480. See also J.C. Favez (ed.), *Nouvelle histoire de la Suisse et des Suisses*, Lausanne, Payot, 3 vols, 1982–3.

41. Rita Thalmann and Emmanuel Feinermann, *Crystal Night, op. cit.*, p. 24.

42. See also what Paul Garde has to say on this subject in *Vie et mort de la Yougoslavie, op.cit.*

43. Sidney Tarrow developed his theory principally from studies of the years of social crisis in Italy at the end of the 1960s. His thesis sets out to measure the degree of openness and vulnerability of a political system to social movements. See Sidney Tarrow, *Power in Movements: Social Movements, Collection Action and Politics*, Cambridge University Press, 1994.

44. Martin Van Creveld, *The Transformation of War*, New York, The Free Press, 1991, p. 163.

45. Joanna Bourke, *An Intimate History of Killing; Face-to-Face Killing in Twentieth-Century Warfare*, London, Granta Books, 1999. Annette Becker and Stéphane Audoin-Rouzeau, *14–18. Retrouver la guerre*, Paris, Gallimard, 2000.

46. Thucydides, *The History of the Peloponnesian War*, Book V, Penguin Classics, 1954.

47. For example, Frank Chalk and Kurt Jonassohn, *The History and Sociology of Genocide, op.cit.*

48. François-René de Chateaubriand, *Mémoires d'outre-tombe*, volume 2, Paris, Librairie Générale Française, 1973, p. 102.

49. John Horne, 'Civilian Populations and Wartime Violence', *International Social Science Journal*, no. 174, Dec. 2002.

50. John Horne and Alan Kramer, *German Atrocites, 1914: A History of Denial*, New Haven, Yale University Press, 2001.

51. Erich Ludendorff, *The Nation at War*, London, Hutchinson, 1936.

52. See Dominique David, 'Douet ou le dernier imaginaire', *Stratégiques*, 49, no. 1, 1991 and his article in Thierry de Monbrial and Jean Klein (eds), *Dictionnaire de Stratégie*, Paris, PUF, 2000, pp. 194–5.

53. John Horne, 'Civilian Populations and Wartime Violence', *op. cit.* p. 487. At the same moment that duke of Brunswick and an army of 80,000 invaded revolutionary France (the taking of Longwy, 22 Aug. 1792), the city of Paris in a state of frenzy, designated refractory priests as traitors to the 'fatherland in peril'. Having already been declared suspect by the law passed on 27 April 1792, some of them were arrested at the end of August in Paris and in the provinces. When the news of the taking of Verdun by the Prussians (1 September) arrived in the capital, the collective psychosis of betrayal from within cast them in the role of representatives of a clergy believed to be linked through multiple interests to the nobility preparing to crush the Revolution. In this climate of psychosis, some were massacred between 2 and 5 September in the capital and in the provinces (Meaux, Provins). The official death toll was 1,100 of whom 260 were ecclesiastics living in Paris (115 at Carmes, 67 at St Firmin, 22 in the abbey).

54. Omer Bartov, *Hitler's Army, op.cit.*, p. 83. During the Russian campaign, it has been estimated that the Germans captured more than 5,700,000 Red Army soldiers, of whom 3,300,000 were killed.

55. Mirko Grmek, 'Un mémoricide', *Le Figaro*, 19 Dec. 1991.

56. Following a declaration of independence in the Bosnian parliament, Europe judged that this could not be legitimately acceptable without a referendum. This was organised on 28 February and 1 March 1992, and with the decision confirmed on 6 April, Bosnia was then able to enter the United Nations, being recognised by a number of member states, including America.

57. Xavier Bougarel, *Bosnie. Anatomie d'un conflit, op.cit.*, p. 13.

58. An example of this is the book published by the French journalist Pierre Pean who strongly supported the thesis that the RPF was responsible for the shooting down of the plane. This book has provoked very heated debate in France. Pierre Pean, *Noires fureurs, blancs menteurs: Rwanda 1990–1994*, Paris, Editions Mille et Une Nuits, 2005. In addition, the investigation led by anti-terrorism judge Jean-Louis Bruguière, following a complaint filed by the families of French victims of this attack, accused Paul Kagamé of having ordred it, purposely unleashing the massares that followed, enabling him to come to power.

On this basis, on 23 November 2006 the magistrate issued nine international arrest warrants for nine of Kagamé's closest aides and recommended that the UN bring Kagamé before the International Criminal Tribunal for Rwanda (ICTR). But as President of Rwanda, he enjoys immunity. The following day, 24 November, Rwanda broke off diplomatic ties with France.

59. Gérard Prunier's hearings before parliamentary commission of the Belgian Senate, concerning the events in Rwanda, 11 June 1997.

60. The figure given here is taken from here the minimal assessment submitted by the Human Rights Watch team in 1999 in *Leave None to Tell the Story, op.cit.*, p. 15. But this figure is arguable, and has often been revised upwards. Some authors speak of 800,000 deaths, or even 1 million or more. Cf. for example, the work of journalists Colette Braeckman, *Rwanda. Histoire d'un génocide*, Paris, Fayard, 1994 and Linda Melvern, *Conspiracy to Murder: The Rwandan Genocide*, London and New York, Verso, 2004. In fact, assessments of the number of victims of mass murder are frequently subject to controversy. In this instance one of the main problems is the reliability of the 1991 census of the Tutsi population in Rwanda.

61. Abdul Ruzibiza, *Rwanda. L'histoire secrète*, Paris, Editions du Panama, 2005, 400 p.

62. Pierre Péan has also argued in support of the theory of a 'double genocide', giving the figure of 280,000 Tutsis slain compared to over a million Hutus (cf. *Noirs terreurs, blancs menteurs, op.cit.*, p. 276). But he gives no definition of what he calls 'genocide' or any justification for these figures.

63. Branka Magas and Ivo Zanic (eds), *The War in Croatia and Bosnia-Herzegovina 1991–1995*, London, Frank Cass, 2001, p. 334.

64. Ervin Staub, *The Roots of Evil: The Origins of Genocide and Other Group Violence*, Cambridge University, Press, 1989, p. 239.

65. Christian Ingrao, 'Violence de guerre, violence génocide: les Einsatzgruppen', in Stéphane Audoin-Rouzeau, Annette Becker, Henry Rousso (eds), *La violence de guerre*, Brussels, Editions Complexe, 2002.

66. Quoted by Christian Gerlach, *Die Wannsee-Konferenz. Das Schicksal der deutschen Juden und Hitlers politische Grundsatzentscheidung all Juden Europas zu ermorden*, Hamburger Edition HIS Verlag, 1998.

67. In March 1999 NATO bombardments in Serbia resulted in just such a situation. Enquiries conducted by the International War Crimes Tribunal for ex-Yugoslavia were able to prove this after the fact, so it was established that as soon as the bombing started, the Serbs executed Albanian prisoners in the Dubrava prison in Kosovo, alleging subsequently that they were killed by American bombs.

68. Report quoted by Yehuda Bauer, 'When Did They Know', *Midstream*, 4, 1968, pp. 54–5 and 57–8.

69. Walter Laqueur, *The Terrible Secret: An investigation into the suppression of information about Hitler's 'Final Solution'*, London, Weidenfeld and Nicolson, 1980, p. 3.

70. *Ibid.*, pp. 74–5.

71. Renée Poznanski, 'Que savait-on dans le monde?' in Stéphane Courtois and Adam Rayski, *Qui savait quoi? L'extermination des juifs (1941–1945)*, Paris, La Découverte, 1987, p. 35.

72. *Ibid.*, p. 37.

73. See Léon Poliakov, *Le procès de Jérusalem*, Paris, Calman-Lévy, 1963, p. 252.

74. David S. Wyman, *The Abandonment of the Jews*, New York, New Press, 1998.

75. With regard to the emergence of this expression and its uses by Western journalists and activists, see the highly original work of linguist Alice Krieg-Planque, *'Purification ethnique'. Une formule et son histoire*, Paris, CNRS Editions, 2003.

76. Roy Gutman, *A Witness to Genocide*, Rockport, Mass., Element Books, 1993.

77. David Rieff, *Slaughterhouse: Bosnia and the Failure of the West*, Simon and Schuster, New York, 1996.

78. Pierre Hassner, 'Les impuissances de la communauté internationale' in Véronique Nahoum-Grappe (ed.), *Vukovar-Sarajevo. La guerre en ex-Yougoslavie*, Paris, Esprit, 1993, pp. 86–118.

79. One of the best analyses of this 'consensual logic of force' I have found is provided by Thierry Tardy, in *La France et la gestion des conflits yougoslaves (1991–1995)*, Brussels, Bruylant, 1999.

80. On the subject of the setting up of this Tribunal, see the well-documented book by Pierre Hazan, *La justice face à la guerre*, Paris, Stock, 2000.

81. On this subject the title of James Gow's book perfectly summarises this analysis, see James Gow, *Triumph of the Lack of Will: International Diplomacy and the Yugoslav War*, London, Hurst, 1997.

82. Quoted by Pierre Hassner, 'Institutions, Etats, sociétés, une culpabilité partagée' in *L'ex-Yougoslavie en Europe. De la faillite des démocraties au processus de paix*, Paris, L'Harmatan, 1996, pp. 57–8.

83. The Serbs seized the opportunity to accuse Bosnian Muslims of having bombarded themselves in order to create a 'media event' to launch a movement of international sympathy in their favour.

84. David Binder, 'Anatomy of a massacre', *Foreign Policy*, Winter 1994–5, no. 97, pp. 70–8.

85. Danielle Birck, 'La télévision et le Rwanda, ou le génocide déprogrammé', *Les Temps Modernes*, no. 583, July–Aug. 1995, pp. 181–97.

86. 'One of the news editors told me in his usual frank tone: "Cover the evacuation of the French, then come home. We're not there to report on Blacks killing each other; anyhow, nobody cares. You go, just do that, and don't take any risks".' See 'Retour sur images' by Philippe Boisserie in *Les Temps Modernes, op. cit.*, p. 201.

87. Among these was his wife, Agathe, who fled to France.

88. In France, 11 and 12 April, three articles by special envoys appeared: Jean-Philippe Ceppi, 'Kigali livré à la fureur des tueurs hutu' (*Libération*, 11 April); Renaud Girard, 'Rwanda. Voyage sur la route de l'horreur' (*Le Figaro*, 12 April) and Jean Hélène, 'Le Rwanda a feu et à sang' (*Le Monde*, 12 April).

89. This *Le Monde* headline is an example of the first type of treatment: 'Forces gouvernementales et rebelles se disputent le contrôle de la capitale' (14 April)

while the headlines in *Libération* and *Figaro* (see the previous footnote) are representative of the second approach.

90. Marc Le Pape, 'Des journalistes au Rwanda. L'histoire immédiate d'un génocide', *Les Temps modernes*, no. 583, July–Aug. 1995, *op. cit.*, p. 175.

91. Johanna Siméant, 'Qu'a-t-on vu quand on ne voyait rien? Sur quelques aspects de la couverture télévisuelle du génocide au Rwanda par TFI et France 2 (April–June 1994)', in Le Pape, Marc, Siméant, Johanna and Vidal, Claudine (eds), *Crises extrêmes. Face aux massacres, guerres et génocides*, Paris, La Découverte, 2006.

92. The same scenes was always shown. These were images taken from afar by a telephoto lens: bodies are seen floating in the Kagera River, or lying beside ransacked houses, the wounded being set upon by the killers wielding clubs and machetes.

93. Quoted by Linda Melvern, *A People Betrayed. The Role of the West in Rwanda's Genocide*, London, Zed Books, 2000, p. 190.

94. One should read Major-General Dallaire's book to grasp fully the sense of disaster that was to inhabit this man, in this situation where he was condemned to powerlessness, an experience that profoundly upset his personal life. See General Romeo Dallaire, *Shake Hands with the Devil: The Failure of Humanity in Rwanda*, New York, Carroll Graf, 2004.

95. Samantha Power, *A Problem from Hell: America and the Age of Genocide*, New York, Basic Books, 2002.

96. *New York Times*, 24 May 1994, p. 1.

97. But, as Samantha Power specifies, not the journalists who channelled the theme of ancestral hatred.

98. Quoted by Samantha Power, *A Problem from Hell. op. cit.*, pp. 371–2.

99. *Ibid.*, p. 196.

100. I have borrowed this expression from Rony Brauman's book *Rwanda. Un génocide en direct.*, Paris, Arléa, 1995, even though its applicability is debatable. In effect the idea of 'live' assumes that radio and television teams covering the event are on the ground—as they are, for example, for an international sporting event. Clearly this is not the case for Rwanda. But the idea of 'live coverage' can nevertheless be upheld because it was possible for journalists from the international press arriving on the scene to quickly bring to light massacres being perpetrated as they spread through the country; and that these reports were picked up quite regularly by the audiovisual media.

101. Edouard Balladur, 'Opération Turquoise: courage et dignité', *Le Figaro*, 18 Aug. 2004. In this article Mr Balladur claims also to be firmly opposed to another scenario: that of a military operation the objective of which would have been to take control of Kigali and so prevent the victory of the RPF.

102. Steven Livingston, Todd Eachus, 'Humanitarian crises and US Foreign Policy: Somalia and the CNN effect reconsidered', *Political Communication*, 12, 4, 1995, pp. 413–29.

103. Johanna Siméant, 'Qu'a-t-on vu quand on ne voyait rien? Sur quelques aspects de la couverture télévisuelle du génocide au Rwanda par TFI et France 2 (April–June 1994)', *op.cit.*

104. Pierre Hassner, *La terreur et l'Empire. La violence et la paix* II, Paris, Seuil, 2003, p. 69.

105. Nicholas J. Wheeler, *Saving Strangers: Humanitarian Intervention and International Society*, Oxford, New York, Oxford University Press, 2000.

106. Richard Holbrooke, *To End a War*, New York, Modern Library, 1999, p. 11. In this accident four French Blue Helmets also died.

107. Samantha Power, *A Problem from Hell*, *op. cit.*, p. 508.

Chapter 4 *The Dynamics of Mass Murder*

1. The next chapter will pursue this line of inquiry in seeing the problem from the point of view of individuals turned mass murderers.

2. Apart from the works of Donald Horowitz already quoted, I am thinking also of those of Steven I. Wilkinson, *Votes and Violence: Electoral Competition and Ethnic riots in India*, Cambridge University Press, 2004. He shows that massacres between Hindus and Muslims tend to escalate just before elections because those who initiate them hope to reap the benefits in terms of votes.

3. Former President of the *Conseil National du Développement* (C.N.D.), i.e. the Rwandan Parliament.

4. In this the analytical framework I used in my research on resistance groups is again useful: it is the stance of the political power unseated by the occupying power that gives the population its keynote, encouraging it to either to collaborate with the occupation authorities or resist them. See in particular Ch. IV 'The question of legitimacy', pp. 47–61 in Jacques Semelin, *Unarmed against Hitler: Civilian Resistance in Europe 1939–1943*, Westport, CT, Praeger, 1993.

5. Mark Roseman, *The Wannsee Conference and the Final Solution: A Reconsideration*, New York, Henry Holt, 2002.

6. Quoted by Dominique Vidal, *Les historiens allemands relisent la Shoah, op.cit.*, p. 118.

7. Götz Aly and Susanne Heim, *Vordenker der Vernichtung. Auschwitz und die deutschen Pläne für eine neue europäische Ordnung*, Hoffman und Campe, Hamburg, 1991.

8. The *Akazu* or '*little house*' refers to a network of people working at the sides of the Rwandan President, all originally from his own region (in the North of Rwanda). His wife and her family were also part of the group. When needed, this network turned directly to Colonel Bagosora, related, moreover, to the President's wife.

9. Cf Filip Reyntjens, 'Akazu, 'escadrons de la mort' et autres 'Réseau Zéro'. Un historique des résistances au changement politique depuis 1990' in André Guichaoua *et al.*, *Les crises politiques au Burundi et au Rwanda (1993–1994), op.cit.*, pp. 265–73.

10. Reported by Alison Des Forges, *Leave None to Tell the Story, op. cit.*, p. 62.

11. *Ibid.*, p. 110.

12. Leon Mugesera provides a typical profile of this inflammatory intellectual as described in Chapter II. Ultimately his speech repeats the extremely threatening content of President Kayibanda's 11 March 1963 'prophecy'. But its expression is much less pompous than that of former Rwandan President,

Mugesera, who had a gift for talking to the people in a very direct style. All the themes he delivers are designed to arouse their destructive passion: the threat of invasion, subversion of religion, destruction of the social tie, bestialisation of the enemy, etc. This speech alone warrants an anthropological and linguistic analysis in Kinyarwandais. It is the very prototype of the discourse that kills in advance with words. Cf. Alison Des Forges, *Leave None to Tell the Story, op. cit.*, pp. 85–6.

13. *Ibid.*, pp. 106–7.
14. Alison Des Forges, *Leave None to Tell the Story, op. cit.*, p. 817.
15. *Ibid.*, p. 134.
16. The journalist Linda Melvern specifies that these machetes (and other agricultural tools that could be used as weapons), mainly imported from China, arrived in Rwanda in eighteen different consignments. Along with the purchase of ammunition, how could Rwanda, one of the poorest countries in the world, have afforded such expenditure, estimated at 100 million dollars? By embezzling World Bank funds, she claims, the Rwandan economy having been since 1990 subject to an IMF structural adjustment programme. Cf Linda Melvern, *Conspiracy to Murder: the Rwandan genocide,* London, New York, Verso, 2004, p. 56.
17. Quoted by Jean-Pierre Chrétien (ed.), *Rwanda. Les médias du génocide, op. cit.*, p. 300.
18. See for example Kalevi J. Holsti, *The State, War, and the State of War,* Cambridge University Press, 1996 or William Zartman (ed.), *Collapsed States: The Disintegration and Restoration of Legitimate Authority,* Boulder, CO, Lynne Rienner, 1995.
19. See Michel Roux, *Les Albanais en Yougoslavie. Minorité nationale, territoire et développement,* Paris, Maison des sciences de l'homme, 1992 and Joël Hubrecht, *Kosovo. Etablir les faits,* Paris, Ed. Esprit, 2001.
20. Interview with Joël Hubrecht (4 Dec. 2003).
21. Joseph Krulic, 'Réflexions sur la singularité serbe', *op.cit.*, p. 111. For an outline of David Easton's theory of political systems refer to David Easton, *A Framework for Political Analysis,* Englewood Cliffs, NJ, Prentice-Hall, 1965.
22. Marina Glamocak *La transition guerrière yougoslave,* Paris, L'Harmattan, 2002.
23. James Gow, *The Serbian Project and its Adversaries: A Strategy of War Crimes,* London, Hurst Co, 2003, p. 12.
24. Tim Judah, *The Serbs: History, Myth and the Destruction of Yugoslavia,* New Haven, Yale University Press, 1997, p. 169.
25. Marina Glamocak, *La transition guerrière, op. cit.*, p. 136.
26. In the eyes of the Serbs, this was the emblem of Pavelic's fascist regime. The Croatian check is in fact a medieval symbol, adopted again in 1991 with a slightly different colour from that of 1941.
27. I discard here the idea put forward by Linda Melvern, that the planning of genocide had begun in October 1990, as she indicates in her chronology in *Conspiracy to Murder: the Rwandan genocide, op. cit.*, pp. 316–17. Although massacres had indeed taken place during this period from the start of the RPF's assault, there is nothing to prove that in Kigali genocide was already being pre-

pared. The recording of massacres from time to time is not synonymous with genocidal intention (Cf. Chapter VI).

28. This is why this notion of *intent* is at the heart of the *Convention on the Prevention and Punishment of the Crime of Genocide* adopted by the UN in 1948. Article 2 starts as follows: 'In the present Convention, genocide means any of the following acts committed with intent to destroy, in whole or in part, a national, ethnical, racial or religious group, as such.' See the key issues arising from this convention in Chapter VI of this book, in the framed excerpt on p. ???.

29. Even though ordinary usage often invites us to, for example when we say 'The United States intends to...'

30. The historian of the Ottoman Empire, Gilles Veinstein, has thus contested their 'genocidal' nature. See 'Trois questions sur un massacre' in *L'Histoire*, no. 187, April 1995, pp. 40–1. This position has aroused lively debate, including a reply from historian Yves Ternon in his book, *Du négationnisme. Mémoire et tabou*, Paris, Ed. Desclée de Brouwer, 1999.

31. Raul Hilberg, *The Destruction of the European Jews*, New York, Holmes and Meier, 1985, 2 vols.

32. Christopher R. Browning, Matthäus Jürgen, *The Origins of the Final Solution: The Evolution of Jewish Nazi Policy (September 1939–March 1942)*, Lincoln, University of Nebraska Press, 2004, p. 309 and ff.

33. Philippe Burrin, *Hitler et les juifs. Genèse d'un génocide*, Paris, Seuil, 1989, p. 169.

34. Following a meeting with Hitler, Himmler noted in his diary on the date in question, the 18 December: 'Jewish question: exterminate like partisans'. See the interpretation offered by Christian Gerlach, *Die Wannsee Konferenz, das Schicksal der Deutschen Juden und Hitlers politische Grundsatzentscheidung...*, *op. cit.*, Hamburger Edition HIS Verlags mbH, 1998.

35. These extracts are taken from Himmler's speech given to the SS generals, in which he made his famous allusion to the extermination of the Jews: 'We must have completed migration of the Jewish people within exactly one year: then there will be none left to wander. They must be totally wiped out, now', quoted by Florent Brayard, *La solution finale de la question juive. La technique, le temps et les catégories de la décisions*, Paris, Fayard, 2004, pp. 16–17.

36. Michael Mann, *The Dark Side of Democracy, op. cit.*, p. 8. To conceptualise this cumulative process, the author has drawn up a series of 'plans' A, B, C, D, etc., that those responsible for ethnic cleansing are supposed to implement, these 'plans' consisting of more and more radical measures against the designated victims. But in trying to apply his plans to the historical cases he treats, Mann himself remarks quite often that his theoretical construction is in the end rather artificial.

37. Raul Hilberg, *The Destruction of the European Jews*, volume 1, New York, Holmes and Meier, 1985, p. 53.

38. Zygmunt Bauman, *Modernity and the Holocaust, op.cit.*

39. Paper presented at Marc Olivier Baruch's seminar at the Ecole des Hautes Etudes en Sciences Sociales (EHESS), 23 Nov. 2003. (See also his book *Nous pouvons vivre sans les juifs. Quand et comment ils décidèrent de la solution finale*, Paris, Perrin, 2005).

40. These units, having first made their appearance during the annexation of Austria, were disbanded twice and then reconstituted before the invasion of Poland and the Soviet Union.

41. See the Avalon Project at Yale Law School, http://www.yale.edu/lawweb/avalon/imt/proc/01-07-46.htm. Viewed 7 Feb. 2006.

42. Omer Bartov, *Hitler's Army, op.cit.*

43. Quoted by Linda Melvern, *Conspiracy to Murder: the Rwandan genocide, op. cit.*, p. 211.

44. Quoted by Linda Melvern, *Conspiracy to Murder: the Rwandan genocide, op. cit.*, p. 191.

45. Alison Des Forges, *Leave None to Tell the Story, op.cit.*, p. 222.

46. Marcel Kabanda, 'Participation populaire à la violence d'Etat. Le cas du Rwanda', paper presented at the seminar *La violence et ses causes*, Paris, 3 Nov. 2003.

47. I refer the reader to my book *La liberté au bout des ondes. Du coup de Prague à la chute du mur de Berlin*, Paris, Belfond, 1997, and the analyses therein of the role the radio played in the Budapest crises in 1956, and in Prague in 1968. In each of these countries the national radios called on the people to resist the Soviet occupying force. In researching the Rwandan RTLM programme, I could not but liken it to the way the Hungarian and Czechoslovak stations had operated during these crises. RTLM also set out to call the people to join a resistance movement, in this case a public appeal to murder the Tutsis.

48. Quoted by Alison Des Forges, *Leave None to Tell the Story, op. cit.*, p. 255.

49. James Gow, *The Serbian Project and its Adversaries, op. cit.*, p. 51.

50. The 'Serbianisation' of the army was also accelerated by the decommissioning of non-Serb officers, or by their departure to early retirement.

51. This dissolution resulted legally from the creation of a new Yugoslavia (Serbia-Montenegro), via the constitution of 27 April 1992.

52. James Gow, *The Serbian Project and its Adversaries, op. cit.*, p. 134.

53. Florence Hartmann, *Milosevic. La diagonale du fou*, Paris, Denoël, 1999, page 206. Bogdanovic was driven to resign following the crushing of the demonstration on 9 March 1991 that left two demonstrators dead. But he remained very active in the corridors of power.

54. See Tim Judah, *The Serbs, op. cit.*, p. 170.

55. This plan was allegedly clearly identified in September 1991, when a secret recording of a conversation between Milosevic and Karadzic was unveiled. See Tim Judah, *The Serbs, op. cit.*, p. 191. But to this day no document has been found confirming the existence of such a plan.

56. See Paul Garde, *Vie et mort de la Yougoslavie, op. cit.*, p. 306.

57. Mark Roseman, *The Wannsee Conference and the Final Solution, op. cit.*, p. 155.

58. Dieter Pohl, *Nationalsozialistische Judenverforlung in Ostgalizien 1941–1944. Organisation und Durchführung eines staatlichen Massenverbrechens*, Studien zur Zeitgeschichte, Oldenbourg, Munich, 1997.

59. Marcel Kabanda 'Participation populaire à la violence d'Etat: le cas du Rwanda', *op.cit.*

60. Cornelia Sorabji, 'Une guerre très moderne. Mémoires identité en Bosnie Herzégovine', *Terrain*, no. 23, Oct. 1994, p. 143.

61. *Ibid.*, pp. 144–5.

62. Note here that the Bosnian Serb government officially recognised this fact in November 2004. The figure of 7,800 victims announced on this occasion by Bernard Fassler, High Representative of the international community, should, according to him, be revised upwards. See *Le Monde*, 10 November 2004.

63. United Nations, *Report of the Secretary-General pursuant to General Assembly Résolution 53/55. The Fall of Srebrenica*, Document A/54/549, 15 Nov. 1999.

64. The Dutch report submitted to the Netherlands Institute of War Documentation, entitled *Srebrenica—a 'safe' area. reconstruction, background, consequences and analyses of the fall of a Safe Area*, can be read on the internet site http://www.srebrenica.nl/en/. The French report written by the Mission d'Information commune sur les événements de Srebrenica, chaired by François Loncle, was published under the title, *Srebrenica, Rapport sur un massacre*, Les documents d'information de l'Assemblée nationale, no. 3413, 2001, Paris, 2 vols. In both cases, if this effort to arrive at the 'truth' was praised by many observers, the results achieved by these commissions of enquiry left many questions unanswered, both because of a lack of cooperation among Defence Ministries in communicating information related to this event, and the impossibility of consulting Serbian archives on the other.

65. See his work in the Appendix of the Dutch report quoted above, and also Ger Duijzings, *History and memory in Eastern Bosnia: Background to the fall of Srebrenica*, Amsterdam, Boom, 2002.

66. One version of this assault was reported in the Benja Luka nationalist daily *Glas Srpski* (The Serbian Voice). This paper reports 49 deaths.

67. Hayat Channel (Sarajevo television) interview with Richard Holbrooke on 10 November 2005. In answer to a question from French journalist Sylvie Matton, he then specified that his instructions came from Tony Lake, Bill Clinton's national security advisor. See *Paris Match*, 2–8 November 2006.

68. Carla del Ponte, 'Seule contre tous', *ibid.*, p. 43.

69. See the hearing of Jean-René Ruez dans *Rapport d'information déposé par la mission d'information commune sur les événement de Srebrenica*, volume II, Paris, Assemblée nationale, 2002, pp. 309–26.

70. Carla del Ponte, 'Seule contre tous', *op. cit.*, p. 44.

71. Quoted by David Rhode, in *Endgame: The Betrayal and Fall of Srebrenica-July 1995*, Boulder, Co, Westview Press, 1997, p. 167. The 'Dahijas rebellion' refers to a Serbian uprising that was brutally repressed by the Turks in 1804.

72. Milosevic's trial led us to believe that he had no special interest in the Srebrenica massacre. The trial of Nazer Oric, sentenced to two years' imprisonment on so June 2006 for 'failing to take steps to prevent the murder and cruel treatment of a number of Serb prisoners in the former UN "safe area"' (http://www.un.org/icty/cases-e/index-e.htm), throws light on how the confrontation throughout this region developed.

73. 'Pessimum facinus auderent pauci, plures vellent, omnes paterentur', quoted by Jan Willem Honig and Norbert Both, *Srebrenica: Record of a War Crime*. London, Penguin Books, 1996.

74. Gustav Janouch, *Conversations with Kafka*, London, Quartet, 1985.
75. Daniel J. Goldhagen, *Hitler's Willing Executioners: Ordinary Germans and the Holocaust*, New York, Random House, 1996.
76. These gruesome illustrations in fact have a large place in Goldhagen's book.
77. Among the more concise critiques, we will cite that of Ch. 5, 'Ordinary Monsters: Perpetrator Motivation and Monocausal Explanations', pp. 122–36, of Omer Bartov's book, *Germany's War and the Holocaust: Disputed Histories*, Ithaca, NY, Cornell University Press, 2003.
78. Daniel Bankier, *The Germans and the Final Solution: Public Opinion under Nazism, op.cit.*
79. The full sermons in French can be found in Yves Ternon and Socrate Helman, *Le massacre des aliénés. Des théoriciens nazis aux praticiens SS*, Tournai, Casterman, 1971.
80. Ian Kershaw, *Popular Opinion and Political Dissent in the Third Reich: Bavaria 1933–1945*, Oxford, Clarendon Press, 1983, p. 277.
81. See the enquiry led by Martin Broszat and Eike Frolich (eds), *Bayern in Der NS-Zeit, op.cit.*
82. Quoted in Michael Pollak, *L'expérience concentrationnaire. Essai sur le maintien de l'identité sociale*, Paris, Ed. Métaillié, 1990, pp. 92–3.
83. Victor Klemperer, *I Will Bear Witness 1942–1945: Diary of the Nazi Years, op. cit.*, p. 48.
84. *Ibid.*, p. 235.
85. Georges Bensoussan, *Histoire de la Shoah*, Paris, PUF, Coll. Que sais-je? 1997, p. 92.
86. RTLM, 3 April 1994, quoted by Alison Des Forges, *Leave None to Tell the Story, op. cit.*, p. 180.
87. Major-General Roméo Dallaire, *Shake Hands with the Devil, op. cit.*
88. Alison Des Forges, *Leave None to Tell the Story, op. cit.*, pp. 245–6.
89. Interview with André Guichaoua (27 May 2003).
90. For a chronology of these events and eye witness reports, see the enquiries led by Rakiya Omaar in *Rwanda: Death, Despair and Defiance*, London, African Rights, 1994.
91. Quoted by Linda Melvern, *Conspiracy to Murder: the Rwandan genocide, op. cit.*, p. 196.
92. See Darryl Li, 'Echoes of violence: considerations on radio and genocide in Rwanda', *Journal of Genocide Research*, vol. 6, no. 1, March 2004, pp. 9–27.
93. I return here to the work of the Laboratoire Communication et Politique of the CNRS, founded by Dominique Wolton and to the excellent journal *Hermès* and its thorough treatment of this question.
94. Danielle de Lame, 'Le génocide rwandais et le vaste monde. Les liens du sang', *Annuaire de l'Afrique des grands lacs*, 1996, *op. cit.*, p. 167. This in-depth research requires, of course, parallel study of these radio programmes in Kinyarwandais.
95. Timothy Longman, 'Genocide and socio-political Change: Massacre in two Rwandan villages', *Journal of Opinion*, vol. XXIII/2, 1995, pp. 18–21.
96. Interview with André Guichaoua (27 May 2003).

97. André Guichaoua, *Rwanda 1994. Les politiques du génocide à Butare*, Paris, Karthala, 2005.

98. Contribution of Pierre-Antoine Braud to the CERI research group 'Faire la paix. Du crime de masse au peacebuliding', 'Lien social, passage au crime de masse et reconstruction' on the CERI website (20 June 1991): www.ceri-sciences-po.org.

99. Jean Hatzfeld, *Machete Season*, New York, Farrar Straus Giroux, 2005.

100. Scott Straus, 'How many perpetrators were there in the Rwandan genocide? An estimate', *Journal of Genocide Research*, vol. 6 (1), March 2004, p. 95. See also by Scott Straus, *The Order of Genocide. Race, Power and War in Rwanda*, Ithaca and London, Cornell University Press, 2006.

101. See Florence Hartmann, *Milosevic: La diagonale du fou, op. cit.*, pp. 271–2.

102. Quoted by Joël Hubrecht, 'Le procès Plavsic, un succès de la justice internationale', *Esprit*, Feb. 2003, p. 138.

103. Slavenka Drakulic, 'L'autisme tragique du peuple serbe', *International Herald Tribune* reprinted in *Courrier International*, 6–14 May 1999.

104. Interview with Jean-Arnault Dérens (22 Sept. 2003), author of *Balkans. La crise*, Paris, Gallimard, 2000.

105. Veljko Kadijevic, *Moje vidjenje raspada. Vojska bez drzave*, Belgrade, Politika, 1993, p. 73, 'My vision of dismantling. An army without a state', p. 108.

106. Marina Glamocak, *La transition guerrière yougoslave, op. cit.*, pp. 117–18.

107. Antony Oberschall, 'The Manipulation of Ethnicity: From Ethnic Co-operation to Violence and War in Yugoslavia', *Ethnic and Racial Studies, op. cit.*, pp. 982–3.

108. Ed Vulliamy, *Seasons in Hell*, London, St Martin's Press, 1994, p. 94.

109. Stathis N. Kalyvas, 'Aspects méthodologiques de la recherche sur les massacres. Le cas de la guerre civile grecque', *Revue Internationale de Politique Comparée*, vol. 8, no. 1, 2001, pp. 23–42.

110. Kupreskic *et al.*, judgement returned 10 Nov. 1998.

111. Marc Bax, 'Warlords, Priests and the Politics of Ethnic Cleansing: A Case Study from Rural Bosnia-Hercegovina', *Ethnic and Racial Studies*, vol. 23, no. 1, 2000, pp. 16–36.

112. See on this subject the enquiry of French anthropologist Elisabeth Claverie, *Les guerres de la Vierge. Anthropologie des apparitions*, Paris, Gallimard, 2003.

113. Bogdan Bogdanovic, 'L'urbicide ritualisé', in Véronique Nahoum-Grappe (ed.), *Vukovar-Sarajevo. La guerre en ex-Yougoslavie, op. cit.*, pp. 33–7.

114. Jean Hatzfeld, *L'ère de la guerre*, Paris, Ed. de l'Olivier, 1994, pp. 56–7. For a more detailed analysis, see John Allcock, 'Rural-urban differences and the break up of Yugolsavia', *Balkanologie*, vol. 6, no. 1–2, Dec. 2002, pp. 101–25.

115. I am thinking here of the exceptional case where Jews from Denmark and Bulgaria were saved, but also of other, less well-known examples. See the ch. 'Civil Resistance Against Genocide' in Semelin, *Unarmed against Hitler, op.cit.*

116. Other villages on this plateau, the Haut Vivarais, joined in hosting refugees, including other groups (such as those 'evacuated' from the east of France, German and Austrian resistance fighters, conscientious objectors working in the Compulsory Labour Service *et al.*). See Patrick Cabanel and Laurent

Jervereau (eds), *La Deuxième Guerre mondiale. Des terres de refuge aux musées*, Vivarais-Lignon, Ed. Sivom, 2003.

117. To all those who saved Jews during the war, in a totally selfless fashion, Israel awards the medal of the Righteous among the Nations. It is engraved with this phrase from the Talmud: 'Whosoever preserves one life—it is as though he has preserved the entire world'.

118. Svetlana Broz, *Good People in an Evil Time: Portraits of Complicity and Resistance in the Bosnian War*, New York, Other Press, 2005.

119. Xavier Bougarel's lecture to the CERI research group, 'From Mass Crime to Peacebuilding', 20 June 2001.

120. Philip Gourevitch, *We Wish to Inform You that Tomorrow We Will Be Killed with our Families: Stories from Rwanda*, New York, Picador, 1999, p. 117.

121. The NGO African Rights published a booklet in 2002 describing the portrait of nineteen of the 'righteous' Rwandans who had selflessly saved Tutsi during the genocide, entitled *Tribute to Courage*, London, African Rights, Aug. 2002.

122. Cf. Gérard Prunier, *The Rwanda Crisis, op. cit.*, p. 307.

123. Jean Hatzfeld, *Dans le nu de la vie, op. cit.*, p. 136.

124. Bruno Bettelheim, *Surviving, and Other Essays*, New York, Knopf, 1979. Although his observations are based on his experience of internment in two Nazi concentration camps (Dachau and Buchenwald) rather than on an extermination camp, and there is clearly a major difference here, this does not seem to me completely to invalidate his analyses.

125. This attack, resulting in sixty-three deaths and more than 200 wounded, immediately gained huge international media coverage. But the investigation launched by the UN showed that in fact the firing came from Serbian positions. The various trials at The Hague touching on this affair have supported this finding.

126. Kalevi J. Holsti, *The State, War, and the State of War, op.cit.*

127. Jean-Pierre Chrétien, *L'Afrique des grands lacs, op. cit.*, p. 293.

128. James Gow, *The Serbian Project and its Adversaries, op. cit.*, p. 135.

129. Joël Hubretch, *Kosovo: Etablir les faits, op. cit.*, pp. 40–1.

130. This is why the extremist newspaper *Kangura* had created an international edition that denounced the danger represented by the Tutsis residing in Burundi and the Congo. What, then, would have prevented Hutu Power from claiming a 'right to pursue' in these countries?

131. Thus in 1898 a British battalion of several hundred soldiers equipped with modern machine-guns attacked several thousand Sudanese soldiers, killing in all about 11,000 of them. See John Ellis, *The Social History of the Machine-Gun*, New York, Pantheon Books, 1975.

132. See Carnegie Endowment for International Peace, *Reports of the International Commission to Inquire into the Causes and Conduct of the Balkan Wars*, Washington, DC, 1914, p. 73.

133. These last two places are considered to be 'mixed institutions' because they were both concentration camps and extermination camps.

134. Quoted by Florent Brayard, *La solution finale de la question juive, op.cit.*, pp. 396–7. English trans http://www.nizkor.org/hweb/people/g/goebbels-joseph/goebbels-1948-excerpts-02.html#1942-mar-27, viewed on 9 Feb. 2006.

135. See in particular Guenter Lewy, *The Nazi Persecution of the Gypsies*, New York, Oxford University Press, 2000.

136. Adolf Hitler, *Mein Kampf*, Zentralverlag der NSDAP, Munich, 1942, p. 772. English trans. http://www.adolfhitler.ws/lib/mk/39index.htm, viewed 7 Feb. 2006.

137. Claudine Vidal, 'Le tueur à la machete comme symbole du génocide des Rwandais Tutsi', contribution to an international seminar '*Face aux crises extrêmes*', University of Lille 2, 21 and 22 Oct. 2004.

138. José Kagabo, 'Rwanda après le génocide, notes de voyage Août 1994', *Les Temps Modernes*, no. 583, July–Aug. 1995, p. 105.

139. Pierre Hassner, *La violence et la paix. De la bombe atomique au nettoyage ethnique*, Paris, Editions Esprit, 1995, p. 262.

Chapter 5 *The Vertigo of Impunity*

1. Pierre Legendre, *La fabrique de l'homme occidental*, followed by *L'homme en meurtrier*, Paris, Mille et Une Nuits, 1996, p. 22.

2. *Ibid.*, p. 15.

3. George Devereux, *Ethnopsychoanalysis: Psychoanalysis and Anthropology as Complement Frames of Reference*, Berkeley, University of California Press, 1978.

4. As part of her doctoral research in history, Natalija Basic interviewed twenty-five ex-combatants involved in the wars in Croatia and Bosnia in 1997 and 1998, in Belgrade, Banja Luka, Bratunac, Crikvenica, Sarajevo, Split, Sremska Mitrovica and Zagreb. Most of those interviewed came from these Croatian, Bosnian and Serbian cities. It is worth mentioning that Natalija Basic prefers the term 'combatants' to militiamen, the former being more appropriate in the context of the popular defence of Yugoslavia. See Natalija Basic, 'Die Akteursperspektive. Soldaten und ethnische Sauberungen in Kroatien und Bosnien-Herzegowina (1991–1995)' in U. Brunnbauer and H. Sundhaussen (eds.), *Definitionsmacht, Utopie, Vergeltung. 'Ethnische Sauberungen' im ostlichen Europa des 20 Jahrhunderts*, Munster, 2006.

5. Chuck Sudetic sketches an interesting picture of Milan Lukic in 'Le criminel de guerre', *Après-guerre(s)*, Ed. Autrement, 2001, pp. 236–53.

6. John Mueller, 'The Banality of Ethnic War', *International Security*, vol. 25, no. 1, summer 2000, pp. 42–70.

7. The mayor's role in the organisation of the massacre can be likened to that of the burgomasters who played exactly the same role in Rwanda (cf. Ch. IV).

8. Jan T. Gross, *Neighbors: The Destruction of the Jewish Community in Jedwabne, Poland*, Princeton University Press, 2001, p. 110.

9. Richard Rhodes, *Masters of Death: The SS-Einsatzgruppen and the Invention of the Holocaust*, New York, Knopf, 2002.

10. Interview with Christian Ingrao, 15 March 2004, author of a remarkable book on the Dirlewanger brigade, an SS unit mainly made up of convicts, formed in

1940 to combat partisans fighting behind German lines on the eastern front, *Les chasseurs noirs. La Brigade Dirlewanger*, Paris, Perrin, 2006.

11. See Michael Mann, 'Were the Perpetrators of Genocide 'Ordinary Men' or 'Real Nazis'? Results from Fifteen Hundred Biographies', *Holocaust and Genocide Studies*, 14 (3): 331–66, 2000. This article is the subject of Ch. 8, entitled 'Fifteen Hundred Perpetrators', of Mann's latest book, already cited.

12. Quoted by Christopher Browning, *Ordinary Men, op.cit.*, p. 2.

13. Scott Straus also conducted a series of interviews with former killers, published in his book *Intimate Enemy: Images and Voices of the Rwandan Genocide*, New York, 2006, Zone Books. The book is illustrated with photographs of the Hutu prisoners taken by Robert Lyons.

14. On condition one can be sure they haven't deliberately tried to disguise certain facts or feelings in order to avoid censorship, which is another problem altogether.

15. "'Once Again I've Got to Play General to the Jews." From the war diary of Blutordenstrager Felix Landau' in Ernst Klee, Willi Dressen and Volker Riess (eds), in Omer Bartov (ed.) *The Holocaust: Origins, Implementation, Aftermath*, London and New York, Routledge, pp. 185–203.

16. Austrian carpenter who participated in the Vienna Putsch of 25 July 1934 against Chancellor Dolfuss, and who afterwards requested German citizenship. He later joined the SS.

17. Letter from Walter Mattner dated 5 Oct. 1941, quoted by Christopher Browning, *The Origins of the Final Solution: The Evolution of Nazi Jewish Policy, September 1939–March 1942*, Lincoln and Jerusalem, University of Nebraska Press, 2004, p. 298.

18. The Nazi propaganda theme of the 'Asian hordes' that threatened to sweep across Europe and destroy Western civilisation is recognisable here.

19. Alexander Laban Hinton, *Why Did They Kill? Cambodia in the Shadow of Genocide*, Berkeley, University of California Press, 2005, p. 31.

20. Leon Festinger, *A Theory of Cognitive Dissonance*, Stanford University Press, 1957.

21. Charles Mironko, '*Igitero*: means and motive in the Rwandan genocide', *Journal of Genocide Research*, vol. 6 (1), March 2004, pp. 47–60.

22. Quoted by Jean Hatzfeld, *Into the Quick of Life, op.cit.*, p. 132.

23. Quoted by Mirko Grmek (ed.), *Le nettoyage ethnique. Documents historiques sur une idéologie serbe, op.cit.*, p. 320.

24. Quoted by Jan T. Gross, *Neighbors, op.cit.*, p. 162.

25. Christopher Browning, *Ordinary Men, op. cit.*, p. 123.

26. Refer to the work of Raul Hilberg for example, *The Destruction of the European Jews*, volume 2, New York, Holmes and Meier, 1985.

27. Intercepted telephone conversation between Colonel Ljubisa Beara (ex-head of military security in 'Republika Srpska' from 1992 to 1996) and General Krstic. This conversation served as evidence used in the Milosevic trial at the International Criminal Tribunal in The Hague, see *Nouvel Observateur*, 'Srebrenica: quand les bourreaux parlent', 18–24 March 2004.

28. Jean-Pierre Chrétien refers to a recording made by the journalist Dominique Makeli of an alleged 'dialogue' between the Virgin Mary and the medium Valentine Nyiramukiza. See Jean Pierre Chrétien, *L'Afrique des Grands Lacs, op.cit.*, p. 294.
29. Elisabeth Claverie, *Les guerres de la Vierge. Anthropologie des apparitions*, Paris, Gallimard, 2003.
30. Quoted by Florence Hartmann, *Milosevic, la diagonale du fou, op.cit.*, p. 208.
31. Omer Bartov, *Hitler's Army, op. cit.*, p. 178.
32. Quoted by Dieter Pohl in Dominique Vidal, *Les historiens allemands relisent la Shoah, op.cit.*, p. 207.
33. John Pomfret, 'Serbs Drive Thousands from Zepa Enclave', *Washington Post*, 27 July 1995.
34. However, in certain cases a discipline of steel can characterise some groups of militiamen, as in Serbia: Arkan's Tigers boasted that their level of discipline was far superior to that of the Yugoslav army.
35. Christopher R. Browning, *Ordinary men, op.cit.*, p. 172.
36. On 21 August 1992, with other police colleagues, he escorted a convoy of Muslims who were travelling in coaches and trucks. But when they arrived near the River Ilomska, they received orders to execute them above a ravine. Thus, according to him, as the guard accompanying the convoy, he was forced in that instant to turn suddenly into a killer.
37. Stanley Milgram, *Obedience to Authority*, New York, Harper Row, 1974. For a discussion of this theory refer to 'Perspectives on Obedience to Authority: The Legacy of the Milgram Experiments', *Journal of Social Issues*, vol. 51, no. 3, Fall 1995.
38. Leonardo Ancona and R. Pareyson, 'Contribution à l'étude de l'agression', *Bulletin de Psychologie*, 1971, XXV, 72, 5–7.
39. Cited in Jean Hatzfeld, *Machete Season, op. cit.*, p. 227.
40. Cited in *ibid.*, p. 224.
41. Anthony Oberschall, 'The Manipulaton of Ethnicity', *art.cit.*, p. 997.
42. Cited in Alison Des Forges, *Leave None to Tell the Story, op.cit.*, p. 323.
43. Christopher Browning, *Ordinary Men, op.cit.*, p. 72.
44. In fact the whole citation reads as follows: 'normal men know that anything is possible. Even if the testimonies force their intelligence to admit, their muscles do not believe.' David Rousset, *L'univers concentrationnaire*, Paris, Editions de Minuit, 1965, republished in paperback by Hachette in 1998, p. 181.
45. Wolfgang Sofsky, *Traité de la violence*, transl. Paris, Gallimard, 1998, p. 163.
46. Robert Lifton has developed his analyses from the study of Nazi doctors; it seems however that his observations are equally relevant when applied to per-petrators in general. Cf. Robert J. Lifton, *The Nazi Doctors. Medical Killing and the Psychology of Genocide*, New York, Basic Books, 1986.
47. For the psychologist James Waller, Milgram's and Lifton's work illustrate what he calls 'the divided self understandings of extraordinary human evil'. He adds, 'a new breed of postmodern psychologists is redirecting the social scientific discussion to the concept of multiple selves. They maintain that we have no single, centralized, unified, coherent self. Rather, we have a community of

selves, each with its own desires and motives which have been created to relate
to different aspects of our multifaceted lives'. James Waller, *Becoming Evil. How
Ordinary People Commit Genocide and Mass Killing*, Oxford University Press,
2002, p. 121.

48. Cited by Christopher R. Browning, *Ordinary Men, op.cit.*, p. 67.

49. Having given himself up voluntarily to the Tribunal in The Hague, his case
    was the first to be dealt with. See the proceedings of his case on the website
    www.un.org/icty

50. See Natalija Basic's presentation to the CERI research group 'Faire la paix. Du
    crime de masse au peace building', (15 Nov. 2001: executioner/victim rela-
    tionships), at www.ceri-sciences-po.org

51. Christopher Browning, *Ordinary Men, op.cit.*, p. 161.

52. Cited by Jean Hatzfeld, *Machete Season, op. cit.*, pp. 21–2.

53. Cited by Gitta Sereny, *Into That Darkness: An Examination of Conscience*, New
    York, Random House, Vintage Books, 1983, p. 201.

54. Knowledge that is transmitted orally, sometimes at the very moment the exe-
    cutions are carried out: for an example of such discussions about the best way
    of aiming to cause immediate death, Cf. Christian Ingrao, 'Violence de
    guerre, violence génocide: les *Einsatzgruppen*', in Stéphane Audoin-Rouzeau,
    Annette Becker, Henry Rousso (eds), *La violence de guerre, op. cit.*, p. 237.

55. *Ibid.*, p. 238.

56. See the contribution of Pierre-Antoine Braud already cited in the CERI
    research group: www.ceri-sciences-po.org. Raiding against various areas only
    ceased in the 1920s, once all of present-day Rwanda was brought under the
    monarchical and colonial powers.

57. Enzo Traverso, *La violence nazie. Généalogie européenne*, Paris, La Fabrique, 2002,
    pp. 54–5.

58. Hannah Arendt, *Eichmann in Jerusalem: A Report on the Banality of Evil*, New
    York, Penguin Books, 1994.

59. Primo Levi, *The Drowned and the Saved*, New York, Vintage Books, 1989,
    p. 52.

60. Henry V. Dicks, *Licensed Mass Murder: A Socio-Psychological Study of Some SS
    Killers*, New York, Basic Books, 1973.

61. Theodor Adorno, *The Authoritarian Personality*, New York, Norton, 1969.

62. See the judgement on the International Criminal Tribunal for the Former
    Yugoslavia website, www.un.org/icty/.

63. Bruno Bettelheim, *The Informed Heart*, London, Penguin, 1988.

64. Ivan Colovic, 'Le football, les hooligans et la guerre' in Nebojsa Popov,
    Radiographie d'un nationalisme, op. cit., pp. 179–204.

65. Cited by Annick Kayitesi, *Les enfants et le génocide rwandais. Implications et pro-
    blèmes de réinsertion*, Master's research dissertation under the direction of Rich-
    ard Banégas, Université Paris I-Sorbonne, 2002–2003, 42 pages. Annick
    Kayitesi is also the author of *Nous existons encore*, Paris, Editions Michel The-
    fon, 2004, a very moving book in which she tells of her combat experience as
    an adolescent at the time of the genocide during which several members of
    her family were killed, including her mother.

66. Alison Des Forges, *Leave None to Tell the Story, op.cit.*, p. 261.

67. Cited by Jean Hatzfeld, *Into the Quick of Life, op.cit.*, p. 50.

68. One of the first reports on this subject is that of the African Rights Association, '*Not so Innocent: When Women become Killers*', London, African Rights,
Aug. 1995. The following lines offer a brief summary of the issue.

69. Annick Kayitesi, *Les enfants et le génocide rwandais. Implications et problèmes de
réinsertion, op.cit.*

70. Cited by Annick Kayitesi, *ibid.*

71. Christopher Browning, *Ordinary Men, op.cit.*, p. 217.

72. Saul Friedlander, *Kurt Gerstein: The Ambiguity of Good*. Translated from the
French and German by Charles Fullman, New York, Knopf, 1969. Due to his
technical and medical background, Kurt Gerstein worked in the Waffen SS
Technical Disinfection Services. In the course of his work he went to Poland
to assess the efficiency of the gassing operations in the Reinhardt programme.
He subsequently attempted to reduce the irritant effects related to the use of
Zyclon B to render the deaths of the victims more 'humane'.

73. The following lines owe a lot to the very enlightening reading of two articles
by Géraldine Muhlman: 'Le comportement des agent de la 'Solution finale'.
Hannah Arendt face à ses contradicteurs', *Revue d'Histoire de la Shoah*, no. 164,
Sept. 1998, pp. 25–52 and 'Pensée et non-pensée selon H. Arendt et
T.W. Adorno. Réflexions sur la question du mal', *Tumultes*, 17–18, 2002,
pp. 278–318.

74. Hannah Arendt, *Eichmann in Jerusalem: A Report on the Banality of Evil, op. cit.*,
pp. 287–8.

75. *Ibid.*, p. 24.

76. Hannah Arendt, '*Thinking and Moral Considerations: A Lecture*', in *Social
Research*, 51, 1984, p. 7.

77. Hannah Arendt, *Eichmann in Jerusalem, op.cit.*, p. 24.

78. Hannah Arendt, *The Life of the Mind*, vol. 1: *Thinking*, New York, Harcourt
Brace Jovanovich, 1978, pp. 19 ff.

79. See the film directed by Ibouka Belgique in 2002.

80. John Horne and Alan Kramer, *German Atrocities: 1914. A History of Denial*,
New Haven and London, Yale University Press, 2001.

81. John Dower, *War Without Mercy: Race and Power in the Pacific War*, Cambridge,
MA, Harvard University Press, 1988.

82. Primo Levi, *The Drowned and the Saved*, op.cit., pp. 105–26.

83. Véronique Nahoum-Grappe, 'L'usage politique de la cruauté. L'épuration
ethnique (ex-Yougoslavie, 1991–1995)' in Françoise Héritier (ed.), *De la violence*, Paris, Odile Jacob, 1996, pp. 273–323.

84. See for example Alexandra Stiglmayer, *Mass Rape: The War against Women in
Bosnia-Herzegovina*, Lincoln, University of Nebraska Press, 1994 and Vesna
Nikolic-Ristanovi's study, *Women, Violence and War. War Time Victimization of
Refugees in the Balkans* (Belgrade 1995), Budapest, Central European Univer-
sity Press, 2000.

85. Such as the former Minister of the Family and Promotion of Women in person, Pauline Nyiramasuhuko. Originating from the Butare area, she encour-

aged the rape of Tutsi women, in particular in the stadium where the Tutsis were assembled (her own son was in the *Interahamwe* militias). See the portrait of her in the *Courrier international*, 14–20 Nov. 2002.

86. Refer to the International Criminal Tribunal for the former Yugoslavia website (judgement Kunarac *et al.*): www.un.org/icty

87. Cited by Tim Judah, *The Serbs: History, Myth and the Destruction of Yugoslavia*, *op. cit.*, p. 236.

88. See in this respect the interesting thoughts of two French authors already renowned for their work on violence: Michel Wieviorka, *La violence*, Paris, Balland, 2004 and Philippe Braud, *Violences politiques*, Paris, Seuil, 2004.

89. Cited by Tim Judah, *The Serbs. History, Myth and the Destruction of Yugoslavia*, *op. cit.*, page 84.

90. Jadranka Cacic-Kumpes, 'La guerre, l'ethnicité et le viol. Le cas des femmes réfugiées de Bosnie' in *Le Livre noir de l'ex-Yougoslavie. Purification ethnique et crimes de guerre*, documents collected by *Le Nouvel Observateur* and Reporters sans Frontières, Paris, Arléa, 1993, pp. 439–44.

91. See Xavier Bougarel's lecture to the CERI research group 'From Mass Crime to Peacebuilding' (15 Nov. 2001: les rapports bourreaux/victims), at www.ceri-sciences-po.org.

92. Other authors have shown the pertinence of an analysis of atrocities as resulting from calculation, such as Paul Richards and Krijn Peters in the Sierra Leone conflict: 'Why We Fight: Voices of Youth Combatants in Sierra Theone', *Africa* 68 (2), 1998, pp. 183–210. In the same line of thought, see Stathis N. Kalyvas, *The Logic of Violence in Civil War*, New York, Cambridge University Press, 2006.

93. Interview with Joël Hubrecht, 14 Oct. 2004.

94. Cited by Gitta Sereny, *Into That Darkness: An Examination of Conscience*, *op.cit.*, p. 101.

95. See the Afterward to Primo Levi, *If This Is a Man*, London, Abacus, 1987, p. 395.

96. Quoted by Jean Hatzfeld, *Machete Season*, *op.cit.*, p. 50.

97. Eric Vogelin, *Hitler and the Germans*, University of Missouri Press, 1999, p. 105.

98. Roger Caillois, *Bellone ou la pente de la guerre*, Paris, 1963, Editions A-G Nizet, p. 211.

99. On 16 August 1870, there was a village fete in Hautefaille, this little village in the north of Perigord where the local farmers traditionally met, but it was also the start of the war against Prussia and France's first defeat. A group of farmers suddenly set about a young nobleman who was passing by and allegedly shouted 'Long live the Republic'. In the party atmosphere, they proceeded to torture him in public and finally kill him like an animal, boasting afterward that they had 'roasted a Prussian'. See Alain Corbin, *Le village des cannibales*, Paris, Aubier, 1990.

100. Alison Des Forges, *Leave None to Tell the Story*, *op.cit.*, p. 212.

101. Jean-Pierre Vernant, *Mortals and Immortals: Collected Essays*, Princeton University Press, 1991.

102. Arjun Appaduraï, 'Dead Certainty: Ethnic Violence in the Era of Globalization', *Public Culture*, vol. 10, no. 2, 1998, p. 909.

103. Christopher Taylor, *Sacrifice as Terror. The Rwandan Genocide of 1994*, Oxford, Berg, 1999, p. 135.

104. *Ibid.*, p. 140.

105. Alexander L. Hinton (ed.), *Genocide: an Anthropological Reader*, Oxford, Blackwell, 2002, and *Annihilating Difference: The Anthropology of Genocide*, Berkeley: California University Press, 2002.

106. Jean Améry, *At the Mind's Limits: Contemplations by a Survivor on Auschwitz and Its Realities*, Bloomington, Indiana University Press, 1980, p. 34.

107. Georges Bataille, *Le procès de Gilles de Rais, Oeuvres complètes*, vol. X, Paris, 1987, pp. 487 ff.

108. Primo Levi, 'The Grey Zone' in *The Drowned and the Saved, op. cit.*, pp. 36–69.

109. Cited by Jean Hatzfeld, *Into the Quick of Life, op.cit.*, p. 81.

110. Jacques Semelin, *Unarmed against Hitler, op. cit.*

111. Raymond Aron, *De la condition historique du sociologue*, Paris, Gallimard, 1970.

Chapter 6 *The Political Uses of Massacre and Genocide*

1. Raphael Lemkin, *Axis Rule in Occupied Europe*, Washington DC, Carnegie Endowment for International Peace, 1944.

2. Barbara Harff and Ted Robert Gurr, 'Toward Empirical Theory of Genocides and Politicides: Identification and Measurement of Cases since 1945', *International Studies Quarterly*, no. 32, 1988, pp. 369–81.

3. Eric J. Hobsbawm, *The Age of Extremes: A History of the World (1914–1991)*, London, Pelham Books, 1994.

4. Lyndall Ryan, 1996: *The Aboriginal Tasmanians*, 2nd edn, Allen Unwin, Sydney, Australia.

5. The passing of a law recognising the 'positive role of [French] colonisation' (article 4 of the law of 23 Feb. 2005) sparked a lively public debate among renowned historians via a series of petitions each revealing different conceptions of the relationship between history, memory and political authority. To end the controversy, the French President repealed the disputed article on 27 January 2006, but other memorial laws were maintained, including the 'Gayssot law' (article 24b of the law on the freedom of the press to combat negationism) and the one recognising the Armenian genocide.

6. See Olivier Masseret, 'La reconnaissance par le Parlement français du génocide arménien de 1915', *Vingtième siècle*, no. 73, Jan.–March 2002, pp. 139–55 and Vincent Duclert, 'Les historiens et la destruction des Arméniens', *Vingtième siècle*, no. 81, Jan.–March 2004, pp. 137–53.

7. Declaration made by Colin Powell on 9 Sept. 2004, before the Senate Foreign Affairs Commission on the basis of an investigation conducted by the Defence Department (in July and Aug.) in refugee camps in Chad. A few hours later the White House published a press release stating that a genocide was under way in Darfur, based on the investigation conducted by the State Department and other information sources. It was the first time a state publicly declared that a genocide was being committed in another state.

8. This report, presented to the Security Council by the High Commissioner for Human Rights and the UN secretary-general's special adviser on the prevention of genocide, concluded that 'crimes against humanity, war crimes and breaches of the laws of war have probably occurred on a large and systematic scale' (30 Sept. 2004).

9. See for instance the article by Jean-Hervé Bradol, president of Médecins sans Frontières, 'D'un génocide à l'autre', *Le Monde*, 14 Sept. 2004.

10. Report of the International Commission of Inquiry on Darfur to the United Nations Secretary-General (Pursuant to Security Council Resolution 1564 of 18 Sept. 2004), United Nations, Geneva, Jan. 2005. http://www.un.org/News/dh/sudan/com_inq_darfur.pdf.

11. Henry R. Huttenbach, 'Locating the Holocaust under the Genocide Spectrum: Towards a Methodology of Definition and Categorization', *Holocaust and Genocide Studies*, vol. 3, no. 3, 1988, p. 297.

12. Israel W. Charny, 'Toward A Generic Definition of Genocide' in George J. Andreopoulos (ed.), *'Genocide: Conceptual and Historical Dimensions'*, Philadelphia, University of Pennsylvania Press, 1994, pp. 64–94.

13. Stephen Katz, *The Holocaust in Historical Context*, vol. 1, New York, Oxford University Press, 1994.

14. Montesquieu, (Charles-Louis de Secondat) *The Spirit of the Laws*, trans. ed. A. Cohler, B. Miller, H. Stone, Cambridge University Press, 1989, p. 139.

15. It is remarkable that Lemkin does not seem to doubt this basic point although he has hardly any reliable evidence for the scope of the extermination of the Jews going on in Europe and the methods used at the very moment he was writing his book. In fact he was basing himself mainly on Hitler's thinking as expressed in *Mein Kampf* and interviews with Rauschnig. For more discussion of Lemkin's thought see the special issue of the *Journal of Genocide Research*, vol. 7, no. 4, Dec. 2005.

16. Maxime Steinberg, 'Le génocide. Histoire d'un imbroglio juridique' in Kathia Boustany and Daniel Dormoy (eds), *Génocide*, Réseau Vitoria, 'International law', Bruxelles, Bruylant/ Éd. de l'Université de Bruxelles, 1999, pp. 161.

17. The word 'Holocaust' comes from the Greek and means an offering to be burned. It expressed the idea of sacrifice, *'Korban'* in Hebrew, and is thus not really an appropriate name for the Nazis' extermination of 6 million Jews. The word 'Shoah' means 'catastrophe' or 'destruction' and has been used in France since 1985, when Claude Lanzman made it the title of his documentary film. The French philosopher Alain Finkielkraut deplored this use of the word 'Holocaust': 'We now refer to the genocide with a misleading word of which the original meaning, we can only hope, has been forgotten and that it will not totally misshape the fact it designates.' Alain Finkielkraut, *L'Avenir d'une négation. Réflexion sur la question du génocide*, Paris, Seuil, 1982, p. 82.

18. Irving Louis Horowitz, *Taking Lives: Genocide and State Power*, 4th edition, New Brunswick, Transaction Publisher, 1976, 1996.

19. A number of book titles attest to this evolution: David E. Stannard, *American Holocaust: The Conquest of the New World*, New York, Oxford University Press, 1992; Jeremy Silvester, Werner H. Illebrecht and Casper Erichsen, 'The

Herero Holocaust? The Disputed History of the 1904 Genocide', *The Nami-bian Weekender,* 20 Aug. 2001; as well as Laurence Mordekhai Thomas, *Vessels of Evil: American Slavery and the Holocaust,* Philadelphia, Temple University Press, 1993.

20. Jean-Michel Chaumont, *La concurrence des victims,* Paris, La Découverte, 1997.
21. But it is less well known that the United States compromised on this point and agreed 'to drop political groups from the definition'. See William A. Schabas, *Genocide in International Law,* Cambridge University Press, 2000, p. 139.
22. Leo Kuper, *Genocide: Its Political Use in the 20th Century, op.cit.*
23. Israel Charny (ed.), *Toward the Understanding and Prevention of Genocide: Proceed-ings of the International Conference on the Holocaust and Genocide,* Boulder, CO, Westview Press, 1984.
24. Frank Chalk and Kurt Jonassohn, *The History and Sociology of Genocide, op.cit.*
25. Helen Fein, 'Genocide: A Sociological Perspective', *Current Sociology,* vol. 38, no. 1, 1990, p. 24.
26. Yves Ternon, *L'Etat criminel. Les génocides au XXème siècle,* Paris, Seuil, 1995. Before this work (which starts with a presentation and discussion of the bene-fits of international law) Yves Ternon had already written, among other things, in collaboration with Socrate Helman, *Le massacre des aliénés. Des théoriciens nazis aux praticiens SS,* Tournai, Casterman, 1971 and also *Les Arméniens. Histoire d'un génocide,* Paris, Seuil, 1977, republished in 1996. Yves Ternon's work has proved, for me, an invaluable reference point from which to move forward in this field of research, so under-explored here in France, and have hence contributed to the maturation of my own research.
27. Scott Straus, 'Contested Meanings and Conflicting Imperatives: A Conceptual Analysis of Genocide', *Journal of Genocide Research,* vol. 3, no. 3, Nov. 2001, pp. 349–75.
28. Barbara Harff and Ted Robert Gurr, 'Genocide and Politicide in Global Per-spective: The Historical Record and Future Risks' in Stan Windass (ed.), *Just War and Genocide: A Symposium,* London, Macmillan Foundation for Inter-national Security, 2001.
29. Rudolph J. Rummel, *Death by Government, op.cit.*
30. Arno J. Mayer, *Why did the heavens not darken?: the 'final solution' in history,* New York, Pantheon Books, 1988.
31. Barry Weisberg, *Ecocide in Indochina: The Ecology of War,* San Francisco, Canfield Press, 1970.
32. Jill Radford and Diana Russell (eds), *Femicide: The politics of Woman Killing,* Buckingham, Open University Press, 1992.
33. Rebecca Knuth, *Libricide: The Regime Sponsored Destruction of Books and Librairies in the Twentieth Century,* Westport, CT, Praeger, 2003.
34. Issiaka-Prosper Laleye, 'Génocide et ethnocide. Comment meurent les cul-tures. Interrogations philosophico-anthropologiques sur le concept de géno-cide culturel' in Katia Boustany and Daniel Dormoy (eds), *Génocide, op.cit.,* pp. 265–93.
35. Defended in France by the French anthropologist Robert Jaulin, *La paix blanche: Introduction à l'ethnocide,* Paris, Seuil, 1970.

36. Christian Gerlach, 'Extremely violent societies—An alternative to the concept of genocide', Lecture given on 26 Nov. 2004 in the EHESS (Ecoles des Hautes en Sciences Sociales) seminar in Paris, 'Histoire et historiographie du nazisme', led by Peter Schöttler, Florent Brayard and Pieter Lagrou.

37. Ben Kiernan and Robert Gellately (eds), *Specter of genocide: Mass Murders in Historical Perspective*, Cambridge University Press, 2003.

38. Eric D. Weitz, *A Century of Genocide: utopias of race and nation*, Princeton University Press, 2003.

39. See primarily William Schabas, *Genocide in International Law*, Cambridge University Press, 2000; Antoine Garapon, *Des crimes qu'on ne peut ni juger ni pardonner. Pour une justice internationale*, Paris, Odile Jacob 2002; Mireille Delmas-Marty (eds), *La justice pénale internationale entre passé et avenir*, Paris, Dalloz, 2004; Mireille Delmas-Marty, *Vers un droit commun de l'Humanité*, Paris, Textuel, 2005; and Guenaël Mettraux, *International crimes and the ad hoc Tribunals*, Oxford University Press, 2005.

40. Frank Chalk and Kurt Jonassohn, *The History and Sociology of Genocide, op.cit.*

41. Bernard Bruneteau, *Le siècle des génocides: violences, massacres et processus génocidaires de l'Arménie in Rwanda*, Paris, Armand Colin, 2004.

42. Marc Levene, *Genocide in the Age of the Nation State*, vol. 1 and 2, I.B. Tauris, 2005 and Martin Shaw, *War and Genocide: Organized Killing in Modern Society*, Cambridge, Polity Press, 2003.

43. Norman M. Naimark, *Fires of Hatred: Ethnic Cleansing in the Twentieth-Century Europe, op.cit.* and Michael Mann, *The Dark Side of Democracy: Explaining Ethnic Cleansing, op.cit.*

44. Benjamin A. Valentino, *Final Solutions: Mass Killing and Genocide in the 20th Century, op.cit.*

45. See Daniel Chirot, Clark McCauley, *Why Not Kill Them All? The Logic of Prevention of Mass Political Murder*, Princeton University Press, 2006.

46. This does not mean that I deny the relevance of the 'UN school'. Beyond theoretical and methodological issues, it is very important for genocide researchers to communicate with one another and agree to discuss their differing approaches. This is not always the case, for the subject of mass violence and hence mass death arouses passions and anathema, even among researchers. But without blotting out their divergences, do they not in a way have a duty to show restraint? In the very name of the memory of the dead, it is essential for those who study genocide and all sorts of massacres to respect one another when confronting their findings, and this in the interest of enabling research to progress.

47. Jacques Semelin, 'Analysis of a Mass Crime. The case of the Former Yugoslavia' in Ben Kiernan and Robert Gellately, *Specter of Genocide: Mass Murders in Historical Perspective*, Cambridge University Press, 2003. This notion also has a history in German research, being particularly favoured by Dieter Pohl. See this author's *Verfolgung und Massenmord in der NS-Zeit 1933–1945*, Darmstadt: Wissenschaftliche Buchgesellschaft, 2003.

48. Some war historians believe it relevant to extend the notion of 'massacre' to the destruction of armed soldiers killed by military power that is overwhelm-

ingly superior to the offensive or defensive capacity of the latter. Thus in the course of the First World War, some have spoken of an 'industrial massacre' when the opponent's artillery could pulverise trenchfuls of soldiers equipped with arms only intended for close combat (bayonets, grenades etc.). This even broader meaning of the word 'massacre' is however problematic in that it puts into the same category armed combatants (who theoretically agreed to fight and hence took the risk of being killed) and civilian non-combatants who made no such choice.

49. I find the notion of mass murder acceptable in the social sciences, in that the word 'murder' has no legal and penal signification.

50. Ervin Staub, *The Roots of Evil: The Origins of Genocide and Other Group Violence, op.cit.*

51. Which is what international law seeks to delimit to incriminate the perpetrators of the act.

52. Max Weber, *Economy and society: An Outline of Interpretive Sociology*, Berkeley, University of California Press, 1978.

53. John Rawls, '50 years after Hiroshima', *Dissent*, summer 1995, pp. 323–7.

54. See for example Bartholomew de Las Casas, *A Short Account of the Destruction of the Indies*, London, Penguin Classics, 1992.

55. Pascal Gueniffey, *La politique de la terreur. Essai sur la violence révolutionnaire (1789–1794)*, Paris Fayard, 2000, p. 46.

56. In the following days the French army, with the help of the colonial settlers, burned and pillaged villages. The number of victims of these massacres remains unknown on the Algerian side (estimates place the dead at 7–8,000). However, the French counted 107 dead.

57. This is the concurring conclusion reached by psychologist Françoise Sironi, *Bourreaux et victimes. Psychologie de la torture*, Paris, Odile Jacob, 1999 and historian Raphaëlle Branche, *La torture et l'armée pendant la guerre d'Algeria, 1954–1962*, Paris, Gallimard, 2001. See also their joint contribution: 'Torture and the borders of humanity', *International Social Science Journal*, Dec. 2002, no. 174, pp. 539–47.

58. Within the FLN itself, several thousand members were eliminated in a series of political purges.

59. Nicolas Werth, 'A State against Its People' in Stéphane Courtois (ed.), *The Black Book of Communism, op.cit.*, p. 149.

60. Such is one of the achievements of the impressive *Histoire du Goulag* undertaken by Russian publisher Rosspen in 6 vols. The first, dealing specifically with Stalin's repressive policies, was compiled by Irina Ziouzina and Nicolas Werth.

61. Report to the second plenary session of the Central Committee of the Seventh Chinese Communist Party Congress, 5 March 49.

62. See in this respect the outline given by Jean-Louis Margolin, 'Communism in Asia: Between Reeducation and Massacre' in Stéphane Courtois (ed.), *The Black Book of Communism, op. cit.*, pp. 457–642.

63. Jean-Luc Domenach, *Chine. L'archipel oubliée*, Paris, Fayard, 1992.

64. Harry Wu, *Laogai: The Chinese Gulag*, Boulder, CO, Westview Press, 1992.

65. Quoted by Bao Ruo-Wang (Jean Pasqualini) and Rudolph Chelminski, *Prisoner of Mao*, London, André Deutsch, 1975, p. 46.

66. Ben Kiernan, *The Pol Pot Regime: Race, Power and Genocide in Cambodia under the Khmer Rouge, 1975–1979*, New Haven, Yale University Press, 1998. See also 'The Ethnic Element in the Cambodian Genocide' in Daniel Chirot and Martin E.P. Seligman, eds, *Ethnopolitical Warfare: Causes, Consequences, and Possible Solutions*, Washington, DC, American Psychological Association Press, 2001, pp. 83–91.

67. Steve Heder, 'Racism, Marxism, labelling and genocide in Ben Kiernan's The Pol Pot Regime' in *The South East Asia Research*, vol. 5, no. 2, pp. 101–53. See also the section dedicated to Cambodia written by Steve Heder in *Encyclopedia of Genocide and Crimes against Humanity*, edited by Dinah L. Shelton *et al.*, Thomson Gale, 2005, vol. 1, pp. 141–6.

68. Essential reading in this respect is the extraordinary dialogue with his gaoler, Duch (who became commander of the sinister S 21 prison) in François Bizot, *Le portail*, Paris, Editions de la Table Ronde, 2000.

69. Quoted by Anthony F.C. Wallace, *Jefferson and the Indians: The Tragic Fate of the First Americans*, Cambridge, Belknap Press, 1999, p. 221.

70. See John Reed, *War in Eastern Europe: Travels through the Balkans in 1915*, New York, C. Scribner's Sons, 1916.

71. The report by the *Carnegie* International Commission published in 1914 gives several telling examples: Carnegie Endowment for International Peace, 1914.

72. I'm thinking primarily of Benny Morris' book, *The Birth of the Palestinian Refugee Problem 1947–1949*, Cambridge University Press, 1987.

73. Ilan Greilsamer, *Une Nouvelle Histoire d'Israel. Essai sur une identité nationale*, Paris, Gallimard, 1998.

74. *Ibid.*, p. 103.

75. Andrew Bell-Fialkoff, *Ethnic Cleansing*, Basingstoke, Macmillan, 1996. Norman Naimark, *Fires of Hatred: Ethnic Cleansing in Twentieth-Century Europe, op. cit.*, and Steven Béla Vardy and T. Hunt Tooley (eds), *Ethnic Cleansing in Twentieth Century Europe*, New York, Columbia University Press, 2003.

76. Donald L. Horowitz, *The Deadly Ethnic Riot*, Berkeley, University of California Press, 2001.

77. Michel Foucault, *Naissance de la biopolitique. Cours au collège de France, 1978–1979*, edited by François Ewald, Alessandro Fontana and Michel Senellart. Paris, Gallimard, 2004.

78. In passing I refer to the gardener metaphor suggested by Zygmunt Bauman. But I don't find it relevant enough to the subject, and so prefer the image of the surgeon, whose craft it is to cut and stitch up to heal.

79. Robert Conquest, *The Great Terror: A Reassessment*, preceded by *Harvests of Sorrow: Soviet Collectivization and Terror-Famine*, New York, Oxford University Press, 1990 and 1986.

80. Claire Mouradian, 'Une pratique soviétique radicalisée par la guerre: les déportations ethniques de masse en URSS' in Stéphane Courtois (ed.), *Une si longue nuit. L'apogée des régimes totalitaires en Europe 1935–1953*, Monaco, Editions du Rocher, 2003, pp. 332–46.

81. See Jürgen Zimmerer, *Deutsche Herrschaft über Afrikaner. Staatlicher Machtanspruch und Wirklichkeit im Kolonialen Namibia*, Münster, LIT Verlag, 2002.

82. The French Historian Olivier Le Cour Grandmaison's book represents a significant contribution in this vein, particularly through his study of France's conquest of Algeria: *Coloniser, Exterminator. Sur la guerre et l'Etat colonial*, Paris, Fayard, 2005.

83. Thus Nicolas Werth (one of the authors of *The Black Book of Communism*) does not consider the famine of 1932–3 as genocide, an option James Macé defends in 'Famine and Nationalism in Soviet Ukraine', *Problems of Communism*, Washington DC, May–June 1984. By the same token, Ben Kiernan asserts the genocidal nature of the violence perpetrated by Pol Pot, which the French historian Henri Locard refutes.

84. François Furet and Ernst Nolte, *Fascism and Communism*, Lincoln, University of Nebraska Press, 2001 (transl. from French edn. of 1998).

85. Ted R. Gurr and Barbara Harff, *Ethnic Conflict in World Politics*, Boulder, CO, Westview Press, 1994.

86. Henri Locard, 'Réflexions sur le livre noir. Le cas du Democratic Kampuchea', *Communisme*, 2000.

87. Jean-Louis Margolin, 'Du cas cambodgien comme enjeu et comme révélateur', *Communisme*, no. 59–60, 1999.

88. David Boyle, *Les Nations Unies et Le Cambodge—1975–2004: La paix et la justice dans la balance*, L'Harmattan, Paris, 2005.

89. Michael Mann, *The Dark Side of Democracy, op. cit.*

90. Michael Mann, *The Dark Side of Democracy, op. cit.*, p. 12. By crossing these various degrees of ethnic cleansing with the procedures of more or less intense violence used to implement them, Mann constructs a dynamic and complex typology presented in Table 1.1 of his book. To do so, he combines several concepts (ethnocide, politicide, fratricide, classicide, genocide). However, it should be noted that he redefines the terms of 'ethnocide' and 'politicide' in his own way, moving away from the meaning generally ascribed to these terms.

91. This however would lead us into an excessively technical discussion. But this is a typical example in which divergent approaches between legal scholars and political scientists can be productive. For the wording of the judgement handed down in appeal, see the tribunal website: www.un.org/icty.

92. Robert Melson, 'Comparative Genocides' in Dinah L. Shelton (ed.), *Encyclopedia of Genocide and Crimes against Humanity*, 3 vols, Thomson Gale, 2005, vol. 1, pp. 188–9.

93. Helen Fein, 'Ethnic Cleansing and Genocide: Definitional Evasion, Fog, Morass or Opportunity?', Minneapolis, paper presented at the *Association of Genocide Scholars Conference* (10–12 June 2001).

94. Eric Markusen, 'The meaning of genocide, as expressed in the jurisprudence of the International Criminal Tribunal for the Former Yugoslavia and Rwanda: a non-legal scholar's perspective', Minneapolis, *op. cit.*

95. The expression 'genocidal process' has already been used by writers such as Leo Kuper, although it was not clearly defined in his book *Genocide and Its Political Uses in the Twentieth Century, op. cit.*

96. Ariel Merari, 'Terrorism as a Strategy of Insurgency', *Terrorism and Political Violence*, vol. 5, no. 4, winter 1993, pp. 213–51. But one should be careful not to conclude, as this author does, that any revolt is terrorist in nature! There are forms of armed insurrection which are not (such as the Liberation of Paris in August 1944), and, even more, non-violent political revolts based on civil disobedience. The 'Salt March' organised by Gandhi in 1930 against British imperial domination is a famous example; as are the Velvet Revolutions that took place in Central Europe in 1989.

97. Didier Bigo, 'L'impossible cartographie du terrorisme', *Cultures et conflits*, autumn 2001. Downloadable at www.conflits.org, Les dossiers de Cultures et Conflits.

98. Anthony Oberschall, 'Explaining Terrorism: The contribution of collective action theory', *Sociological Theory*, 22 (1) March 2004.

99. Michel Wieviorka, *The Making of Terrorism*, University of Chicago Press, 2004, p. 9.

100. Walter Laqueur, *The Age of Terrorism*, Boston, Little, Brown, 1987, p. 72.

101. The first word of 'Irgun Zvai Leumi' meaning 'National Military Organisation'.

102. Isabelle Sommier, *Le terrorisme*, Paris, Flammarion, coll. Dominos, 2000.

103. Christian Mellon, 'Face au terrorisme, quelques repères', *Esprit et Vie*, March 2003, pp. 3–7.

104. Christian Mellon, 'Face au terrorisme, quelques repères', *Esprit et Vie, op. cit.*

105. Didier Bigo and Daniel Hermant, 'Guerre et terrorisme', *Cultures et Conflits*, autumn 2001. Article downloadable at www.conflits.org, Les dossiers de Cultures et Conflits.

106. See Brian Jenkins, *International Terrorism: A New Mode of Conflict*, Los Angeles, Crescent Publications, 1975.

107. We could speak of World Terror, as does the sociologist Edgar Morin in *Le Monde* of 22 Nov. 2001. But this would again be demonstrating western-centrism. Although the event caused an emotional shock in many countries, some, most notably China, remained rather insensitive to it.

108. The attacks by the Army for the Liberation of Holy Places on 7 Aug. 1998, against the American embassies in Nairobi and Dar Es Salaam.

109. See *International Herald Tribune*, 25 Sept. 2001.

110. http://www.fas.org/irp/world/para/docs/980223-fatwa.htm. Consulted 29 Dec. 2005.

111. Abdelwahab Meddeb, *The Malady of Islam* (trans. Pierre Joris and Ann Ried), New York, Basic Books, 2003 p. 43.

112. Bruce Hoffman, 'La terreur sacrée' in *Politique internationale*, no. 77, autumn 1997, pp. 345–55.

113. Nietzsche, *Gesammelte Werke*, volume XV, Frankfurt, Kroener Verlag, 1905, p. 137. Cf. *The Internet Encyclopedia of Philosophy*, http://www.iep.utm.edu/, 29 Dec. 2005.

114. Nietzsche, *Gesammelte Werke*, volume V, *op. cit.*, p. 271.

115. Herman Rauschning, *The Revolution of Nihilism*, trad. New York, Alliance Book Corp., 1939.

116. Brian Jenkins, 'The New Age of Terrorism', Chpt. 8 of the *McGraw-Hill Homeland Security Handbook*. Available at http://www.rand.org/pubs/reprints/RP1215.

117. Raymond Aron, *Peace and War: A Theory of International Relations*, London, Weidenfeld Nicolson, 1966.

118. Xavier Crettiez, Isabelle Sommier, 'Les attentats du 11 September. Continuité et rupture du terrorisme' in *Annuaire Français de Relations Internationales*, vol. 3, 2002.

119. A total of 2,823 died or disappeared in the World Trade Center and 184 died or disappeared at the Pentagon. See *New York Times*, 24 April 2002.

120. Gérard Chaliand, 'Les attentats du 11 September' in Gérard Chaliand (ed.), *Les stratégies du terrorisme, op. cit.*, p. 5.

121. See Sylvaine Trinh's interesting study, 'Aum Shinrikyô. Secte et violence' in Michel Wieviorka (ed.), 'Un nouveau paradigme de la violence?', *Cultures et Conflits*, no. 29–30. Downloadable at www.conflits.org

122. This specialist on strategy and psychological warfare shows how this type of operation should not be confused with the sacrifice of Japanese kamikazes in the context of battle. Cf François Geré, 'Les opérations suicides entre guerre et terrorisme' in Gérard Chaliand and Arnauld Blin, *Histoire du Terrorisme, op. cit.*, p. 399.

123. Farhad Khosrokhavar, 'La victoire d'Oussama Ben Laden', *Le Monde*, 23 Nov. 2001. See also his book *Suicide Bombers: Allah's New Martyrs*, London, Pluto Press, 2005.

124. Marc Sageman, *Understanding Terror Networks*, Philadelphia, University of Pennsylvania Press, 2004.

125. Jean Delumeau, *Sin and Fear: The Emergence of the Western Guilt Culture, 13th-eighteenth centuries*, New York, Palgrave Macmillan, 1990 (transl. of French edn. of 1978).

Conclusion *The 'Never Again' Refrain*

1. F. Scott Fitzgerald, *The Crack-Up*, ed. Edmund Wilson, New York, New Directions, 1956 (1945), p. 69.

2. Luc Boltanski, *Distant Suffering: Morality, Media, and Politics*, Cambridge University Press, 1999.

3. See the writings of Bernard Kouchner, and particularly *Charité Business*, Paris, Le Pré aux Clercs, 1986 and *Le malheur des autres*, Paris, Odile Jacob, 1991.

4. Joyce Apsel (ed.), *Darfur: Genocide before Our Eyes*, 2nd ed., New York, Institute for the Study of Genocide, 2006. See also the action initiated by Jerry Fowler through the United States Holocaust Memorial Museum Committee on Conscience in Washington, D.C.

5. The latter notion in particular was described by Boutros Boutros–Ghali, the UN's former Secretary-General, in his *Agenda for Peace*: 'Preventive diplomacy is action to prevent disputes from arising between parties, to prevent existing disputes from escalating into conflicts and to limit the spread of the latter when they occur'. Boutros Boutros Ghali, *Agenda for Peace. Preventive diplomacy, peacemaking, and peace-keeping*, New York, United Nations Editions, 2nd edn, 1995, p. 48.

6. Kofi Annan, *Prevention of Armed Conflict*, UN Secretary General's report to the Security Council, 7 June 2001.

7. Point 256 of the report *A More Secure World: Our Shared Responsibility*, High-Level Panel on Threats, Challenges and Change, New York, United Nations, 2004. This can be viewed at http://www.un.org/secureworld/.

8. *International Convention on the Prevention and Repression of the Crime of Genocide*, passed in Paris on 9 Dec. 1948. See the framed excerpt in Ch. VI of this book.

9. Barbara Harf, 'No Lessons Learned from the Holocaust: Assessing Risks of Genocide and Political Mass Murder since 1955', *American Political Science Review*, vol. 97, no. 1, Feb. 2003, pp. 57–73. Ted R. Gurr, 'Containing Internal War in the 21st Century', Fen Osler Hampson and David M. Malone (eds), *From Reaction to Conflict Prevention Opportunities for the UN System*, Boulder, CO: Lynne Rienner for the International Peace Academy, 2001, pp. 41–62.

10. Helen Fein, 'The Three P's of Genocide Prevention: With Application to a Genocide Foretold—Rwanda' in Neal Riemer (ed.), *Protection Against Genocide: Mission Impossible?*, Westport, CT, Praeger, 2000, pp. 41–66. Note also the systematic approach of Gregory Stanton in 'Early Warning' in Dinah L. Shelton (ed.), *Encyclopedia of Genocide and Crimes against Humanity, op. cit.*, pp. 271–3.

11. Interesting in this regard is the NGO initiative Search for Common Ground, founded by the journalist John Marks, who in particular assigned himself the objective of working towards creating various radio and TV broadcasts and programmes favouring cooperation between ethnic and religious groups in conflict.

12. On this subject historian Frank Chalk maintains that in 1944 the BBC could have warned Jews in Hungary as soon as the Germans occupied the country of the fate that awaited them, and of the fact that Eichmann was preparing their deportation. Warnings broadcast over the radio encouraging them to hide could, Chalk maintains, have saved a large number of lives.

13. Cf. Barnett R. Rubin (ed.), *Cases and Strategies for Preventive Action*, New York, Century Foundation Press, 1998.

14. See especially Chapter 4 in Daniel Chirot, Clark McCauley, *Why Not Kill Them All?, op.cit.*

15. This point of view is developed by Michael Walzer in his article 'Au-delà de l'intervention humanitaire, les droits de l'homme dans la société globale', *Esprit*, Aug.–Sept. 2004, pp. 8–27, an article expanding on his lecture entitled 'Beyond Humanitarian Intervention: Human Rights in Global society,' given at the Institute for Advanced Study at Princeton on 11 March 2004.

16. See Arthur C. Helton, *The Price of Indifference: Refugees and Humanitarian Action in the New Century*, Oxford University Press, 2002.

17. Carnegie Commission on Preventing Deadly Conflict, *Final Report*, Carnegie Corporation of New York, Dec. 1997.

18. See, for example, the argumentation defended in the introduction to Benjamin A. Valentino's book, *Final Solutions: Mass Killing and Genocide in the 20th Century, op.cit.*

19. Marc Levene, 'A Dissenting Voice: or how current assumptions of deterring and preventing genocide may be looking at the problem through the wrong

end of the telescope', Part I, *Journal of Genocide Research*, vol 6, no. 2, June 2004, pp. 153–66.

20. *Ibid.*, p. 163. Read also the second part of his article in *Journal of Genocide Research*, vol. 6, no. 3, Sept. 2004, pp. 431–45.

21. See David Hamburg, *No More Killing Fields: Preventing Deadly Conflict.* Lanham, MD, Rowman and Littlefield, 2002, and more recently D.A Hamburg and A. George, *Never again: practical steps toward prevention of genocide*, Oxford University Press, forthcoming.

22. Hannah Arendt, 'On the Nature of Totalitarianism: An Essay in Understanding', Hannah Arendt Papers at the Library of Congress: Essays and Lectures (Series: Speeches and Writings File, 1923–1975, n.d.), p. 7.

23. Jean-Claude Passeron, *Le raisonnement sociologique*, Paris, Nathan, 1991.

24. Michael Freeman, 'The Theory and Prevention of Genocide', *Holocaust and Genocide Studies*, vol. 6, no. 2, 1991, pp. 185–99.

25. Thomas Cushman, 'Is genocide preventable? Some theoretical considerations', *Journal of Genocide Research*, vol. 6, no. 4, Dec. 2003, pp. 523–42.

26. In September 2000 Canada and a group of major foundations announced to the UN the creation of an International Commission on Intervention and State Sovereignty, the chairmanship of which was assigned to the Australian Gareth Evans and the Algerian Mohamed Sahnoun. The Commission was invited to tackle all legal, moral, political and operational issues in this area, to gather as wide a range as possible of opinions from every part of the world, and to submit a report that would help the UN Secretary General and all the other participants to forge a new basis for mutual understanding.

27. G. Evans and M. Sahnoun, 'The Responsibility to Protect', *Foreign Affairs*, vol. 81, no. 6, Nov. 2002. The report can be consulted at the site www.crisisweb.org.

28. For example, as regards reconstruction, see the comparative enquiries conducted by Béatrice Pouligny, *Peace Operations Seen from Below*, London, Hurst, 2006 (French edn. 2004).

29. See Valérie Rosoux's interesting approach in *Les usages de la mémoire dans les relations internationales. Le recours au passé dans la politique étrangère de la France à l'égard de l'Allemagne et de l'Algérie de 1962 à nos jours*, Bruxelles, Ed. Bruylant, 2001. This work on memory can draw on Paul Ricoeur's philosophical approach in *Memory, History, Forgetting*, Chicago University Press, 2004.

30. See the http://www.cidcm.umd.edu. website.

31. In France, the *Centre de Recherche sur la Paix (C.R.P.)* at the Catholic University of Paris has undertaken such work under the leadership of François Mabille. Such research must, however, be paired with specific course offerings. In this regard, in 2005 Andrea Bartoli and Henry Huttenbach designed a course on the prevention of genocide at Columbia University. I myself initiated a multidisciplinary course of study on genocide (which also broaches the question of prevention at the end of the syllabus) at Sciences Po, Paris.

32. Pierre Hassner, 'Une anthropologie des passions', *Commentaires*, N. 110, summer 2005, pp. 299–312.

33. Because the training of groups controlled by Bin Laden was set up in Afghanistan under the protection of the Taliban Islamist regime.

34. Stanley Hoffmann, 'Clash of Globalizations', *Foreign Affairs*, vol. 81, no. 4, July–August 2002, pp. 104–115. See also *Chaos and Violence. What Globalization, Failed States and Terrorism Mean for U.S. Foreign Policy*, Lanham, MD, Boulder Co, Rowman and Littlefield, 2006.
35. The conference specified that this list should without doubt be extended to other countries: www.preventinggenocide.com

Appendix B *Comparing Massacres*

1. See Stephen Kalberg's excellent book, *Max Weber's Comparative-Historical Sociology*, University of Chicago Press, 1994.
2. Stéphane Courtois (ed.), *The Black Book of Communism, op.cit.*, p. 9.
3. Ian Kershaw and Moshe Lewin, *Stalinism and Nazism: Dictatorship in Comparison*, Cambridge University Press, 1997 and Henry Rousso (ed.), *Stalinisme et nazisme. Histoires et mémoires comparées*. Bruxelles, Complexes/IHTP, 1999.
4. Yehuda Bauer, *Rethinking the Holocaust*, New Haven, Yale University Press, 2001.
5. A reading of her book, *Auschwitz Explained to My Child*, suggests this. In it she mentions the existence of two other genocides: those of the Armenians and of the Tutsis in Rwanda (New York, Marlowe Co., 2002, p. 26).
6. Omer Bartov, 'Seeking the Roots of Modern Genocide: On the Macro- and Micro-History of Mass Murder', in Ben Kiernan and Robert Gellately, *The Specter of Genocide: Mass Murder in Historical Perspective*, Cambridge University Press, 2003, pp. 75–96.
7. On these major points that define my approach, and more generally my position in the field of genocide studies, see the discussion in Ch. VI of this book.
8. Robert Melson, *Revolution and Genocide: On the Origins of the Armenian Genocide and the Holocaust*, University of Chicago Press, 1992.
9. Norman Naimark, *Fires of Hatred, op.cit.*; Eric D. Weitz, *A Century of Genocide, op.cit.*

NAME INDEX

SUBJECT INDEX